Public Administration and Information Technology

Volume 36

More information about this series at http://www.springer.com/series/10796

Christopher G. Reddick
Manuel Pedro Rodríguez-Bolívar
Hans Jochen Scholl
Editors

Blockchain and the Public Sector

Theories, Reforms, and Case Studies

Springer

Editors
Christopher G. Reddick
Department of Public Administration
The University of Texas at San Antonio
San Antonio, TX, USA

Manuel Pedro Rodríguez-Bolívar
Department of Accounting and Finance
University of Granada
Granada, Spain

Hans Jochen Scholl
The Information School
University of Washington
Seattle, WA, USA

ISSN 2512-1812 ISSN 2512-1839 (electronic)
Public Administration and Information Technology
ISBN 978-3-030-55745-4 ISBN 978-3-030-55746-1 (eBook)
https://doi.org/10.1007/978-3-030-55746-1

This Springer imprint is published by the registered company Springer Nature Switzerland AG
The registered company address is: Gewerbestrasse 11, 6330 Cham, Switzerland

Preface

Introduction

Blockchain has received significant attention in the area of financial technology (Fintech). As potentially disruptive innovation of the Internet era, it combines several computer technologies, including distributed data storage, point-to-point transmission, consensus mechanisms, and encryption algorithms (Zhang, 2016). Initially, blockchain technology has been used to record historical transactions of encrypted digital currency such as Bitcoin (Nakamoto, 2008). However, due to its key characteristic of immutability, i.e., an append-only record system, blockchain technology has further developed beyond virtual currencies combining existing technologies for recording a range of different types of business transactions.

Blockchain is transforming industries by enabling innovative business practices in areas such as remittance, payment, banking, financing, trading, manufacturing, supply chain management, legal service, among others. Recently, public administrations have been introducing blockchain technologies to areas, in which actors must reliably record decentralized transactions, in particular, in environments where not all parties, whether humans or machines, can be fully trusted. Blockchain technology has been portrayed as a universal, evolving, open and transparent, robust infrastructure that cannot be easily corrupted (Ølnes & Jansen, 2018). Given the trustworthiness and security, the use of blockchain can help increase citizens' trust in government information. It might enable the coordination of transactions and information exchanges within the emerging "Internet of Things" or it also might have uses in digital identification and voting systems (Pilkington, 2016).

However, while many potential benefits in digital government have been identified, it is important that researchers begin discussing challenges, benefits, regulations, frameworks, taxonomies, and applications of blockchain technologies in the public domain.

Objectives and Audience

This edited book, *Blockchain and the Public Sector: Theories, Reforms, and Case Studies*, has high-quality chapter contributions from leading scholars and practitioners on the theoretical, empirical, and application-oriented research on blockchain and other distributed ledger technologies (DLT) and the public sector. The chapters present cases and applications of blockchain addressing challenges and/or presenting information frameworks or taxonomies for government transparency, accountability, and security and/or describing the role of blockchain architectures and applications to comply with societal needs and public values and/or describing experiences in designing, implementing, and using blockchain applications to solve real-world problems through theory, case studies, and reforms.

This book is a convenient source of information on the need to define blockchain and the need of transforming governments to foster public policies with the aim of creating greater public value. In this regard, the book provides the most up-to-date information on important developments regarding blockchain in government around the world.

This book should prove valuable to many different stakeholders such as academics, researchers, policy-makers, public managers, international organizations, and technical experts in understanding how blockchain can enhance public service delivery. Therefore, this book focuses on understanding how to define blockchain by improving transparency, efficiency, and overall good governance. This book provides insightful analysis about the organizational issues that public managers and politicians have to deal with the introduction of blockchain technologies to achieve better public service delivery.

The collection of chapters in this book are written by leading international academic experts and practitioners on the implementation and study of blockchain technologies in different countries. These chapters show the importance of the use of case studies to illustrate reforms as a result of blockchain initiatives. The chapters are able to push important theoretical explanations of blockchain for its application to the public sector. Each of the chapters and their contributions is discussed in our overview.

Overview of Chapters

In Chap. 1, Rodríguez Bolívar, Scholl, and Pomeshchikov indicate that prior research has shown that institutional stakeholders influence the elaboration of regulatory frameworks by seeking to maximize their institutional power to achieve favorable policy outcomes. In recent years, blockchain services regulation has been issued with the aim of influencing the process of technological change and diffusion. Based on stakeholder theory and empirical data collected from key stakeholders, this chapter seeks to contribute to the literature on stakeholder involvement in formulating and enacting regulatory frameworks and understanding the perspectives and needs of different key stakeholders regarding benefits, challenges, and expected outcomes of legislative initiatives to regulate services based on blockchain technology/distributed ledger technology (BCT/DLT). The major findings show that the various stakeholders analyzed have competing views and interests in the respective service regulation that ranges from the functioning of BCT/DLT services inside financial markets (financial regulators and government decision-makers), to safety, security, and practical risk-management and operational measures for their conducting business (lobbyists and Fintech firms).

In Chap. 2, Ølnes and Jansen explore how and to what extent blockchain technologies can grow into an information infrastructure for various types of applications in the public sector, e.g., secure document/digital asset management. The chapter is partly conceptual and analytical, but the analysis will be illustrated by some existing use cases. Firstly, the authors explore different types of blockchains, their characteristics, strengths, and weaknesses. Secondly, the authors compare possible architectural development trajectories of blockchain technologies with those of the Internet. Thirdly, the authors address some essential and critical challenges related to interoperability between different types of blockchain implementations. Ølnes and Jansen describe some use cases to discuss possible changes and future work that need to be done for blockchain technology to evolve from platforms into an information infrastructure.

Prager, Martinez, and Cagle in Chap. 3 show that blockchain technology has the potential to transform public and private organizations worldwide, and its development and implementation in a given region will depend on legacy industries and infrastructure, developer and managerial talent, and local demand for the technology. Public organizations such as workforce development agencies and universities can identify employment opportunities and training needs around blockchain systems and facilitate the growth of regional blockchain clusters. This chapter explores: projections of future development in blockchain technology; potential impacts on South Bay, California, USA, occupations and sectors; and proposals for educational and workforce training programs that can be implemented by local public organizations. Interviews with industry-sector experts emphasize the potential for blockchain investment to increase operational efficiency and reduce transaction costs. Interviews with blockchain technology experts highlight high demand for expertise in blockchain software development, finance and accounting, and strategic development, as well as opportunities for entrepreneurs to develop innovative software and enterprise solutions.

Chapter 4, by Rieger, Stohr, Wenninger, and Fridgen, argues that blockchain solutions are a promising alternative for use in the public sector when the delegation of workflow governance to a central authority is not possible or desirable. In particular, blockchain supports the retention of decentralized structures and allows individual authorities to share process information over the blockchain while simultaneously maintaining control over their own data and data repositories. However, the use of blockchain solutions also introduces challenges, such as reconciling blockchain with the general data protection regulation (GDPR). The GDPR demands that blockchain solutions involve clear responsibilities for compliance, rely on specific lawful bases for processing personal data, and observe rights to rectification and erasure. Here, we describe how Germany's Federal Office for Migration and Refugees managed these challenges and created a GDPR-compliant blockchain solution for the coordination of the German asylum procedure.

In Chap. 5, Sobolewski and Allesssie in their chapter analyze the benefits of blockchain technology for the public sector by looking at the outcomes of ongoing experimentation with distributed ledgers by governments. These authors use an evidence-based approach by analyzing seven pioneering projects in Europe in different stages of implementation, including two services in the production phase. The study uses a structured framework for the case study analysis and a horizontal comparison on the functionalities, governance aspects, the usage, the technical aspects, and the benefits. The study shows that current blockchain-driven innovation in the public sector mainly consists of automating the enforcement of transactions. The ongoing experimentation demonstrates the capacity of blockchain to reduce bureaucracy and costs of administrative processes, like record-keeping or financial management. However, a lack of standards and trusted hosting infrastructure and gaps in essential functionality are strong indications that technology has yet to mature. Without addressing scalability, governance, and interoperability, blockchain will not become a transformative technology for governments.

Johnson and Krueger in Chap. 6 show that in the decade following the introduction of blockchain distributed ledger technology and cryptocurrencies, adoption of the technology lags far behind its potential. Past research identifies knowledge-based trust and understanding as critical to the adoption of technological innovations, particularly in regard to individual willingness to use online financial instruments. Despite negative perceptions of technology identified as key barriers to individual adoption, to the best of our knowledge, little systematic research examines individual attitudes towards the use of blockchain technology or cryptocurrency. The authors utilize a survey experiment to examine how common discussion contexts surrounding cryptocurrencies influence openness to adoption in comparison with the U.S. dollar. The authors found that an increased openness to cryptocurrency adoption is associated with messages reflecting (1) the independence of cryptocurrency from political or central bank management and (2) when information describing the security features of blockchain are included. This is consistent with prior research that the socio-technical complexity of a system requires process description in responses. A second important finding suggests that individuals most open to cryptocurrencies as a substitute for the dollar are those benefitting the least from the existing financial system.

Chapter 7, by Petroni and Pfitzner, examines artificial intelligence and blockchain will be the most relevant technologies in Brazil within the next 10 years. They may cope with social challenges like corruption, violence, and bureaucracy. Blockchain and smart contracts are "models of trust" that enable secure data transfer in a peer network. The widespread of blockchain and smart contracts will reduce frauds and errors for all information that is registered in the network. They are supposed to improve public services provision, bringing more efficiency, transparency, and fairness. This chapter aims at analyzing the main problems of public services in Brazil, namely the uncertainty of delivery and lack of universality, by means of a comprehensive ethnography and literature review. Then, the chapter proposes a scalable blockchain framework, using as examples the current processes of healthcare and tax refund. This technology framework is based on the business process management (BPM) approach and can be applied in other routines of public services.

Datta, in Chap. 8, conducts a survey of vision and white papers and reports from industry as well as private industry actors, along with academic literature, to understand how blockchain is being used for digital government and public services. The purpose of this survey is to explore which fundamental properties of blockchain technology are being harnessed, and how, putting it in perspective by reviewing technological alternatives when pertinent and by also discussing the cautions one needs to take to use blockchains in a prudent and correct manner. The case studies discussed in this chapter are thus not exhaustive, nor is any individual case discussed in great depth. Instead, we focus on capturing a wide spectrum of representative use cases to expose the efficacy as well as limitations of integrating blockchains in the government technology stack.

In Chap. 9, Sullivan shows that digital identity is now required for virtually all transactions and is fundamental to individual standing for most activities. The authenticity and accuracy of identity are important to governments, businesses, and individuals. Because of the increased economic and legal significance of digital identity, there is interest by governments around the world in using blockchain and other distributed ledger technologies to replace paper-based identity records for identity authentication and verification. A number of governments are considering moving to a blockchain-based system, while others have already moved to this new technology. There are advantages in doing so, but there are implications that have not been adequately analyzed. This chapter examines the advantages and challenges presented by blockchain identity systems and the implications for governments, private sector organizations, and individuals relying on blockchain-based identity. The chapter concludes with a framework for a new approach to support the use of blockchain for identity authentication.

Finally, in Chap. 10, Reddick examines distributed ledger technology (DLT), a type of blockchain technology poised to transform central banks. The potential impact of disruptive blockchain/DLT technologies on central banks worldwide is unimaginably large and would have significant implications for financial and monetary transactions and economic stability. Strong public interest in cryptocurrencies such as Bitcoin has popularized the term blockchain/DLT. The goal of DLT is to remove the costly and time-consuming back-office processes and the need for third-party "middlemen" in many transactions. The core question addressed in this paper is: what is the potential impact of DLT on improving central banks' performance? To address this question, the paper presents the major findings from the Bank of Canada's Project Jasper which consists of four phases. The first two phases explore and compare two distinct DLT platforms: an Ethereum platform and the R3 Corda platform. The four-main areas of focus for guiding hypotheses in Phase I are cost, resilience, accessibility, and control, while Phase 2 focuses on improvement in regard to privacy. Phase 3 explored the potential role for DLT in the Canadian financial market and determined if the new business value in terms of greater speed and efficiency can be achieved through the DLT-based automation of the securities settlement process. Phase 4 focuses on managing issues in the cross-border payment and settlement space because of the lack of standardization between jurisdictions in terms of regulatory requirements, data standards, and operating hours. The overall analysis of Bank of Canada innovations into DLT noted challenges of security and privacy but the key challenge is moving from highly complex centralized payment systems to new near-real-time payment platforms.

Acknowledgments must go to the expert peer reviewers of the draft chapters in this book. Their valuable comments have greatly improved the contributions of authors and enabled this book to provide leading-edge theory and practice in the field.

San Antonio, TX, USA — Christopher G. Reddick
Granada, Spain — Manuel Pedro Rodríguez-Bolívar
Seattle, WA, USA — Hans Jochen Scholl

References

Nakamoto, S. (2008). *Bitcoin: A peer-to-peer electronic cash system.*

Ølnes, S., & Jansen, A. (2018, May). Blockchain technology as infrastructure in public sector: An analytical framework. In *Proceedings of the 19th annual international conference on digital government research: Governance in the data age*. ACM, p. 77.

Pilkington, M. (2016). Blockchain technology: principles and applications. In: F. Xavier Olleros & Z. Majlinda (Eds.) *Research handbook on digital transformations*. Cheltenham, UK: Edward Elgar.

Zhang, E. (2016). *Antshares Whitepaper1.0.*

Contents

Chapter 1
Stakeholders' Perspectives on Benefits and Challenges in Blockchain Regulatory Frameworks

Manuel Pedro Rodríguez Bolívar, Hans Jochen Scholl, and Roman Pomeshchikov

1 Introduction

Around the world both private and public organizations have increasingly implemented blockchain technologies (BCTs), or more generally, distributed ledger technologies (DLTs) in different areas and industries like finance, tourism, supply chain among others. From a user perspective, BCTs/DLTs are expected not only to provide some benefits like a shared decentralized database or the immutability of data and smart contracts, but rather also some challenges such as scalability or resilience that BCT/DLT application and service providers need to resolve. BCTs/DLTs are not neutral to the context, in which they are applied. Rather consensus-supportive incentives for BCT/DLT providers and users are critical for its successful implementation (Beck, Müller-Bloch, & King, 2018).

In addition, contrary to other emerging technologies, BCT/DLT is not a passive technology. By contrast, BCT/DLT platforms require the interaction of different stakeholders of the ecosystem because the automation of smart contracts and the transfer of values raise important legal and regulatory questions (Schwabe, 2019). Legislation can profoundly influence the process of technological change and diffusion when imposing regulatory enablers and barriers for the uses of emerging technologies, also paving the path for generating new value (Hacker, Lianos, Dimitropoulos, & Eich, 2019). Thus, BCT regulation has attracted the attention of different stakeholders with diverse and even conflicting preferences over multiple

M. P. Rodríguez Bolívar (✉)
Department of Accounting and Finance, University of Granada, Granada, Spain
e-mail: manuelp@ugr.es

H. J. Scholl · R. Pomeshchikov
The Information School, University of Washington, Seattle, WA, USA
e-mail: jscholl@uw.edu; romanpom@uw.edu

C. G. Reddick et al. (eds.), *Blockchain and the Public Sector*, Public Administration and Information Technology 36,
https://doi.org/10.1007/978-3-030-55746-1_1

issues (Meijers, Schneider, & Zhelyazkova, 2019) on domestic levels (Quaglia & Spendzharova, 2019), and especially with public agencies that are necessarily involved in the creation of a regulatory framework process (Ølnes, Ubacht, & Janssen, 2017).

It has been argued that institutional stakeholders influence the elaboration of regulatory frameworks by seeking to maximize their institutional power to achieve favorable policy outcomes (Quaglia & Spendzharova, 2019; Schoeller & Héritier, 2019). However, this interest has not been exerted in the particular case of BCT/DLT regulation and, contrary to expectation, BCT/DLT service regulation has not yet materialized in an international setting. So far, regulatory frameworks for BCT/DLT have not been a primary goal for regulators, except for those focused both on the financial area (Hacker et al., 2019) and on some local markets in specific locations around the world, mainly in countries or areas considered as tax havens.

In addition, according to the OECD (2014), achieving good regulatory outcomes is almost always a co-operative effort. This way, Arras and Braun (2018) have pointed out that regulators are also interested in involving non-state stakeholders into the regulatory process for incorporating expertise into their decisions, for improving their organizational capacity as well as for a reputation-building process. Therefore, the blockchain regulatory frameworks introduced by various jurisdictions cannot be seen as either static or uniform. Regulatory effectiveness will rather depend on its continuous improvement process that accommodates the regulations to non-governmental stakeholder needs.

As the non-governmental stakeholders can vary among different institutional contexts, patterns of regulatory frameworks could tend to be different according to both the institutional context and the stakeholders involved. This chapter seeks to contribute to the literature on stakeholder involvement in formulating and enacting regulatory frameworks, in particular with regard to the perception and needs of various stakeholder groups in the context of BCT/DLT. The chapter further aims at better understanding the perspectives and needs of different key stakeholders regarding benefits, challenges, and expected outcomes of a legislative initiative. This was accomplished by collecting empirical data via surveys from key stakeholders of BCT/DLT service regulations.

The remainder of this chapter is organized as follows: The next section analyzes select blockchain regulatory frameworks and identifies the key stakeholders involved in a particular case of BCT/DLT service regulation. Then, the relevance of the involvement of each stakeholder in the regulatory process is examined (before and after the regulation was put into force). The third section describes the empirical research carried out with different main actors in regulatory processes in a sample of some tax havens with BCT/DLT service regulations in force, followed by the final discussion and conclusion sections.

2 Stakeholders and Blockchain Regulatory Frameworks

2.1 Blockchain Regulatory Frameworks and the Needs of Key Actors

Several theories support the involvement of stakeholders into the decision-making processes (rational choice theory, agency theory, or stakeholder theory, for example). This chapter is mainly based on stakeholder theory, which is prone to consider the interests of salient stakeholders in decisions affecting them or decision that salient stakeholders can affect (Phillips, Freeman, & Wicks, 2003; Scholl, 2001, 2004). Stakeholder theory also recognizes the involvement of different stakeholders with competing views and different moral approaches-endogenous perspective of the theory (Freeman, Harrison, Wicks, Parmar, & DeColle, 2010). According to Freeman et al. (2010), ethical regulations cannot be performed if one attempts an ex-ante solution. By contrast, procedures must be in place, by which to adjudicate the multitude of interests that stakeholders bring to the table (Kline & McDermott, 2019). It provides stakeholders with the power of making their voices heard in the legal arena.

In addition, according to rational choice theory, a political decision is previously analyzed regarding its positive and negative consequences of their potential acts, and politicians prefer not to take any risky decisions if they are not sure about possible outcomes (Amadife, 1999; Rosenau, 1980). Under this presumption the regulator of blockchain would act in a purely rational manner; however, this presumption cannot always hold due to limited information available for taking the decisions, along with pre-existing beliefs, perceptions, etc. Furthermore, in the financial sector, in which regulation for BCT/DLT-based services has been provided, regulators are not purely technocratic or bureaucratic actors that are insulated from the economy or politics of the national context, in which they are embedded (Singer, 2007).

Futhermore, blockchain is a potentially disruptive technology with the capability of introducing and requiring novel governance models regarding how data are conceived and stored along with potentially unintended consequences prompting regulatory authorities to consider the need for intervention (Yeoh, 2017). As has been pointed out technology itself can lead market participants to a specific mode of governance in the system (Lessig, 2006), which leads to distinguishing between the "code *of* law" and the "code *as* law" (De Filippi & Hassan, 2018; Dwyer, 2017; Yeung, 2019), also known as "functional equivalence" (Collomb, De Filippi, & Klara, 2019). Although technology neutrality is an acclaimed approach to ICT regulation, regulatory authorities take decisions regarding technology-neutral or technology-specific approaches (Reed, 2007). The variety of BCT/DLT service regulations is reflective of the diversity and decentralized nature of the systems implemented, which has limited any single one-size-fits-all legislation (Peters, Panayi, & Chapelle, 2015).

As a result, it appears that regulatory frameworks of blockchain technologies are in their early stages of appearance and development, where each system used for regulating blockchain activities (code *of* law *vs.* code *as* law) presents some inconveniences that need to be addressed in future versions of regulation with both the help of regulators and the involvement of salient stakeholders. In this way, technical systems used for regulation promise to ensure that stakeholders' interests are included in the technical code of BCTs/DLTs but, at the same time, regulators need to consider and ensure that the respective operating system is resilient against systemic risks and market failures (Yeoh, 2017). In this vein, BCT/DLT service regulations at the early stage might already have unnecessarily constrained the technology's full potential, which further illustrates the need for stakeholder involvement when adjusting legal frameworks to technical codes and desired goals, and vice versa.

In this regard, past experiences suggest that cautious regulation of new technology-based services works better and functions as a collaborative peer to other constituents of society rather than the heavy hand of law (Ojo, 2019; Tapscott & Tapscott, 2016). This suggests the need of legal and technical codes of blockchain technologies to come together (Yeoh, 2017) and, by this way, the need of articulating means for interaction and collaboration of stakeholders in the blockchain regulatory frameworks. In this regard, the institutionalization and harmonization of formal and informal multi-stakeholder processes are essential when crafting technical codes along with regulatory frameworks to achieve desired regulatory goals. Among the different stakeholders interacting in the policy cycle when framing and selecting the regulatory details, prior research has identified government decision makers, the regulating agency, Fintech firms, the lobbyists, law firms and legal advisors, BCT/DLT developers, and the BCT/DLT firms/licensees as the main ones (Scholl & Rodríguez Bolívar, 2019).

Within this context, the emerging BCT-based ecology can be considered a novel socio-technical system (Fuenfschilling & Truffer, 2016), in which government is an important player among others in a multi-stakeholder approach with the aim of orchestrating appropriate and non-harmful behavior of market participants by boosting transparency and civic engagements as complements to existing systems (Yeoh, 2017). In brief, blockchain environments provide benefits, but also pose challenges, to both governments and stakeholders when working on creating a framework that needs to be defined, formulated, and selected from a legal perspective using a multi-stakeholder approach, also considering global ramifications of the regulation. The chapter contributes to the improved understanding of this particular problem space.

2.2 *The Importance of Key Stakeholders in Evaluating Regulatory Frameworks (Stage of Involvement)*

According to Breu (2018), cooperation and interaction between stakeholders is necessary to take full advantage of blockchain technologies, mainly for the sheer difficulty to implement effective regulations around a decentralized technology. In addition, under these decentralized frameworks, regulated stakeholders often know more about their business than regulators do (Magnuson, 2018a) and the discussions among them is important to assess issues from different angles and to exchange information (Puccio & Harte, 2019). While regulation is a necessity for BCTs/DLTs to be legally sound, nevertheless it is the stakeholders (and their networks) involved in the market who are critical to the operation and maintenance of the blockchain technologies (Islam, Mäntymäki, & Turunen, 2019).

This way, the OECD (2018) indicates that the stakeholder engagement in regulatory processes can help regulators collect better evidence of stakeholders' needs, to improve compliance of legislations through an increased sense of ownership, and to strengthen legitimacy of decision-making processes. This engagement is seen crucial not only before, but also after the adoption of rules, forcing governments to check if regulations work in practice and have not become outdated. Evaluations of implemented legislation regarding their impact on the regulated BCT/DLT services provide effective learning and transparency (Stern, 2009), also ensuring effective and analysis-based next-round legislation (Poptcheva, 2019).

Under this cooperative framework, the regulation facilitates new modes of interaction between stakeholders by establishing rules to support both trust and fairness, avoiding unilateral appropriation and utilization of power by unregulated platforms and financial entities (Hacker et al., 2019). The regulation seeks to direct stakeholders towards reaching this goal through a learning process leading to the transformation of stakeholders' preferences (Jacobsson, 2004; Sabel & Zeitlin, 2008) and their interaction despite diverging interests within the regulated market.

In this regard, one of the essential premises of stakeholder theory is that it focuses on managerial decision-making (Jones & Wicks, 1999). An instrumental stakeholder theory posits that certain outcomes will obtain if certain behaviors are adopted. Under this framework, basis of mutual trust and cooperation will produce a competitive advantage over other contexts, or countries, that do not (Jones, 1995). By this way, the collaboration among the main stakeholders in the blockchain market could help jurisdictions to have competitive advantage over the rest of markets.

Therefore, the application of this theory to the blockchain regulation puts the blockchain system at the center of the discourse, discouraging both the consideration of stakeholders in their own right and the balanced viewing of the stakeholder relation (Friedman & Miles, 2002). Stakeholders' relationships are here included into the necessary compatible relationship defined by Friedman and Miles (2002), where all parties seek to be protectionist because they think that their relationship is important and have something to lose by disruption to the relationship.

Under this assumption, traditionally, financial regulators (regulatory agencies) are used to having full control of rule-making and enforcement processes. However, blockchain frameworks do not fit well into regulatory systems with a central authority due to their decentralized nature, nor with the diverse coding processes that can be used in these frameworks (Ozili, 2019). To face this issue, some authors indicate that regulators can follow different strategies (Finck, 2018), although some of them think that the immature stage of blockchain technology forces the blockchain market not to be regulated yet (Finck, 2018), while others indicate the need of striking a balance between supporting innovation and ensuring consumers to be adequately protected (Financial Conduct Authority, 2017).

Finding the right moment for regulation appears as one of the main challenges for regulators (Walch, 2016), and regulators are supposed to take a learning-mode approach with this new technology environment (Jamison & Tariq, 2018) forcing them to be cautious with their regulations due to the risks that blockchain-based markets potentially introduce to customers. In addition, regulators not only regulate the blockchain market from similar perspectives based on a shared body of technical knowledge (Financial ConductAuthority, 2017; Tsingou, 2015), but they rather also use the technology for promoting new blockchain-based developments. As a key stakeholder group, governmental actors tend to be more focused on the containment of risks for market participants as well as on addressing the challenges than on the benefits of BCT in regulatory approaches.

Moreover, they craft public polices for anticipating, intercepting, mitigating, and managing threats (Stanton & Webster, 2014) shaping how firms conduct business (Larkin et al., 2015) under a blockchain framework. Regulation enforcement, it is understood, has to facilitate government decision makers with means not only to respond, if necessary, but rather also to send a strong message to potentially harmful actors in the blockchain market (Burns, 2017).

As for Fintech firms, although more flexible in adopting to and shaping new financial markets (Magnuson, 2018a) along with taking an early lead in them, these firms are more vulnerable to rapid and adverse market shocks, and their operations are significantly more opaque and less restricted by reputational constraints than those of traditional, large financial institutions (Magnuson, 2018b). This way, these firms usually force financial regulation to require both more information production and cybersecurity procedures (Magnuson, 2018a), which may include incentives for Fintech firms to provide information about their business and to voluntarily seek guidance on the applicability of current regulations (Magnuson, 2018b).

Fintech regulation, however, it has been argued, should be humble and light-touch to promote innovation for improving digital financial inclusion, albeit under the premise of containing potentially systemic risks and protecting consumer interest against those risks at the same time (Magnuson, 2018b; Tsai & Kuan-Jung, 2017; Zetzsche, Buckley, Barberis, & Arner, 2017). In this regard, Fintech firms appear to prefer light regulations for smoothly transforming their services into regulated activities within a flexible work and innovation environment.

Lobbyists represent another group of salient stakeholders that contributes to regulatory effort in this context. Lobby associations comprise market participants and other actors with similar interests in financial matters. For example, in Gibraltar, the Gibraltar Bankers Association (GBA) seeks to promote and protect the local banking industry providing financial services for traders and international commerce at the Western entrance to the Mediterranean Sea, and they are in regular contact with the Gibraltar Financial Services Commission to co-ordinate and consult on the implementation of current and future regulations (see http://www.gba.gi/).

By so doing, the lobbyists have been directly involved in crafting regulation for decentralized financial services (Dorofeyev et al., 2018; Scholl & Rodríguez

Bolívar, 2019), or indirectly through the learning process, in which they were involved in training politicians regarding BCTs (Warnez & Jõesaar, 2018). The influence of these lobby groups is even more relevant when implementing disruptive technologies that inherently introduce certain degrees of uncertainty (Allen & Berg, 2018; Lacity, 2018). Elected officials and politicians appear to follow the lobbyists' advice in favor of Fintech-friendly regulation, although the effect of this influence (positive vs. negative) (Karajovic, Kim, & Laskowski, 2019) and its overall impact (quantity measure) on regulatory processes is not clear (Baumgartner, Berry, Hojnacki, Leech, & Kimball, 2009). In any case, the function of lobbyists is seen as necessary for advancing novel regulations or changing existing regulations with the aim of improving the policy-making process, which contributes to enhancing the legislative and economic framework (Anastasiadis, 2014). With regard to BCT-related regulation, this group can be expected to seek involvement in the regulatory process, although the lobby influence may vary depending on the type of lobbyist and lobbied interest.

Another important stakeholder group are lawyers and legal advisors, law firms, and lawyer associations, hereafter in summary referred to as 'lawyers' who have dual interest in BCT/DLT. On the one hand, lawyers are aware of the adoption of BCTs/DLTs to their business and the potential for improving client engagement and satisfaction (Fenwick, Kaal, & Vermeulen, 2017). On the other hand, lawyers have to advise clients on their legal rights and responsibilities in business transactions performed in a blockchain framework. Therefore, as both users and advisors concerning BCTs/DLTs, lawyers are interested in having a say on blockchain regulation. In their roles of representing clients, lawyers likely favor light regulations for enabling and maintaining flexibility of interpretation for the sake of improving their business and advising clients.

BCT/DLT developers, another salient stakeholder group, have to assure and demonstrate the safety and security to users and market participants before these commit their data and transactions to BCT/DLT-based services (Campbell, 2019). In addition, within the regulatory framework, while governments are setting the standards, they are delegating the means for meeting these standards to the developers themselves (Clarke, 2019). In this regard, prior research has indicated that this industry has shown to be a good partner for government to develop new technologies efficiently (Ghaffari, Lagzian, Kazemi, & Malekzadeh, 2019). In this role, BCT/DLT developers support governments and regulators in order to assure efficient and secure blockchain environments. Therefore, it is expected that this group of stakeholders are more focused on benefits than on challenges about BCT/DLT regulation because they control the code and shape it in ways that obtain efficient and secure blockchain environments mandated by governments and regulators.

Last, but not least, BCT/DLT service firms, another salient stakeholder group, and their roles regarding regulation are multifaceted for a number of reasons including their competitive positions within the BCT/DLT ecosystem (Hileman & Rauchs, 2017). Nonetheless, these firms have a need to ensure the maintenance of robust and accurate records of transactions (Breu, 2018). BCT/DLT firms have often been linked to innovation in financial markets, and regulatory agencies have worked alongside BCT/DLT firms when designing and testing new products and services (Lewis, McPartland, & Ranjan, 2017). Therefore, one might expect that these firms seek light regulations and legal environments that enable continued innovation without unsurmountable barriers to the further development of their novel businesses.

3 Methodology

3.1 *Case Study Approach, Sample, Instrument, and Data Collection*

This research used a case-study approach to capture the views, behaviors, and articulated needs of the salient stakeholders in the regulatory processes about benefits and challenges of blockchain regulation provision. In general, case studies have been used in social science research for a range of purposes, in many instances for exploring for the first-time phenomena within their real-life social settings (Flyvbjerg, 2006; Yin, 2009). Comparing the various salient stakeholders' perspectives on the regulation of BCT/DLT-based service provision helps understand the practical problems of such regulation and potentially paves the path towards an initial development of a theory (Eisenhardt, 1989) on BCT/DLT service provision regulation.

In terms of the case sample, this chapter focused on the jurisdictions of Gibraltar, Liechtenstein, and Malta, which were purposefully chosen for their roles as early issuers of BCT/DLT service provision regulations (Scholl, Pomeshchikov, & Rodríguez Bolívar, 2020). For this particular research, a total of twenty individuals from these jurisdictions were interviewed representing primary stakeholders such as regulators, government officials, legal advisors, lobbyists, Fintech firms, developers, and licensees. These individuals held top management positions in each one of their organizations, and they were specialists in blockchain technology, specially, in blockchain technology regulation. The interviews were conducted either in person or via a videoconferencing tool (Zoom, version 4.1.34801.1116) during the end of 2018 and mid-summer of 2019. The interviews lasted between 41 and 128 minutes. Based on extant literature , on benefits and challenges in the realm of regulating BCT/DLT service provisiona semi-structured interview protocol was devised, which covered the areas of (1) general information, (2) benefits of DLT provision and DLT provider/provision regulation, (3) challenges of DLT provision and DLT provider/provision regulation, and (4) the governance of DLT provider/provision regulation. The instrument incorporated a total of twenty interview questions plus forty-one pre-conceived probes, which were designed to fathom and further render the main question. Interviews were recorded, transcribed, and coded for analysis, which for this chapter mainly focused on the benefits and challenges of BCT/DLT service provision regulation. The initial codebook was developed from the questions on the questionnaire, and additional codes were inductively added during the data analysis and interpretation process (Glaser, 1999; Strauss & Corbin, 1998), finally containing a total of 57 sub-categories.

4 Analysis of Results

The findings in all three cases indicate that financial regulators (regulatory agencies) intended to move fast and decisively on establishing rules in the emerging financial markets, which were providing innovative assets and services. Regulators appeared to sense that BCT/DLT service provision could help democratize financial markets allowing for small and medium financial operators to involve themselves on a more equal footing with larger and longer-established financial institutions. In addition, regulators appeared to be interested in issuing legislation with high degrees of agility and flexibility that allowed fast moving for necessary correction, if needed. In this way, regulatory and supervisory attempts were made to swiftly and flexibly adapt to the emerging procedures and codes and types of assets created in BCT/DLT service markets assuring that participants could work in safe market environments. In other words, regulators expressed to mainly focus on guaranteeing transparency and fair transaction practices geared at protecting customers, transactions, and the reputation of local financial markets.

In addition, they appear to have found themselves in a competitive race for early and effective BCT/DLT service regulation that was meant to quickly and firmly produce a safe environment for long-term sustainability of service providers as well as for protecting customers along with the international reputation of the respective domestic financial market. Therefore, the early move towards BCT/DLT service regulation was seen as a vehicle for putting a stake in the ground and maintaining a favorable competitive position in a market that was expected to thrive.

In this regard, government decision makers in the sample of respondents also expressed their hopes and intents to attract early adopters in BCT/DLT service markets as a means to quickly attract financial investments to their jurisdictions before larger jurisdictions would take over the emerging markets. As a high-ranking government official in Liechtenstein stated,

> ...There is a race in Europe, I would say, from many participants to be the first one to offer a marketplace where you really can exchange all types of tokens and cryptos and fiat currencies, traditional assets so that that's the next development...
> (quote #1)

Lobbyists had experience with working on markets similar to those created by BCT/DLT-based services (for example, online gaming markets), and they suspected that regulatory conditions for these new service models would not be much different from those previously established service models. Therefore, they thought they were aware of the benefits that the regulation of this type of markets could bring to them.

On the other hand, law firms have mostly been involved in helping BCT/DLT service firms secure their business licenses, but they also reported on the windy path full of unforeseen surprises before finally acquiring these licenses (mainly in the early phases of the new markets). Legal advisors also confirmed that licensing firms operating in the online gaming sector had previously presented similar legal challenges. With this experience in mind, some lawyers stated that the main benefit of BCT/DLT service regulation was related to avoiding abuses such as money laundering, tax evasion, and the financing of terrorists.

Regarding blockchain developers, this stakeholder group indicated that a long-term transition from traditional centralized infrastructures to decentralized BCT/DLT infrastructures in financial and securities markets would be necessary, since time was needed not only for changing the current technology platforms but also for people to accept the new emerging frameworks brought about by distributed ledger technologies. The greatest benefit that developers identified in BCT/DLT service regulation was the improvement of information transparency in the financial markets, which would help avoid information asymmetries and lead to better decision-taking processes. In this regard, one interviewee said:

> With blockchain, you can trust the information to high levels and high extents…
>
> …So, I see this whole blockchain and digital innovation space completely changing the landscape in terms of regulatory reporting and the way that people use data…
>
> (quote #5)

Finally, BCT/DLT service licensees expressed their support for being regulated since they saw service and market regulation as presenting them with attractive business opportunity. Licensees appeared to perceive regulation also as an effective barrier to entry, since obtaining BCT/DLT service licenses required to pass a very strict vetting process, which kept some less committed competitors away from the market. In other words, the regulation was seen as a protective shield not only for service users and customers but rather also for developers and service operators themselves.

Despite previous comments, interviewers also expressed some main challenges associated to BCT/DLT regulations. To begin with, regulators were concerned with challenges that were linked to either administrative non-compliance or criminal non-compliance, or both, with regard to BCT/DLT service regulation. Initially, the supervisory and monitoring tasks were mostly performed on an individual basis with a low number of BCT/DLT service licensees. However, with the growth in approved licensees and respective new business operations, the complexity of tokens and business models appeared to have made it more difficult to perform the necessary monitoring functions. For achieving and maintaining the objective of tight and consultative supervision, an increased number of skilled personnel along with innovative technology-based monitoring tools were considered to be an effective remedy.

In addition, the main challenges in BCT/DLT service provision, as seen by regulators, government agencies, and government officials were legal and technological risks translating into potentially harmful outcomes for market participants.

Cross-border transactions and respective legislation and the legal definition of digital assets were seen as major challenges. Moreover, crypto-currencies and smart contracts, which have been created in recent years without appropriate track records, were found to be potentially highly problematic and in need of further scrutiny. As an Officer of the Financial Market Innovation agency in Liechtenstein said:

> ...the handling of technologies is not easy...But you have to just go through this process, and see if the final solution is awesome <meaning "viable," interpretive insertion by authors> for companies, and it's not threatening to business, and in parallel, it ensures the interests of the state, the government...
> (quote #2)

The regulators and government officials in the three case-study jurisdictions appeared to expect the evolution of a harmonized European BCT/DLT legislation over time, which they hoped their own DLT legislation would influence, this way appealing to other European member states to advance their respective BCT/DLT regulation along similar lines.

The case data also suggested that Fintech firms had collaborated with government and regulators to bring about BCT/DLT regulation, through which they highlighted the need for protection of players in the new financial markets and the business opportunities introduced by this emergent technology in this new scenario.

According to these firms, the great volatility of assets traded in these novel service markets was a major challenge. In this regard, service regulation was seen as indispensable rules for introducing viable norms and verifiable criteria that helped foster transparent and accountable business practices in these highly volatile environments. Fintech firms basically agreed with both government decision makers and the regulator regarding regulation as the most pragmatic and effective way to meet the various challenges associated with BCT/DLT service provision.

By contrast, lobbyists' concerns regarding the effectiveness of any regulation were more focused on physical-asset tokenization and on both the viability and the soundness of players inside the markets and, specifically, regarding how new players gain access to novel and traditional financial markets. Therefore, from their perspective regulation was supposed to establish rigid criteria regarding the access points to financial markets, and the regulation had to extend to methods and asset types, by which transactions of tokenized assets could be performed.

As for legal advisors in contrast, this stakeholder group held that BCT/DLT service regulations were too early a shot absent any experience with the emerging technology and the services built thereupon. The legal advisors also considered and proposed the combination and assimilation of regulation of Initial Coin Offerings (ICOs) with more general BCT/DLT service regulation. While finding themselves on a steep learning curve regarding the enabling technology and the respective novel services, legal advisors also considered ways to integrate this regulation into the overarching regulatory system of financial markets. However, legal advisors also recognized the dynamic nature of technology development in the BCT/DLT arena, which makes regulatory efforts challenging. As a partner of leading law firm in Malta explained:

...but I believe that there is still a lot of work to be done even though sometimes we will rush into things...

... When it comes to technology law you need to ensure that the technology is sufficiently mature before you make any legislature...

(quote #3)

Finally, law firms and legal advisors warned against overregulation due to a lack of understating of the phenomena. Overregulation they argued had stifled some industries and prevented their growth in harmful ways. An attorney from Liechtenstein remarked that the inclusion of BCT/DLT service regulation in the legal systems would complicate the smooth functioning of markets, which would also require the introduction and study of and familiarity with law and legal processes on part of the service providers. While study and legal instruction could do so much, the lawyers foresaw that the service providers' learning process would ultimately also be complemented from the litigation side. As the attorney explained:

...I have seen a lot of things that did not go well. So, this is also my approach on all these matters. I did 12 years of litigation already before. So, I know when s*** hits the fan, and how this looks like, which helps a lot in advising because you know, what doesn't work...

(quote #4)

When taking into account the various emerging regulations on BCT/DLT service provision and the lack of international guidelines on the issue, as a key stakeholder group the developers found themselves in immediate need for close monitoring and strictness of compliance with the pertaining regulation but also, at the same time, they had to identify the requirements for necessary and adequate capital resources to cover the material risks of compliance with the BCT/DLT service-related legislation using a three-layer model (finance team, risk assessment team, and compliance team).

What could have been an ardent challenge for an effective and enforced regulation, however, was overcome by the tight collaboration between BCT/DLT service providers and the regulators as well as other government agencies at the time when the license went into effect and the BCT/DLT-based service was started. Already during the licensing process, prospective service providers had been asked to disclose the elements and details of their respective business models along with the physical safeguards and monitoring tools necessary for establishing and maintaining safety and security measures in their business operations. In this fashion, the regulators helped the prospective service provides think through various risk scenarios and harden their business model before operating under license in the blockchain service environment. Based in this positive consultancy-type and quasi-business development experience the licensed service providers expressed their concern regarding the potential loss of highly qualified expert staffers at the regulatory agency since these support provided and the measures agreed upon were of great importance, and a change in the quality of staffers would likely have negative impacts and hamper future business and necessary security processes.

As one worker of the licensed service provider said:

> Challenge one is making sure that the regulator maintains their level of expertise and competency...
> ...the great thing about our regulator is, not only did they understand our business, they were able to challenge us on things, some of which we had not considered. And that is unusual for a regulator...
> (quote #6)

5 Discussion and Conclusion

Technology has become a principal means to distribute power in contemporary society (Brey, 2008). Nonetheless, although the approach taken to the legislative process in blockchain regulation has varied in the three analyzed jurisdictions (Scholl et al., 2020), this research confirms the predictions of stakeholder theory and other recent research, which documented that strong stakeholder involvement in regulatory processes assured the balancing of different, including opposing, interests when regulating an emerging market although at the risk of some dependency on the regulated industry (Arras & Braun, 2018).

As this chapter also illustrates, when government and financial regulators face new challenges with the implementation of emerging technologies in, for example, financial markets, they can successfully develop policies and regulatory frameworks in a collaborative way involving salient stakeholders like Fintech firms and BCT/DLT developers among others in the regulatory process. What this research has also shown is that the views were widely shared and consensus on needs and necessity of regulation on part of the interviewees was uncontested in each stakeholder group irrespective of the jurisdiction, to which the interviewee belonged. This finding could be the result of the application of the stakeholder theory underlying the thinking that collaboration among the main stakeholders in BCT regulation could help their jurisdiction to have competitive advantage.

In addition, the findings indicate that stakeholders sought to bring their institutional weight to bear in order to increase their influence over regulatory outcomes in the BCT/DLT service markets. Whereas regulators, government decision makers, and law firms were mainly concerned with regard to legal compliance, other stakeholders such as the developers were interested in areas of self-regulation, for example, due to technological and legal risks such as cross-border legislation, overregulation, among other aspects. Yet others, such as lobbyists and Fintech firms emphasized their interest in the performance and safety of BCT/DLT service markets both at the access points and with respect to volatility of traded assets.

According to Hacker et al. (2019), the foremost challenge for the future legal frameworks of the blockchain universe would be to precisely specify how the evolved diverse blockchain-based service applications can cope and comply with technologically neutral general provisions of legislation in major jurisdictions, in which these services are provided, and to point to novel forms of legal intervention, from self-regulation to new hard laws where existing regulation fails. These two main challenges are recognized by all stakeholders, but mainly by regulators, government decision makers, and legal advisors who have indicated the need for adapting legislation, which is reflective of the mounting experiences when working in BCT/DLT service environments. Although initially created in a collaborative way, early BCT/DLT service legislations must be considered provisional waiting for the completion of a learning process in day-to-day operations, which could suggest changes and improvements of legislation in the future.

The findings presented in this chapter also confirm prior literature, which indicates that financial regulators have at least two (at times competing) objectives: to safeguard financial stability and to promote the competitiveness of their national financial sector (Kapstein, 1989). As the data from the three cases suggest, regulators in all jurisdictions put an explicit emphasis on establishing rules for transparent and fair transactions in the emerging financial markets for protecting customers and the international reputation of their respective markets. They also supported the idea of democratizing financial markets and, as noted previously, they were aware of the need for adjusting regulations to rapid changes in emerging financial markets, or to changes in international BCT/DLT service regulations, which requires high degrees of agility and flexibility when updating financial regulation as fast as possible.

In summary, as the cases suggest, initially regulators and government decision makers were mainly concerned with the functioning of BCT/DLT services inside financial markets (protection of participants, transparent operations, etc.), while other salient stakeholders were more interested in safety, security, and practical risk-management and operational measures for their conducting business, although these stakeholders highly valued the business opportunity that BCT/DLT service markets provided and the effort of regulators and government agencies to adopt the opportunities presented by the emerging technologies and cater them to the needs of the all market participants in this new service environment.

Future research will need to widen this research in two main areas: other jurisdictions need to be included, and the sample of cases, in general, needs to be larger. It will be informative to analyze how the regulations will have evolved over time due to the issuance of international regulations and guidelines, as well as relative to the experience accumulated with the functioning BCT/DLT service markets. Finally, future studies may analyze the evolution of stakeholder perceptions after gaining experience with operations in these novel and emerging service markets along with an analysis of the observable effects of early regulations on their businesses.

References

Allen, D. W., & Berg, C. (2018). Regulation and technological change. In *Australia's red tape crisis* (pp. 218–230). Brisbane: Connor Court Publishing.

Amadife, E. N. (1999). *Pre-theories and theories of foreign policy-making*. Lanham: University Press of Amer.

Anastasiadis, S. (2014). Toward a view of citizenship and lobbying: Corporate engagement in the political process. *Business & Society, 53*(2), 260–299.

Arras, S., & Braun, C. (2018). Stakeholders wanted! Why and how European Union agencies involve non-state stakeholders. *Journal of European Public Policy, 25*(9), 1257–1275.
Financial Conduct Authority. (2017). *Discussion Paper on distributed ledger technology*. DP17/3. Retrieved from https://www.fca.org.uk/publication/discussion/dp17-03.pdf
Baumgartner, F. R., Berry, J. M., Hojnacki, M., Leech, B. L., & Kimball, D. C. (2009). *Lobbying and policy change: Who wins, who loses, and why*. Chicago: University of Chicago Press.
Beck, R., Müller-Bloch, C., & King, J. L. (2018). Governance in the blockchain economy: A framework and research agenda. *Journal of the Association for Information Systems, 19*(10), 1020–1034.
Breu, S. (2018). Are blockchains and cybercurrencies demanding a new legislative framework. *Journal Law and Digital Economy, 1*(1), 12–18.
Brey, P. (2008). The technological construction of social power. *Social Epistemology, 22*(1), 71–95.
Burns, J. (2017). Breach of faith: A lack of policy for responding to data breaches and what the government should do about it. *Florida Law Review, 69*, 959.
Campbell, R. E. (2019). Research transitioning to a hyperledger fabric hybrid quantum resistant-classical public key infrastructure. *The Journal of British Blockchain Association, 2*(2), 15–25.
Clarke, R. (2019). Principles and business processes for responsible AI. *Computer Law & Security Review, 35*(4), 410–422.
Collomb, A., De Filippi, P., & Klara, S. O. K. (2019). Blockchain technology and financial regulation: A risk-based approach to the regulation of ICOs. *European Journal of Risk Regulation, 10*(2), 263–314.
De Filippi, P., & Hassan, S. (2018). Blockchain technology as a regulatory technology: From code is law to law is code. arXiv preprint arXiv:1801.02507.
Dorofeyev, M., Kosov, M., Ponkratov, V., Masterov, A., Karaev, A., & Vasyunina, M. (2018). Trends and prospects for the development of blockchain and cryptocurrencies in the digital economy. *European Research Studies Journal, 21*(3), 429–445.
Dwyer, R. (2017). Code!= Law: Explorations of the Blockchain as a Mode of Algorithmic Governance.
Eisenhardt, K. M. (1989). Building theories from case study research. *Academy of Management Review, 14*(4), 532–550.
Fenwick, M., Kaal, W. A., & Vermeulen, E. P. (2017). Legal education in the Blockchain revolution. *Vanderbilt Journal of Entertainment & Technology Law, 20*, 351.
Finck, M. (2018). Blockchains: Regulating the unknown. *German Law Journal, 19*(4), 665–692.
Freeman, R. E., Harrison, J. S., Wicks, A. C., Parmar, B. L., & DeColle, S. (2010). *Stakeholder theory: The state of the art*. Cambridge, UK: Cambridge University Press.
Friedman, A. L., & Miles, S. (2002). Developing stakeholder theory. *Journal of Management Studies, 39*(1), 1–21.
Fuenfschilling, L., & Truffer, B. (2016). The interplay of institutions, actors and technologies in socio-technical systems—An analysis of transformations in the Australian urban water sector. *Technological Forecasting and Social Change, 103*, 298–312.
Flyvbjerg, B. (2006). Five misunderstandings about case-study research. *Qualitative inquiry, 12*(2), 219–245.
Ghaffari, K., Lagzian, M., Kazemi, M., & Malekzadeh, G. (2019). A socio-technical analysis of internet of things development: An interplay of technologies, tasks, structures and actors. *Foresight, 21*(6), 640–653.
Glaser, B. G. (1999). The future of grounded theory. *Qualitative Health Research, 9*(6), 836–845.
Hacker, P., Lianos, I., Dimitropoulos, G., & Eich, S. (2019). Regulating blockchain: Techno-social and legal challenges – an introduction. In *Regulating blockchain. Techno-social and legal challenges* (pp. 3–24). Oxford: Oxford University Press.
Hileman, G., & Rauchs, M. (2017). *2017 global blockchain benchmarking study*. Available at SSRN 3040224.
Islam, N., Mäntymäki, M., & Turunen, M. (2019, January). *Understanding the role of actor heterogeneity in blockchain splits: An actor-network perspective of bitcoin forks*, in Proceedings of the 52nd Hawaii International Conference on system sciences.

Jacobsson, K. (2004). Soft regulation and the subtle transformation of states: The case of EU employment policy. *Journal of European Social Policy, 14*, 355–370.
Jamison, M. A., & Tariq, P. (2018). Five things regulators should know about blockchain (and three myths to forget). *The Electricity Journal, 31*(9), 20–23.
Jones, T. M. (1995). Instrumental stakeholder theory: A synthesis of ethics and economics. *Academy of Management Review, 20*(2), 404–437.
Jones, T. M., & Wicks, A. C. (1999). Convergent stakeholder theory. *Academy of Management Review, 24*(2), 206–221.
Kapstein, E. B. (1989). Resolving the regulator's dilemma: International coordination of banking regulations. *International Organization, 43*(2), 323–347.
Karajovic, M., Kim, H. M., & Laskowski, M. (2019). Thinking outside the block: Projected phases of blockchain integration in the accounting industry. *Australian Accounting Review, 29*(2), 319–330.
Kline, W., & McDermott, K. (2019). Evolutionary stakeholder theory and public utility regulation. *Business and Society Review, 124*(2), 283–298.
Lacity, M. C. (2018). Addressing key challenges to making enterprise blockchain applications a reality. *MIS Quarterly Executive, 17*(3), 201–222.
Larkin, S., Fox-Lent, C., Eisenberg, D. A., Trump, B. D., Wallace, S., Chadderton, C., et al. (2015). Benchmarking agency and organizational practices in resilience decision making. *Environment Systems and Decisions, 35*(2), 185–195.
Lessig, L. (2006). *Code: and other laws of cyberspace, version 2.0*. New York, NY: Basic Books.
Lewis, R., McPartland, J., & Ranjan, R. (2017). Blockchain and financial market innovation. *Economic Perspectives, 41*(7), 1–17.
Magnuson, W. (2018a). Financial regulation in the Bitcoin era. *Stanford Journal of Law, Business & Finance, 23*(2), 159–209.
Magnuson, W. (2018b). Regulating fintech. *Vanderbilt Law Review, 71*(4), 1167–1226.
Meijers, M. J., Schneider, C. J., & Zhelyazkova, A. (2019). Dimensions of input responsiveness in the EU: Actors, publics, venues. *Journal of European Public Policy, 26*(11), 1724–1736.
OECD. (2014). *OECD best practice principles for regulatory policy*. Paris: OECD Publishing.
OECD. (2018). *OECD regulatory policy outlook*. Paris: OECD.
Ojo, M. (2019). Facilitating artificial intelligence and block chain systems, partnerships and technologies: Emerging global actors and players in the financial reporting framework. *Center & Institute for Innovation and Sustainable Development Economic Review, 1*, 1.
Ølnes, S., Ubacht, J., & Janssen, M. (2017). Blockchain in government: Benefits and implications of distributed ledger technology for information sharing. *Government Information Quarterly, 34*(3), 255–364.
Ozili, P. K. (2019). *Blockchain finance: Questions regulators ask. Disruptive innovation in business and finance in the digital world* (Vol. 20, pp. 123–129). Bingley: Emerald Publishing Limited.
Peters, G., Panayi, E., & Chapelle, A. (2015). Trends in cryptocurrencies and blockchain technologies: A monetary theory and regulation perspective. *Journal of Financial Perspectives, 3*, 3.
Phillips, R., Freeman, R. E., & Wicks, A. C. (2003). What stakeholder theory is not. *Business Ethics Quarterly, 13*(4), 479–502.
Poptcheva, E. M. (2019). Parliamentary oversight: Challenges facing classic scrutiny instruments and the emergence of new forms of 'steering' scrutiny. In *The European Parliament in times of EU crisis* (pp. 25–52). Cham: Palgrave Macmillan.
Puccio, L., & Harte, R. (2019). The European parliament's role in monitoring the implementation of EU trade policy. In *The European Parliament in times of EU crisis* (pp. 387–412). Cham: Palgrave Macmillan.
Quaglia, L., & Spendzharova, A. (2019). Regulators and the quest for coherence in finance: The case of loss absorbing capacity for banks. *Public Administration, 97*(3), 499–512.
Reed, C. (2007). Taking sides on technology neutrality. *SCRIPTed, 4*(3), 263–284.
Rosenau, J. N. (1980). *The scientific study of foreign policy*. London/New York: Frances Pinter Publishers Ltd..

Sabel, C. F., & Zeitlin, J. (2008). Learning from difference: The new architecture of experimentalist governance in the EU. *European Law Journal, 14*(3), 271–327.
Schoeller, M. G., & Héritier, A. (2019). Driving informal institutional change: The European Parliament and the reform of the Economic and Monetary Union. *Journal of European Integration, 41*(3), 277–292.
Scholl, H. J. (2001). Applying stakeholder theory to e-government: benefits and limits. In B. Schmid, K. Stanoevska-Slabeva, & V. Tschammer (Eds.), *1st IFIP conference on e-commerce, e-business, and e-government (I3E 2001)* (pp. 735–747). Alphen aan den Rijn: Kluwer.
Scholl, H. J. (2004). Involving salient stakeholders: Beyond the technocratic view on change. *Action Research, 2*(3), 281–308.
Scholl, H. J., Pomeshchikov, R., & Rodríguez Bolívar, M. P. (2020, January). *Early regulations of distributed ledger technology/blockchain providers: A comparative case study*, in Proceedings of the 53rd Hawaii International Conference on System Sciences.
Scholl, H. J., & Rodríguez Bolívar, M. P. (2019). Regulation as both enabler of technology use and global competitive tool: The Gibraltar case. *Government Information Quarterly, 36*(3), 601–613.
Schwabe, G. (2019). The role of public agencies in blockchain consortia: Learning from the Cardossier. *Information Polity, 2019*, 1–15.
Singer, D. A. (2007). *Regulating capital: Setting standards for the international financial system*. Ithaca, NY: Cornell University Press.
Stanton, T., & Webster, D. W. (Eds.). (2014). *Managing risk and performance: A guide for government decision makers*. Hoboken: John Wiley & Sons.
Stern, E. (2009). Evaluation policy in the European Union and its institutions. *New Directions for Evaluation, 2009*(123), 67–85.
Strauss, A., & Corbin, J. (1998). *Basics of qualitative research techniques*. Thousand Oaks, CA: Sage Publications.
Tapscott, D., & Tapscott, A. (2016). *Blockchain revolution: How the technology behind bitcoin is changing money, business, and the world*. New York: Penguin.
Tsai, C. H., & Kuan-Jung, P. (2017). The FinTech revolution and financial regulation: The case of online supply-chain financing. *Asian Journal of Law and Society, 4*(1), 109–132.
Tsingou, E. (2015). Club governance and the making of global financial rules. *Review of International Political Economy, 22*(2), 225–256.
Walch, A. (2016). The path of the blockchain lexicon (and the law). *The Review of Banking and Financial Law, 36*, 713–765.
Warnez, J. & Jõesaar, S. (2018). Regulating and taxing platform businesses. Copenhagen, Denmark: Master's Thesis, MSc in Social Sciences in Service Management.
Yeoh, P. (2017). Regulatory issues in blockchain technology. *Journal of Financial Regulation and Compliance, 25*(2), 196–208.
Yeung, K. (2019). Regulation by blockchain: The emerging battle for supremacy between the code of law and code as law. *The Modern Law Review, 82*(2), 207–239.
Yin, R. K. (2009). How to do better case studies. *The SAGE handbook of applied social research methods, 2*, 254–282.
Zetzsche, D. A., Buckley, R. P., Barberis, J. N., & Arner, D. W. (2017). Regulating a revolution: From regulatory sandboxes to smart regulation. *The Fordham Journal of Corporate & Financial Law, 1*, 31–103.

Manuel Pedro Rodríguez Bolívar is Professor of Accounting at the University of Granada. His research interests are mainly related to e-government and smart cities. He is the author of more than 55 papers published in JCR indexed journals and more than 35 book chapters published in international publishers. He holds the position of Editor in Chief of the Public Administration and Information Technology (PAIT) book series in Springer and the International Journal of Public Administration in the Digital Age (IJPADA), and he is a member of the Editorial Board of Government Information Quarterly and other relevant international journals like Informatics.

Hans Jochen Scholl serves as a Full Professor in the Information School at the University of Washington, Seattle, WA. He earned a Ph.D. in Information Science from the University at Albany, State University of New York, and also holds a Master's degree in Business Administration from the GSBA Zurich, Switzerland. His research interests focus on the information perspective for understanding human-originated complex systems. He employs quantitative and qualitative approaches ranging from System Dynamics to Situational Action Analysis and Action Research among other methods. Areas of study include information management, in general, and Digital Government, disaster studies (Disaster Information Management), information artifact evaluation, and pro sports information management, in particular. Jochen is a past president of the Digital Government Society, of which he was a founding member. He also serves as Past Chair of the IFIP WG 8.5 (IS and Public Administration) and as Board Member of the International Association for Information Systems for Crisis Response and Management (ISCRAM organization). With help of iSchool graduate assistants he maintains and publishes the Digital Government Reference Library (DGRL) and the Disaster Information Reference Library (DIRL). Furthermore, Jochen served as founding chair for over a decade and later as co-chair of the renowned Digital Government Track at HICSS (until 2020). He serves as Associate Editor and Editorial Board Member on a number of leading journals.

Roman Pomeshchikov is currently a Ph.D. candidate at the Near and Middle Eastern Studies (NMES) Interdisciplinary Program at the University of Washington. His academic interests include qualitative comparative research, politics of digital transformation, digital government, state-society relations, and institutional change in developing countries.

Chapter 2
Blockchain Technology as Information Infrastructure in the Public Sector

Svein Ølnes and Arild Jansen

1 Introduction

Blockchain technology (BCT) has met with significant acceptance in recent years. After first being applied exclusively to financial operations (payments and value transfer), the benefits derived from applying this technology in other sectors has attracted increasing interest. Blockchain technology has already developed into platforms that foster a wide range of applications (Ølnes, Ubacht, & Janssen, 2017). In this section, we will explore the potential for BCT to evolve into a broader concept—namely, an information infrastructure.

Fundamentally, blockchain is a combination of already existing technologies that together can create networks that are able to ensure trust between people or parties who otherwise have no reason to trust each other. Specifically, it utilizes distributed ledger technology (DLT) to store information verified by cryptography among a group of users. The current state of the blockchain is agreed upon through a network protocol without a central, controlling authority. Through the combination of core technologies like peer-to-peer network, digital signatures, hash functions and proof of work (POW), trust is not removed but replaced by a new architecture for trust based on these technologies (Werbach, 2018).

The most important features of the open blockchain technology are its global nature and scope, its decentralized and distributed character, its built-in transparency, and independence of trusted parties. Although BCT has grown remarkably as a foundation for many innovations, it is still a somewhat immature technological

S. Ølnes (✉)
Western Norway Research Institute, Sogndal, Norway
e-mail: sol@vestforsk.no

A. Jansen
University of Oslo, Oslo, Norway
e-mail: arildj@jus.uio.no

C. G. Reddick et al. (eds.), *Blockchain and the Public Sector*, Public Administration and Information Technology 36,
https://doi.org/10.1007/978-3-030-55746-1_2

platform. Accordingly, it is most likely that future BCT-based platforms will be comprised of a variety of different implementations, including both permissioned (controlled) and permissionless (no central control) as well as public and private blockchains (see e.g. Hardjono, Lipton, & Pentland, 2018). Thus, it is highly relevant to investigate how such different, distinct platforms may grow into a coherent infrastructure that allows for interaction between different BCT-based applications. One crucial issue is how to achieve interoperability. We will enquire into how we can use the experiences from the development of the Internet in building a BCT-based infrastructure architecture that supports interoperability.

Our methodological approach is mainly theoretical and conceptual, analyzing the potential for adopting BCT through the lens of information infrastructure. Our use of literature mainly relies on the general body of blockchain literature that has grown substantially in recent years. The literature on blockchain technology used in the public sector is more limited. We have used the extensive DGRL library (previously EGRL) v. 15.5 with more than 12,500 references of peer-reviewed publications within the digital government domain. Searching for the keyword 'blockchain' in this library resulted in 84 articles, a sign that research on BCT in digital government is still in an early stage.

2 Blockchain Typology: Themes, Terms, and Concepts

This section presents some of the core elements and functions of blockchain technology. However, we discuss only the parts and details that are considered relevant for the question of BCT as a possible information infrastructure (also) in the public sector. These parts include a discussion of terminology and important characteristics of BCT including consensus methods, immutability and data quality, trust and governance, security, and smart contracts and tokens.

Fundamentally, blockchain technology is a combination of already existing technologies. What is innovative is the way these technologies are combined, not least the consensus method.

Bitcoin was built on well-proven technologies. The new way these were combined resulted in a breakthrough for addressing the problem of value transfer on the Internet without the need for a trusted third party. As stated by Satoshi Nakamoto in the seminal white paper (Nakamoto, 2008), cryptography (e.g. digital signatures and hash functions) is an important part of the solution, but will not in itself remove the need for a trusted third party. It is the combination of cryptography and consensus methods—in Bitcoin's case, the proof of work method (PoW)—that eliminates the need for a trusted third party to prevent double spending. Trust is shifted from a central authority to a distributed system of nodes, all working independently of one other.

Figure 2.1 illustrates the basic concept of linking blocks in a blockchain by using hashes. The "nonce" field contains just a counter for the miners to change in order to calculate a new hash in their ongoing effort to meet the defined difficulty.

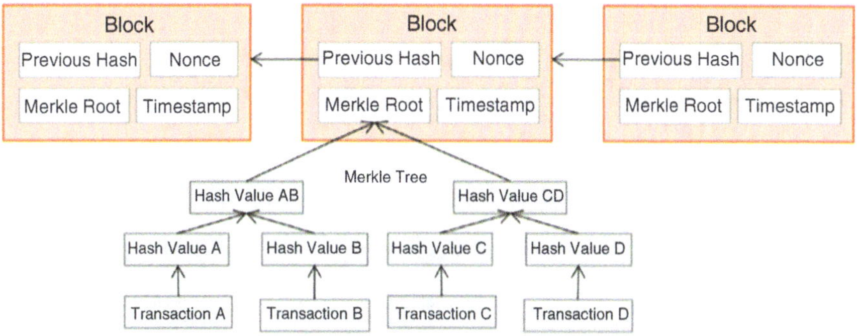

Fig. 2.1 Illustration of hash-linked blocks in a blockchain (Bahga & Madisetti, 2016)

This is the "proof of work" part of the consensus method (see more about consensus methods later in the section). The Merkle root is a combined hash value of a pairwise hashing of all the transactions in the block.

2.1 *Distributed and Decentralized Systems*

In blockchain literature the terms "distributed" and "decentralized" are often used interchangeably. However, these terms should be distinguished to highlight their special characteristics and to avoid misunderstandings. One of the Internet pioneers, Baran (1964) distinguishes between centralized, decentralized, and distributed communications networks, see Fig. 2.2.

To our understanding, a *decentralized system* [in systems theory] is a system in which lower level components operate on local information to accomplish global goals, whereas a *distributed system* (more precisely a *network)* consists of a collection of autonomous units/components. All components in a decentralized system are linked to the central level and will not be able to function entirely without the central unit functioning. An example of a decentralized system is Internet's Domain Name System (DNS) where ICANN serves as the authoritative, central organization, while the administration of country-specific domain names is delegated to the individual countries.

On the other hand, a distributed architecture consists of a collection of autonomous systems linked by a network and operating according to a set of common rules. Accordingly, such distributed autonomous "systems" can function without a central unit in the network (as e.g. in the case of Internet). However, for distributed systems as well, some type of "entity" must define and maintain the necessary common rules, as is the case for Internet (like e.g. IETF, a large open international community concerned with the evolution of the Internet architecture) and for blockchain based network such as Bitcoin. Following from this, a decentralized system is still bounded, while a distributed architecture is that of an (open) network: it can be

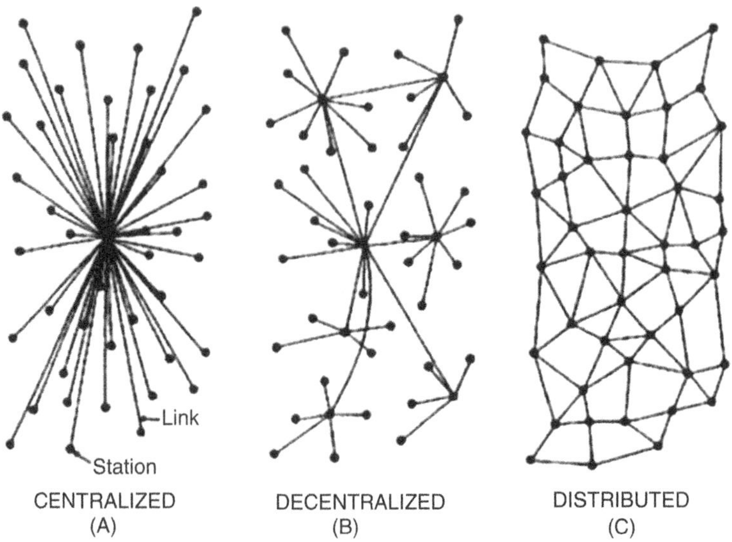

Fig. 2.2 Paul Baran's illustration of a centralized, decentralized, and distributed system (Baran, 1964)

extended continuously without changing its way of functioning. This understanding of "decentralized" and "distributed" corresponds well with Baran's definitions.

2.2 *Blockchain Typologies*

Blockchains are "append-only" databases where transactions are grouped in blocks that are connected by hash linking. The hash linking is done by hashing some of the meta-data information in a block header including the hash of the previous block, see Fig. 2.1. By doing this, the content of a block cannot be changed without changing the hash, and any such change will therefore be easy to detect. BCs are therefore tamper-evident meaning that it is easy to detect any attempt to change information that is already stored on the blockchain. However, this is not what makes a blockchain secure. The hash linking of blocks in a blockchain makes it tamper *evident*, but it is the consensus method that defines the degree of tamper *resistance* and hence its immutability (Narayanan, Bonneau, Felten, Miller, & Goldfeder, 2016).

All blockchain systems are updated though transactions. A transaction alters the blockchain's state from one state to a new state. A blockchain thus needs to keep track of its state, contrary to traditional databases, which are mostly stateless (Wüst & Gervais, 2018). The openness and type of permission is related to what an ordinary user can do. The openness ranges from completely *open* in all parts of the transaction process, to being completely *closed*. Table 2.1 below shows the typical properties of open and closed, and permissionless and permissioned blockchains.

Table 2.1 Types of blockchains, revised from (Hileman & Rauchs, 2017, in OECD (2018))

			Read	Write	Commit	Example
Blockchain Types	Open	Public permissionless	Open to anyone	Anyone	Anyone	Bitcoin, Ethereum
		Public permissioned	Open to anyone	All or authorised participants	Authorised participants	Supply chain ledger for retail brand viewable by public
	Closed	Consortium	Restricted to an authorised set of participants	Authorised participants	All or subset of authorised participants	Multiple banks operating a shared ledger
		Private permissioned "enterprise"	Fully private or restricted to a limited set of authorised nodes	Network operator only	Network operator only	External bank ledger shared between parent company and subsidiaries

In the table above 'Read' applies to whether the transactions in the blockchain are open to access. 'Write' means who can perform transactions in the blockchain system and 'Commit' means who can append the transactions to the blockchain, thereby finalizing the transactions. The commit part is tightly coupled to the consensus method of the blockchain. We should note that the term *public* is also used as a synonym for *open and permissionless blockchains, and private is often used to denote a permissioned blockchain.*

The permissioned/permissionless aspect refers to the degree of control of the blockchain and who is granted the right to store information. However, it also affects the governance of the blockchain, e.g. the changing of rules for the blockchain. Openness, or public/closed, refers to whether the information on the blockchain is accessible to the public.

It should be noted that a blockchain like Bitcoin is permissionless even when the proof of work method used is highly specialized with specific hardware and software. Anyone who can afford to invest in the equipment, large or small, can also participate in the consensus procedures, e.g. the 'commit' part.

2.3 Consensus Methods

A consensus method is used for the distributed parties to come to agreement on the present state of the system. In a distributed system there needs to be a way of agreeing on which transactions are valid and how to order them (timestamping). Lamport, Shostak, and Pease (1982) first identified the problem of reaching consensus in a distributed environment through their description of the Byzantine Generals Problem. Out of their work, the Byzantine Agreement was developed. The Byzantine Generals Problem is an imagined situation involving a group of generals surrounding an enemy city. The problem is to find an algorithm that can ensure that the loyal generals reach a concerted agreement, because there may be traitors among them. The generals pass a simple message among themselves with either "attack" or "retreat". Lamport et al. (ibid.) showed that there is no solution to the problem unless more than 2/3 of the generals are loyal. Lamport et al.'s work was about reliability in computer systems with malfunctioning components giving conflicting information (ibid.). However, the problem is at the core of BCTs' consensus methods.

In Bitcoin and several other open, permissionless blockchains, the proof of work method is the central part of the consensus method. To get the permission to add transactions to the blockchain, it is necessary to solve a mathematic puzzle in the form of a hash function. The puzzle can only be solved by a trial-and-error method and the difficulty of the puzzle is dependent on the amount of computing capacity in the network. The PoW method was first suggested to combat spam in emails by Dwork and Naor (1992) and later in a combination with digital cash by Back (2002).

Open, permissionless systems need incentives to compensate for the costs incurred by the consensus method. All open and permissionless blockchains therefore need a built-in currency, a cryptocurrency, to pay for the consensus work being done. The combination of the stochastic proof of work method and the incentives by generating new bitcoins is also a way to randomly distribute the currency supply.

Controlled blockchains, in which only a limited set of actors have the right to store transactions on the blockchain, do not need incentives, and therefore need no cryptocurrency. These systems typically have different consensus methods because of the controlled environment.

Table 2.2 below lists some of the most relevant consensus methods in blockchain technology and their properties.

Proof of work (PoW) is the only exogenous consensus method of those listed above. An exogenous method means that the method relies on external factors; in PoW that is computing capacity by energy consumption. An endogenous method means that the consensus method is based on internal factors, e.g. proof of stake's staking ("risking") a part of your cryptocurrency investment. The tolerated power of

Table 2.2 Comparison of some typical consensus methods (derived and modified from Zheng, Xie, Dai, Chen, & Wang, 2017)

Property	Proof of work	Proof of stake	Practical byzantine fault tolerance (PBFT)
Openness	Open	Open	Permissioned
Exogenous/endogenous	Exogenous	Endogenous	Endogenous
Tolerated power of adversary	<50%	<50%	<33%
Example	Bitcoin, ethereum	Dash, tezos	Hyperledger fabric

adversary in the open blockchains above is related to the challenge of avoiding double-spending, e.g. spending the same "coin" more than once.

2.4 Security

As discussed in the previous section, it is the consensus method rather than the hash linking that secures a blockchain. The hash linking makes a blockchain tamper evident; the consensus method makes the blockchain tamper resistant. Tamper resistance is the crucial factor for obtaining immutability; that is the impossibility of making changes to data once they are stored on the blockchain.

The most common change of data on a blockchain is the double-spend situation where the same coins can be spent more than once. Bitcoin proposed a solution to the double-spending problem and Nakamoto described the solution this way (Nakamoto, 2008):

> We propose a solution to the double-spending problem using a peer-to-peer network.
>
> The network timestamps transactions by hashing them into an ongoing chain of hash-based proof-of-work, forming a record that cannot be changed without redoing the proof-of-work.

It is the ongoing verification process based on hash-based proof of work that secures against double-spending. To tamper with the blockchain with an intention to double-spend, the attacker will have to muster more than half of the total computing power in the network and thereby be able to redo the proof of work and spend the coins twice. The double-spend attack concerns both the economic and the informational part of an open, permissionless blockchain. Information e.g. a hash of a document, can be changed as a result of a double-spending attack. In a controlled blockchain a double-spend attack can be carried out by more than a third of the consortium partners colluding.

The immutability property of a blockchain is not a yes or no, but rather a spectrum. The Ethereum Classic blockchain, one of the top 20 cryptocurrencies in market capitalization, suffered a 51% attack in January 2019 (Walch, 2019), an incident showing that a 51% attack is not merely a theoretical discussion. Therefore, the Bitcoin and Ethereum mining pool concentrations have raised concerns since individual pools have come close to, and even above, the critical 50% limit of cumulative PoW resources (ibid.).

2.5 Immutability and Data Quality

Immutability is sometimes interpreted as a guarantee of high data quality. But immutability is just as much a case of erroneous data as it is of correct data (garbage in gives garbage out). A blockchain can just as easily store false data as it can store correct data. A blockchain that stores data other than its internal cryptocurrency needs a trusted party to ensure the correctness and validity of the data to be stored. This might appear to be a contradiction since blockchain technology is supposed to remove the need for a central authority, or a trusted third party. However, the elimination of a trusted third party only concerns the transaction process inside the blockchain system, not the content of the transaction that is created outside the blockchain. All "external" information stored on a blockchain needs to be verified by a trusted authority to ensure the quality.

If we take the use case of publishing academic credentials on the blockchain (discussed later in this chapter), it is obvious that each student cannot be given the permission to upload his or her credentials to a blockchain. We would have no guarantee that the information uploaded was not tampered with and changed in favor of the student. The university would have to issue the credentials and upload them together with their own certificate to ensure the quality of the data.

The immutability of data on the blockchain is dependent on the overall security of the blockchain. As discussed in the previous section, the most important part of the security is the consensus method. In a PoW-based consensus method, the amount of computer power needed to solve the puzzle, e.g. the hash rate, is a clear indicator of the tamper resistance of the blockchain.

However, the governance model and the built-in "ethos" of the blockchain are also, as discussed later, important factors for preserving data integrity and quality and mitigating the risk of data being compromised.

2.6 Trust, Transparency and Blockchain Governance

Blockchains operate under the slogan "Don't trust, verify", a twist on the famous quote from former president Reagan when he described USA's relation to the Soviet Union: "Trust, but verify". In open (public) blockchains everybody needs to know everything to be able to perform the necessary verification. All nodes (peers) have all information and can independently verify the correctness of the blockchain's state.

However, we must not confuse the distribution of data in blockchain systems with decentralization of power. It is possible to have data distributed among many nodes, but still have a centrally controlled and coordinated system. As Walch (2019) points out, decentralization comes in many flavors and must be analyzed on many levels to get a broader picture of the governance model of a blockchain and its degree of decentralization. We need to look at the distribution of power among different constituencies such as developers, miners, users, and exchanges, to name the most important groups.

Different blockchains also have different visions ("ethos") for development, further complicating interoperability between blockchain systems. As an example, we can compare Bitcoin's conservative philosophy, "move slow, do not break things", with Ethereum's philosophy of "move fast, break things". Bitcoin's philosophy is reminiscent of the development of the core Internet protocols where backwards compatibility had, and still has? the highest priority, thus in sharp contrast to Ethereum's philosophy where regularly performed "hard forks" are an important part of the development plans. A hard fork is a change in the protocol that is not backwards compatible. A soft fork, which is Bitcoin's preferred method of updates, is a change in protocol that is backwards compatible. A hard fork in a permissionless blockchain will increase the risk of creating a chain-split and thereby creating two currencies. This is what happened in the infamous DAO incident in 2016, see below (Walch, 2019).

2.7 Interoperability Between Blockchains

The blockchain universe has evolved from the original Bitcoin blockchain to a heavily fragmented landscape of numerous un-interoperable blockchains (Schulte, Sigwart, Frauenthaler, & Borkowski, 2019). New use cases with new requirements have been met during the development of new blockchain systems, most often modified versions of existing ones (ibid.). The open source culture of almost all blockchain systems facilitates making modifications, but this also implies a greater challenge regarding interoperability between systems. The constant increase in new, independent, and unconnected blockchain technologies causes significant problems for cross-blockchain operations (ibid.). This is discussed in more detail below.

2.8 Smart Contracts, Token Economy, and Digital Assets

Another area in which the two major permissionless blockchains Bitcoin and Ethereum differ is smart contracts. The term smart contracts was first used and described by Szabo (1997) and a definition of the term is "... an automatable and enforceable agreement" (Clack, Bakshi, & Braine, 2016). Automatable refers to the execution by computers and enforceable agreement refers to legal enforcement of rights and obligations (ibid.).

Although Bitcoin also provides the opportunity to create smart contracts on its blockchain Ethereum is the blockchain recognized for introducing smart contracts. This is mostly because Ethereum has a Turing-complete programming language that Bitcoin does not have. For Bitcoin, this was a deliberate choice related to security, while for Ethereum it is included to provide more functionality and is thus also a deliberate choice.

Critics have claimed that smart contracts are neither smart nor contracts (O'hara, 2017) and the notion that they would make a radical change in many sectors experienced a shot across the bow when the decentralized autonomous organization The DAO failed in 2016 (ibid.). The DAO was a smart contract on the Ethereum blockchain that gathered $150 mill. worth of the cryptocurrency *ether* (in 2016) and was hacked immediately after the launch. The hack resulted in a hard fork to save the funds, and that again resulted in a chain-split with two incompatible blockchains; Ethereum and Ethereum Classic. The idea of removing human control from contracts proved to be complicated and dangerous. This incident raised serious questions about the claim of blockchains' immutability (Walch, 2019).

Despite the setback from the DAO, smart contracts are believed to hold a great potential. However, there is need for a better understanding of the risks involved. A smart contract is essentially a small computer program and storing it on the blockchain requires developers to "make the program right the first time". There is no way to correct the program once it is stored on the blockchain; it can only be replaced by a new (smart) contract. Another challenge with smart contracts is that they most often rely on data input from external sources. Even the input of a simple observation like the exchange rate of a currency can be subject to debate because of the source used.

Closely linked with smart contracts are tokens and the token economy. The term "token economy" is well established and predates the cryptocurrency era (Ivy, Meindl, Overley, & Robson, 2017). However, in the blockchain sphere, the term tokenization describes the process of transferring rights to a real world asset into a digital representation – or token – on the blockchain (OECD, 2018). Being in possession of that digital token then gives you the right to that asset and the ability to trade and track it digitally.

There are three main types of tokens (ibid.):

1. *Payment tokens*: Commonly known as a cryptocurrency. A payment token can be a store of value and a unit of measurement, e.g. Bitcoin.
2. *Utility tokens*: Tokens that represent a right to a good or service, like a gift card, e.g. StorjCoin provides one with access to a distributed storage.
3. *Security tokens*: Token that are digital representations of traditional securities such as equities, bonds, and options. The holder of the token has rights to the company's future profits, e.g. tZERO.

Tokens will probably also play an important role in the public sector, mostly in the form of utility tokens. One example of its use might be as a bearer of information such as various credentials and evidence of identity. This is discussed later in this chapter.

The topics, terms, and concepts presented above provide the necessary foundation for studying the possibilities for how blockchain technology can evolve from today's various platforms into a universal information infrastructure.

3 Information Infrastructures

This section will discuss BCT platform developments in an infrastructure perspective and explore the extent to which they may grow into information infrastructures. We will address issues like installed base, bootstrapping and how to design an information infrastructure, focusing in particular on challenges related to IIs in public sector

3.1 Platforms Versus Information Infrastructures

The growing number of BC based implementations illustrates that blockchains already comprise platforms supporting various types of applications.

Infrastructures are different from platforms. An ICT platform can be described as a set of basic software components and services that are used as a base upon which other applications, processes etc. are developed. Once established, it remains rather stable, and they are primarily designed to support a limited set of systems and applications, as e.g. Microsoft MS Windows. An infrastructure has broader scope and is more dynamic; it is aimed at supporting a wide range of systems and applications across many platforms and technologies.

An ICT infrastructure comprising various networking components and software is primarily understood as a technical facility. However, the growth of the Internet, including the World Wide Web created a need for a holistic, socio-technical and evolutionary approach when studying such networks of distributed, but interlinked information systems, therefore denoted as *information infrastructure* (II). Following e.g. Hanseth and Lyytinen (2010) and Star and Ruhleder (1996), we understand an information infrastructure (II) as "a *shared, open* and *unbounded, heterogeneous and evolving socio-technical system consisting of a set of IT capabilities and their user, operations, and design communities*." Contrary to platforms, infrastructures are being built over time in a step-wise manner where "different actors shape, maintain, and extend it in modular increments, not all at once or globally" (Star & Ruhleder, 1996). Because of this dispersed and distributed ownership, the lack of centralized control is a fundamental attribute of an infrastructure. This also applies to public sector, as their infrastructures will be built, extended, and maintained by different agencies, sometimes through shared responsibilities between public and private partners. This certainly applies to public sector blockchain applications, which most likely will be based on systems and platforms operated by commercial actors. For example, a national ID-gateway often comprises both private and public systems for identification, authentication, and authorization. Similarly, a public register may be accessed through private APIs.

It should be noted, however, that the distinction between platforms and infrastructures is diffuse; a platform may be a hub for a number of different applications and therefore gradually inherit some characteristics of an II, such as a national health service platform that supports a large variety of applications and has the flexibility to support future needs. But there are also many platforms that do not qualify as infrastructure at all, because they are centralized and often too specialized, or they lack necessary flexibility. Accordingly, a crucial question in our context is how and to what extent blockchain based platforms will grow into infrastructures.

3.2 The Installed Base and Blockchain Technology

Of importance in an infrastructure is its *installed base (IB)*, including both technical and non-technical elements. The evolution of infrastructures are path-dependent due to the "living legacy" of existing technical solutions along with organizational, economic and legal elements, interconnected practices and regulations that are often institutionalized in the organization, as part of the installed base (Hanseth & Lyytinen, 2010). An adequate understanding of this installed base is particularly important in building an II in governments (eGovII), as an increasing number of platforms and information systems (also legacy systems) are shared in order to provide online government services, and the dynamics related to these systems often require both forward flexibility and backward compatibility.

The "living legacy" of the blockchain technology is currently limited, as its applications have a short history. However, even after just 10 years we see an increasing social and technical diversity where new applications and various platforms are emerging, e.g. new altcoins, smart contracts, sidechains (Back et al., 2014). Thus, blockchains are evolving beyond their primary application area and comprise platforms that already support a range of applications, including secure document and asset management in other areas; see also Ølnes and Jansen (2017). By comparison, Internet had to wait more than 20 years to gain acceptance on a broader scale.

The limited installed base of blockchain may both stimulate and inhibit innovations. On the one hand, it may enable the development and diffusion of new applications as there are few "technical debts" such as legacy systems. New users can therefore start to use innovative solutions if they are sufficiently attractive or meet specific needs. The growth of cryptocurrency and various electronic cash systems clearly illustrates this. On the other hand, the lack of bonds to existing installed bases, for example, users of existing applications in relevant areas (such as payment systems, secure document handling and asset management etc.), may imply that there are few incentives for adoption of new applications based on blockchain technology unless they are made more attractive. The growth of the Internet is a good illustration. From the outset, it had no "legacy" applications to tackle. On the other hand, Internet benefitted from using the existing (technical) infrastructure of telecommunications. For blockchain technologies, the challenge is to stimulate the development and use of BC applications that can gain momentum and through network effects build a sufficient installed base, and at the same time benefit from existing infrastructure elements in government, see also the discussion of bootstrapping below. One possible strategy can be to develop gateways (a node in a network that comprises an interface to other networks that use different protocols by translating between the protocols).

A BCT-based infrastructure [in public sector] will not replace existing infrastructure. Instead, the opposite is true; it will be built by extending the existing systems and functional components. Currently, most BCT-based application outside cryptocurrencies systems combines blockchains and traditional (off-chain) databased.

Typically, blockchains are used for securing integrity, authentication, and authorization by only storing the hash value (fingerprint) of the system state, while user data are stored off-chain, see e.g. Allessie et al. (2019).

A promising application is decentralized identities. Work is currently being done to build an identity framework that allows for self-sovereign identity (SSI), which puts the user at the centre of the framework and thereby removes the need for the existing third parties. In this framework, the user can "create" his/her own unique identifier and the attaching identity information to that identifier. By associating verifiable credentials from recognized authorities, for instance governments, users can create digital national IDs, driving licenses etc.,

Current studies of blockchain implementations show that blockchain is always just one layer of a more developed service. It usually depends on a non-DTL layer which runs on top a legacy-type centralized database. (ibid). Thus, the blockchain part of government II will comprise modules that offer functionalities like notarization, shared databases, and workflow automation. In particular, a blockchain-based decentralized identity can support an infrastructure for access control and data use consent, and potentially linking credentials to smart contracts etc. (EU Blockchain Observatory and Forum, 2019a).

3.3 Different Types of Prospective Blockchain Infrastructures

However, although an infrastructure is assumed to be open, it does not necessarily mean universal openness. Hanseth and Lyytinen (2004) distinguish between three types of [vertical] information infrastructures (1) universal [service] infrastructure (as e.g. Internet), (2) business sector infrastructure, and (3) corporate information infrastructure. *A universal II* is open to everybody, supporting a wide range of applications, standardization takes place through open processes involving many stakeholders and its governance is shared by many organizations. A business sector II is shared by a limited number of organizations (e.g. companies within one sector), supporting primarily limited applications for information exchange between involved organizations and standardization is part of the its governance by selected stakeholders.

Contrary to this, a corporate II is aimed at its employees and selected collaborating partner; it supports mainly relevant applications within this closed network. Standardization is usually pragmatic and ad hoc, and its governance is an integral part of corporate management. Internet is a successful *universal II*, while the payment system in the financial sector, for example, is a well-functioning *business II*. The development of their appurtenant installed bases follows different patterns: for a universal II, the IB can grow exponentially (without any central control). A corporate II will have a limited and controlled IB, mainly comprising current applications, their users and developers, and the practices they are supporting. Its typical ad hoc-oriented standardization may thus imply challenges. In Table 2.3, we

Table 2.3 The characteristics of different types of BCT based platforms

Property	Open (universal) permissionless blockchains	Public (business) permissioned blockchains	Private permissioned blockchains
Open	Open to any users in offering a platform for e.g. payment system, secure document/ asset handling etc.	Public BC may be open to most citizens and other relevant actors	Restricted to members in relevant organizations
Shared(write/ commit)	Potentially shared among those who are involved in building the platform	Possibly restricted to some involved public agencies	Restricted to active private BCs
Installed base	The present, limited installed includes few legacy systems which can stimulate innovations, but few networks effects	Very limited, and it depends on the type of application it is aimed at.	The challenge is to transfer/convert old applications
Evolving	Yes, in many directions. Although as a new technology, Bitcoin has demonstrated innovative potential	So far, we have limited experience. May face problems in matching the development of permissionless BCs	We see a growth in private blockchain, e.g. related to logistics
Control	Distributed control based on OSS software. Updates are negotiated among user. No standardization procedures	Centralized, but to a limited set of stakeholders	Centralized, often by a a consortium of stakeholders
Examples	Bitcoin, Ethereum	Ripple, Libra	Corda

compare the different types of BCT platforms along the typical dimensions of an infrastructure.

We see that these distinct types of blockchain platforms are significantly different according to these distinct characteristics, and we must expect significant innovations for all of them.

3.4 How to Build a BCT-Based Infrastructure?

We believe it is possible that some of the evolving blockchain platforms can fulfil such requirements that they qualify as an infrastructure. However, it is not obvious what type that may be. A prospective universal blockchain-based infrastructure should be able to support all (most?) types of BCT implementations, while a business-type infrastructure can be limited to bridge permissioned but public BCTs. On the other hand, a corporate-like blockchain infrastructure will most likely be restricted to comprise a small number of private blockchains. It can thus be argued that a blockchain-based infrastructure can be built merely on permissionless blockchains, in which gateways offers interaction with permissioned blockchain. So far, we believe it is hard to predict how the blockchains will evolve, but most likely in many, somewhat un-coordinated directions.

An important dimension of an infrastructure is its control structure. The *control* of a universal II is distributed and dynamically negotiated (Weil & Broadbent, 1998). Permissionless blockchains have clearly distributed their control functions (usually denoted the mining process) to all nodes in a peer-to-peer network, as the main purpose of its design has been to avoid central control (Nakamoto, 2008). On the other hand, permissioned blockchains will at most be decentralized, in that some of the control mechanisms may be delegated to lower levels in a hierarchy. Accordingly, there will be several technical as well as organizational challenges if permissionless blockchains are be part of a universal II.

When analyzing the Internet development in retrospect, it was not at all self-evident that WWW would become an open and universal II. Similarly, it is not evident that Blockchain technology platforms will grow into infrastructures. BCT was designed to support electronic money transfer and similar applications and was not intended to comprise a general-purpose platform. First, a permissionless BCT is generally available to everybody, which demonstrates its *openness*. Furthermore, as we have described above, many new applications have been built on blockchain platforms, clearly indicating the potential of this technology to be *shared* across multiple communities in various ways. These developments also demonstrate its *evolving* nature, including a growing number of new platforms.

However, when building an II, there are two major challenges: *bootstrapping* and *adaptation*. The bootstrapping problem may be defined as "*[a] design process taking as its starting point the challenge of enrolling the first users and then drawing upon the existing base of users and technology as a resource to extend the network*" (Hanseth & Lyytinen, 2010). They suggest these design principles: (1) design initially for usefulness, (2) build upon the installed base, (3) expand installed base by persuasive tactics to gain momentum. The adaptability problem is understood as making the system maximally adaptive and variety generating to avoid "technology traps", that is, being locked into a less fruitful development trajectory. They suggest (1) making the IT capability as simple as possible and (2) modularizing the infrastructure.

We may study how Tim Berners-Lee designed the first WWW services, initially intended to meet information-sharing needs among high energy physicists. However, their applications expanded quickly to a growing, worldwide community, as there were no corresponding services (Star & Ruhleder, 1996). We believe that a similar bootstrapping approach is useful to foster the growth of BCT-based applications. Such application may be Self Sovereign Identity (SSI) and academic certificates on the blockchain, see next section. Although this technology is not yet mature, it has demonstrated significant developments from being used by a handful of persons to today's millions of users and links (Kondor, Pósfai, Csabai, & Vattay, 2014), We see a significant investment rate, indicating lots of start-ups, and expansion in terms of diversity of components and services added to the technology (Pilkington, 2016), for example, new platforms such as Ethereum (Wood, 2014) and off-chain scaling solutions like Lightning Network (Poon & Dryja, 2015).

However, there are also some fundamental differences between Internet and blockchains. The design of Internet was based on strictly layered and modular architecture. This implies that each layer has a limited set of capabilities and offers a well-defined (functional) interface. Although blockchain technology can be (conceptually) described in a similar manner, see Table 2.3, its development trajectory does not strictly follow such principles, in that applications on a higher level (layer in the protocol stack) do not build on identical lower level functionality, which may imply that horizontal interoperability (direct exchange of transactions between peer nodes at the platform layer) may not be possible, see next section. We must bear in mind, however, that the present Internet architecture is the result of long period of development. It is likely that BCT will undergo a similar development trajectory, including standardization of basic procedures and mechanisms.

4 Blockchain Platform Architectures and Interoperability

Section 4 addresses the need for harmonization and standardization of blockchain development, and we suggest a rough proposal for an architecture. Furthermore, some fundamental design strategies related to interoperability will be discussed.

4.1 Blockchain Based Platform Developments

So far, the growth of blockchains has been rather uncoordinated, which has been unavoidable when allowing for the wide range of innovations. However, if this technology is going to grow into more general/universal platforms, and eventually into an information infrastructure, it is a requirement that the different implementations follow some generally accepted architectural principles. This will become a necessary requirement if interoperability between different BCT implementations are made possible. An EU report (EU Blockchain Observatory and Forum, 2019b) predicts "*that the first wave of blockchain will be characterized by a large number of permissioned, purpose-built blockchain platforms geared towards a specific use case or user base*". These blockchains will clearly need to interact with each other as well as with the off-chain world. The report furthermore suggests that *a small number of global blockchain networks will emerge as the backbone of a Web of Value.* At least 3 types of challenges must be faced: *scalability, interoperability, and sustainability*. Below, we will focus on architectures to achieve the interoperability requirement.

The structure and development trajectory of the blockchain technology has been compared to that of the Internet, see e.g. van Valkenburgh (2016), Ølnes and Jansen (2017). Although such comparisons may result in misleading associations, we believe there are some lessons to be learned from the history of building the Internet. The Internet was designed according to a 4-layered architectural model in which each layer builds on the functionality of the previous one, and it provides a well-defined interface for the next layer. The main idea is that the content in one layer may be replaced without modifying the others. The kernel of Internet architecture is the TCP/IP protocol suite, built in a layered and modular way, as illustrated in Sect. 2. The IP–protocol architecture allows for arbitrarily many different physical network technologies ranging from Ethernet to wireless to single point-to-point links. Similarly, we see that TCP offers sufficient functionality to support a nearly unlimited set of applications. This layered architecture allows horizontal interaction between two corresponding layers that offer corresponding functionality, such as, for example, between two different LANs.

Furthermore, its basic characteristics are important: being open, global, and borderless with no censorship. The Internet is transparent and neutral to any type of information being sent across the network (as unfiltered data). Thus, based on the end-to-end-principle (see e.g. Saltzer, Reed, & Clark, 1984), the Internet may be considered an "unintelligent" network, meaning that there is minimum functionality inside the network, making it efficient, flexible and dynamic. This result in that that each node is as simple as possible and has minimum functionality. One consequence is that security functions (other than that those necessary to guaranty secure delivery of IP packages) were not part of the original Internet, but are taken care of on top of the TCP protocol (Wikipedia, 2018).

Similarly, the blockchain platform, including consensus and security mechanisms, is a transaction-processing network because it pushes much of its "intelligence" to the edges, thus being able to support various smart devices. It does not offer a range of financial services and products, but it has some basic support functions at lower levels, thus making the interfaces simpler and thereby capable of supporting innovations (Antonopoulos, 2016). Furthermore, security functions aimed at data quality assurance (beyond tamper-resident and immutability) are not part of the core blockchain technology but must be implemented in each individual application. There is no common standard for such functionality across different BCT applications, as e.g. cryptocurrencies. Thus, if a BCT platform is going to constitute the basis for an infrastructure that allows for interoperability, some standardization is required. These issues are discussed below.

An adequate architecture comprising a fruitful framework must fulfill many requirements. First, it must allow for further development and growth and at the same time define necessary standards. Next, it must be simple and flexible. The blockchain technology is still immature and should therefore stimulate innovations in various directions. At the same time, a flexible architecture should support implementations that facilitate interoperability. Thus, it should not be linked to a specific platform, and should entail quality as a distributed, peer-to-peer network. Thus, the architecture must support different blockchains such as the permissionless protocols like Bitcoin and Ethereum as well as permissioned protocols like Ripple, Hyperledger and R3's Corda, some of them not even fully peer-to-peer and not using POW consensus methods.

The literature on blockchains provides several architectural models. A preliminary ISO report (ISO TC 307/WG X, reference ISO 2017) outlines a draft proposal for a 4-layered references architecture. This work is not yet finished. An OECD primer briefly discusses another, simpler 3-layered model) (OECD, 2018). A somewhat more complicated model is outlined in "Towards common blockchain architecture—an "ISO OSI for blockchain" primer (Scan Pay, 2017) comprising 5 layers: Application, API, Virtual Machine layer (with e.g. smart contracts), Consensus layer and P2P Network layer. Correspondingly, an EU report om Interoperability (EU Blockchain Observatory and Forum, 2019b), suggests the following layers: (1) a blockchain and database layer, (2) a platform management layer, (3) a middle layer of services, (4) a platform presentation layer and an application and service ecosystem layer.

First, we believe that a layered and modular architecture is fruitful, resembling that of Internet and other data communication models. Some layers are common in the various models. Firstly, the blockchain platforms must rely on a basic (network) infrastructure layer, limited to include storage, computation (including crypto services) and protocols for securing internode communications (between peer-to-peer nodes), somewhat similar to the IP layers in Internet. Next, there must be a consensus layer, which (conceptually) must include several different procedures (e.g. permissionless versus permissioned blockchains). Above this layer, we suggest a virtual machine layer, including a currency platform layer, a set of APIs, and then a value/token layer. A revised version of a 4-layered model suggested by Ølnes and Jansen (2017) is presented in Table 2.4.

When designing a blockchain architecture (framework) we should learn from the experiences in the early architectural debates on the different approaches to network architectures, e.g. Internet versus the OSI model. Therefore, we suggest a stepwise and experimental approach when building an architecture, based on a "minimum-standard" philosophy, balancing bottom-up and top-down approaches.

Table 2.4 The layered architecture of blockchain technologies

Layer	Functionality	Bitcoin example		Ethereum example
User layer	Applications	Ordinary bitcoin wallet	BTCPay server	A range of token applications
Platform service layer	API, management functions (e.g. on-/off-chain)		Lightning network	ERC-20/ ERC-721
Blockchain virtual layer	Currency, tokens, virtual machine	Bitcoin and script (Bitcoin programming language)		Ether/Ethereum virtual machine (Solidity–Ethereum prog. lang.)
Consensus layer	PoW, POS	PoW		PoW (migrating to PoS)
Network/ infrastructure	Peer-to-peer, routing, hash, encryption,	Bitcoin blockchain		Ethereum blockchain

4.2 Governance of Blockchain Technology Platforms

At present, each BCT platform and its applications is managed separately, and their governance model differs between various blockchain systems; e.g. for Bitcoin, there is so far no formal governing body, as the main constituencies comprising the Bitcoin community including the (full node) users, the miners, the developers, the service providers, and the merchants must agree on changes to have them deployed (Antonopoulos, 2017). De Filippi and Loveluck (2016) distinguish between two distinct coordination mechanisms: governance by the infrastructure and governance of the infrastructure. The former is primarily achieved through technical coordination as is the case in permissionless blockchains, e.g. the consensus method in Bitcoin. The latter, permissioned blockchains, is more a matter of ownership and management; it needs consensus between the primary interests (constituencies) on various questions. De Filippi and Loveluck [ibid] conclude that the lessons from the past, both the successes and failures of Internet governance should be considered when developing the BCT governance structure. If we are going to have interoperability between platforms, or even integration towards a growing BCT infrastructure, far more developed governance regimes will be required to resolve harmonization and standardization issues.

An EU-report (EU Blockchain Observatory and Forum, 2019b) predicts that "*the first wave of blockchain adoption will be characterized by a large number of permissioned, purpose-built blockchain platforms geared towards specific use cases*". Whether it is building or running a corporation or a consortium, successful collaboration requires strong governance, not least when it is based on a distributed network architecture (The governance paradox.) This can be challenging, particularly since the question of governance in collaborative consortia for decentralized technologies is still relatively new, and a lot remains to be learned. Having said that, we believe this is important, not least to secure interoperability between distinct blockchain implementations.

Even if we can trust each individual blockchain, this does not imply necessarily that we can trust transaction across blockchains. Important requirements will be a mapping of the on-chain proofs with the relevant off-chain legal and regulatory frameworks, along with clear service-level agreements spelling out each stakeholder's rights and duties. Moreover, there should be clear criteria as to who can vote on consensus, who is allowed to have a complete copy of the chain (which may contain sensitive data), who can put data into the chain and who can process that data. Thus, much work, partly experimental, must be done to explore various governance models.

4.3 Interoperability

As stated above, interoperability between different platforms is necessary if blockchains are to gain wider acceptance as a "Web of value". The blockchain technology "family" has evolved from the original Bitcoin to a heavily fragmented landscape of numerous non-interoperable blockchains (Schulte et al., 2019). New requirements have been met in the development of new blockchain systems, most often modified versions of existing ones (ibid.). The open source approach that has been used for most blockchain systems makes it easy to make modifications and has created new, independent, and unconnected blockchain platforms. The consequence, however, has been great challenges regarding interactions across blockchains providing quite different services.

As illustrated in the previous section, there are many lessons to be learned from the development of Internet. (Hardjono et al., 2018) remind us of the three primary (design) goals of the Internet: *(1) Survivability, (2) Variety of service types, and (3) Variety of networks*. They argue that the architecture of blockchain technology must satisfy the same fundamental goals if it is to become a fundamental component of the future global distributed network of commerce and value (ibid.). They offer the following definition of an "interoperable blockchain architecture":

> An interoperable blockchain architecture is a composition of distinguishable blockchain systems, each representing a distributed data ledger, where transaction execution may span multiple blockchain systems, and where data recorded in one Blockchain is reachable and verifiable by another possibly foreign transaction in a semantically compatible manner (Hardjono et al., 2018).

Thus, the large variety of blockchains, not least permissionless versus controlled permissioned, becomes a major hindrance. One strategy may be to utilize the "end-to-end" principle.

4.4 BCT and the "End-to-End" Principle

The end-to-end principle is an essential element in the Internet architecture, along with the "minimum assumption", in that the transport of datagrams (packets) as the lowest common denominator unit. In networks designed according to this principle, application-specific features reside in the communicating end nodes of the network, rather than in intermediary nodes, such as gateways and routers, that exist to establish the network. The basic argument is that a lower (network) level subsystem that supports a distributed application may be wasting its effort in providing a function that must be implemented at the application level anyway (Hardjono et al., 2018). The argument for applying the end-to-end principle is: "*The function in question can completely and correctly be implemented only with the knowledge and help of the application standing at the end points of the communication system. Therefore, providing that questioned function as a feature of the communication system itself is not possible* (Saltzer et al., 1984)".

Another fundamental principle in the Internet design is the "*Autonomous systems*", including domain level control with distributed topology, (uniquely identifiable entities, autonomous reachability, and operation by legal entities). These autonomous systems were interconnected through gateways (bridges, routers, and higher levels gateways) accepting that it was necessary to incorporate the (at the time) existing network architecture (as LAN, WAN, telecom and satellite communication systems etc.), each of them representing boundaries of control.

Today, there is a similar situation, in which multiple Blockchain designs are being proposed. Thus, the question is how we can achieve survivability in a BCT context, meaning "the completion of an application-level transaction" understood as sub-transaction confirmed on a spread of Blockchain systems being opaque to the user application (Hardjono et al., 2018). In the context of very heterogeneous BCT systems, the functions in question include among others reliability, semantic type of a blockchain etc., in addition to the degree of permissibility and the degree of anonymity, all of which are discussed in the next section.

One possible re-interpretation of this original problem, according to Hardjono et al., 2018), is as follows: how can multiple types of blockchain systems support the completion of a two-way transaction between two applications, involving computer resources across blockchain systems where some may be operated (or owned) by different entities. Their suggestion of what implies «minimal assumption» for interoperable Blockchain systems is stated to be "*the transaction unit that is semantically understandable between multiple different blockchain system*". So far, to our knowledge, there is no common agreement across existing blockchain implementations as to what this transaction unit might be.

Two other important questions closely related to the minimal assumption principle is (1) the degree of permissibility, that is, the degree to which data recorded on one ledger can be referenced by transactions in another blockchain system, and (2) the degrees of anonymity, both pertaining to identity-anonymity of the users and that of the nodes participating in processing transactions.

There are several blockchain-based interoperability solutions on the market. One example of such a solution is *Cosmos*. Cosmos has sought to separate the technology stack so that the network and consensus layers are separated from the application layer into a generic engine based on the Tendermint BFT (Kwon & Buchman, 2019). Cosmos has also developed an Inter-Blockchain Communication protocol (IBC) to allow heterogeneous blockchains to transfer value (i.e. tokens) or data to each other (ibid.). Cosmos has a built-in token, or cryptocurrency, called atom.

5 Blockchain Applications for the Public Sector

In this chapter, we present relevant initiatives and use cases for the public sector: the broader EU initiative to create a blockchain-based service infrastructure and the more specific cases of using BCT as a secure store of academic certificates and BCT for self-sovereign identity. The EU initiative and the use cases highlight the transformation to self-sovereign handling of important information.

5.1 The European Blockchain Service Infrastructure (EBSI)

The European Blockchain Partnership (EBP) was established in 2018 and most of the EU and EEA member countries are partners. Its aim is to align policies and regulatory approaches to blockchain and other distributed ledger technologies, and develop a trusted, secure and resilient European Blockchain Services Infrastructure (EBSI) which will deliver EU-wide cross-border public services leveraging blockchain technology (European Commission, 2019). The EBSI is part of the Connecting Europe Facility (CEF) as a core building block. The EBSI consists of four layers: (1) Network layer, (2) Chain layer, (3) Core service layer, and (4) Application layer. The first version (v. 1.0) is intended to be a self-contained infrastructure that delivers all components within three computing hosts; a master host and two hosts for blockchain protocols and distributed storage (European Commission, n.d.). The EBSI will be based on the Hyperledger suite of tools for developing enterprise-grade blockchain solutions. These are tools for developing permissioned DLTs and blockchain systems. The proof of authority consensus method will be used, with one authorizing node per member state (Doerk, 2020).

For 2019 the EBP agreed to develop these four use case pilots as part of the EBSI v. 1.0: (1) Notarization, (2) Diplomas, (3) European Self-Sovereign Identity, and (4) Trusted Data Sharing. For 2020 new use cases will be selected as an upgrade to EBSI v. 2.0. However, EBSI 1.0 is a proof of concept and will not be a production-ready solution. That is planned to be achieved with EBSI 2.0. The self-sovereign identity part is called the European Self-Sovereign Identity Framework eSSIF, and the goal is that it should provide seamless cross-border services for the citizens. An important part of the work with eSSIF is to link the framework to an existing legal framework such as eIDAS, the EU regulation on electronic identification and trust services for electronic transactions in the European Single Market.

5.2 Academic Certificates on the Blockchain

The pilot on diplomas in the EBSI 1.0 is only a proof of concept at this stage. However, there are already several other solutions for using blockchain technology to secure and validate academic certificates.

Blockchain technology is ideal as a new infrastructure to secure, share, and verify learning achievements (Smolenski, 2016). Using this technology, individuals can take control of their own credentials through the possession of verified records, which they can then use as needed. Because such credentials can be easily verified, employers or others who rely on them can have greater trust in their veracity.

The potential of such an approach has been widely recognized (Blockchain Observatory and Forum, 2018; Grech & Camilleri, 2017) and many projects other than the EBSI initiative have already started and provided working solutions. The University of Nicosia, for instance, already issues academic certificates on the

Bitcoin blockchain that can be verified online (Grech & Camilleri, 2017). MIT has developed a system called Blockcerts for self-management of educational credentials (ibid.). Blockcerts is an open standard for creating, issuing, viewing and verifying blockchain-based certificates and is available as open source software. The system includes modules for storing verified "fingerprints" of credentials (e.g. hashes of the credentials) to the Bitcoin blockchain, together with an app for checking the validity of the corresponding credential held by the owner. Blockcerts also handles revocation of credentials (ibid.)

We will here describe MIT's solution BlockCerts developed by the MIT Media Lab and the company Learning Machine (MIT Media Lab, 2016). MIT's primary motivation was to empower students to manage their own credentials and thereby relieve the universities of a burdensome task. The system is based on the Open Badge standard for representing credentials from higher education and works this way:

1. The university first publishes the student's credentials on the Bitcoin blockchain and signs it with their own digital certificate.
2. The application BlockCerts Wallet, specially developed for the verification of the credentials, needs to be downloaded from those who receive an academic credential they wish to verify.
3. The BlockCerts app computes a SHA256 digest of the received certificate (=A).
4. The hash stored on the Bitcoin blockchain (=A′) is fetched and compared to the hash produced locally. The two hashes, A and A′, should be identical.
5. The university's signature is checked and verified.
6. Finally, the app checks that the certificate has not been revoked by the issuer.

5.3 *Identity on the Blockchain*

The EU report "Blockchain and Digital Identity" (Blockchain Observatory and Forum, 2019a) launched an important application area; to build an identity framework based on the concept of decentralized identities, potentially including an interesting subset of decentralized identities known as self-sovereign identity (SSID). The idea is to put the user at the center to remove the need for third parties. In this world, the user "creates" his or her own identity, generally by creating his or her own unique identifier (or several them), and then attaching identity information to that identifier. By associating verifiable credentials from recognized authorities, for instance governments, users can in effect create the digital equivalents of physical world credentials like national IDs and driving licenses. Since these are digital, they will, however, be more flexible and easier to manage than their physical counterparts. The user has both a means of generating and controlling unique identifiers as well as some facility to store identity data. Users are then free to make use of whatever identity data they choose.

Another EU report, "Blockchain for government and public services" (Blockchain Observatory and Forum, 2018), points to the potential for using blockchains in creating trust in information and processes in situations where there are large, heterogeneous sets of stakeholders or users. As blockchain is good at creating trusted audit trails of information and, depending on how a system is designed, it makes it relatively easy to keep data both private and shareable. The report points to several promising areas of application from reconciling blockchain's data sharing properties with the data protection provisions of the GDPR to addressing the legal status of smart contracts and digital assets. It is suggested that a key infrastructure for blockchain in government be set up to allow governments to deploy blockchain technology for themselves. This will be challenging with a technology as new as blockchain, one that is evolving rapidly and for which there are still few standards or clear examples of best practice. Furthermore, the previously mentioned EBSI initiative from EU, is working with a European framework for self-sovereign IDs, the eSSIF.

There are different takes on the problem of developing self-sovereign ID solutions. One is to take a top-down approach, developing one blockchain platform for all agencies and mandating its use. This can serve the cause of standardization but runs the risk of not being adequate to meet the real needs of the agencies or locking the government into a single vendor or single technology and hence potentially missing out on new developments. Another alternative is to let the agencies experiment and build blockchain platforms themselves, but that runs the risk of fragmentation of platforms and knowledge, creating a whole that is less than the sum of its parts. As a middle ground between these two extremes, Blockchain Platform as a Service model (BPaaS) is suggested, which should allow for evaluation to choose the preferred technology or standard functionality, build proofs of concept and test the results. These and other efforts in this area clearly illustrate that there is no lack of vision for the potential use of this technology, but at the same time highlights significant pitfalls entailed by moving too fast.

The eSSIF initiative from the EU is an example of a top down strategy. However, the centrally defined components will be combined with nationally adapted ID provisions. A core requirement is that the solution has to be interoperable with the eIDAS regulation, both on a technical and a regulatory level.

There are also several market-driven initiatives for SSIDs. Microsoft has presented an SSID framework called IoN—Identity Overlay Network based on the Bitcoin blockchain. Microsoft IoN uses the Sidetree protocol, a protocol for creating scalable 'Layer 2' Decentralized Identifier/DPKI networks that can run atop any decentralized ledger system (e.g. Bitcoin) and be as open, public, and permissionless as the underlying ledger they utilize (Buchner, 2020b). The Sidetree protocol is blockchain agnostic, however, Microsoft chose to develop the IoN system based on the Bitcoin blockchain. The advantage of using Bitcoin is the decentralized aspect, and the advantage of using a layer 2 solution is scalability. IoN can handle tens of thousands of DID operations per second (Buchner, 2020a). The development of IoN is done through the Digital Identity Foundation collaboration.

The IoN solution from Microsoft supports W3C's Digital Identifiers (DIDs) recommendations (Reed et al., 2020). Digital identifiers is a broader concept than SSIDs. W3C defines DIDs as a new type of identifier that enables verifiable, decentralized digital identity. A DID identifies any subject (e.g., a person, organization, thing, data model, abstract entity, etc.) that the controller of the DID decides that it identifies (ibid.). Although decentralization is at the core of the recommendation, DIDs can also be developed for identifiers registered in federated or centralized identity management systems. Indeed, all types of identifier systems can add support for DIDs. This creates an interoperability bridge between the worlds of centralized, federated, and decentralized identifiers (ibid.).

6 Conclusions

We have shown the vital ecosystem of blockchain technologies and platforms and the potential this technology has to evolve into an information infrastructure. However, the blockchain technology is still in its emergent phase, 11 years after its inception. As a comparison, the Internet was developed over a period spanning two to three decades before its breakthrough.

For blockchain technology to evolve into an II, interoperability issues in particular need to be solved. In addition to interoperability, there are also important issues like harmonizing, standardizing, and architectural development as well as regulation that need to be addressed.

BCT is a very promising technology that can bring about a digital transformation in the public as well as the private sector provided that most of the issues mentioned above are solved.

References

Antonopoulos, A. (2016). *The internet of money*. Columbia: Merkle Bloom LLC.

Antonopoulos, A. M. (2017). *Mastering Bitcoin: Programming the open blockchain*. O'Reilly Media, Inc. Retrieved from https://www.google.com/books?hl=en&lr=&id=tponDwAAQBAJ&oi=fnd&pg=PT7&dq=mastering+bitcoin&ots=QrqUXR08fO&sig=ghLouY2kFirwQ9wpOK4g8olbn10

Allessie, D., Sobolewski, M., & Vaccari, L. (2019). *Blockchain for digital government: An assessment of pioneering implementations in public services*. Joint Research Centre (Seville site).

Back, A. (2002). *Hashcash—a senial of service counter-measure*. Retrieved from http://c65mcoididjlt3zo.onion.city/pdf/hashcash.pdf

Back, A., Corallo, M., Dashjr, L., Friedenbach, M., Maxwell, G., Miller, A., Poelstra, A., Timón, J., & Wuille, P. (2014). *Enabling blockchain innovations with pegged sidechains*. Retrieved from http://www.opensciencereview.com/Papers/123/Enablingblockchain-Innovations-with-Pegged-Sidechains; http://www.bitcoin.fr/public/divers/docs/sidechains.pdf

Bahga, A., & Madisetti, V. K. (2016). Blockchain platform for industrial internet of things. *Journal of Software Engineering and Applications, 9*(10), 533–546.

Baran, P. (1964). On distributed communications networks. *IEEE Transactions on Communications Systems, 12*(1), 1–9.

Buchner, D. (2020a, May 13). *Toward scalable decentralized identifier systems [Blog']. Azure active directory identity blog.* Retrieved from https://techcommunity.microsoft.com/t5/azure-active-directory-identity/toward-scalable-decentralized-identifier-systems/ba-p/560168

Buchner, D. (2020b, September 5). *Decentralized identity—sidetree [open source software repository]. Github.* Retrieved from https://github.com/decentralized-identity/sidetree/blob/master/docs/spec/abstract.md

Clack, C. D., Bakshi, V. A., & Braine, L. (2016). Smart contract templates: Foundations, design landscape and research directions. ArXiv Preprint ArXiv:1608.00771

De Filippi, P., & Loveluck, B. (2016). *The invisible politics of bitcoin: Governance crisis of a decentralized infrastructure.* Retrieved from https://papers.ssrn.com/sol3/papers.cfm?abstract_id=2852691

Doerk, A. (2020, February 2). *ESSIF: The European self-sovereign identity framework [Blog platform (Medium)]. SSI Ambassador.* Retrieved from https://medium.com/@SSI_Ambassador/essif-the-european-self-sovereign-identity-framework-4572f6875e12

Dwork, C., & Naor, M. (1992). Pricing via processing or combatting junk mail, in *Annual International Cryptology Conference* (pp. 139–147).

EU Blockchain Observatory and Forum. (2018). Blockchain for government and public services. *European Commission.* Retrieved from https://www.eublockchainforum.eu/sites/default/files/reports/eu_observatory_blockchain_in_government_services_v1_2018-12-07.pdf

EU Blockchain Observatory and Forum. (2019a). Blockchain and digital identity. *European Commission.* Retrieved from https://www.eublockchainforum.eu/sites/default/files/report_identity_v0.9.4.pdf

EU Blockchain Observatory and Forum. (2019b). *Scalability, interoperability, and sustainability of blockchains.* Retrieved from https://www.eublockchainforum.eu/sites/default/files/reports/report_scalaibility_06_03_2019.pdf

European Commission. (n.d.). *Documentation EBSI [News on technology].* CEF Digital - EBSI - Docmemtation EBSI. Retrieved from https://ec.europa.eu/cefdigital/wiki/display/CEFDIGITAL/Minimum+Technical+Requirements+for+an+EBSI+v1.0+NODE+Deployment

European Commission. (2019, September 25). The European Blockchain Services Infrastructure is on its way [News on technology]. *CEF Digital - News.* Retrieved from https://ec.europa.eu/cefdigital/wiki/display/CEFDIGITAL/2019/09/25/The+European+Blockchain+Services+Infrastructure+is+on+its+way

Grech, A., & Camilleri, A. F. (2017). *Blockchain in education.* Luxembourg: Publications Office of the European Union.

Hanseth, O., & Lyytinen, K. (2004). Theorizing about the design of information infrastructures: Design kernel theories and principles. *Sprouts: Working Papers on Information Environments, Systems and Organizations, 4*(4), 207–241.

Hanseth, O., & Lyytinen, K. (2010). Design theory for dynamic complexity in information infrastructures: The case of building internet. *Journal of Information Technology, 25*(1), 1–19.

Hardjono, T., Lipton, A., & Pentland, A. (2018). Towards a design philosophy for interoperable blockchain systems. ArXiv Preprint ArXiv:1805.05934.

Hileman, G., & Rauchs, M. (2017). 2017 Global blockchain benchmarking study.

Ivy, J. W., Meindl, J. N., Overley, E., & Robson, K. M. (2017). Token economy: A systematic review of procedural descriptions. *Behavior Modification, 41*(5), 708–737.

Kondor, D., Pósfai, M., Csabai, I., & Vattay, G. (2014). Do the rich get richer? An empirical analysis of the Bitcoin transaction network. *PloS One, 9*(2), e86197.

Kwon, J., & Buchman, E. (2019). Cosmos Whitepaper. Jan.

Lamport, L., Shostak, R., & Pease, M. (1982). The Byzantine generals problem. *ACM Transactions on Programming Languages and Systems, 4*(3), 382–401.

MIT Media Lab. (2016). What we learned from designing an academic certificates system on the blockchain. *MIT Media Lab.* Retrieved from https://medium.com/mit-media-lab/what-we-learned-from-designing-an-academic-certificates-system-on-the-blockchain-34ba5874f196

Nakamoto, S. (2008). Bitcoin: A peer-to-peer electronic cash system. *Consulted, 1*(2012), 28.
Narayanan, A., Bonneau, J., Felten, E., Miller, A., & Goldfeder, S. (2016). *Bitcoin and cryptocurrency technologies: A comprehensive introduction*. Princeton: Princeton University Press.
OECD. (2018). *OECD Blockchain primer*. Retrieved from https://www.oecd.org/finance/blockchain
O'hara, K. (2017). Smart contracts-dumb idea. *IEEE Internet Computing, 21*(2), 97–101.
Ølnes, S., & Jansen, A. (2017). Blockchain technology as a support infrastructure in e-government. *Electronic Government, 2017*, 215–227. https://doi.org/10.1007/978-3-319-64677-0
Ølnes, S., Ubacht, J., & Janssen, M. (2017). *Blockchain in government: Benefits and implications of distributed ledger technology for information sharing*. London: Elsevier.
Pilkington, M. (2016). Blockchain technology: Principles and applications. In F. X. Olleros & M. Zhegu (Eds.), *Research handbook on digital transformations*. Cheltenham: Edward Elgar.
Poon, J., & Dryja, T. (2015). *The Bitcoin lightning network: Scalable off-chain instant payments*. Technical Report (draft). Retrieved from http://lightning.network/lightning-network-paper.pdf
Reed, D., Sporny, M., Longley, D., Allen, C., Grant, R., & Sabadello, M. (2020). *Decentralized identifiers (DIDs) v1.0. W3C*. Retrieved from https://www.w3.org/TR/did-core/
Saltzer, J. H., Reed, D. P., & Clark, D. D. (1984). End-to-end arguments in system design. *ACM Transactions on Computer Systems (TOCS), 2*(4), 277–288.
Scan Pay. (2017, November 23). *Towards common blockchain architecture—An "ISO OSI for blockchain" primer [Blog platform (Medium)]*. Retrieved from https://medium.com/@scanpayasia/towards-common-blockchain-architecture-an-iso-osi-for-blockchain-primer-778db4e5b35c
Schulte, S., Sigwart, M., Frauenthaler, P., & Borkowski, M. (2019). Towards blockchain interoperability, in *International conference on business process management* (pp. 3–10).
Smolenski, N. (2016). Academic credentials in an era of digital decentralisation. Learning Machine Research.
Star, S. L., & Ruhleder, K. (1996). Steps toward an ecology of infrastructure: Design and access for large information spaces. *Information Systems Research, 7*(1), 111–134.
Szabo, N. (1997). Formalizing and securing relationships on public networks. *First Monday, 2*(9), 548.
van Valkenburgh, P. (2016). Open Matters—why permissionless blockchains are essential to the future of the internet (p. 62). *Coin Center*. Retrieved from https://coincenter.org/files/2016-12/openmattersv1-1.pdf
Walch, A. (2019). *Deconstructing 'decentralization': Exploring the core claim of crypto systems. Crypto assets: Legal and monetary perspectives*. Oxford: OUP.
Weil, P., & Broadbent, M. (1998). *Leveraging the new Infrastructure*. Boston: Harvard Business School Press.
Werbach, K. (2018). *The blockchain and the new architecture of trust*. Cambridge: MIT Press.
Wikipedia. (2018). Internet security. *Wikipedia, the free encyclopedia*. Retrieved from https://en.wikipedia.org/wiki/Internet_security
Wood, G. (2014). Ethereum: A Secure Decentralized Transaction Ledger. *Ethereum*. Retrieved from http://gavwood.com/paper.pdf
Wüst, K., & Gervais, A. (2018). Do you need a Blockchain? *2018 Crypto Valley Conference on Blockchain Technology (CVCBT)* (pp. 45–54).
Zheng, Z., Xie, S., Dai, H., Chen, X., & Wang, H. (2017). An overview of blockchain technology: Architecture, consensus, and future trends, in *2017 IEEE International Congress on Big Data (BigData Congress)* (pp. 557–564).

Svein Ølnes has more than 20 years of experience as a researcher at Western Norway Research Institute. His main field of research has been digitalization in the public sector (e-Government). The last years blockchain technology has taken over as the main research interest. It is primarily the use of the technology in the public sector, as a possible information infrastructure, that has been the research focus and the subject for publications.

Arild Jansen is Professor emeritus, Norwegian Research Center for Computers and Law, Department of Private Law, University of Oslo. Jansen's research activities include a number of studies of eGovernment projects in Norway, and he was heading a cross-disciplinary research program in eGovernment at the University of Oslo from 2008 to 2013. Jansen was also active in organizing the Norwegian and Nordic University computer network cooperation and was instrumental in implementing Internet in the Nordic countries from 1982 to 1990. He has also been deputy director in the Norwegian government, including heading the secretariat for the national ICT advisory policy board. Current research includes ICT-governance, information infrastructures, IS implementations and organizational change, and more recently, studying the use of blockchain technologies in public sector. His has published several books and a large number of scientific papers.

Chapter 3
Blockchain and Regional Workforce Development: Identifying Opportunities and Training Needs

Fynnwin Prager, Jose Martinez, and Chris Cagle

1 Introduction

This paper explores the role of workforce development in facilitating regional development and adoption of Blockchain technology, using the South Bay region of Los Angeles, California as a case study. Blockchain and distributed ledger technology (DLT) have the potential to transform the modern workplace, as well as the economic regions that develop and implement it. Originally developed to support the Bitcoin digital currency, Blockchain distributes digital information across networks of computers and servers, and updates information to maintain standardization across all links, while maintaining transparency and not allowing corruption by a single user. These characteristics mean that Blockchain has the potential to contribute to numerous areas of business and government activity, including online finance and e-commerce, contracting and title registration, accounting, supply-chain management, cyber-security and anti-money laundering, file storage and data management, intellectual property rights protection, and the Internet of Things.

Such changes could change organizational practices within economic regions, as well as the fortunes of those regions spearheading Blockchain innovations and implementations. However, the future of Blockchain in specific regions is uncertain as the technology is still in the early development stages and sector clusters have yet to solidify (Davies and Likens, 2018; Kharif, 2018), and it is important that regional

F. Prager (✉)
Public Administration, CSU Dominguez Hills, Carson, CA, USA
e-mail: fprager@csudh.edu

J. Martinez
Economics, CSU Dominguez Hills, Carson, CA, USA

C. Cagle
South Bay Workforce Investment Board, Hawthorne, CA, USA

C. G. Reddick et al. (eds.), *Blockchain and the Public Sector*, Public Administration and Information Technology 36,
https://doi.org/10.1007/978-3-030-55746-1_3

public organizations anticipate such changes. Specifically, regional public organizations such as workforce development agencies and universities can explore how Blockchain might change the future workforce and demand for labor—including in the areas of software development, systems implementation and management, and technology usage—and develop training and education programs that provide workers in such organizations with the skills needed to succeed in this environment. Moreover, regional public organizations can also help to foster the development of new technologies and organizational solutions by training future entrepreneurs and software developers in this technology.This paper focuses on the workforce development aspects that contribute to regional innovations and adoptions of Blockchain as a new technology through a case study of the South Bay region of Los Angeles County.[1] This region provides a useful location to study this phenomenon because the Los Angeles economy is larger than many global markets, and it is a technologically innovative region with advanced manufacturing and a highly educated workforce (LAEDC, 2020).

As Blockchain technology is still largely in the research and development stages, this study is exploratory in nature, and seeks to apply core principles, identify likely trends, and propose education and training programs. Following discussion of the economic principles behind Blockchain, and how they might contribute to economic development in the South Bay, the case study explores:

1. Projections of future development in Blockchain technology;
2. Potential impacts on South Bay occupations and sectors;
3. Proposals for educational and workforce training programs that can be implemented by local public organizations.

This case study is informed by interviews with experts in the areas of Blockchain technology and industry-sector workforce, alongside literature review and analysis of workforce trends for the region. This paper aims to inform public officials and policy makers working on the issues of new technology, regional economic development, and workforce investment.

Prior studies have often focused on how Blockchain might affect specific economic sectors (Deloitte, 2016, 2017a, 2017b; Hileman & Rauchs, 2017; Killmeyer, White & Chew, 2017) rather than impacts to economic regions or workforce development concerns. There is an emerging literature examining the economic development aspects of Blockchain, both in general (Pisa & Juden, 2017; Swan, 2017), and in terms of the potential for sustainable development (Adams, Kewell, & Parry, 2018), and smart city development (Sun, Yan, & Zhang, 2016). However, there have been no prior efforts to explore the strategies available to public organizations to facilitate Blockchain-related regional economic and workforce development. This paper contributes to the literature by exploring strategies for regional workforce development around Blockchain technology.

[1]The South Bay is a region of Los Angeles County that includes the cities of Avalon, Carson, El Segundo, Gardena, Hawthorne, Hermosa Beach, Inglewood, Lawndale, Lomita, Portions of the City of Los Angeles (Harbor City/Harbor Gateway, San Pedro and Wilmington), Manhattan Beach, Palos Verdes Estates, Ranch Palos Verdes, Redondo Beach, Rolling Hills, Rolling Hills Estates and Torrance.

The paper is organized as follows: Sect. 2 presents a literature review that explores regional economic and workforce development, new technology development and adoption, and the role of public organizations within these areas. These areas are explored with respect to workforce development. Section 3 presents the research methods used, namely open-ended semi-structured interviews featuring questions and topics based on areas identified in the literature review. Section 4 explores projections of Blockchain growth in general, based on interviews with subject matter experts and reference to the literature. Section 5 presents a case study of Blockchain's potential impact on the South Bay region's economy. Section 6 concludes the paper and provides recommendations to regional policy makers and agencies.

2 Literature Review

This paper intersects three areas of the literature: (1) regional economic and workforce development (Giloth, 2000; Jacobs & Hawley, 2009); (2) new technology development and adoption (Hall & Khan, 2003; Hoppe, 2002; Lai, 2017; Oliveira & Martins, 2011; Van Ittersum & Feinberg, 2010) and; (3) the role of public organizations within these areas (Asheim, Smith, & Oughton, 2011; Bramwell & Wolfe, 2008; D'Allura, Galvagno, & Mocciaro Li Destri, 2012; Drucker & Goldstein, 2007; Gibbs, 2000; Lee, 2010; Siau & Long, 2005). This literature review examines first the potential for Blockchain to influence regional economic and workforce development, in terms of the general economic principles that create the conditions for the technology to emerge and develop, as well as the outcomes and workforce needs of an emerging Blockchain eco-system. Second, the literature review examines Blockchain as a new technology, and especially the ways in which Regional Innovation Systems—a combination of regional institutions that are public and private, educational and entrepreneurial (Asheim et al., 2011; D'Allura et al., 2012)—can create value and benefit for individuals, corporations, and the broader welfare of a region. Third, the literature review will highlight the role of public-serving institutions in supporting new technology development, especially in terms of workforce development, but also in terms of entrepreneurial support, product trialing, and implementation. This literature review will inform the research questions framing this exploratory study.

2.1 Blockchain and Regional Economic Development

There are numerous economic rationales for Blockchain development and adoption, such that the technology can help to address critical problems within organizations and across industries. Major corporations such as IBM, Microsoft, Oracle, Facebook, and Overstock have invested significantly in Blockchain technology research and development. For example, IBM is reported to have over 1500 employees working on Blockchain (Campbell, 2019a). This current interest is partly due to recent notable events such as media attention to initial coin offerings (ICOs), cryptocurrencies (Long, 2019), and cyberattacks (Julian, 2014), all of which are linked to Blockchain. Yet the investment is due to more than just media hype. It can also be explained by important economic principles behind the technology—such as the potential to reduce transaction costs, lessen information asymmetry, improve trust, and enhance efficiencies and economies of scale into decentralized systems (for further discussion, please see Catalini & Gans, 2016; Davidson, De Filippi, & Potts, 2016; Nofer, Gomber, Hinz, & Schiereck, 2017). This section discusses these economic principles with respect to Blockchain, and what issues they raise for regional economic and workforce development.

Blockchain is attractive to investors because it has the potential to help address the problem of information asymmetry within marketplaces. When a buyer and seller in a marketplace have significantly different levels of information, there are incentives to cheat, which creates a lack of trust between those transacting (Akerlof, 1978). Information asymmetries can also provide justification for government interventions to require that information is revealed to the public through an independent body. The downside for these government interventions is that they add cost to the transaction. In sum, information asymmetries add costs and inefficiencies to the marketplace.

Blockchain technology can help to address some of these information asymmetry problems by providing immutable and transparent information to all market actors. Blockchain technology could provide a trustworthy and easily accessible register of used-car characteristics that both the buyer and seller could see, and the system could either enhance government registry systems by making them more accessible, or be employed in the private sector through collaboration between industry stakeholders or a third-party vendor. This same principles could also apply to property information records, contracts, and supply chain management.

In each of these areas, Blockchain could potentially reduce transaction costs, and hence benefit the companies or individuals engaged directly in the trade, as well as the market as a whole. Either approach could reduce the uncertainty for buyers and, by implication, their transaction costs. However, the extent of such transaction cost reductions would depend on the particular Blockchain design, and may be offset by charges to access the information. An important distinction here is between private and public Blockchain systems. In private Blockchain systems, the information stored would only be available behind a firewall and hence within an organization or mutually-beneficial network. Private Blockchains could reduce transaction costs within and between organizations, especially through supply chains. In contrast, public Blockchain systems provide information to any stakeholder, either as a consequence of cultural norms—such as those evidenced in "open-source software"—or government regulation. Considering our case study region, such market improvements could provide opportunities for entrepreneurs in the South Bay to develop new technologies and solutions, and benefit South Bay companies through enterprise solutions that reduce costs and improve process automation and efficiency.

Another set of economic principles that helps to explain the appeal of Blockchain is the tension between economies of scale and decentralization. As first highlighted in Ronald Coase's Nature of the Firm Coase (1937), individuals group into firms in order to gain the benefits of economies of scale, improved information, and lower risks within an organization. Yet such collaboration comes with costs, including bureaucratic systems, inefficient management structures, and the limitation of innovation and risk-taking. In other words, there are benefits and costs to large, centralized firms on the one hand, and decentralized networks of individuals on the other. In recent years, technological innovations—such as those used in the "gig economy" platforms around rideshares and vacation rentals—have enabled companies and individuals to benefit from combining the best elements of both centralized and decentralized systems (Tasca, 2018).

Blockchain has the potential to provide centralizing forces that are similar in effect to economies of scale, while taking advantage of the benefits of decentralization. Supply chain management provides an interesting example of these forces (Denmark & Ny, 2018; Gonzalez, 2015). Due to the global nature of supply chains, with productive activities linked across industry sectors and nations, supply chains are often decentralized in nature. While there are good reasons for this condition, including the unique practices and regulations of each industry and nation, this condition creates numerous layers of transaction costs. Blockchain can facilitate the management of supply chains by providing standardized and transparent contracts, improving the speed of information flows through the system, and facilitating the ability of corporations and regulators to track and manage productive processes.

The distinction between public and private Blockchain systems is important here too. Private systems can be employed across established networks to ensure that companies can integrate their processes and improve information flows. There is also potential for information from private systems to be provided to regulatory agencies as needed—potentially through a "single-window"—to facilitate cross-border exams, inspections, and document processing. Public Blockchain systems are less likely to emerge given the competitive nature of the industry; however, there are potential benefits for regional consortia of stakeholders to share information publicly when in competition with other regions, to facilitate regional infrastructure and transportation planners, port systems, and hence regional economic development. In terms of our case study, South Bay has significant potential to benefit from these changes, due to its proximity to the major ports of Los Angeles and Long Beach, and its significant manufacturing base, for which supply chain management plays a key role.

2.2 *New Technology Development and Regional Innovation Systems*

Focusing on IT software and systems development, there are notable conceptual frameworks in the literature that can guide our understanding of how Blockchain might develop within a region. The concept of "Regional Innovation Systems" (Asheim et al., 2011; D'Allura et al., 2012) can help to explain how technological innovations such as Blockchain can emerge and prosper within regional economies.

This literature posits that place-based agglomerations of interacting organizations "provide the best context for an innovation-based globalizing economy" (D'Allura et al., 2012). These organizations include private industry, investors, and science and technology parks, as well as public and non-profit organizations that promote and facilitate innovation (such as incubators, economic development agencies, and workforce development agencies), and educational institutions that conduct research and develop human capital through training. The closeness of these organizations appears to generate interactive learning, knowledge production and sharing, and social embeddedness through personal relations and networks (Doloreux, 2004). Numerous empirical studies have confirmed that regional locations significantly influences firm innovation (summarized in Becheikh, Landry, & Amara, 2006), which results from beneficial regional infrastructure, an educated regional workforce, and proximity to partners in the supply chain, research institutions, and investors.[2]

A new technology such as Blockchain could therefore influence the economic development of regions by improving the productivity and processes of major public and private organizations, as well as by creating opportunities for start-up activity and the development of regional eco-systems. The success of Blockchain in a given region is likely to depend on factors such as legacy industries, entrepreneurial culture, and IT infrastructure, as well as its ability to train, attract and retain Blockchain developer and managerial talent, and local organization willingness to invest in and implement the technology. Workforce development agencies and educational institutions in particular can play a role in providing training and education to future software developers, managers, and entrepreneurs in the IT sector, as well as for the broader workforce that will be implementing, managing, and operating Blockchain systems.

When considering Regional Innovation Systems, and the workforce development implications of Blockchain, there are also both opportunities and risks. Technological change is a key element of macroeconomic growth; after major technological innovations, significant economic development follows (Acemoglu & Robinson, 2012). While the economy as a whole benefits, such disruption creates winners and losers. If Blockchain is successful, the winners are likely to be those first adopters who invest in the technology, as either innovating IT start-ups, or organizations implementing enterprise solutions. Similarly, regions and institutions that invest early in Blockchain by supporting innovators, facilitating investors, and educating workers, can reap the rewards of the technological change. In this respect,

[2]There are parallels here with "Social Innovation Theory," which is prominent in the public administration literature as it focuses on the place-based inter-organizational collaborations between public agencies and social entrepreneurs to address social problems (Caulier-Grice, Davies, Patrick, & Norman, 2012; Moulaert et al., 2013; Phills Jr, Deiglmeier, & Miller, 2008; Westley, 2008). This theory is relevant to our study with respect to Blockchain technology being an opportunity to provide employment, as well as the numerous social entrepreneurship programs (Tillemann, Price, Tillemann-Dick, & Knight, 2019).

governments and educational institutions have the potential to become a first adopter and first investor in this space and hence benefit while other regions lag behind.

As with any new technology, there is significant uncertainty that might limit the level of investment and can possibly create market distortions. However, this uncertainty also creates opportunity for new market entrants. Blockchain is currently in the relatively early stages of development, and was initially both inefficient computationally and clunky to use (Kharif, 2018). Moreover, while there are many ideas about how Blockchain might be implemented across different sectors of the economy, these ideas need to be developed and delivered in ways that are practical and meaningful to customers. This development and delivery is both uncertain and costly, leading to hesitancy among decision makers. This uncertainty is also present for potential future entrepreneurs and workers in Blockchain, who may not wish to pay the opportunity cost of product development or retraining. As new technologies emerge in the marketplace, regional workforce development agencies and universities can play an important role providing information to regional organizations, facilitating collaborations and information sharing, and training workers in the new technology.

2.3 New Technology Adoption and Public-Serving Institutions

Theories and studies of new technology adoption can also provide important insights about the future of Blockchain (Hall & Khan, 2003; Hoppe, 2002; Lai, 2017; Lee, Trimi, and Kim, 2013; MacVaugh & Schiavone, 2010; Oliveira & Martins, 2011). New technologies are seen to pass through five key stages of diffusion and adoption: knowledge, persuasion, decision, implementation, and confirmation (Rogers, 2010). Blockchain is currently largely in the early development stages of this process, and a relative small section of the market has advanced on to the later stages of implementation and confirmation. A PWC survey found that 20% of responding companies were in the research phase, 30% in the development phase, 10% in the pilot phase, and 15% were running live Blockchain projects (Davies & Likens, 2018).

Studies in this field have highlighted the numerous factors influencing technology adoption or non-adoption by firms (MacVaugh & Schiavone, 2010) including external factors such as industry characteristics, technology infrastructure, and government regulation, organizational factors such as communication processes, size, and slack, and leadership characteristics (Oliveira & Martins, 2011). Applying these factors to Blockchain, a number of points arise. First, in order for Blockchain to be implemented broadly, there need to be sufficient numbers of innovators and entrepreneurs and a level of competition between them. These individuals and start-ups entering the marketplace face the risk of investing their time and money in the ideas that can create technological change, but with uncertain outcomes and payoffs to them. Such risks are always present for entrepreneurs, yet are heightened given the unproven nature of Blockchain technology. Second, organizational executives face uncertainty around investing in Blockchain at this early stage of development. The benefits of these enterprise solutions could be transformative to such organizations, but decision makers need to balance the risks and rewards of adopting the technology early at a possibly cheaper level—and gaining an advantage over competitors—as opposed to waiting for other firms to take the risk and learn from others' mistakes, despite possibly losing out to competitors.

Third, there is a risk for individual workers and students with respect to investing time and money in training, either around Blockchain in general, or specifically around software development, as the outcomes are uncertain. Currently, there are not enough workers and students with the sufficient levels of training to contribute to the emerging Blockchain industry. This creates labor market distortions, with the demand for labor outweighing the supply, creating artificially inflated wages, and hence further-stymieing investment levels. In terms of our case study region, Blockchain professionals are lacking in the South Bay, and most South Bay companies have not yet developed business plans to support Blockchain. While those companies advance with this new technology, smaller companies, and companies in the South Bay, may miss out on emerging opportunities due to their lack of knowledge and resources. For example, the South Bay has many medical and medical insurance facilities not using Blockchain management because of many political factors dealing with the security of personal information, and the fear of change (Slabodkin, 2018).

Local educational institutions—that in the South Bay are predominantly public organizations—can play a key role in preparing students and workers for a career in the Blockchain field. Small businesses need a workforce that is ready to meet the demands of the ever-changing dynamics of Blockchain, especially professionals with specific knowledge of Blockchain utility and construction. Educational institutions can also highlight the potential job opportunities for a knowledgeable workforce to build applications to run on the network.

3 Methods

Interviews were conducted with experts on numerous industry sectors and Blockchain using an open-ended, semi-structured approach (Hammer and Wildavsky, 2018), which allows the interviewees to answer questions with deeper meaning and insight about Blockchain systems (Rapley, 2001) and is appropriate for the exploratory nature of this research. Questions and topics covered projections of Blockchain development and implementation, specific industries in the South Bay, and training and curriculum development required to support the emergence of a Blockchain industry in the region. These questions and topics were identified through the literature review above, which prompts a number of areas for inquiry related to Blockchain and workforce development, especially as they relate to our case study area of the South Bay region of Los Angeles County. The first area relates to the potential development and diffusion of Blockchain technologies within the South Bay:

- What factors are likely to influence Blockchain adoption and diffusion?
- Is Blockchain likely to develop across multiple sectors, including government?
- Is Blockchain likely to develop within the South Bay region?

The second area relates to the workforce needs to facilitate a Blockchain ecosystem and for organizations—public and private—implementing Blockchain technology:

- What are the workforce needs and opportunities related to Blockchain software and system technology?
- What are the workforce needs and opportunities related to the implementation of Blockchain across sectors of a regional economy?
- How can public organizations support regional workforce development to facilitate Blockchain implementation?

The interviewees are from a wide variety of different occupations. Thirty four interviews were conducted with industry-sector experts representing sectors such as Aerospace & Defense, Manufacturing, Entertainment, Sports Management, Health Care, Education, International Trade, Professional and Business Services, Government, Technical Services, Transportation/Utilities, and Finance. These interviews tended to focus on the likely impact of Blockchain on their industry and related occupations. Of this group, 23 had knowledge of Blockchain prior to the interview, 13 had experience of Blockchain in their workplace. Of those who had prior knowledge of Blockchain, seven had experienced it in their workplace. The responses suggest that those in a majority of the industry sectors see the potential for Blockchain to be both a disruptive and a positive force in their workplace. Many responses highlight the potential for Blockchain investment to develop their workplaces, whether through increasing operational efficiency, reducing transaction costs, or creating new opportunities for growth. Interviews were also conducted with 19 Blockchain experts from around the U.S., whose responses informed discussion in the following section.

4 Projections of Blockchain Growth

This section looks at projections of Blockchain in the coming years. Based on interviews with experts and review of industry literature, a model of factors influencing the rate of Blockchain implementation both globally and in the South Bay is proposed in Table 3.1. Further discussion of projected implementation and outcomes are presented before an exploration of the implementation challenges.

The impacts of Blockchain could be many and varied. Blockchain can affect people across a wide range of industries and within numerous occupations. In the short-term impacts are expected to be small. Public awareness is likely to increase with growing media coverage of cryptocurrency (Tapscott & Tapscott, 2018); individuals are likely begin to know basics of Blockchain and how it will be used. It is

Table 3.1 Proposed Model of Factors Influencing the Rate of Blockchain Implementation

	External factors to the industry	Internal factors to the industry
Global	• Success of ICOs and cryptocurrencies and potential regulation • Economic conditions	• Blockchain technology overcoming interoperability and user experience issues • Labor supply—education and training of developers and managers
South Bay	• Competition from other regions within the US—e.g. Bay Area, New York, St. Louis, Oregon—And internationally, such as EU and Asia • Obstacles to attract workers, including housing costs	• Implementation issues: Success at enterprise level • Company partnerships • Cost of labor • Entrepreneurial and innovative ideas

Source: Author's proposal, based on interviews with Blockchain experts and literature review

likely that implementation will take a longer period. According to a recent survey by KPMG, 41% of responding companies perceived that it is "very likely/likely" Blockchain will be implemented within their company over the next 3 years. On the other hand, 28% of responding companies said that it was "not likely/not at all likely." Over the same period, a further 48% noted that it is "very likely/likely" that Blockchain will change business practices, while on the other hand, 27% stated that it was "not likely/not at all likely" (Campbell, 2019a).

Recently, concerns have been raised about the "hype" surrounding Blockchain, with some market analysts suggesting the possibility of a "blockchain winter" (Bennett, 2018; Campbell, 2019c). As the promise of new ideas has given way to the reality of research, development, piloting, and implementation, there remains uncertainty about whether Blockchain solutions can deliver on the potential. Rajesh Kandaswamy, an analyst at Gartner Inc. argues "the disconnection between the hype and reality is significant—I've never seen anything like it. In terms of actual production use, it's very rare" (Kharif, 2018). Numerous planned projects have either been shelved or faced delays. For example, ASX, the operator of Australia's national stock exchange, announced in 2016 that they would release a commercial Blockchain platform by 2018. The expected rollout is now 2021 (Kharif, 2018). Similarly, Australian mining company BHP Billiton announced plans in 2016 of a 2017 Blockchain rollout to monitor rock and fluid samples. That company currently has no Blockchain projects or experiments underway (Kharif, 2018). All that said, in a new field with high degrees of innovation and entrepreneurialism, it is expected that failures and subsequent problem solving will be a common feature of the marketplace (Aitken, 2019; Campbell, 2019a).

Much of the current work is at the proof-of-concept stage, and within universities; while the IT and tech sectors are not as crowded currently, this means that there is lots space for growth in regions such as Los Angeles that have less-developed tech sectors compared with regions such as the Bay Area of California (B. Maurer, Personal Communication, June 9, 2018). Within the US, there is notable interest in the St Louis, especially in the shipping industry, while in Orange County, there is more work around finance and legal tech/smart contracts. There is also notable work in Oregon, especially with respect to mobile payment systems and contracts, for example in bike share and goods movement. Internationally, there have been substantial efforts to develop and implement Blockchain in the area of identity management, especially in Estonia, Singapore, and Sweden (B. Maurer, Personal Communication, June 9, 2018).

In the medium term, impacts might be more significant on businesses and government that are implementing Blockchain in operating practices. Some experts believe that this period will see the major development and implementation of Blockchain as benefits are noted and shared adoption will grow significantly over this period by major players who are followers (S. Brakeville, Personal Communication, June 14, 2018; C. Zhao, Personal Communication, June 12, 2018). Over the longer-term, we are likely to see a full integration of Blockchain be widely used for securing valuable information like financial, medical, and personal information (Tapscott & Tapscott, 2016). Some experts believe that broader implementation of Blockchain will take place during this period, since this is a disruptive technology and the workforce is an aging population, implying that acceptance and implementation will be slow (S. Murty, Personal Communication, June 14, 2018). It is argued that once 10% market share adopts the technology, a major adoption wave will follow, which is likely to be during this period (S. Brakeville, Personal Communication, June 14, 2018).

It is anticipated by some experts that a new eco-system would take 10–20 year time horizon to be achieved. It would take longer still for different interests to agree to a single system (S. Brakeville, Personal Communication, June 14, 2018). This eco-system would require the complete redesign of logistics networks on the technology with undetermined consequences in terms of efficiency. These challenges are framed by the questions posed by one Blockchain expert interviewed: "How do companies determine if they should implement it? How should the architecture be developed? When we have the road map, who has the technology skills to develop it? If innovation solutions are developed, what are the other issues surrounding them—e.g. legal, accounting, economics?"

The same Blockchain expert identified further challenges facing the technology. When considering investments in the technology, business leaders might find the concept confusing, have caution about the lack of current proof of concepts, or be wary of investing before a common standard is established. In terms of technology development, they argued that computational efficiency improvements were needed to address "clunky" operations. Moreover, Blockchain technologies would need to be integrated with "legacy" IT systems within organizations which can be challenging, especially in older systems. Particularly important for workforce development, this expert identified a "lack of available technical and software development talent," especially in the South Bay, which drives up the labor wage rate for innovation start-ups.

Another Blockchain expert highlighted the rollout challenges within organizations, each of which highlights an important area of potential workforce development. They argued that business processes and practices would need to adapt to the new approaches required with Blockchain systems. More specifically, IT systems would need to be implemented with respect to integration, communication, and security. In addition, users may be unaware of Blockchain adoption beyond occasional new software, creating a disconnection between IT offices and the end users. This expert suggested there may be resistance from skeptics, especially among less flexible or tech-savvy employees. As a result, this expert anticipated that hardware and software solutions and training would be required for organizations to benefit fully from the new technology and processes. The expert finally argued that organizations should pay attention to the legal and ethical implications of new data and identity management and contractual approaches. These elements can all offer material for workforce development agencies and universities when considering development of training programs in Blockchain.

5 Case Study of Blockchain Impacts on the South Bay

This case study explores the potential for Blockchain impacts on the South Bay using a combination of interviews with industry experts and assessments of each industry's presence in the South Bay. These efforts can provide a model for other regions to use when exploring workforce needs around emerging technologies.

Blockchain technology has the potential to benefit and affect numerous different private and public-sector establishments that are operating in the South Bay. The South Bay is a major economic engine of the Los Angeles region. Industries in the South Bay—including aerospace and defense, manufacturing, international trade, government, healthcare, business and professional services, and hospitality/tourism—employed 570,000 and paid $36.8 billion in wages in 2018 (CSUDH, 2018). Most of the sectors shown in Table 3.2 (which presents 2015 data) are relevant to Blockchain. There is a relatively small IT sector compared to the rest of Los Angeles County. However, there is potential for growth as the "Silicon Beach" IT start-up hub in the West Los Angeles areas of Santa Monica, Venice, and Playa Vista spreads south into El Segundo and other South Bay cities. There are notable financial and business-services sectors, both of which are at the forefront of Blockchain implementation. There is a significant legacy of manufacturing in the South Bay, including high value, capital-intensive aerospace and defense industries, which could have specific needs for Blockchain in terms of supply chain management and cybersecurity. There are also numerous, small health care establishments with large employment numbers, and which have potential for implementation of Blockchain in the area of data and identity management (Randall, Goel, & Abujamra, 2017).

The DLT properties of Blockchain technology have the potential to change significantly the workplace in general, but the potential impacts from its adoption are expected to differ significantly in speed and magnitude among sectors, industries, and specific occupations. Disruptions to the workplace might imply merely forcing the workforce to acquire basic skills through a brief training about the challenges and opportunities from Blockchain technology or, in a more severe case; it might

Table 3.2 South Bay Economic Indicators by Industry, 2015

Industry	Companies	Jobs	Average wage	Output ($M)	Output per worker ($'000 s)	Total value added ($M)
Natural resources	60	1,500	67,100	20,349.9	17,986.3[a]	118.3
Construction	1,541	17,400	63,600	4,362.1	169.1	1,967.3
Manufacturing	1,390	75,700	107,100	29,995.2	427.4	16,679.1
Wholesale trade	1,990	26,500	74,500	7,978.2	249.2	5,041.0
Retail trade	3,030	51,900	34,000	5,341.2	93.7	3,732.3
Transportation/ utilities	1,620	57,600	63,000	8,458.3	259.7	4,213.6
Information	590	11,500	122,000	7,294.9	362.4	3,767.5
Financial activities	2,800	24,300	82,300	5,087.6	234.3	2,831.1
Professional/ business services	5,120	83,100	66,400	17,545.1	147.7	10,903.3
Educational services	390	8,600	47,500	446.1	55.1	295.0
Health care	18,970	65,300	45,900	6,101.8	84.1	3,919.2
Leisure and hospitality	3,070	67,000	28,500	7,361.0	75.5	4,569.7
Other services and unclassified	4,600	18,500	35,500	13,797.8	272.0	9,835.8
Government	730	46,100	63,600	1,376.1	287.1	796.9
Total	45,890	555,000	62,200	135,495.3	221.0	68,670.1

Source: Author calculations based on California Employment Development Department and IMPLAN data

[a]This outlier reflects the capital-intensive petroleum refining industry sector, which is prominent in the South Bay

imply significant reductions in employment due to disruptions from a wide adoption of Blockchain technology.

Furthermore, some sectors and industries seem to be more willing and able to embrace the change than others are. Based on this research project findings, interviews, and industry experts' opinions, a wide adoption of Blockchain technology is most likely to have a significant impact on Financial Activities, Government, Health Care, Information, and Transportation/Utilities industries. Consequently, the higher dependence on these particular economic sectors, the higher the expected employment and economic impacts from the adoption of Blockchain technology (Table 3.3).

It is typically difficult to map occupational data with industry level data, but Healthcare practitioners and technical, Healthcare support, Education, training, and library, Business and financial operations, Transportation and material moving, and Management occupations might be more likely to be significantly impacted from the adoption of Blockchain technology. According to estimates for the U.S., healthcare, management, and business and financial operations occupations are projected to grow at a significant rate, and these occupations are likely to be considerably changed if Blockchain technology is widely adopted.

Table 3.3 Los Angeles County Employment and Projections by Industry (Thousands)

Industry	2016	2026[a]	Change	% Change
Educational services, health care, and social assistance	721	930	209	29.0
Leisure and hospitality	467	577	110	23.6
Professional and business services	599	680	81	13.6
Trade, transportation, and utilities	799	876	77	9.7
Retail trade	413	450	37	8.9
Self-employment	284	319	35	12.2
Construction	120	147	27	22.7
Government	556	582	26	4.6
Wholesale trade	223	243	20	9.1
Transportation, warehousing, and utilities	163	184	20	12.3
Other services	151	167	17	11.0
Information	198	214	16	7.8
Financial activities	211	219	8	3.7
Private household workers	14	15	2	12.5
Mining and logging	4	5	0.2	4.7
Total farm	5	5	−0.5	-9.6
Durable goods manufacturing	203	189	−14	-6.9
Nondurable goods manufacturing	161	140	−21	−13.0
Manufacturing	364	329	−35	-9.6
Total employment	4,492	5,063	572	12.7
Total nonfarm	4,189	4,725	536	12.8

Source: California EDD-Labor Market Information Division
aProjections by the California EDD

5.1 *Blockchain Impacts on South Bay Industry Sectors*

This section discusses the current and future uses and impacts of Blockchain technology across the following South Bay industry sectors of information technology, finance and insurance, manufacturing (including aerospace and defense), real estate, wholesale and foreign trade, and government. These sectors were selected due to their prominence in the South Bay economy and their potential to develop or adopt Blockchain technology systems.

5.1.1 Information Technology

This sector is at the heart of the Blockchain industry. Major corporations such as IBM, Microsoft, Oracle, Facebook and Overstock have made significant investments in Blockchain (Campbell, 2019a, 2019b; Disparte, 2019a, 2019b; La Monica, 2019; Slocum, 2018). In order for Blockchain to be broadly implemented, IT solutions need to be created, in particular, software technology development, server and hardware investment, and logistics. In these respects, the South Bay region is in a unique situation. The presence of "Silicon Beach"—an IT and software agglomeration in West LA that is spreading into the South Bay region—offers notable potential for economic development. The emergence of this innovation hub has attracted and nurtured entrepreneurs, developers, and business analysts within the region. These skills are all transferrable to Blockchain products and services, and it is expected that many of the companies within the "Silicon Beach" space will also implement Blockchain technology. For example, the Venice Beach start-up Gem is engaged in software development related to Blockchain.

It is unclear what area of specializations might emerge for Blockchain in the Los Angeles and South Bay regions. According to Heidi Pease of BlockchainLA, the financial applications of Blockchain are expected to emerge in the New York area, while Silicon Valley is anticipated to generate IT solutions and social media-oriented Blockchain applications. This provides Los Angeles and the South Bay with the opportunity to become a hub for the development of enterprise solutions so that organizations across numerous industries can take advantage of Blockchain's potential. The international connections of the region also offer promise for enterprise products to be developed and exported. The Los Angeles and South Bay economies are well placed for such interactions, given their diversity in terms of economic sectors, ethnicities, and long-term investments from international companies.

5.1.2 Finance

In the banking and financial services industries, Blockchain technology has the potential to introduce secure and efficient alternatives to current banking processes (Treleaven, Brown, & Yang, 2017). Firms like JPMorgan Chase, Citigroup, and Credit Suisse are currently investing in the technology in order to streamline their transaction processing, and hence reduce the expenses associated with their current practices (Orran & Irrera, 2016). U.S. markets will also experience the benefits of Blockchain as discussed by Capgemini, which estimates that the automation of tasks within the organization, increased trustworthiness of digital legal documents, and incorporating external information sources into the Blockchain can result in estimated minimum savings of $1.5 billion and $6 billion in the U.S. market (Maity, 2016). This reduction in costs for all participants is possible due to a distributed ledger's system of peer-to-peer collaboration that simplifies operational processes.

Smart contracts can also both accelerate clearing activities and streamline regulatory compliance. The self-executing contract process begins with one end of the contract using data from a Blockchain record as an input and generating an output reaction that is then written to the same or a different Blockchain (Magazzeni, McBurney, & Nash, 2017). By mapping more than 50 operational cost metrics in a joint survey with McLagan, a Connecticut based financial services consulting firm, Accenture estimates that investment banks could save up to $10 billion by using Blockchain technology to improve the processes involved in clearing and settlements. (Treat et al., 2017). Blockchain's immutable data storage feature allows for fast and accurate reporting by automating processes, making smart contracts an adequate source for proof of regulatory compliance (World Economic Forum, 2016).

While many industries expect to benefit from Blockchain implementation, traditional banks may be disrupted in some important ways. Blockchain is a threat to them as intermediaries of most financial transactions. According to the company Blockchain Capital, "Blockchain technology holds the promise to disrupt legacy businesses and create entirely new markets and business models" (Cuen, 2018). Using Blockchain as a public ledger allows financial transactions to be completed without contemporary intermediaries such as banks. Similarly, the insurance industry can benefit from smart contracts, peer-to-peer insurance mechanisms, and improved processes following disasters.

5.1.3 Manufacturing

Blockchain shows large potential in manufacturing, specifically in the field of "Just-In-Time" inventory and production. This would be advantageous to small manufacturers and even more so with large manufacturers, such as Boeing, who deal with a large number of vendors and sites (M. MacDonald, personal communication, April 21, 2018). There is a lack of understanding of Blockchain, and at the time of interview there were no "off the shelf" solutions that allowed small business such as Mac's Lift Gate in Long Beach, California to easily take advantage of a Blockchain solution for their inventory and production.

The intersection of supply chains and manufacturing also offers interesting insights into the use of Blockchain. Evelozcity (now Canoo) is a South Bay company using Blockchain to augment their design and manufacturing processes, as well as their supply chain management. Car manufacturing is a complex multiple step process from design to assembly and inspection. It would be beneficial for manufacturers in the vehicle industry and beyond to identify whether parts are defective or counterfeit and trace them through the supply chain (Jones, 2017). Traceability would also make it easier for a manufacturer warranty team to identify counterfeit parts quickly to deter fraudulent acts across the supply chain. Furthermore, being able to target recalls would save the manufacturer time and money compared to an entire fleet of cars being recalled (E. Mika, personal communication, May 14, 2018). Key questions remain among industry experts as to how Blockchain is going to be implemented. As with other industries, a major concern is their ability to attract talent. One car manufacturer interviewed believed that most of the talent is based up in Silicon Valley rather than Los Angeles.

Boeing, Honeywell, Lisi, Lockheed Martin, Northrop Grumman, Raytheon, and SpaceX makeup a large part of South Bay's aerospace sector. Recent development and research have hypothesized the benefits of large companies such as these if they implemented Blockchain technology to their current industry. Boeing, Honeywell, and Lockheed Martin have publicly announced their intention to integrate Blockchain technology within their procedures. This could improve and maintain proficient operations in manufacturing (specifically for parts life cycle tracking and maintenance), supply chain, after market, management, and customer transparency (Gutierrez, 2017).

5.1.4 Real Estate

In real estate, a great amount of time and effort is spent examining the financial and legal activities that would outline the specifics of a transaction. This is largely due to the need for physical identification documents (World Economic Forum, 2016). The use of such documents may result in lengthy verification processes or encounters with insufficient or inaccurate data. In some cases, third-party intermediaries are required, which increase the time spent on the due diligence part of a transaction. Blockchain-based systems offer a space for digital identities to be created which could transfer user data across a distributed ledger to which market participants can have permissioned access. This digital identifier, combined with a Blockchain MLS could potentially result in a shortened property search process and an expedited pre-lease analysis.

Moreover, access to government property records at the county level can be cumbersome, creating market inefficiencies that are plugged by brokers, lawyers, or other occupations that add cost to the process. Government offices, such as Cook County, Illinois have trialed the use of Blockchain for property records, with the aim of reducing citizen costs and increasing market efficiency. Key market participants in the real estate industry such as brokers, owners, and tenants typically use multiple listing service (MLS) platforms that can carry high access fees in order to find data on property listings. The information found through online platforms might be inaccurate, out-of-date, or incomplete due to a dependency on broker preference, a lack of standardization, and user intervention (Deloitte, 2017b). This results in a lack of trust in the information, which can increase the transaction processing time. Blockchain-based platforms can enable the data to spread throughout a distributed ledger that would allow increased transparency, availability, and shared control of information (Imbrex, 2018).

5.1.5 Wholesale and Foreign Trade

The potentially profound effects of Blockchain on the supply chain management described above are likely to also impact the wholesale industry. Using Blockchain in global trade can lead to "fast and secure access to information, verifiable authenticity and immutability of digital documents, trusted cross-organizational workflows, better risk assessments and fewer unnecessary intervention, and lower administrative expenses and elimination of costs to move physical paper across international borders" (White, 2018). An example of a company that is already benefiting from Blockchain is Maersk Line. According to Katherine Mosquera, the Strategic Communications Manager at the Maersk Line for the Greater New York City Area, "Maersk and IBM have been at the forefront of digitizing global trade since last year when we first announced our partnerships" (Personal communication, April 2018). The South Bay's location between the Port of Los Angeles and LAX international airport and large trade and logistics industries mean the region can benefit from Blockchain implementation. In addition, Blockchain has the potential to contribute to government efforts to implement "Single Window" systems to monitor and inspect goods crossing borders.

5.1.6 Government

The public sector can also readily incorporate Blockchain solutions to address issues like fraud and risk minimization, streamlining of operations, data and identity management, monitoring and assessment of regulated goods and operations, and emergency management (Ølnes, Ubacht, & Janssen, 2017). Government agencies are increasingly collaborating with technology companies to innovate and develop Blockchain-based platforms for public services and internal use applications. The US, Estonia, and the United Arab Emirates are currently among the top nations to explore a wide range of potential Blockchain applications. These range from business registration and banking operations to voting and share issuance (Allison, 2016; Higgins, 2017; Irrera, 2017; Lohade, 2017). In the US, several agencies, including the Department of Homeland Security and the Health and Human Services Department, have announced Blockchain programs aimed at proving the integrity of data captured by border devices and to protect and share health records (DHS, 2016; Ravindranath, 2017).

There is also the potential for government agencies to use Blockchain applications to facilitate movement towards "single-window" approaches, such as those provided by the Estonian government. These approaches enable citizens and businesses to conduct all of their interactions with numerous different government agencies through single portals. This has long been a "holy grail" for e-government advocates. While a full system is unlikely to be adopted in the US, regulated Blockchain systems—whether private or public—could enable governments to improve internal operational efficiency and reduce administrative costs for businesses.

Government policy makers can also promote the use of Blockchain and related cryptocurrencies for their own organizations. Blockchain can significantly improve government operations, data and identity management, cyber-security, and citizen interactions. Furthermore there is the potential for government agencies across the state of California to use cryptocurrencies for accounts and in tax collection. This would allow the nascent cannabis industry easier access to banking systems and facilitate tax collection.

6 Conclusions and Recommendations

The future of Blockchain is uncertain, yet promising. There is great potential for the technology to be applied in numerous ways across numerous industries, and as such is experiencing substantial interest and investment across numerous economic sectors. The success of Blockchain in regions such as the South Bay will hinge on the region's ability to attract and retain developer talent, local organization willingness to invest in and implement the technology, and to connect with state-level institutions to create a more unified stance when in competition with U.S. regions such as the Bay Area and New York. Regional public organizations such as workforce agencies, city governments, and educational institutions can play a pivotal role in the development of Blockchain technology innovation ecosystems, including facilitating industry stakeholder interactions and information sharing, developing local talent, and investing in regional infrastructure. As the technology develops, information sharing around Blockchain systems implementation best practices and workforce needs can help government and industry leaders to make better-informed decisions.

Interviews with industry-sector experts emphasize the potential for Blockchain investment to develop their workplaces, whether through increasing operational efficiency, reducing transaction costs, or creating new opportunities for growth. Interviews with Blockchain technology experts highlight the substantial demand for workers with experience and knowledge of Blockchain, especially in the areas of software development, finance and accounting, and strategic development. They also emphasize significant opportunity for entrepreneurs to contribute to the development of innovative software and enterprise solutions designed around organizational needs and legacy technology. Blockchain could also displace or increase competition for numerous occupations, especially those currently involved in the verification of contracts and supply chain operations, trade brokerage, data management and processing, and accounting systems management. Hence, public organizations—especially workforce agencies and educational institutions—can play a key role in informing regional graduates and workers about their threats and opportunities.

The broad scope of industries potentially impacted by Blockchain highlights the need for students from most disciplines and workers in most occupations and industry sectors to be aware of the ways in which this new technology will be implemented into workplace systems. Based on this research project findings, interviews, and industry experts' opinions, a wide adoption of Blockchain technology is most likely to have a significant impact on Financial Activities, Government, Health Care, Information, and Transportation/Utilities industries. There is substantial opportunity for those in executive, managerial or operations positions to develop their careers through experience and knowledge of delivering, using, and evaluating Blockchain systems. On the other hand, Blockchain systems might also be developed in such a way that reduces the need for human interactions, with operations either being automated or based on artificial intelligence programs. If Blockchain is implemented to its potential, some of these positions will be renegotiated or eliminated, highlighting the need for individuals to anticipate such market changes. There is also a significant opportunity for software developers to find employment in this area. With this in mind, local educational institutions should facilitate market development by providing courses and certificates on Blockchain. Interviews with Blockchain experts suggest that courses and certificates should focus on the following:

- Increasing knowledge about the basic functions of Blockchain.
- Providing those in a broad range of occupations (including managers, administrators, data analysts, sales representatives, etc.) and industries with an under-

standing of the practical implementation of Blockchain and the ways in which it might reshape the workplace and organizational structures.
- Exploring Blockchain from different perspectives, including legal, ethical, security, and entrepreneurial.
- Providing Blockchain software development training classes with a computer science perspective that highlight the interactions between entrepreneurs, managers, and operators within organizations.

Focusing on our case study region, Blockchain has the potential to create jobs within the South Bay case, both within the information technology sector and within the organizations implementing the technology. Analysis above suggests that Blockchain development is likely to differ between sectors; therefore any training should account for such variance. There is opportunity for Blockchain to be established as a hub within the South Bay, especially when considering broad applications across numerous industry sectors. The Southern California region is unique nationally due to its economic dynamism and diversity, as well as the number of educational establishments and lifestyle. If the South Bay can build upon the success of the "Silicon Beach" area that has a high rate of startups and science and technological innovation, and a Blockchain hub can emerge in the region, there is significant potential for the technology to spread across the wide range of industry sectors present in the South Bay. These levels of implementation would create jobs for the companies developing the technology, and would create new opportunities in the implementing organizations, to manage the technology and to take advantage of the efficiency gains.

In line with the "Regional Innovation Systems" theory explored in the literature review, there is the potential for the regional government agencies to invest in infrastructure that in turn facilitates development and adoption of Blockchain technology. The implementation of a high-speed broadband internet system in the South Bay, similar to that employed in the City of Santa Monica—one of the attractions for IT firms in that region—could boost the appeal of the South Bay for Blockchain entrepreneurs. The South Bay Fiber Network is a regional broadband project being developed by the South Bay Workforce Investment Board and the South Bay Cities Council of Governments. The South Bay Fiber Network would connect 15 cities in the South Bay to a fiber-optic network offering capacity and speeds much faster than what is currently available in many areas. The project aims to ensure the South Bay region has the Broadband infrastructure needed to stay globally competitive and to facilitate Smart-City services. Providing competitive broadband speed and capacity to the South Bay is also important for business retention and consequently saving jobs (SBWIB, 2019).

Local businesses are already investing in Blockchain to identify both enterprise and innovation solutions. South Bay governments can further support these efforts by connecting innovative entrepreneurs with more established firms, and by informing both of the opportunities for IT solutions in this space. There is a developing network of Blockchain developers and experts in the broader Los Angeles region that can inform and support South Bay organizations.

In order for Blockchain technology to develop in the region, talented entrepreneurs and developers would need to be nurtured and attracted to the region. The South Bay is a desirable location in terms of lifestyle, yet housing costs and transportation issues are notable concerns for many employees in the region. To address these concerns, South Bay organizations and governments could possibly take a holistic approach and promote alternative solutions to these opportunities, including telework programs, housing developments in local cities, and improved transportation infrastructure. Educational institutions can also play and important role in nurturing the development of the local workforce and students. However, the costs and benefits of such investments would need to be weighed.

Future research on this subject could go in a number of directions. One avenue would be the study of Blockchain agglomerations within particular regions. Another could be the possible impacts of Blockchain on business practices and outcomes in key sectors—such as supply chain management, manufacturing, and health care. A third would be to explore the effectiveness of Blockchain training and educational programs in terms of pedagogy and job market outcomes.

Acknowledgements This research was funded by a grant from the South Bay Workforce Investment Board, Inc. to the South Bay Economics Institute at CSU Dominguez Hills.

The authors would like to thank Aliah Cadena, Brian Daniels, Ashlyn Chapman, Selaini Ikahihifo, Stacie LaFargue, Ryan Quesenberry, and Samuel Rodgers for their research assistance on this project.

References

Acemoglu, D., & Robinson, J. A. (2012). Why nations fail: The origins of power, prosperity, and poverty. Currency.

Adams, R., Kewell, B., & Parry, G. (2018). Blockchain for good? Digital ledger technology and sustainable development goals. In *Handbook of sustainability and social science research* (pp. 127-140). Springer, Cham.

Aitken, R. (2019). Solving Blockchain's Current Flaws And Enabling Future Mainstream Adoption. *Forbes.* Retrieved from https://www.forbes.com/sites/rogeraitken/2019/02/28/solving-blockchains-current-flaws-enabling-future-mainstream-adoption/#6a31e3ad274b

Akerlof, G. A. (1978). The market for "lemons": Quality uncertainty and the market mechanism. In *Uncertainty in Economics* (pp. 235-251).

Allison, I. (2016) Consensus 2016: State of Delaware open for blockchain business. *International Business Times.* Retrieved from https://www.ibtimes.co.uk/consensus-2016-state-delaware-open-blockchain-business-1557851

Asheim, B. T., Smith, H. L., & Oughton, C. (2011). Regional innovation systems: theory, empirics and policy. *Regional studies, 45*(7), 875–891.

Becheikh, N., Landry, R., & Amara, N. (2006). Lessons from innovation empirical studies in the manufacturing sector: A systematic review of the literature from 1993–2003. *Technovation, 26*(5-6), 644–664.

Bennett, M. (2018, November 18). Predictions 2019: Steady Evolution In Blockchain Will Continue, Unless Disillusionment Causes A "Winter". Retrieved from https://go.forrester.com/blogs/predictions-2019-blockchain-distributed-ledger-technology/

Bramwell, A., & Wolfe, D. A. (2008). Universities and regional economic development: The entrepreneurial University of Waterloo. *Research policy, 37*(8), 1175–1187.
California State University, Dominguez Hills (CSUDH). (2018). South Bay Economic Forecast and Industry Outlook. Retrieved from https://www.csudh.edu/Assets/csudh-sites/uce/docs/forecast/csudh_south-bay-economic-forecast-report_2017.pdf
Campbell, R. (2019a, March 1). KPMG: 41% of Tech Leaders in Favor of Adopting Blockchain for Business in the Next 3 Years. *Forbes*. Retrieved from https://www.forbes.com/sites/rebeccacampbell1/2019/03/01/kpmg-blockchain-adoption/#56b173c53b5d
Campbell, R. (2019b, February 22). Industry Experts Weigh In On Zuckerberg's Data Sharing Blockchain System Plans. *Forbes*. Retrieved from https://www.forbes.com/sites/rebeccacampbell1/2019/02/22/industry-experts-weigh-in-on-zuckerbergs-data-sharing-blockchain-system-plans/#2ff7735e2d17
Campbell, R. (2019c, January 14). See How This Non-Profit is Using the Blockchain to Clean Up the Niger Delta. *Forbes*. Retrieved from https://www.forbes.com/sites/rebeccacampbell1/2019/01/14/see-how-this-non-profit-is-using-the-blockchain-to-clean-up-the-niger-delta/#54a3bba83302
Catalini, C., & Gans, J. S. (2016). *Some Simple Economics of the Blockchain* (No. w22952). National Bureau of Economic Research.
Caulier-Grice, J. Davies, A. Patrick, R. Norman, W. (2012) Defining Social Innovation. A deliverable of the project: "The theoretical, empirical and policy foundations for building social innovation in Europe" (TEPSIE), European Commission – 7th Framework Programme, Brussels: European Commission, DG Research.
Coase, R. H. (1937). The Nature of the Firm. *Economica, 4*(16), 386–405.
Cuen, L. (2018, March 22) Blockchain Capital Raises $150 Million, Looks Beyond Financial Services. *Coindesk*. Retrieved from https://www.coindesk.com/blockchain-capital-raises-150-million-looks-beyond-financial-services/
D'Allura, G., Galvagno, M., & Mocciaro Li Destri, A. (2012). Regional innovation systems: a literature review. *Business Systems Review, 1*(1), 139–156.
Davies, S. and Likens, S. (2018). Blockchain is here. What's your next move? Retrieved from: https://www.pwc.com/gx/en/issues/blockchain/blockchain-in-business.html
Davidson, S., De Filippi, P., & Potts, J. (2016). Economics of Blockchain. *Available at SSRN 2744751*.
Denmark, C., & Ny, A., (2018). Maersk and IBM to Form Joint Venture Applying Blockchain to Improve Global Trade and Digitize Supply Chains. *IBM*. Retrieved from https://www-03.ibm.com/press/us/en/pressrelease/53602.wss
Deloitte (2016) Blockchain Technology – Speeding Up and Simplifying Cross-Border Payments. https://www2.deloitte.com/nl/nl/pages/financial-services/articles/1-blockchain-speeding-up-and-simplifying-cross-border-payments.html
Deloitte (2017a) Blockchain Technology: A Game-Changer in Accounting? Retrieved from: https://www2.deloitte.com/content/dam/Deloitte/de/Documents/Innovation/Blockchain_A%20game-changer%20in%20accounting.pdf
Deloitte (2017b) Blockchain in Commercial Real Estate: The Future is Here! *Deloitte Center for Financial Services*. Retrieved from: https://www2.deloitte.com/content/dam/Deloitte/us/Documents/financial-services/us-fsi-rec-blockchain-in-commercial-real-estate.pdf
Disparte, D. (2019a, March 5) IBM X-Force Red Launches Blockchain Cybersecurity Service. *Forbes*. Retrieved from https://www.forbes.com/sites/dantedisparte/2019/03/05/ibm-x-force-red-launches-blockchain-cybersecurity-service/?ss=crypto-blockchain#513da35c1602
Disparte, D. (2019b, February 28) Oracle: On The World's Data Lake, A Blockchain Swan. *Forbes*. Retrieved from https://www.forbes.com/sites/dantedisparte/2019/02/28/oracle-on-the-worlds-data-lake-a-blockchain-swan/?ss=crypto-blockchain#3d3066dc2763
DHS (2016) DHS S&T Awards $199K to Austin Based Factom Inc. for Internet of Things Systems Security. Department of Homeland Security, Science and Technology. Retrieved from: https://www.dhs.gov/science-and-technology/news/2016/06/17/st-awards-199k-austin-based-factom-inc-iot-systems-security

Doloreux, D. (2004). Regional innovation systems in Canada: a comparative study. *Regional studies, 38*(5), 479–492.
Drucker, J., & Goldstein, H. (2007). Assessing the regional economic development impacts of universities: A review of current approaches. *International Regional Science, 30*(1), 20–46.
Gibbs, D. (2000). Ecological modernisation, regional economic development and regional development agencies. *Geoforum, 31*(1), 9–19.
Giloth, R. P. (2000). Learning from the field: Economic growth and workforce development in the 1990s. *Economic Development Quarterly, 14*(4), 340–359.
Gonzalez, A. (2015, December 21) One More Prediction for 2016: Blockchain Technology Will Make Its Debut in Supply Chain Management. *Talking Logistics*. Retrieved from: https://talkinglogistics.com/2015/12/21/one-more-prediction-for-2016-blockchain-technology-will-make-its-debut-in-supply-chain-management/
Gutierrez, C. (2017). Boeing improves operations with blockchain and the internet of things. *Altoros*. Retrieved from https://www.altoros.com/blog/boeing-improves-operations-with-blockchain-and-the-internet-of-things/
Hall, B. H., & Khan, B. (2003). *Adoption of new technology* (No. w9730). National bureau of economic research.
Hammer, D., & Wildavsky, A. (2018). The open-ended, semistructured interview: An (almost) operational guide. In Craftways (pp. 57–101). Routledge.
Higgins, S. (2017, March 29) Emirates NBD Enlists UAE Central Bank in Blockchain Check Trial. *Coindesk*. Retrieved from https://www.coindesk.com/emirates-nbd-enlists-uae-central-bank-blockchain-check-trial/
Hileman, G., & Rauchs, M. (2017). Global blockchain benchmarking study. Cambridge Centre for Alternative Finance, University of Cambridge, 122. Retrieved from: https://j2-capital.com/wp-content/uploads/2017/11/GLOBAL-BLOCKCHAIN.pdf
Hoppe, H. C. (2002). The timing of new technology adoption: theoretical models and empirical evidence. *The Manchester School, 70*(1), 56–76.
Imbrex (2018) Imbrex company website. Retrieved from https://imbrex.io/
Irrera, A. (2017, January 23) Nasdaq successfully completes blockchain test in Estonia. *Reuters*. Retrieved from https://www.reuters.com/article/nasdaq-blockchain/nasdaq-successfully-completes-blockchain-test-in-estonia-idUSL1N1FA1XK
Jacobs, R. L., & Hawley, J. D. (2009). The emergence of 'workforce development': Definition, conceptual boundaries and implications. In *International handbook of education for the changing world of work* (pp. 2537-2552). Springer, Dordrecht.
Jones, M. (2017, June 21). Blockchain for Automotive: spare parts and warranty. Retrieved from: https://www.ibm.com/blogs/internet-of-things/iot-blockchain-automotive-industry/
Julian, T. (2014, December 4). Defining Moments in the History of Cyber-Security and the Rise of Incident Response. *Infosecurity-Magazine*. Retrieved from: https://www.infosecurity-magazine.com/opinions/the-history-of-cybersecurity/
Kharif, O. (2018, August 1). Blockchain, Once Seen as a Corporate Cure-All, Suffers a Slowdown. *Los Angeles Times*. Retrieved from: https://www.latimes.com/business/la-fi-blockchain-corporations-20180801-story.html
Killmeyer, J., White, M., & Chew, B. (2017) Will blockchain transform the public sector? Deloitte University Press, Deloitte Center for Government Insights. Retrieved from: https://www2.deloitte.com/content/dam/insights/us/articles/4185_blockchain-public-sector/DUP_will-blockchain-transform-public-sector.pdf
La Monica, P. R. (2019, February 25) Overstock is still a retailer but it wants to be a blockchain company. *CNN*. Retrieved from: https://www.cnn.com/2019/02/25/investing/overstock-retail-sale-blockchain/index.html
Lai, P. C. (2017). The literature review of technology adoption models and theories for the novelty technology. *JISTEM-Journal of Information Systems and Technology Management, 14*(1), 21–38.

Lee, J. (2010). 10 year retrospect on stage models of e-Government: A qualitative meta-synthesis. *Government Information Quarterly, 27*(3), 220–230.

Lee, S. G., Trimi, S., & Kim, C. (2013). The impact of cultural differences on technology adoption. *Journal of world business, 48*(1), 20–29.

Lohade, N. (2017, April 24) Dubai Aims to be a City Built on Blockchain. *Wall Street Journal.* Retrieved from https://www.wsj.com/articles/dubai-aims-to-be-a-city-built-on-blockchain-1493086080

Long, C. (2019, March 4). What Do Wyoming's New Blockchain Laws Mean? *Forbes.* Retrieved from: https://www.forbes.com/sites/caitlinlong/2019/03/04/what-do-wyomings-new-blockchain-laws-mean/?ss=crypto-blockchain#358f11185fde

Los Angeles Economic Development Corporation (LAEDC). (2020). Discover LA. Retrieved February 2020, from https://laedc.org/wp-content/uploads/2019/02/LAEDC-2019-Economic-Forecast-Report.pdf

MacVaugh, J., & Schiavone, F. (2010). Limits to the diffusion of innovation: A literature review and integrative model. *European journal of innovation management, 13*(2), 197–221.

Magazzeni, D., McBurney, P., & Nash, W. (2017). Validation and verification of smart contracts: A research agenda. *Computer, 50*(9), 50–57.

Maity, S. (2016) Consumers Set to Save up to Sixteen Billion Dollars on Banking and Insurance Fees Thanks to Blockchain-Based Smart Contracts Says Capgemini Report. Retrieved from https://www.capgemini.com/news/consumers-set-to-save-up-to-sixteen-billion-dollars-on-banking-and-insurance-fees-thanks-to/#

Moulaert, F., et al. (Eds.). (2013). *The International Handbook on Social Innovation.* Cheltenham: Edward Elgar Publishing Limited.

Nofer, M., Gomber, P., Hinz, O., & Schiereck, D. (2017). Blockchain. *Business & Information Systems Engineering, 59*(3), 183–187.

Oliveira, T., & Martins, M. F. (2011). Literature review of information technology adoption models at firm level. *Electronic Journal of Information Systems Evaluation, 14*(1), 110.

Ølnes, S., Ubacht, J., & Janssen, M. (2017). Blockchain in government: Benefits and implications of distributed ledger technology for information sharing. *Government Information Quarterly, 34*(3), 355–364.

Orran, O., & Irrera, A. (2016). Goldman, JPMorgan to invest in blockchain startup Axoni: sources. Reuters. Retrieved from https://www.reuters.com/article/us-axoni-blockchain/goldman-jpmorgan-to-invest-in-blockchain-startup-axoni-sources-idUSKBN149073

Phills Jr., J. R., Deiglmeier, K., & Miller, D. T. (2008). Rediscovering Social Innovation. *Stanford Social Innovation Review, 6*(4), 34–43.

Pisa, M., & Juden, M. (2017). Blockchain and economic development: Hype vs. reality. *Center for Global Development Policy Paper, 107*, 150.

Randall, D., Goel, P., & Abujamra, R. (2017). Blockchain applications and use cases in health information technology. *J Health Med Informat, 8*(276), 2.

Rapley, T. J. (2001). The art (fulness) of open-ended interviewing: some considerations on analysing interviews. *Qualitative research, 1*(3), 303–323.

Ravindranath, M. (2017, March 23) HHS Wants More Blockchain in Health Records – Eventually. *Nextgov.* Retrieved from https://www.nextgov.com/cio-briefing/2017/03/hhs-wants-more-blockchain-health-records-eventually/136393/

Rogers, E. M. (2010). *Diffusion of innovations.* Simon and Schuster, New York, US.

Siau, K., & Long, Y. (2005). Synthesizing e-government stage models–a meta-synthesis based on meta-ethnography approach. *Industrial Management & Data Systems, 105*(4), 443–458.

Slabodkin, G. (2018, February 15) Blockchain Not a Panacea for Managing Health Records, Fed Expert Says. *Health Data Management,* www.healthdatamanagement.com/news/blockchain-is-not-a-panacea-technology-for-managing-health-records

Slocum, H. (2018, November 19) IBM and Columbia University Launch Two Accelerator Programs for Blockchain Startups. *IBM Newsroom.* Retrieved from https://newsroom.ibm.com/2018-11-19-IBM-and-Columbia-University-Launch-Two-Accelerator-Programs-for-Blockchain-Startups

South Bay Workforce Investment Board (SBWIB) (2019). The South Bay Regional Broadband Fiber Optic Master Plan. Retrieved from https://www.sbwib.org/broadband
Sun, J., Yan, J., & Zhang, K. Z. (2016). Blockchain-based sharing services: What blockchain technology can contribute to smart cities. *Financial Innovation, 2*(1), 26.
Swan, M. (2017). Anticipating the economic benefits of blockchain. *Technology innovation management review, 7*(10), 6–13.
Tapscott, D., & Tapscott, A. (2016, May 10). *The Impact of the Blockchain Goes Beyond Financial Services*. Retrieved from https://hbr.org/2016/05/the-impact-of-the-blockchain-goes-beyond-financial-services
Tapscott, D., & Tapscott, A. (2018). *Blockchain Revolution: How the Technology Behind Bitcoin and Other Cryptocurrencies Is Changing the World*. New York: Portfolio/Penguin.
Tasca, P. (2018). The Hope and Betrayal of Blockchain. *New York Times*. Retrieved from: https://www.nytimes.com/2018/12/04/opinion/blockchain-bitcoin-technology-revolution.html
Tillemann, T., Price, A., Tillemann-Dick, G., and Knight, A. (2019). The Blueprint for Blockchain and Social Innovation. *New America*. Retrieved from: https://www.newamerica.org/bretton-woods-ii/blockchain-trust-accelerator/reports/blueprint-blockchain-and-social-innovation/
Treat, D., Brodersen, C., Blain, C., & Kurbanov, R. (2017) Banking on Blockchain: A value analysis for investment banks. Accenture Consulting. Retrieved from https://www.accenture.com/_acnmedia/Accenture/Conversion-Assets/DotCom/Documents/Global/PDF/Consulting/Accenture-Banking-on-Blockchain.pdf
Treleaven, P., Brown, R. G., & Yang, D. (2017). Blockchain technology in finance. *Computer, 50*(9), 14–17.
Van Ittersum, K., & Feinberg, F. M. (2010). Cumulative timed intent: A new predictive tool for technology adoption. *Journal of Marketing Research, 47*(5), 808–822.
Westley, F. (2008, 2008. Retrieved from http://sig.uwaterloo.ca/researchpublications). The Social Innovation Dynamic, Social Innovation Generation. *University of Waterloo*. http://www3.weforum.org/docs/WEF_The_future_of_financial_infrastructure.pdf
White, M., (2018). Digitizing Global Trade with Maersk and IBM. *BlockChain Unleashed: IBM BlockChain Block*. Retrieved from https://www.ibm.com/blogs/blockchain/2018/01/digitizing-global-trade-maersk-ibm/
World Economic Forum (2016) A Blueprint for Digital Identity: The Role of Financial Institutions in Building Digital Identity. Future of Financial Services Series. Retrieved from: http://www3.weforum.org/docs/WEF_A_Blueprint_for_Digital_Identity.pdf

Dr. Fynnwin Prager is Assistant Professor of Public Administration and Co-Director of the South Bay Economics Institute at CSU Dominguez Hills. He received his PhD from—and undertook a Postdoc at—the USC Price School of Public Policy and the Center for Risk and Economic Analysis of Terrorism Events. His research and publications in journals such as *Risk Analysis, International Journal of Disaster Risk Reduction, Transportation Research Part A, Contemporary Economic Policy, and Transport Policy* have focused on the policy and economics of disasters, particularly environmental and terrorism policy, as well as regional economies and transportation systems. Dr. Prager has published two books: *Terrorism: An International Perspective* with Professor Gus Martin at CSUDH and *Economic Consequence Analysis of Disasters* with Professor Adam Rose and colleagues at USC. Dr. Prager is committed to teaching, research, and service at CSUDH, and interconnects his classroom with research for numerous regional and national organizations, including U.S. Customs and Border Protection, U.S. National Biosurveillance Integration Center, World Trade Center, Los Angeles, South Bay Workforce Investment Board, and the CSU Transportation Center.

Dr. Jose Martinez is Associate Professor of Economics at California State University, Dominguez Hills. His academic research and interests focus on international migration, labor informality, econometrics, and time series forecasting. Dr. Martinez has expertise on the South Bay economy through his role of Co-Director of the South Bay Economics Institute at CSUDH, the CSUDH Economic Forecast, and projects and presentations with Los Angeles Economic Development Corporation, World Trade Center Los Angeles, and the SBCCOG.

Chris Cagle is the Regional Affairs Manager for the SBWIB and also serves as the organization's Marketing Director. Additionally, his duties include grant writing, program design and apprenticeship development. Chris has designed an apprenticeship model for engineering as part of a team that became the first to successfully register an Aerospace Engineering Apprenticeship occupation in the United States with the US Department of Labor. He also established an online business portal for the region, SouthBayBusiness.org, which provides user-friendly profiles of each city in the South Bay area. Chris was also instrumental in establishing a workforce office at the Los Angeles Air Force Base in El Segundo, California, to provide enhanced workforce transition assistance for veterans exiting the military into civilian careers. Chris is frequently a guest speaker on workforce development issues at many community events and was previously a two-term city council member, representing the residents of District 2 in Redondo Beach. He holds a master's degree in Political Science.

Chapter 4
Reconciling Blockchain with the GDPR: Insights from the German Asylum Procedure

Alexander Rieger, Alexander Stohr, Annette Wenninger, and Gilbert Fridgen

1 Introduction

Blockchains are distributed databases that use peer-to-peer protocols and cryptographic hash functions to propagate as well as store data in a tamper-resistant and consistent manner among the organizations in a blockchain network (Beck, Müller-Bloch, & King, 2018; Glaser, 2017). The use of blockchain technology is commonly understood to reduce trust concerns in various cross-organizational contexts and processes (Pedersen, Risius, & Beck, 2019). Blockchain solutions allow the organizations of a blockchain network to maintain control over their activities but, at the same time, enable them to establish a "shared and persistent truth" on the state of the process at any given time. This truth allows the resolution of possible conflicts that may occur at a later point. It also allows the use of updates on the blockchain as reliable triggers for subsequent activities. Further, the organizations can deploy so-called smart contracts that allow for the automated activation of certain steps of the process and its monitoring, if required. In a nutshell, blockchain affords

A. Rieger (✉) · G. Fridgen
SnT - Interdisciplinary Center for Security, Reliability and Trust, University of Luxembourg, Luxembourg, Luxembourg
e-mail: alexander.rieger@uni.lu; gilbert.fridgen@uni.lu

A. Stohr
Project Group Business and Information Systems Engineering of the Fraunhofer FIT, Augsburg, Germany
e-mail: alexander.stohr@fit.fraunhofer.de

A. Wenninger
FIM Research Center, University of Bayreuth, Project Group Business & Information Systems Engineering of the Fraunhofer FIT, Bayreuth, Germany
e-mail: annette.wenninger@fim.rc.de

C. G. Reddick et al. (eds.), *Blockchain and the Public Sector*, Public Administration and Information Technology 36,
https://doi.org/10.1007/978-3-030-55746-1_4

an alternative when the delegation of process governance to a central authority is not possible or desireable (Beck et al., 2018; Mendling et al., 2018).

Despite the promising benefits, technical challenges and regulatory uncertainties have limited the adoption of blockchain-based process management (Lacity, 2018). Whereas many technical challenges, such as high energy consumption, slow and cumbersome usage, and scalability, can be mitigated by appropriate designs and modern blockchain frameworks (Carson, Romanelli, Walsh, & Zhumaev, 2018; Lacity, 2018), regulatory uncertainties are more difficult to address. Foremost among such uncertainties are those arising from Europe's General Data Protection Regulation (GDPR). The GDPR standardizes the rules for the processing of personal data throughout the member states of the European Union (EU). It encodes several essential rights of natural persons. Most importantly, it establishes the need to establish clear responsibilities for compliance with the regulation, and outlaws any processing of personal data unless the processor has a lawful basis, for example, if the processing is necessary for compliance with a legal obligation of the controller. Also, the GDPR grants natural persons the right to have inaccurate personal data rectified (or completed, if it is incomplete) and to have their personal data erased (General Data Protection Regulation (GDPR), 2016).

At first glance, the GDPR requirements appear to conflict with the basic properties of blockchain. For instance, the decentralized nature of blockchain networks seems to prevent the designation of clear responsibilities. Moreover, the need to obtain a lawful basis for processing personal data at each node appears daunting. Also, blockchain does not envisage the data being erased at a later point (Lyons, Courcelas, & Timsit, 2018).

In this context, the blockchain pilot undertaken by Germany's Federal Office for Migration and Refugees (BAMF) represents an interesting case study. The pilot evaluates the use of blockchain to coordinate cross-authority processes in the German asylum procedure. In Germany, the asylum procedure requires close collaboration between multiple authorities at the municipal, state, and federal levels. Blockchain provides a particularly promising technological approach because various organizational and legal hurdles have so far prevented the delegation of process governance to a single authority.

One of the core objectives of the project is to develop a blockchain-based solution that complies fully with the GDPR requirements (Fridgen et al., 2019a, 2019b). For this purpose, the BAMF is working closely with the Federal Commissioner for Data Protection and Freedom of Information (BfDI), Germany's GDPR supervisory authority. Learnings and results emerging from this cooperation are disseminated regularly. They offer an insightful point of reference for the development of GDPR-compliant blockchain solutions, both in the public sector and beyond.

The remainder of this chapter is structured as follows: First, we briefly outline the German asylum procedure and describe the context of the pilot project. We then illustrate the implemented process and functionality of the blockchain solution. Next, we discuss in detail how the BAMF addresses the most critical requirements of the GDPR. Lastly, we provide an outlook on other challenges that the project will have to address in the future.

2 The German Asylum Procedure

The right to asylum for politically persecuted individuals is laid down in the *Grundgesetz*, the constitution of the Federal Republic of Germany. The German Asylum Act extends this right to anyone who flees from violence, war, or terrorism. The act governs the general design of asylum procedures and specifies the necessary competences and responsibilities of the authorities involved. Figure 4.1 provides a simplified version of the German asylum procedure.

Upon arrival in Germany, asylum seekers must immediately report to federal or state police to make a request for asylum. The police will transfer asylum seekers to the nearest registration agency, which will provide them with access to medical care and with a proof-of-arrival document that grants a temporary right to stay. Asylum seekers can also register their application with the BAMF during their stay at the registration agency. The BAMF will then determine if another EU member state is responsible for the examination of the asylum application, for instance, because the applicant has first entered the European Union in this member state. Should this prove to be the case, the asylum seeker must, in accordance with the Dublin Regulation, return to the responsible member state. However, the review process may take several days.

Meanwhile, Germany's federal quota system may require applicants to be transferred to another registration agency. This quota system is recalculated annually and distributes refugees in accordance with the so-called 'Königstein Key', which is based on the tax revenue and population of each of Germany's federal states. If the Dublin review does not reveal that another EU member state is resposible for the applicant, the BAMF will hold a personal interview at the closest appropriate registration agency or regional office. Based on the interview, a BAMF caseworker will approve or reject the asylum application and provide the applicant with a written justification for this decision. If the application is rejected, the applicant can appeal the decision in court. If either the applicant does not appeal or the court confirms the rejection, the relevant immigration authority will repatriate the applicant. Approvals, on the other hand, result in the applicant being granted a residence permit.[1]

The German asylum procedure requires close collaboration and the exchange of information between various authorities at the municipal, state, and federal levels. While the BAMF plays a pivotal role and issues decisions regarding asylum applications, state-level migration authorities and municipal governments are responsible for the initial registration, distribution, accommodation and care, and the

Fig. 4.1 The German asylum procedure

[1] Please refer to Federal Office for Migration and Refugees (2019) for a more detailed description of the German asylum procedure.

eventual integration or repatriation of the applicant. Moreover, several security agencies conduct background checks and various health authorities provide medical care.

3 Project Context

The delegation of governance over the German asylum procedure to a central authority, such as the BAMF, is not desirable because it would undermine the procedure's separation of competencies. Having said that, such seperation also leads to a significant degree of variation between instances of the procedure at different regional authorities and offices, which makes the creation of a common process model difficult. Moreover, it means that the exchange of certain procedural data still takes place using paper records or excel files, which, in many cases, are still considered a practical method of information sharing.

One essential step in managing the resulting complexities was the transformation of the Central Register of Foreign Nationals (AZR) into a shared repository for certain master data, such as names and fingerprints. The AZR now stores data on more than 26 million foreign nationals and grants more than 14,000 authorities access to read and write in these records. However, the transformation did not add process management features. Moreover, it revealed three challenges to the creation and operation of centralized IT solutions for the German asylum procedure: Firstly, centralization requires considerable legislative action. Secondly, it creates unbalanced data guardianship arrangements. Thirdly, a centralized solution will often be hard-pressed to support the various local instances of the procedure.

Thus, the BAMF began to explore decentralized technological alternatives that would not require it to delegate governance over the procedure to a single authority. Based on a preliminary evaluation, the BAMF narrowed down its technological options and decided to evaluate the prospects of blockchain technology in a Proof-of-Concept (PoC) project. In this PoC project, the BAMF created a blockchain prototype for a simplified asylum procedure involving three authorities. The prototype used blockchain to log and propagate the completion of essential steps in the procedure. Moreover, an IT provider working for the BAMF coded the simplified asylum procedure into a smart contract to allow for automated monitoring of the steps of the procedure and the automated triggering of subsequent steps. The PoC exemplified several functional and technical benefits of blockchain. Firstly, blockchain could establish a shared truth on the status and course of asylum applications across various authorities with great speed and security. Secondly, blockchain technology could facilitate the coordination of the many authorities involved in the asylum procedure. Thirdly, blockchain could support decentralized structures by leaving data in the respective repositories while using status messages to document when and where a status change in an application occurred.

Following the positive evaluation of the PoC, the BAMF decided to advance its blockchain efforts and test the technology in a pilot project. Due to the complexity of the German asylum procedure, the BAMF limited the scope of its pilot project to two authorities (the BAMF and Saxony's central immigration authority (LDS)) and the AnkER facility in Dresden, Germany. The AnkER concept bundles all functions and responsibilities in one place: from arrival, asylum application and the decision to local distribution, integration and the repatriation of asylum seekers. Moreover, the scope was limited to three so-called application areas: 'registration, creation of an application file, and personal interview' (application area I), 'referral' (application area II), and' ruling and next steps' (application area III).

Since blockchain is a new technology to most authorities and users, educational workshops with partner authorities other than the LDS and continuous engagement of prospective users were integral aspects of the pilot project.

4 Implemented Procedure and Functionality of the Blockchain Solution

The BAMF implemented a process model with a hierarchical structure of application areas, status categories, and status messages. Specifically, the three application areas supported by the BAMF's blockchain solution are subdivided into functional status categories (e.g., for application area I: asylum application, registration, consultation, organization of the creation of an application file, creation of an application file, organization of the personal interview, personal interview). The functional categories reflect the mandatory elements of any asylum application according to the German Asylum Act. A functional status category can comprise one or more status messages that may differ between regional authorities and offices. Each status message is either a general or a local status message. General status messages are transferred when responsibilities for asylum applications shift due to Germany's quota system; local status messages are not. This distinction is relevant as it enables storage limitation and data minimization (see Sect. 5).

Each application area has a distinct set of dependencies and rules regarding status messages, status transitions, and the corresponding effects (e.g., new status, parallel status messages, no changes). These dependencies and rules are implemented in a status machine and can be changed via simple configuration files. Figure 4.2 displays an excerpt from this status machine for application area I.

The pilot's status machine reflects the typical asylum procedure in the context of the AnkER facility in Dresden. It performs three basic process functions: "forward", "warning" and "critical error" as indicated in Table 4.1. The forward function informs caseworkers of the status of asylum applications. The warning and the critical error function inform caseworkers of minor and serious deviations from the typical procedure coded into the status machine. Whereas caseworkers can overrule this information, the blockchain solution records any such deviations from the typical procedure.

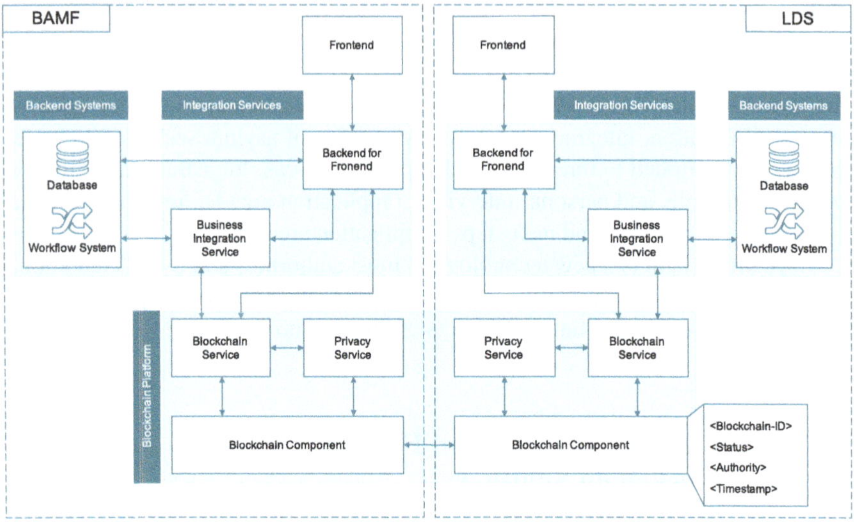

Fig. 4.2 Status machine of the blockchain solution

Table 4.1 Basic process logic functions of the blockchain solution

Forward function (green)	Basis for continuing with the next step in the procedure
Warning function (yellow)	Notification to the affected authority that there are minor deviations from the typical procedure
Critical error function (red)	(Push) notification to the affected authority that there are serious deviations from the typical procedure

5 GDPR Compliance

An essential non-functional requirement of the blockchain solution is data privacy. In particular, the blockchain solution has to comply with the requirements of the General Data Protection Regulation as the regulation applies to any act of processing information related to an identified or identifiable natural person in the EU, and to any such act by a data processor operating in the EU.

The GDPR was designed to allow data subjects to hold to account controllers and processors of their data, and it enshrines privacy by design and by default. At the same time, it aims to foster the free movement of personal data across the EU member states. Chief among the requirements of the GDPR are the need to establish clear responsibilities, the need to secure lawful bases for the processing of personal data, and the need to comply with the rights to rectification and erasure (Rieger, Guggenmos, Lockl, Fridgen, & Urbach, 2019).

In general, meeting these requirements requires both organizational and technical means. The design and combination of these means, however, are highly context-specific (Guggenmos, Wenninger, Rieger, Fridgen, & Lockl, 2020; Rieger et al.,

2019). The BAMF opted for an approach that emphasizes the use of technical means. For instance, it addressed the right to erasure through a design that pseudonymizes all data on the blockchain. Specifically, the BAMF uses specialized software components – so-called privacy services – to store and exchange ID mappings that allow the pseudonymized data on the blockchain to be attributed to asylum applications. In the following, we detail this design and discuss how the BAMF addressed the requirements of the core chapters and articles of the GDRP (see Table 4.2).

5.1 Solution Architecture

The BAMF implemented a software architecture with two layers (see Fig. 4.1), which extends the existing workflow management systems and data repositories of the authorities involved (Rieger et al., 2019). The blockchain solution does not need to be closely integrated with these backend systems; instead, it can be loosely coupled through a set of application programming interfaces (APIs). These interfaces enable the blockchain solution to interact with various backend systems in a well-defined manner (e.g., by exchanging status messages). The integration layer (layer 2: integration services) connects the blockchain platform (layer 1: blockchain platform) with both these backend systems and human users. It has two elements: the business integration service and the backend for frontend. The blockchain platform consists of three elements: the blockchain component, the blockchain service, and the privacy service (Fig. 4.3).

5.1.1 Blockchain Component

The blockchain component propagates pseudonymized status messages, which each consist of four attributes: a status update, a timestamp, the ID of the authority that created the status update, and a pseudonymous identifier (ID). From a functional perspective, these attributes reflect the minimum amount of data required for effective use. From a GDPR perspective, they are coarse enough to limit the risk of inadvertent attribution, for example, through the analysis of the trail of status messages.

Table 4.2 Overview of the GDPR elements addressed by the BAMF's blockchain solution

Solution architecture	Sect. 5.1
Observance of principles relating to the processing of personal data	Sect. 5.2
Observance of the rights of the data subject	Sect. 5.3
Processor and controller	Sect. 5.4

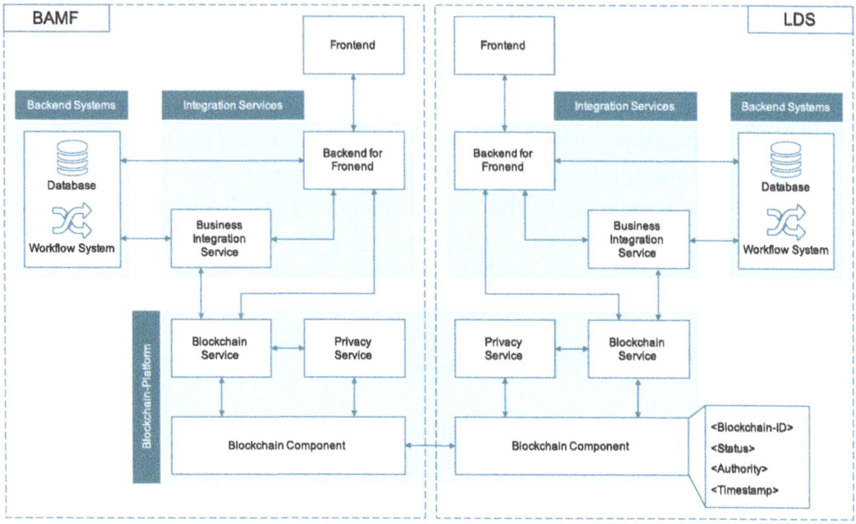

Fig. 4.3 Architecture of the blockchain solution

The blockchain component comprises a private, permissioned blockchain based on Hyperledger Fabric. Hyperledger Fabric is one of the Hyperledger projects currently under development by the Linux Foundation (Linux Foundation, 2017). Unlike the Bitcoin blockchain and Ethereum, Hyperledger Fabric uses a private and permissioned design. Such a design allows only selected participants to join the network, and only authorized nodes can view, execute, and validate transactions.

Specifically, Hyperledger Fabric has a modular and flexible structure that supports easy adaptation of individual components to the requirements of the application. It also supports targeted expansion to include new approaches and technological possibilities. Also, Hyperledger Fabric is well scalable (Linux Foundation, 2017; Osterland & Rose, 2018), and the fact that it is anchored in the Linux Foundation promises reliable long-term development. What is more, Hyperledger Fabric can easily be operated on various physical and virtual infrastructures and supports a range of programming languages that can be used to implement smart contracts (Androulaki et al., 2018; Linux Foundation, 2017; Sajana, Sindhu, & Sethumadhavan, 2018). Thus, it addresses many of the technical challenges commonly associated with blockchain technology (see Sect. 1), such as performance and scalability. Moreover, it employs Raft (Linux Foundation, 2017), a lightweight consensus mechanism that does not require an energy-intensive proof-of-work (Carson et al., 2018).

In the Hyperledger Fabric framework, the distribution of data through the global ledger, that is, the common ledger of all organizations in the network, is based on three different roles: *client*, *peer*, and *orderer*. The peer role can be further differentiated into *endorser* and *committer* (Linux Foundation, 2017). The client creates transactions on behalf of the end-user, which are then submitted to endorsers for verification. Endorsers simulate the transactions and give the client feedback on the transaction's validity. They also give the client a read/write set. Subsequently, the client forwards the verified transaction proposals to orderers (also known as ordering services), who perform a syntactical verification in line with the endorsement policy before grouping transactions into blocks. The finished blocks are sent back to the peers or, more specifically, to the committers. The committers run checks to ensure that all previous steps in the consensus mechanism were executed correctly and that no changes made to the blockchain in the meantime have rendered the transactions invalid. Only then are the new blocks added to the global ledger (Le Hors, Ferris, & Singh, 2018). As a rule, all transactions are included in the global ledger, but invalid transactions are flagged. Figure 4.4 illustrates the transaction flow for adding a new transaction to the global ledger.

In certain cases, organizations might want to share confidential data with only specific organizations and not have it disclosed to all organizations in the network. Hyperledger Fabric offers two features to address this issue. Firstly, developers can create separate channels (i.e., sub-networks) with separate rules and separate global ledgers. However, creating separate channels necessarily entails significant additional administrative effort because it requires, among other things, maintaining separate chain code, that is, smart contract versions as well as endorsement policies (Hyperledger, 2019). Secondly, as an alternative, Hyperledger Fabric offers the feature of private data collections (PDCs). These collections are private ledgers that allow data to be shared between a subset of organizations on the same channel. The data is then stored only on the nodes of the organizations involved. All other organizations can only see a hash, i.e., a cryptographic value, of the data on the channel's global ledger. This hash can serve as evidence of the transactions for state validation or audit purposes (Hyperledger, 2019). Private data collections can be given a

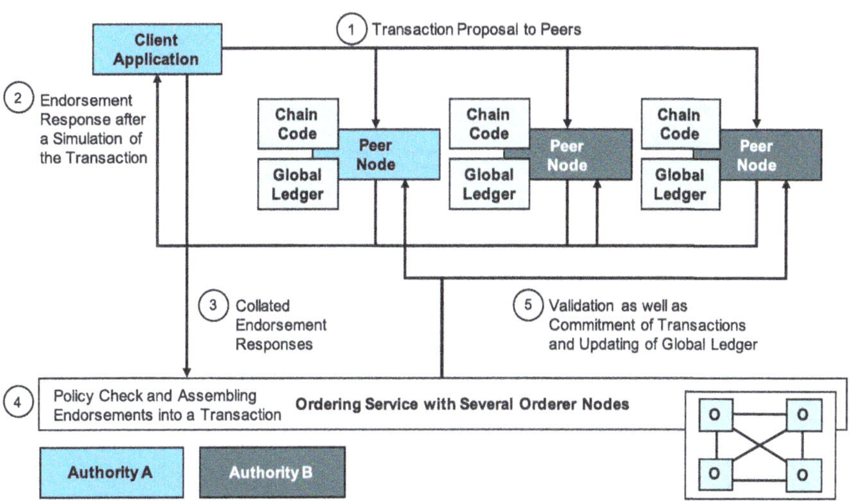

Fig. 4.4 Transaction flow for adding a new transaction to Hyperledger Fabric's global ledger

so-called "time to live" feature, which ensures that the ledger of a private data collection always has the same number of blocks by erasing the oldest block when adding a new one.

The BAMF' blockchain solution uses private data collections as the exclusive means for the sharing and persistent storing of status messages (persistent PDCs) and the sharing of mapping information (temporary PDCs). Specifically, private collections are used to limit the exchange of status messages and mapping information to the particular set of authorities that are involved in handling a particular asylum application at a particular point in time. All other network participants can only view the hash values of these transactions on the global ledger.

5.1.2 Privacy Services

In order to attribute the status messages on the blockchain, the BAMF created so-called privacy services. Each authority has its own privacy service, which contains databases that map the pseudonymous blockchain IDs to Functional IDs. These allow the clear identification of individual asylum applications across all authorities involved in the asylum procedure. The privacy services exchange mapping information via temporary private data collections. Such exchanges are important for the handover of an asylum application to a new authority. The services can also exchange requests for the erasure of mappings related to a pseudonymous

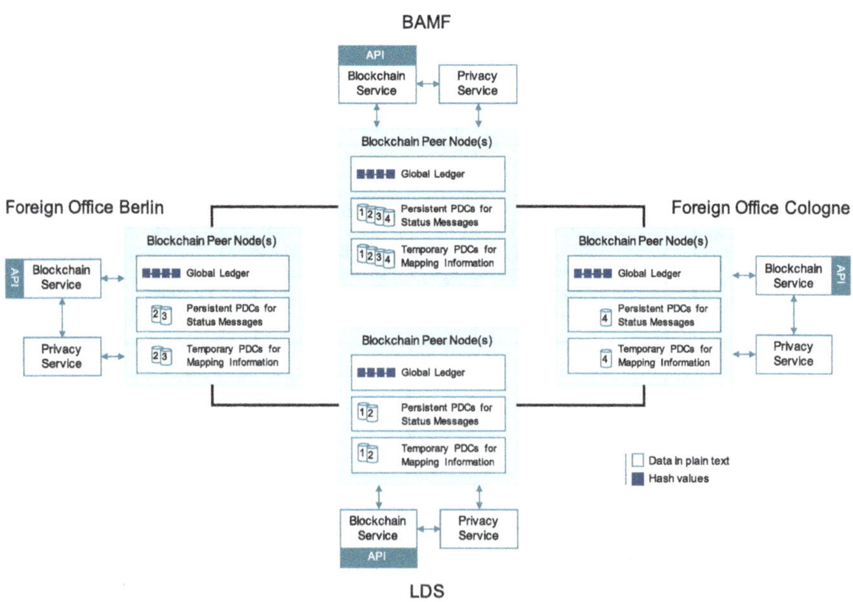

Fig. 4.5 Network architecture of the blockchain solution

ID. Figure 4.5 gives an example of an asylum application that is transferred from Dresden to Berlin.

Status messages up to the point of transfer are saved in a persistent private data collection that only the BAMF and the local migration authority in Dresden, the LDS, can access (persistent private data collections 1). The mapping information that needs to be exchanged for the first handover between the BAMF and the LDS is shared through a temporary private data collection (temporary private data collection 1). The subsequent status message and mapping information that concern the transfer of responsibilities from Dresden to the local migration authority in Berlin – known as the Foreigners' Office (FO) Berlin – are shared between the BAMF, the LDS, and the FO Berlin (persistent and private data collections 2). Status messages and mapping information are only visible to the BAMF and FO Berlin after the transfer (persistent and temporary private data collections 3). The local migration authority in Cologne can only see hashes of these transactions on the global ledger. Its private data collections with the BAMF (persistent and temporary private data collections 4) do not receive status messages and mapping information.

5.1.3 Blockchain Services

To enable the submission of status messages to the blockchain component and their later display, the BAMF implemented so-called blockchain services. Technically speaking, the blockchain services offer communication interfaces with the blockchain platform.

The blockchain services can write to the blockchain component status messages that they receive from the backend for frontends (in case of manual entry in the frontend) or the business integration services (in case of automatic data transfer from the backend systems). Also, they can read and forward status messages from the blockchain component to the backend for frontends.

5.1.4 Backend for Frontends, Business Integration Services, and Frontends

The backend for frontends integrate the backend systems with the blockchain services and the frontends. They can forward status messages from the frontends to the blockchain services. Moreover, they can enrich status messages from the blockchain services with data from the backend systems, and forward this enriched data to the frontends.

The business integration services can forward status messages from the backend systems to the blockchain services. Moreover, they contain databases that map the Functional IDs used in the blockchain platform to the IDs used in the authorities' backend systems, such as application or personal identification numbers. This mapping is necessary since each backend system might organize data on applications differently, and identifiers in the backend systems may change over time.

Moreover, it improves data privacy through the introduction of a second layer of pseudonymization. Status message in the blockchain component can only be attributed to a specific person through two mappings, namely, blockchain ID to Functional ID and Functional ID to the ID used in one of the backend systems.

The frontends can display to users (enriched) status messages. Moreover, they can be used to create specific status messages.

5.1.5 Simple Example

In terms of a simple example: For data display, users can access their authority's frontend through a web browser and enter, using the IDs used in their backend systems, various commands, for example, instructing it to display the history of a certain application or to display all applications that meet certain conditions. The frontend will pass these instructions to the backend for frontend, which then invokes the business integration service to exchange the IDs of the backend systems with the Functional IDs used in the blockchain platform, and instructs the blockchain service to provide the required status messages from the blockchain component. Subsequently, the blockchain service collects – in accordance with the access rights of the user and the mapping information in the privacy service – the required status messages and forwards these to the backend for frontend. The backend for frontend then compliments the returned status messages with further data from the backend system, if required, and forwards the (enriched) status messages to the frontend for display to the user. Importantly, a user can only view information for which the authority and the user have clearance and a lawful basis for access.

5.2 Principles Relating to Processing of Personal Data

The General Data Protection Regulation applies to the processing of personal data. Consequently, data processors need to establish whether or not the data they process is classed as personal. Personal data includes all information relating to an identified or identifiable natural person. A natural person is identifiable if he or she "can be identified, directly or indirectly, in particular by reference to an identifier such as a name, an identification number, location data, an online identifier, or to one or more factors specific to the physical, physiological, genetic, mental, economic, cultural or social identity of that natural person" (General Data Protection Regulation (GDPR), 2016, Art. 4(1)). Data in the BAMF case is *personal* because asylum applicants are natural persons, and all data explicitly mapped to an application can be attributed to them - either directly or indirectly.

According to Art. 4(2) of the GDPR, the concept of data processing is very broad and concerns "any operation or set of operations which is performed on personal data or on sets of personal data" (General Data Protection Regulation (GDPR), 2016, Art. 4(2)). It is irrelevant if the data is processed via automatic means. In accordance with this definition, the BAMF's blockchain solution *processes* personal data. For instance, each submission of an attributable status message results in personal data being collected, recorded, ordered, and stored. Authorities with reading rights can then access this data. The use of the blockchain solution may include various additional data processing operations, such as the exporting of attributable status data from the blockchain for further use in asylum procedures.

The BAMF's blockchain solution is thus fully subject to the requirements of the GDPR. In particular, the solution has to uphold the seven principles related to the processing of personal data coded in Art. 5 of the GDPR. We discuss these principles and their observance in the following.

5.2.1 Lawfulness, Fairness and Transparency

The GDPR requires data to be "processed lawfully, fairly and in a transparent manner in relation to the data subject" (General Data Protection Regulation (GDPR), 2016, Art. 5). In particular, it forbids processing that does not have at least one of the six legal bases defined in Art. 6, such as consent by the data subject or data processing required to meet legal obligations of the data processor (General Data Protection Regulation (GDPR), 2016, Art. 6). In particular, Art. 6(1e) of the GDPR regards the processing of personal data as justifiable if it is necessary to fulfill a task which is carried out either in the public interest or in the exercise of public authority vested in the controller. This, however, must be laid down in either EU law or the law of the corresponding member state (General Data Protection Regulation (GDPR), 2016, Art. 6(3)).

The conduct of the asylum procedure, as well as the associated data processing, are in the public interest, and the competent authorities exercise public authority according to the relevant laws (such as the German Asylum Act, the German Residence Act, and the European Convention on Human Rights). The BAMF's solution ensures fairness by processing only those data that have been collected in good faith and according to due procedure. It ensures transparency by providing data subjects with accessible documentation of its design and operation. Thus, the BAMF's blockchain solution complies fully with the principle of lawfulness, fairness and transparency.

5.2.2 Purpose Limitation and Data Minimization

The GDPR principle of purpose limitation restricts the collection of personal data to "specified, explicit and legitimate purposes" (General Data Protection Regulation (GDPR), 2016, Art. 5). Data minimization restricts data processing to an adequate, relevant, and limited level that is necessary for the respective purpose.

The BAMF's blockchain solution uses several components of the Hyperledger Fabric framework, described in Sect. 5.1, to address the principles of purpose limitation and data minimization. More specifically, the solution's private and permissioned design and its use of private collections ensure that only authorities and users with explicit authorization can view and enter data. In particular, the private design of the solution enables the establishment of a controlled onboarding process during which new authorities can be added to the solution. The permissioned design facilitates the creation of a model for the allocation of access rights – namely, the rights to read and/or write status updates – that is both dynamic and specific to the authority-type. A dynamic model is required as responsibilities can shift between regional authorities and offices in the course of the asylum application.

The use of private data collections ensures that authorities which are no longer responsible for an application can only view data gathered up to the point where responsibility was transferred. Authorities which responsibility is transferred to can view all data from the change of responsibility onward but can also request data from the past. In technical terms, the transferring authority submits to the receiving authorities the relevant global status messages through a shared persistent private data collection and the relevant mapping information through a shared temporary private data collection. One of the receiving authorities copies these status messages to the persistent private data collection of the receiving authorities under a new application area ID and adds a matching mapping information to the temporary private data collection of the receiving authorities. Only the (now) responsible authorities have the new mapping and can access the status messages in the new persistent private data collection. The authority that transferred responsibility and other authorities that were responsible before the transfer cannot see the new status messages because they lack both the mapping and access to the new private data collection. This also further reduces the risk of inadvertent attribution.

The use of private data collections thus supports purpose limitation and data minimization. Arguably, storing data in the blockchain component leads to additional data processing that is not strictly necessary for the respective purpose. More specifically, additional status messages (e.g., 'application for asylum requested'), which reflect the current status of the procedure, are created and written to the blockchain component. However, the additional data processing can be justified as necessary because it ultimately aims at replacing the error-prone paper lists and excel files that authorities currently exchange.

5.2.3 Accuracy

The GDPR requires data to be accurate and kept up-to-date where necessary. Therefore, processors and controllers must ensure that inaccurate data can be erased or rectified (General Data Protection Regulation (GDPR), 2016, Art. 5).

The BAMF's blockchain ensures that status messages are immediately shared with the entire network (or its relevant sub-parts). As such, it keeps data up-to-date throughout the network. The right to erasure and rectification, however, require dedicated measures. In Sect. 5.3, we describe these measures in more detail.

5.2.4 Storage Limitation

The principle of storage limitation requires that personal data is only stored "in a form which permits identification of data subjects for no longer than is necessary for the purposes for which the personal data are processed" (General Data Protection Regulation (GDPR), 2016, Art. 5).

To address this issue, the BAMF's blockchain solution permits the erasure of single application areas ('registration, creation of an application file and personal interview', 'referral', and' ruling and next steps'). Moreover, each application area has an independent erasure timer for automatic erasure (see Table 4.3). The erasure timers are detailed in a specific smart contract and are observed by the privacy services of all authorities involved.

5.2.5 Integrity and Confidentiality

The principle of integrity and confidentiality requires personal data to be "processed in a manner that ensures appropriate security of the personal data, including protection against unauthorized or unlawful processing and against accidental loss, destruction or damage, using appropriate technical or organizational measures" (General Data Protection Regulation (GDPR), 2016, Art. 5).

Immutability is one of the main features of blockchain technology. Thus, blockchain, by default, prevents accidental loss, destruction, or damage of data. Moreover, the blockchain solution's private and permissioned design prevents unauthorized or unlawful processing.

5.2.6 Accountability

Lastly, the GDPR holds controllers responsible for compliance with the first six principles and requires that they are able to demonstrate their compliance. While most of these principles can be observed through technical means, accountability is an organizational issue. Therefore, the BAMF has drafted a joint control arrangement with the LDS, which specifies the respective responsibilities for compliance with the GDPR and for establishing lawful bases for data processing.

Table 4.3 Implementation of different erasure timers

Functional ID	Blockchain ID	Application area	Erasure timer
00012345	35,729,843	0[a]	15.12.2019
00012345	46,273,895	I	01.01.2030

[a]The formal expression of an application for asylum is modeled as application area 0

5.3 *Rights of the Data Subject*

Chap. 3 of the GDPR regulates the rights of data subjects. In particular, it governs the information that has to be provided to the data subject and the data subject's access rights (Articles 13 to 15). Articles 16 and 17 regulate the rights to rectification and erasure (General Data Protection Regulation (GDPR), 2016).

5.3.1 Information and Access to Personal Data

The GDPR requires data controllers to provide data subjects with certain information concerning the processing of their personal data. Among other things, controllers should provide information on the identity and contact details of the controller, the purposes and legal basis for the processing, and the recipients or categories of recipients of the personal data. Moreover, controllers should provide additional information to ensure fair and transparent processing, such as the period of storage and the consequences of not providing the personal data (General Data Protection Regulation (GDPR), 2016, Art. 5). Additionally, controllers must, upon request, inform data subjects of the processing of any of their personal data, disclose additional information such as the purpose and category of personal data, and provide a copy of the personal data undergoing processing (General Data Protection Regulation (GDPR), 2016, Art. 5).

In general, the BAMF's blockchain solution enables authorities to establish a "shared and persistent truth" on the state of an asylum application at any given time. This truth can act as a point of reference in cases where process forensics are required to observe information and access rights of asylum applicants. When an asylum applicant approaches one of the authorities that use the blockchain solution, the authority can easily export the status messages of the application areas they were involved in. Technically speaking, each network participant can query their persistent private data collections and export the status messages related to the blockchain IDs mapped to an application.

5.3.2 Rights to Rectification and Erasure

The GDPR requires controllers to rectify inaccurate personal data and to complete incomplete personal data (General Data Protection Regulation (GDPR), 2016, Art. 16).

The BAMF's solution addresses this requirement through technical means by enabling the submission of rectification transactions to the blockchain. More specifically, a rectification transaction invalidates the original transaction, which, however, remains on the blockchain.

The right to erasure stipulates that personal data must be erased if the purpose for which it was collected no longer exists (General Data Protection Regulation (GDPR), 2016, Art. 17). In the context of the asylum procedure, this is the case when, for instance, the asylum procedure has been completed. Specifically, the German Asylum Act stipulates that data must be deleted no later than ten years after the asylum procedure has been completed (Asylum Act, 2008, §7(3)).

The BAMF's blockchain solution enables 'erasure by anonymization' through the erasure of mapping information in the privacy services. Without the mapping in the privacy services, authorities can no longer attribute data stored in the blockchain component to a specific application or person. Moreover, the erasure triggers in the smart contracts allow the automatic observance of storage limitations. Specifically, the BAMF's blockchain solution ensures by design, that all legitimate (manual and automatic) erasure requests are executed in all privacy services. The BAMF's blockchain solution does so by triggering the erasure of mapping information related to a certain application in all privacy services, once at least one privacy service has submitted an erasure request related to the application. Without the mapping in the privacy services, authorities can no longer attribute data stored in the blockchain component to a specific application or person.

5.4 Processor and Controller

Chap. 4 of the GDPR governs the obligations of data controllers and processors. Most importantly, the chapter specifies controllers' responsibilities to demonstrate compliance with the GDPR (Art. 24), data protection by design and by default (Art. 25), and joint controllership (Art. 26).

5.4.1 Responsibilities of the Controller

Firstly, the GDPR requires controllers to "implement appropriate technical and organizational measures to ensure and enable the demonstration that processing is performed in accordance with [the regulation of the GDPR]" (General Data Protection Regulation (GDPR), 2016, Art. 24).

For this purpose, the BAMF closely collaborates with the German Federal Commissioner for Data Protection and Freedom of Information (BfDI) to establish, demonstrate, and obtain confirmation of the appropriateness of its organizational and technical measures, that is, of the administrative agreement and the design of the blockchain solution. The BfDI is an independent federal authority responsible for data protection supervision in accordance with Art. 51 of the GDPR.

5.4.2 Data Protection by Design and by Default

The GDRP establishes rules on data protection both by design and by default. More specifically, the GDPR requires controllers to implement appropriate technical and organizational measures which are designed to meet data protection principles (by design) and "for ensuring that, by default, only personal data which are necessary for each specific purpose of the processing are processed" (General Data Protection Regulation (GDPR), 2016, Art. 25).

The BAMF implemented several such measures that ensure protection by both design and default. For instance, the BAMF's blockchain solution uses a private and permissioned design, pseudonymization, and private data collections to address purpose and storage limitation as well as data minimization requirements. The Asylum Act provides the legal basis for the processing of personal data in the context of asylum procedures. Moreover, the blockchain solution includes certain mechanisms that enforce, by default, the regulations of the Asylum Act and the GDRP, such as automatic erasure triggers.

5.4.3 Joint Controllership

The GDPR further specifies that in cases "where two or more controllers jointly determine the purposes and means of processing, they shall be joint controllers" (General Data Protection Regulation (GDPR), 2016, Art. 26). The German asylum procedure entails several such instances wherein the BAMF works together with other organizations to determine the purpose and means of processing.

In the pilot project, the BAMF addressed this issue by creating a joint control arrangement through an administrative agreement with the LDS, which established the purpose and means of processing and assigned responsibilities for GDPR compliance. More specifically, the agreement detailed, as the means and purpose of data processing, the storage and exchange of status messages via the blockchain solution for collaborating across AnkER procedures. The agreement also determined that the BAMF hosts and assumes responsibility for data stored on the blockchain and for privacy services. However, the LDS and the BAMF have to independently verify if they have a lawful basis for submission for each status message. Rieger et al. (2019) provide more detail on the procedure. Additionally, the BAMF and the LDS worked closely with legal experts to ensure the existence of the required lawful bases for each conceivable type of data exchange.

6 Outlook

The BAMF's blockchain pilot provides valuable insights into the opportunities and challenges of using blockchain in the public sector. In particular, the pilot offers best practices and design recommendations for meeting the requirements of the GDPR.[2] The most important of these design requirements is that personal data should not be stored on a blockchain. Tamper-resistant storage is one of blockchain's core fea-

[2] We discuss many of these practices in detail in Rieger et al. (2019) and Guggenmos et al. (2020).

tures, yet seriously conflicts with the rights to rectification and erasure. If the context nevertheless requires processing that allows for the attribution of the processed data to a natural person, blockchain solutions should use a pseudonymization approach and have a highly secure off-chain attribution mechanism. Additionally, the attribution information is to be exclusively exchanged via secure channels and protocols.

The BAMF's blockchain pilot demonstrates that with such a GDPR-compliant architecture, a blockchain solution can enable the efficient and frictionless exchange of information between authorities in countries that use a federal model of government. Moreover, it could also contribute to the standardization and harmonization of the exchange of information. That is, authorities could use the status messages in the blockchain component to request, from other authorities, the transfer of complementary data through complementary channels (pull), or to send complimentary data through these channels to all authorities affected by this status message (push). In this way, the BAMF's blockchain solution could increase the usefulness of standards for these channels, such as XAusländer, in the context of Germany's asylum procedure.[3]

In summary, the BAMF case demonstrates that blockchain solutions are a promising alternative in the public sector when the delegation of process governance to a central authority is not possible or desirable. In particular, modern blockchain technologies support the retention of decentralized structures and allow individual authorities to share process information while simultaneously maintaining control over their respective data and data repositories. Consequently, the BAMF is contemplating various expansion scenarios. For instance, future releases of the blockchain solution could also support parts of the three application areas that have so far been excluded or include additional areas (such as the process of canceling and withdrawing protection). Another expansion option is the inclusion of other authorities. To this end, further AnkER-facilities, or authorities with similar functions, could be connected to the blockchain solution, in both Saxony and other German states. Another possibility is the use of the blockchain solution for other purposes (such as the integration process) or, indeed, in entirely different contexts in which the concepts and design principles developed in the BAMF's pilot project can serve as a blueprint and guideline.

At the international level, the BAMF is actively disseminating its experiences and learnings. In the BAMF's vision, blockchain could become a digital enabler of European federalism. For instance, blockchain could support parts of the Dublin procedure and support EU member states in organizing transfers – without having to transfer sovereignty over national data to a centralized EU server. These expansion scenarios, however, require effective governance as well as a scalable blockchain solution.

[3] XAusländer is an XML-based data exchange format that supports the electronic exchange of identical data between the authorities in the foreigners administration in Germany.

6.1 Governance

The implementation and operation of a blockchain solution require coordination at several levels. To minimize the attendant complexity, authorities need to effectively delegate decision-making competencies and responsibilities, i.e., they need to ensure effective governance. Such delegation is particularly crucial at the technical and organizational levels.

At the technical level, effective governance structures ensure the smooth development, reliable operation, and efficacious maintenance of the blockchain solution. They require developers to consider the technical requirements of all parties involved and ensure that the respective IT departments cooperate closely. Moreover, an effective technical governance framework must clearly specify the delegation of responsibilities and implementation competencies and ensure that this delegation is sustainable. The framework should not only specify delegation on a conceptual level but should also include a development model that corresponds to the desired design of the blockchain. In addition, effective technical governance must address operational questions about the blockchain layer as well as the underlying software and hardware layers. Within federal structures, the authorities/organizations involved should be granted certain flexibility to enable them to address such operational questions. However, the functionality and security of a blockchain solution are highly dependent on even its weakest link. Therefore, the technical governance framework should specify certain minimum requirements for the selection of potential operating models and their operators.

At the organizational level, effective governance must ensure that both the general and functional requirements of all parties involved are reliably incorporated into the development of the blockchain solution. For instance, organizational governance should consider the federal framework as a general requirement of public administration in Germany.

Governance has, so far, been a secondary focus of the BAMF's blockchain project but will become more important if the blockchain solution is more widely adopted. For the initial setup of the pilot project, the BAMF and the LDS chose a joint provider to develop and supply the blockchain solution. However, the project envisages that different authorities may choose different providers in the future. Therefore, the BAMF and its partners will need to establish minimum requirements for the onboarding of other operators. The BAMF and its partners will also need to formalize review meetings and joint decision-making with regard to both the general and the specific functional requirements.

6.2 Scalability

In order to minimize complexity, the BAMF's pilot solution connects only two authorities. Nevertheless, technical scalability was considered from the beginning of the project, and the solution was designed for future use in which it would accommodate other authorities and multiple variations of the asylum procedure.

In the first step, the BAMF performed an in-depth evaluation of existing public sector blockchain solutions in Germany and Europe. One of these projects is the European Blockchain Services Infrastructure, the development of which has been actively promoted by the European Blockchain Partnership (EBP) since 2018. Prospectively, this infrastructure will provide various services and enable the implementation of various applications. However, the EBP did not provide actionable specifications or recommendations in 2018 or 2019 that could have served as a guideline for the implementation of a scalable blockchain solution in the public sector. Therefore, the BAMF's blockchain solution drew best practices from successful projects in the private sector.

Specifically, the blockchain solution makes it easy for other authorities to connect thanks to its use of standardized application programming interfaces, common technologies, and a flexible data model. Responsibility for the integration of the blockchain solution with the individual backend system rests with each new authority joining the blockchain system. That is, each authority has the sovereignty to decide on which of the data stored in the blockchain component it wants to process and on the means of processing (e.g., individual warning functions regarding process deviations). As a result, the blockchain solution can accommodate a large number of authorities without a substantial increase in its complexity. The blockchain solution also incorporates different hosting models and provides default configurations, which enable the integration of authorities that have no prior knowledge of blockchain technology.

Finally, if it is to ensure scalability from an organizational perspective, the BAMF must still develop a scalability concept that addresses two essential aspects. Firstly, the blockchain solution requires safeguards that ensure conformity with the requirements of other authorities, such as security authorities. Secondly, the solution needs additional safeguards that ensure new authorities are given the opportunity to participate in shaping the overall process without impeding agility in the decision-making process.

Acknowledgments Supported by PayPal and the Luxembourg National Research Fund FNR (P17/IS/13342933/PayPal-FNR/Chair in DFS/Gilbert Fridgen).

References

Androulaki, E., Barger, A., Bortnikov, V., Cachin, C., Christidis, K., Caro, A. de, Enyeart, D., Ferris, C., Laventman, G., Manevich, Y., Muralidharan, S., Murthy, C., Nguyen, B., Sethi, M., Singh, G., Smith, K., Sorniotti, A., Stathakopoulou, C., Vukolic, M.,. Yellick, J. (2018). Hyperledger fabric: A distributed operating system for permissioned blockchains. In *Proceedings of the 13th EuroSys Conference,* Porto, Portugal.

Asylum Act in the version promulgated on 2 September 2008 (Federal Law Gazette I, p. 1798), last amended by Article 48 of the Act of 20 November 2019 (Federal Law Gazette I, p. 1626) (2008).

Beck, R., Müller-Bloch, C., & King, J. L. (2018). Governance in the Blockchain economy: A framework and research agenda. *Journal of the Association for Information Systems, 19*(10), 1020–1034.

Carson, B., Romanelli, G., Walsh, P., & Zhumaev, A. (2018). Blockchain beyond the hype: What is the strategic business value? McKinsey&Company. Retrieved from https://www.mckinsey.com/business-functions/mckinsey-digital/our-insights/blockchain-beyond-the-hype-what-is-the-strategic-business-value#

Federal Office for Migration and Refugees. (2019). *The stages of the German asylum procedure: An overview of the individual procedural steps and the legal basis.*

Fridgen, G., Guggenmos, F., Lockl, J., Rieger, A., & Urbach, N. (2019a). Supporting communication and cooperation in the asylum procedure with Blockchain technology– A proof of concept by the Federal Office for Migration and Refugees. Retrieved from https://www.fit.fraunhofer.de/content/dam/fit/de/documents/BAMF_FhG_Whitepaper_en_final.pdf

Fridgen, G., Guggenmos, F., Lockl, J., Rieger, A., Urbach, N., & Wenninger, A. (2019b). Development of a GDPR-compliant Blockchain Solution for the German Asylum Procedure: A pilot project in the context of the AnkER-facility in Dresden. Retrieved from https://www.bamf.de/SharedDocs/Anlagen/EN/Digitalisierung/blockchain-whitepaper.pdf;jsessionid=342CBBDED20ADA6FB04FBF71E4DDDE4D.internet532?__blob=publicationFile&v=2

Glaser, F. (2017). Pervasive decentralisation of digital infrastructures: A framework for Blockchain enabled system and use case analysis. In *Proceedings of the 50th Hawaii International Conference on System Sciences,* Waikoloa, Hawaii, USA.

Guggenmos, F., Wenninger, A., Rieger, A., Fridgen, G., & Lockl, J. (2020). How to develop a GDPR-compliant Blockchain solution for cross-organizational workflow management: Evidence from the German asylum procedure. In *Proceedings of the 53rd Hawaii International Conference on System Sciences,* Wailea, Hawaii, USA.

Hyperledger. (2019). *Private data.* Retrieved from https://hyperledger-fabric.readthedocs.io/en/release-1.4/private-data/private-data.html#what-is-a-private-data-collection

Lacity, M. C. (2018). Addressing key challenges to making enterprise blockchain applications a reality. *MIS Quarterly Executive, 17*(3), 201–222.

Le Hors, A., Ferris, C., & Singh, G. (2018). Hyperleder Fabric. *Architecture Explained.* Retrieved from http://hyperledger-fabric.readthedocs.io/en/release-1.1/arch-deep-dive.html

Linux Foundation. (2017). Hyperledger architecture Vol.. *I. Introduction to Hyperledger Business Blockchain Design Philosophy and Consensus.* Retrieved from https://www.hyperledger.org/wp-content/uploads/2017/08/Hyperledger_Arch_WG_Paper_1_Consensus.pdf

Lyons, T., Courcelas, L., & Timsit, K. (2018). *Blockchain and the GDPR.* Retrieved from https://www.eublockchainforum.eu/sites/default/files/reports/20181016_report_gdpr.pdf

Mendling, J., Weber, I., Aalst, W. V. D., Brocke, J. V., Cabanillas, C., Daniel, F., et al. (2018). Blockchains for business process management - challenges and opportunities. *ACM Transactions on Management Information Systems (TMIS), 9*(1), 4–20.

Osterland, T., & Rose, T. (2018). Engineering sustainable Blockchain applications. In *Proceedings of the 1st ERCIM Blockchain Workshop,* Amsterdam, Netherland. Retrieved from https://dl.eusset.eu/handle/20.500.12015/3161

Pedersen, A. B., Risius, M., & Beck, R. (2019). A ten-step decision path to DetermineWhen to use Blockchain technologies. *MIS Quarterly Executive, 18*(2), 99–115.

Regulation (EU) 2016/679 of the European Parliament and of the council of 27 April 2016 on the protection of natural persons with regard to the processing of personal data and on the free movement of such data, and repealing Directive 95/46/EC, L 119 Official Journal of the European Union (OJ) 1 (2016). Retrieved from https://eur-lex.europa.eu/legal-content/EN/TXT/PDF/?uri=CELEX:32016R0679&from=EN

Rieger, A., Guggenmos, F., Lockl, J., Fridgen, G., & Urbach, N. (2019). Building a Blockchain application that complies with the EU general data protection regulation. *MIS Quarterly Executive, 18*(4), 263–279.

Sajana, P., Sindhu, M., & Sethumadhavan, M. (2018). On Blockchain applications: Hyperledger fabric and Ethereum. *International Journal of Pure and Applied Mathematics, 18*(118), 2965–2970.

Alexander Rieger is a researcher at the Interdisciplinary Center for Security, Reliability and Trust (SnT) at the University of Luxembourg. His research interests include innovative digital technologies such as blockchain, digital identitites, and artificial intelligence, and, more specifically, their strategic implications and adoption. He acts as advisor to the European Blockchain Partnership and various public and private sector partners in Germany and Luxembourg. Before joining the SnT, Alex was the operational lead of the Fraunhofer Blockchain Lab and spent several years working in industry and consulting. He joined the BAMF's blockchain project in January 2018.

Alexander Stohr is a doctoral candidate at the Finance & Information Management (FIM) Research Center, University of Bayreuth, and the Project Group Business & Information Systems Engineering of the Fraunhofer FIT. His current research focuses on the adoption of emerging technologies, such as blockchain and artificial intelligence, and their socio-technical implications. Alex has worked as a consultant on a variety of industry projects before joining the BAMF's blockchain project in August 2019.

Annette Wenninger is a doctoral candidate at the Finance & Information Management (FIM) Research Center and the Project Group Business & Information Systems Engineering of the Fraunhofer FIT, University of Bayreuth. Her current research focuses on the adoption of emerging technologies or services, such as blockchain or proactive services, and their socio-technical implications. Annette joined the BAMF's blockchain project as a consultant in February 2019.

Gilbert Fridgen is PayPal-FNR PEARL Chair in Digital Financial Services at the Interdisciplinary Center for Security, Reliability and Trust (SnT) at the University of Luxembourg. His work focuses on smart grids, the machine economy, and blockchain technology in both the public and private sectors. Gilbert's work has been published in several prominent IS, management, computer science and engineering journals. He has also managed various industry research projects and received multiple research grants. Gilbert has served as expert counsel to many government bodies, including the German Bundestag and six German federal ministries, and also to the European Commission through its European Blockchain Partnership.

Chapter 5
Blockchain Applications in the Public Sector: Investigating Seven Real-Life Blockchain Deployments and Their Benefits

Maciej Sobolewski and David Allessie

Highlights

- The study uses an empirical approach to analyze the deployment characteristics and benefits of real-life blockchain deployments in the public sector
- A horizontal comparison of case studies is conducted based on a novel structured framework
- The analysis shows that the benefits are currently mainly in the domain of automating the enforcement of transactions
- The study shows that key inhibitors like a lack of standards and trusted hosting infrastructure are to be addressed to fully realize the benefits of this technology

1 Introduction

Blockchain (BC) technology was initially recognized as a typical business sector innovation offering a new, lower-cost solution for transaction settlement (Casino, Dasaklis, & Patsakis, 2019; Konstantinidis et al., 2018). Eruption of use cases across nearly all sectors of the economy, particularly in finance, logistics and energy, created high expectations towards distributed ledgers (DL) technology becoming new information and business infrastructure. Recently, in economic and political

The content of this publication does not reflect the official opinion of the European Union. Responsibility for the information and views expressed herein lies entirely with the authors.

M. Sobolewski (✉)
European Commission, Joint Research Centre, Seville, Spain
e-mail: maciej.sobolewski@ec.europa.eu

D. Allessie
Gartner Consulting, Amsterdam, The Netherlands
e-mail: david.allessie@gartner.com

C. G. Reddick et al. (eds.), *Blockchain and the Public Sector*, Public Administration and Information Technology 36,
https://doi.org/10.1007/978-3-030-55746-1_5

debates, the attention is shifted to the more fundamental implications of decentralisation and transformative role of blockchain in the public sector. Decentralisation is a core property of distributed ledgers that enables fundamentally different way of establishing trusted relationships between various actors in the ecosystem. Blockchain technology, is a 'trust machine', that has a potential to transform organizations, enterprises and governmental institutions, undermining the role of intermediaries and giving rise to new business models and forms of cooperation (Boucher, 2017). To what extent blockchain technology will reach technical maturity and a practical capability to generate these benefits is still an open question that can be answered only by referring to empirical evidence.

Existing literature on the use of blockchain by governments provides mainly conceptual insights. Recent systematic literature reviews adopt technology perspective, focusing on design, development and evaluation of system architecture (Batubara, Ubacht, & Janssen, 2018; Hughes et al., 2019). Due to the scarcity of development efforts, research papers speculate about 'promised' or 'potential' benefits of blockchains for government. Consequently, after 10 years from its advent, little is known about practical applicability of blockchain technology and real-value it may bring to the public sector. In order to move forward, the discussion on potential benefits of blockchain needs to be supported by empirical argumentation (Ølnes, Ubacht, & Janssen, 2017). There is a growing consensus in the in the research community, that a shift towards empirical research is needed to inform about actual advantages and disadvantages of distributed ledger technology (Batubara et al., 2018).

Present paper aims to take a first minor step in moving the research agenda in the new direction. Growing experimentation with blockchain by governments and the emergence of first operational implementations provide an opportunity to understand better, how blockchain technology may practically affect public sector. The study analyses seven projects, active in 2018, with a participation of governments. The projects are in different stages of the life cycle, ranging from early-stage experimentation pilots to production deployments. We developed a custom case-study assessment framework to provide a comparative analysis of information collected from project teams via structured interviews. The study asks two research questions:

1. What patterns emerge from the current experimentation of governments with blockchain?
2. What benefits blockchain may bring to the public sector?

The added value of the present study is twofold. First, this is one of the first attempts undertaking a rigorous and comparative analysis of ongoing blockchain projects in the public sector. The sample represents a diverse range of services, functionalities and blockchain architectures. Moreover, projects differ in life-cycle maturity. To cope with these challenges and compare different projects in a meaningful a structured analytical framework is needed. To gain clearer insights, our framework distinguishes institutional, functional, technical and economic aspects and compares project across these dimensions. Our results might be of interest to public administrations that consider implementation of blockchain-based services and for the policy makers who are responsible for policy agenda supporting adoption of blockchain technology in the public sector. Moreover, practical observations and generalizations from the study can serve as a reference point for future assessment of blockchain implementations by governments.

The rest of the paper is organized as follows. Section 2 elaborates on the innovative features of distributed ledgers and provides literature on blockchain the public sector. In Sect. 3, analytical framework is introduced, followed by the horizontal analysis of seven case studies. Section 4 presents main findings and answers both research questions. Section 5 concludes.

2 Background

2.1 *Understanding Blockchain Driven Innovation*

A distributed ledger is a database technology that facilitates an expanding, chronologically ordered list of irrevocable transactional records, shared by all participants in a network. For convenience, transactions are often grouped in blocks prior to recording on a ledger. In such case, a ledger takes the form of a chain of blocks, in which each new block is linked via a cryptographic signature referring to the exact content of the previous block. The ledger is stored in multiple nodes and validated by some form of consensus in the network, which makes it resistant to unilateral change or tweaking. The ledger must also be tamper-resistant to attack of a coalition of malicious nodes.

In the so-called, permissionless blockchains, that are anonymous and open to everyone, this is ensured by using computationally heavy consensus or consensus participation mechanism that selects nodes in the network that have the greatest stake and thus greatest incentive to behave honestly. In permissioned blockchains, tamper-resistance is not an issue and is ensured by transparency and gatekeeping—entry is restricted, and all nodes have identity. Within these limits, distributed ledgers safeguard transactions and eliminate the risk of double spending just as traditional third-party intermediation does. The main difference, according to enthusiasts of blockchain technology, is that decentralised intermediation is cheaper, more effective and does not lead to concentration of power in hands of one institution that may than start to push for its own agenda (rent seeking).

Practical use cases leverage two innovative enablers of distributed ledgers. First, because of resistance to tweaking, a ledger can serve well for notarization purposes, providing solid proof of existence, ownership and originality of any digital or physical asset or a statement. Smart contract functionality is the second enabler of blockchains, coming on top of notarization. Smart contract is a piece of computer code that formalizes governance rules for transaction and executes it. A workflow might be conditional on statements signed by various human or machine agents, including sensors and connected things. Programmability of smart contracts makes them very flexible and adjustable to much wider range of arrangements than could be handled in traditional paper-based contracts. Smart contract functionality enables enforcement of commitments and automation of complex arrangements among multiple parties that otherwise would be too risky and too costly to execute (Szabo, 1997). Hence, it potentially generates huge efficiency gains.

The emergence of algorithmic trust has far-reaching implications from the broader economic and political perspective. If the technology itself can eliminate uncertainty related to intentions and identity of the transacting parties, then the role of institutional intermediaries is seriously undermined. Decentralized intermediation holds a promise to reduce transaction costs and shift the balance of control and power from economic and political institutions towards the ecosystem. For example, blockchain supports creation of decentralized autonomous organizations (DAO). These systems can effectively self-organize, create own sustainable business models and enforce own governance rules. DAO might challenge the current role of firms and governments as providers of private and public goods. The distributed nature of the blockchain technology may be highly disruptive for a large number of industries. At the same time, it evokes strong resistance from private and public institutions that have built their economic position on the provision of central intermediation.

The first application of blockchain, Bitcoin, illustrate both issues very well. The concept of Bitcoin, "A Peer-to-Peer Electronic Cash System" proposed by an anonymous (group of) author(s) called Satoshi Nakamoto (Nakamoto, 2008) proved to be robust in practice and essentially created a global and independent payment system.[1] The idea of a peer-to-peer cash system and accompanying cryptocurrency is still leading to resistance from regulators, legislators and the media, given the border-less nature of the financial system, its' pseudonymous properties and the fact that traditional financial institutions like banks are not part of the system. The success of Bitcoin inspired recent revolutionary concepts of private stable coins or central banks crypto currencies, which may seriously hit the business of private retail banking sector.

Currently, the majority of blockchain applications and explorations focus on financial and business sectors. The interest in this technology is also increasing in the public sector, as can be seen from the growing scientific literature. Emerging experimentation that involves governments is fueled by the expectations that blockchain technology may bring efficiency improvements to the informative and administrative functions of governments and perhaps also transform relations between citizens and administration (Berryhill, Bourgery, & Hanson, 2018; Swan, 2017).

[1] Bitcoin application demonstrates also very well the general property of public, permissionless blockchains, namely that they need to have a built-in cryptocurrency to provide incentives to run the ledger. We thank one of the reviewers for pointing this observation to us.

2.2 Related Literature

Technology-driven innovation has been a topic of research since the early 1990s. Public administrations have experienced organizational and institutional transformations, caused by developments of information technology. As Gasco concluded in 2003 that technology will change public administrations in their technological managerial, and political structures (Gascó, 2003). Over the years, the public sector has seen an increasing amount of IT embedded in public services, initially merely digitizing the manual paper-based processes and later fundamentally changing the way public services are delivered (Janssen & Van Veenstra, 2005). Many researchers have created or analysed maturity models in the domain of e-government. Recently, public sector modernisation strategies have shifted towards digital government paradigm (OECD, 2016). Contrary to e-government that focused on the use of digital technologies by governments, the new approach adopts citizen-centric and problem-focused perspective. Over the last 5 years, an increase in variety of potentially disruptive technologies is observed in the public sector, included the Internet of Things, Big Data, Robotic Process Automation and Blockchain (Leitner & Stiefmueller, 2019). Our study fits into the new digital government approach by taking a closer look at how blockchain technology can transform administrative processes as well as end-user service design and delivery.

The interest of scientific community in the research on blockchain and government has originated in 2015. Early studies presented blockchain as a disruptive, holistic governance system that will redefine the role of governments (Atzori, 2017; Davidson, De Filippi, & Potts, 2016). Initially, the disintermediation argument was taken to the extreme. Blockchain was naïvely claimed to compete away contemporary political and economic institutions due to their chronical inefficiency. These claims ignored the subtle difference between rule enforcement and rule making (Lehdonvirta & Robleh, 2016). In the public sector context, permissioned blockchains seem to resolve this centralization paradox reasonably well. This particular type of distributed ledgers introduces efficient enforcement but setting the governance rules remains under control of a single organization or a consortium. Soon researchers started to focus on more operational issues looking at how governments could modernize administrative processes by substituting human-based bureaucratic procedures with machine-based automated enforcement (Ølnes et al., 2017). Specific attention has been dedicated to healthcare (McGhin, Choo, Liu, & He, 2019) and education (Alammary, Alhazmi, Almasri, & Gillani, 2019; Grech & Camilleri, 2017). This literature concentrates on theoretical use cases and therefore only speculates about potential or promised effects of blockchain technology applied to public services. So far there are no empirical papers that link this conceptual perspective with real implementations (Batubara et al., 2018).

There is a strong conviction that blockchain-enabled automation and information sharing could support several administrative functions of governments. The list of main applications, based on existing literature, includes provision of identity, facilitation of voting, management of benefits and pensions, management of tax liabilities, combating frauds, management of citizen records and state registries and facilitation of regulatory oversight. Several positive effects from adoption of blockchain are expected across public administration: increased process efficiency and flexibility, reduced bureaucracy and corruption and broken siloes between agencies (Berryhill et al., 2018; Ølnes, 2016).

The list of specific public sector use cases continuously expands and it is impossible to provide an actual overview off all ideas. Use cases can be found in almost sections of broadly defined public sector, including healthcare, education and public administration (Casino et al., 2019). Functional typology is more informative and recognizes few broad groups of potential use cases: provision of identity, facilitation of voting, management of benefits and pensions, management of tax liabilities, combating corruption and frauds, management of citizen records and state registries, facilitation of regulatory oversight and introducing central bank cryptocurrencies (Berryhill et al., 2018).

In the context of public administration blockchain-enabled automation and information sharing is expected to bring several operational benefits: increase process efficiency, reduce bureaucracy, break siloes between agencies and eliminate corruption (Ølnes & Jansen, 2017). Blockchain technologies can also potentially be used as an information infrastructure to provide the exchange of information by public administrations, for example the exchange of criminality information, the distribution of grants and the exchange of information regarding academic degrees (Davidson et al., 2016). Potential impact of blockchain technology in the public sector goes far beyond efficiency gains enabled by database innovation in recordkeeping and information exchanges. Blockchain technology could have more transformative impact, taking over a large part of the administrative roles that governments fulfil in society nowadays. Smart contracts are likely to trigger a new wave of public sector innovation in governance generating new service delivery models and disruptive business architectures of governments (Reijers, O'Brolcháin, & Haynes, 2016). Full traceability and transparency of transactions on the ledger creates an additional layer of algorithmic trust and algorithmic control over governmental organizations, which may shift the balance of power between administration and citizens (Meijer & Ubacht, 2018). To what extent these more ambitious impacts will be realized is still to be seen.

Some critiques argue that in reality, these projected effects are unlikely because of genetic incompatibility between public administrations and blockchains, but this claim mostly holds only for public permissionless blockchains. From the governmental point of view, public permissionless blockchains have several undesirable properties. They allow for unrestricted participation and anonymous identities and do not provide any level of transaction secrecy (Mik, 2018). Moreover, transaction intensive public services based on existing public permissionless blockchains would not only be expensive, due to involvement of cryptocurrencies, but also difficult to scale-up because of technical constraints (Hughes et al., 2019).

On the other hand, private blockchains are compatible with centralized governance as they mandate known identities and approval of users by the system administrator. Much smaller number of writing nodes, lack of untrusted participants and lower latency in the network favor a combination of high throughput and light consensus that are required to deliver cheap mass-scale services. Nevertheless, the list of potential technical and organizational issues that make integration of private blockchains with the legacy systems questionable is long. Distributed nature of blockchain systems creates concerns regarding stability in the network and lack of one point of control. Certain public services, such as pension management or vat tax collection not only involve extremely high transaction volumes but are particularly challenging for maintaining privacy and security of data (Allessie, Sobolewski, Vaccari, & Pignatelli, 2019; Batubara et al., 2018). Governments should consider that blockchain implementations have fundamental differences in comparison with traditional, centrally managed information infrastructures. Most importantly, blockchain rely on the network of nodes that require some form of consensus to agree on the state of the system. This introduces latency and other implementation challenges related to integration of storage on mobile devices or the need for interoperability to generate cross-border network effects.

3 Empirical Analysis

3.1 Methodology

The analysis of blockchain projects is based on data collected from structured interviews with the representatives of the project development teams. During interviews, we have explored both technical and institutional part of the project. Given qualitative nature of primary data sources, large diversity of developed services and a limited number of projects in the sample, our methodological choice is the case study analysis (Eisenhardt, 1989). The protocol to study multiple case studies requires that data on each individual case is systematic and comparable to ensure external validity and enable discovery of patterns via cross-case comparison. Drawing on the insights from literature, we have elaborated a case study assessment framework. The assessment framework was derived based on the two strands of literature: (1) technology acceptance models adapted for governmental organizations and (2) digital government paradigm. From the first strand, we took classical factors that affect adoption and usage intensions: technology and organizational dimensions, and perceived benefits (Davis, 1989). Technology adoption models provide however an incomplete analytical framework A digital government project is a multidimensional phenomenon that extends beyond pure technology adoption (Sandoval-Almazán et al., 2017) to a set of contextual, application-specific impacts, such as external relations between stakeholders, project governance, openness and transparency (Janowski, 2015). Given these guidelines, in our analysis we have accounted for governance, openness, efficiency and ecosystem perspective. Our analytical framework has six 'bins'. They cover institutional, functional, technical and economic aspects of individual projects (see Fig. 5.1). Institutional aspect.

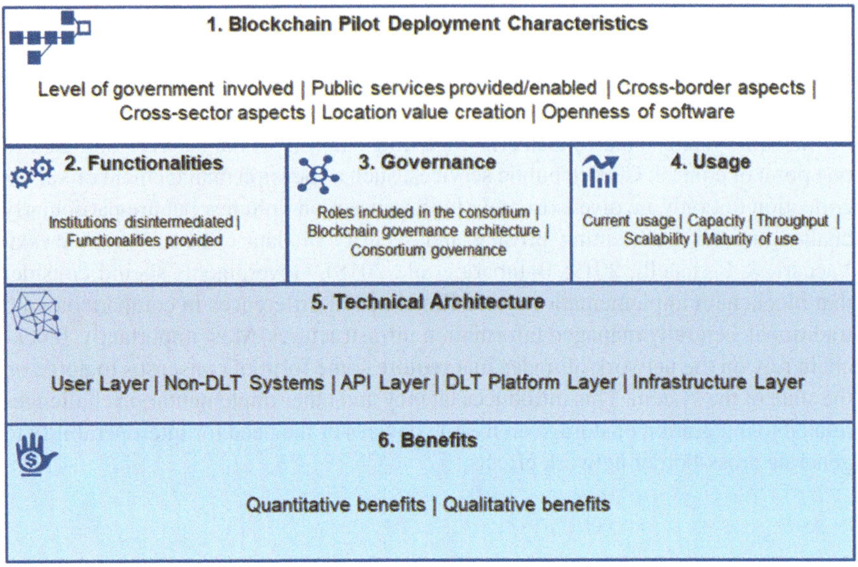

Fig. 5.1 Analytical framework

This aspect focuses on project and technology governance. Project governance refers to the way it is controlled and directed. Decentralized governance means that all consortium stakeholders have an equal say in the decision-making and centralized governance means that a central party has the ability to take decisions on the direction and implementation of the service deployment. The rules of consortium governance directly affect the speed of development and the future evolution of the service. By looking at these issues, we wanted to check if there is any relation between governance model and the complexity of the service developed. Another objective was to see if the way public institutions position themselves within consortium has any impact on the maturity of the developed service. Regarding blockchain governance, the openness of transaction validation (validate/commit) and openness of participation (read/write) in the transactions is analyzed. These principles determine how the distributed database is maintained and directly affect service performance, scalability and the level of trust (Casino et al., 2019). Public permissionless blockchains are largely incompatible with the requirements set out in real-life applications which require an oversight from governmental organizations (Mik, 2018). The main limitations here are pseudo-anonymity, non-compliance with privacy and impractical security model based on public-private key cryptography (Hughes et al., 2019). We therefore expect to observe some form of restrictions concerning who can access the ledger and participate in consensus mechanism.

3.1.1 Functional Aspect

We begin with identification of core blockchain functionalities that are leveraged to provide a public service. Based on the literature, the three main groups of innovative enablers of blockchain are differentiated: notarization of transactions (proof of existence), automatic execution of transactions (smart contracts) and identity verification (proof of identity). These enablers are then mapped onto specific functionalities developed by the projects. In this way, one can see which blockchain innovations are being leveraged in practice and if any of existing institutions are at risk of disintermediation.

3.1.2 Technical Aspect

Digital architectures are usually analyzed with hierarchical approach, focusing on different layers of a service. We follow this approach, building on existing models of blockchain architectures (Tasca & Tessone, 2019). Given the practical objectives of the study, our model is much simpler and differentiates only five main layers. User and API layers refer to how the service interfaces with the end users and the ecosystem. Usually blockchain technology facilitates selected functions provided within a service, while for example storage of data or authentication use external, possibly centralized non-DLT systems. The DLT part of the service design is examined in detail by separately looking at the type blockchain platform blockchain and underlying infrastructure. We also consider project choice regarding the openness of software developed within a project. This choice is important because it affects the speed of development and adoption of the service. The openness of the software can range between fully open source to completely proprietary software. In reality, mixed situation can be expected as well. For example, parts of the system, such as user interfaces or application protocol interfaces (API) can be proprietary, while the core elements of the system may adapt existing open source solutions. Technical aspect explores also current usage parameters, such number of users and number of transactions per second. The teams provided also information on the system capacity, understood as a number of users that the blockchain system can comfortably facilitate. Capacity and usage parameters will be informative mostly for services in production stage, because pilot projects use non-scalable test environments.

3.1.3 Economic Aspect

Economic aspect will be explored by looking at benefits involved in the development and operation of blockchain service. We did not include the costs involved in this analysis, as for projects in experimentation phase it was impossible to collect quantitative information on costs and development risks.

The catalogue of potential benefits from deployment of blockchain technology is well elaborated in the literature (Hughes et al., 2019). We have introduced a distinction between quantitative and qualitative benefits. Quantitative benefits include cost savings (reduced costs of processing transactions without intermediary as compared to the traditional system) and efficiency gains (reduced time of completing a transaction compared the traditional system). Qualitative benefits include reliability gains (decreased risk of cyber-attack, system breakdown or data leakage), transparency and accountability gains (an increased oversight of the current state of the system and transaction history).

3.2 Sample Selection

The initial list of candidate projects was created from several publicly available sources. Only those projects qualified, in which governmental agency was listed among consortium partners and the kick-start date was at least 6 months prior to data collection. The list was restricted to projects implemented in Europe, but consortia could be composed of technological or scientific partners from outside Europe. Selection was carried in such a way as to ensure sufficient variability across three dimensions:

- Field of implementation;
- Country of implementation;
- Level of government involved in the project (local vs national).

The final sample contained seven projects, listed in Table 5.1. The fieldwork took place in February-April 2018.

The sample contains projects implementing services from three broad groups: (1) public aid and social transfers, (2) citizen's records and public registries and (3) foundational components related to user identity and regulatory compliance. Short characterizations of individual projects can be found in the Annex. For a detailed overview a reader is referred to (Allessie et al., 2019). Projects in the sample were implemented in six different European countries. Five projects involved national governments while the remaining two had local authorities in the consortia. In the next section, we present the results of horizontal analysis of case studies based on structured in-depth interviews. The questionnaire explored all elements of the analytical framework from Fig. 5.1.

3.3 Horizontal Analysis of Case Studies

Horizontal comparison of case studies is an established method for the analysis of qualitative data. It enables to explore diversities and similarities among individual projects and to uncover patterns. In what follows we compare projects along six dimensions set out in the case study assessment framework.

Table 5.1 Final sample composition and general features of blockchain projects

Project name	Country of implementation	Field of implementation	Level of government involved	Openness of software
1. Exonum land title registry	Georgia	Land title registry; property transactions	National	Open source
2. Blockcerts academic credentials	Malta	Academic certificates verification; personal documents storage and sharing	National	Open source
3. Chromaway property transactions	Sweden	Property transactions; transfer of land titles	National	Proprietary
4. uPort decentralized identity	Switzerland	Digital identity for proof of residency, eVoting, payments for bike rental and parking	Local (municipality of Zug)	Open source
5. Infrachain governance framework	Luxemburg	Blockchain governance	National	Open source
6. Pension infrastructure	The Netherlands	Pension system management	National	Hybrid: open standards, proprietary software
7. Stadjerspas smart vouchers	The Netherlands	Benefit management for low-income residents	Local (municipality of Groningen)	Hybrid: open blockchain protocol, proprietary smart contract layer

3.3.1 Project Characteristics

Currently public governments experiment with a number of specific services like registration, verification and transfer of land titles, verification of personal certificates and attestation of identity or allocation of benefits, as indicated in Table 5.1. These concrete services support the three main functions of governments: (1) management of governmental and citizen registries (2) management of social transfers / benefits and (3) provision of verified information for facilitation of economic transactions and regulation. Majority of services are targeted at citizens as end-users. A few projects develop foundational building blocks of blockchain: government-attested decentralized identity and governance framework. The decentralized identity solution developed locally in Zug, can serve for authentication to a wide range of services including electronic voting, access to public infrastructure or rentals. The level of government involved varies across case studies, yet dominantly the national government is involved. Two projects where local governments participate in the consortia are relatively advanced in the lifecycle, despite leveraging advanced blockchain functionalities on top of notarization. Most likely, their higher maturity is related with smaller scale. The majority of projects use open source software at the blockchain protocol level, but not necessarily at the application level. Only one implementation, the Postchain system in Chromaway property transactions, is fully proprietary. Few projects combine open source blockchain protocols and proprietary software. Proprietary parts include specific implementations of smart contracts or user wallets, which are not available on-shelve.

3.3.2 Functionalities

Most services will take over particular tasks from public organization, but none of them assumes full intermediation of the institution. In Chromaway system for property transactions, a private institution will be redundant. The notary will not be involved in registration and attestation of documents as this will be done directly provided by the smart contract. The humane tasks that can be handed over from public administration to blockchain protocol include attestation of identity, verification of documents or eligibility check-up. These transfers will likely reduce paper work and speed up administrative workflows by removing existing bottlenecks.

Analyzed projects differ with respect to the scope of implemented blockchain functionalities (Table 5.2). Blockchain-based notarization allows for attestation and verification of the originality and ownership of a document by storing its hash. A hash is a fixed-length cryptographic extract of a document, which can be conveniently stored on blockchain without disclosing its content or personal details.

Table 5.2 Functionalities overview

Project	Institutions disintermediated: full/partial	Blockchain functionalities leveraged: notarization/smart contract shared database/automation
1. Exonum land title registry	None/none	Notarization
2. Blockcerts academic credentials	None/yes: reduced tasks for admin office at university	Notarization
3. Chromaway property transactions	Yes: notaries/yes: reduced tasks for banks and land registry back offices	Smart contract automation/shared database
4. uPort decentralised identity	None:/yes: reduced tasks for municipality	Notarization/smart contract shared database
5. Infrachain governance framework	None	Notarization/shared database/smart contract automation
6. Pension infrastructure	None/yes: reduced tasks for pension funds back offices	Notarization/shared database/smart contract automation
7. Stadjerspas smart vouchers	None/yes: reduced tasks for municipality	Notarization/smart contract automation

Exonum system records hashes of land titles on public blockchain to create an independent verification layer. Distributed notarization alone generates rather limited gains compared to traditional services. Other projects, like Blockcerts or uport, combine notarization with non-DLT functionalities, such as local mobile wallets. These wallets create additional value, because users may store and share personal certificates. Five projects in the sample implement DLT functionalities, based on programmable smart contracts. Smart contracts introduce automated workflows on running on a shared database between different actors such as (1) employees, employers and pension funds (Pension Infrastructure); (2) citizens using decentralized identity and service providers (uPort); (3) property agents, sellers, buyers, banks and title registry (Chromaway); (4) voucher holders, municipality and providers of subsidized services (Stadjerspas). Projects, which utilize smart contracts for shared databases and automated workflows, are less advanced in their life cycle. These implementations have to reconcile different needs in the ecosystem, integrate legacy systems of various actors through APIs and deliver mobile interfaces.

3.3.3 Governance

The governance of the project consortia are mostly centralized or hybrid as shown in Table 5.3. In the centralized model, usually government has a vast amount of decision-making power. In the hybrid model, few large players can steer the consortium in certain directions, often with a strong influence of the technology provider. In around half of the case studies, an open source software community contributes

Table 5.3 Governance overview

Governance	Roles in the consortium	Blockchain governance	Consortium governance
1. Exonum land title registry	Government; open source community; tech provider	Private permissioned and public permissionless	Centralized (NAPR)
2. Blockcerts academic credentials	Government; open source community; tech provider	Private permissionless	Hybrid—various consortium partners
3. Chromaway property transactions	Government; tech provider; banks	Private permissioned	Hybrid—various consortium partners
4. uPort decentralized identity	Government; open source community, tech provider	Private permissionless	Hybrid
5. Infrachain governance framework	Government; businesses, tech provider	Private and public permissioned	Decentralized
6. Pension infrastructure	Government; open source community; pension funds; tech provider	Private permissioned	Hybrid
7. Stadjerspas smart vouchers	Government; businesses, tech provider	Private permissionless	Centralized (City of Groningen)

technically to the solution, which requires stronger coordination from the technological partner. Once services enter to production, governments naturally start to play a dominant role in the consortium acting also in a capacity of the client. The choices of blockchain governance architectures are not clear-cut. No single project uses solely a public permissionless archetype. There is always some type of restriction: either on who can transact in the system or on who can validate transactions. Four projects display elements of a private permissioned design, with limited number of known nodes participating in the validation. Permissioned blockchains are by definition closer to centralized systems. They do not reproduce trust and hence do not run heavy consensus. Permissioned blockchains are a default choice in case of services targeted at increasing operational capacities of governments, like introducing automated enforcement of voluminous transactions (pension system, property transfers). Projects, which use permissionless design, either operate in a small (municipal) scale or experiment with test environments.

3.3.4 Usage Overview

The current usage differs greatly per project and is logically largely dependent on the lifecycle phase. At the time of writing, the majority of projects were in a conceptual or pilot phase. Only two services were already operational. Usually pools of test users do not exceed few hundreds, but for operational services they reach several thousands. Georgian authorities have registered over 100 thousand land titles hashed on the Exonum blockchain. Voucher system of the Municipality of Groningen already has over 20 thousand users. As can be seen from Table 5.4, pilot projects have very limited account of the current throughput parameter of their blockchain systems. This is not surprising in early stage, when the objective is to develop a functional service in a test environment. Stability and scalability of the system are considered at later stages of experimentation. Although impossible to verify, the declared scalability in current environments (understood as a maximal number of transactions in a given time interval) ranges from 7 transactions to 5 thousand transactions per second. Generally, projects, which utilize permissioned blockchains, do not report scalability constraints. Transaction speed, latency and maintenance costs are often considered to be impediments for scalability of permissionless blockchain (Casino et al., 2019), but in case of analyzed implementations they do not seem to be the major obstacles. All projects with permissionless design have developed ways to overcome throughput bottleneck. For example, Blockcerts records transactions in batches and Exonum hashes the whole state of the system, instead of individual land titles.

3.3.5 Technical Architecture

An overview of the architecture layers is displayed in Table 5.5. User layer provides mobile wallets or web portals. Mobile applications are a dominant form of interface because they greatly enhance user experience. Looking at the non-DLT systems, a

Table 5.4 Usage overview

Project	Current usage	Current throughput	Scalability (per April 2018)	Maturity
1. Exonum land title registry	Over 100,000 titles	Unknown	5000 tps (private permissioned part)	Production
2. Blockcerts academic credentials	Hundreds of users	7 tps (Bitcoin)	7 tps (Bitcoin)	Early stage pilot
3. Chromaway property transactions	Unknown	Unknown	160 tps	Proof-of-concept
4. uPort decentralized identity	300 users	Unknown	7 tps	Early stage pilot
5. Infrachain governance framework	Unknown	Depending on blockchain	Depending on blockchain	Early stage pilot
6. Pension infrastructure	5000 users	Unknown	Unknown	Proof-of-concept
7. Stadjerspas smart vouchers	20,000 users, 4000 transactions monthly	7 tps	7 tps	Production

separate registry or database is always found to which blockchain system connects, like credential database or state registry. Blockchain pilots dominantly use APIs to connect the blockchain layer to the existing systems of project participants. The most complex blockchain pilots display a range of different APIs with varying exchange, authentication and admin functions. The physical storage of the transaction data heavily depends on the architecture. Private blockchain infrastructures often allow participants to host blockchain nodes and participate in the consensus. In public blockchain architectures, the physical location of transaction data is usually unknown.

Varying consensus mechanisms currently occur in the pilot deployments. In permissionless blockchain deployments, Proof-Of-Work and Proof-Of-Stake are mostly available. This will however change with transition of service from infancy towards production phase. Services in production establish consensus among known nodes that are owned by consortium participants including government institutions. In such cases a more efficient consensus model will be deployed, such as PBFT or Proof-Of-Authority. The organization of infrastructure layer on which the consensus mechanism is running is largely determined by blockchain design. In permissioned blockchains, consortium participants often own the nodes. In permissionless deployments, anyone can theoretically establish a node. If a service anchors hashes in the Bitcoin blockchain, these would be stored in all full Bitcoin nodes spread all over the globe.

Table 5.5 Architecture overview

Project	User layer	Non-DLT systems	API layer	DLT platform layer	Infrastructure layer
1. Exonum land title registry	Admin NAPR application	NAPR land title registry system	Admin API to land title registry	Private consensus (private blockchain) and Proof-Of-Work (Bitcoin)	Known nodes and Bitcoin blockchain
2. Blockcerts academic credentials	Wallet (mobile app) and issuer software	Certification database of institutions	Blockchain APIs for confirmation and searching	Proof-Of-Work consensus	Bitcoin blockchain
3. Chromaway property transactions	Smart contract interface (mobile app)	Swedish Land Registry	Internode API, client API and legacy API	Proof-Of-Authority with PBFT (private) consensus	Storage is in PostgreSQL or another RDBMS with known nodes
4. uPort decentralized identity	uPort (mobile app)	Front-end portal (municipal webpage)	uPort Connect API	Proof-Of-Stake consensus	Hash is stored in Ethereum (test net) blockchain, user data stored locally
5. Infrachain governance framework	Not applicable	Not applicable	Not applicable	Private consensus (currently Proof-Of-Work)	Nodes based on Ethereum protocol
6. Pension infrastructure	User group specific application	Exiting salary and pension databases	Currently unknown	Private consensus (currently Proof-Of-Work)	Hash stored in Ethereum blockchain with known nodes, storage of transaction unknown
7. Stadjerspas smart vouchers	QR code, browser (mobile app)	Municipal registries	Admin API	Proof-Of-Authority consensus	Nodes using the Zcash protocol

3.3.6 Benefits

Experimentation projects focus mainly on the functional development. Economic and technical efficiency is not considered at this stage. While data from pilot projects may not serve as a proxy for the deployment costs of production services, experimental projects already have reflected about the expected benefits. In Table 5.6, we have collected insights about the types of benefits foreseen by the project teams from implementation of their services.

Table 5.6 Benefits overview

Project	Quantitative benefits	Qualitative benefits
1. Exonum land title registry	400 times faster registration of extract; reduction of operational costs (over 90%)	Improved transparency; higher fault-tolerance; increased reliability of data
2. Blockcerts academic credentials	Lower operation cost; efficiency gains; lower integration cost	Citizens' ownership of data, convenient storage; quick and selective sharing; identity and privacy protected; no hard copies; elimination of fake certificates; self-management
3. Chromaway property transactions	Est. €100M/annum; reduced transaction time (over 95%); reduced transaction cost (90%); faster registration and transfer of land title	Increased trust; higher liquidity of assets; improved market operation; improved resilience to record modification and fraud
4. uPort decentralized identity	Lower administration cost; lower storage cost; lower infrastructure cost; efficiency gains for administration; efficiency gains for citizens	Citizens' ownership of data; reduced risk of cyberattacks; self-management
5. Infrachain governance framework	Not applicable	Increased reliability and resilience; increased transparency and flexibility
6. Pension infrastructure	Est. €500M/annum; lower storage cost; efficiency gains for pension funds; efficiency gains for administration; lower transaction costs for citizens	Increased transparency; increased security of data; improved regulatory oversight
7. Stadjerspas smart vouchers	Lower administration cost; efficiency gains for administration; lower transaction costs for citizens	Effective redistribution; improved auditability of public funds

Process efficiency is the most frequently declared benefit from introducing blockchain. Elimination of human-based registration and verification of documents and reduction of hard copies will reduce operational cost of administration. This is particularly expected from projects that establish shared databases, like Chromaway or Pension Infrastructure avoid endless copying of the same data between different IT systems. Smart contracts enable to streamline various business processes and hence create efficiency by reducing the uncertainty and automating transactions. Quicker and more reliable settlement of transactions reduces transaction costs also for citizens. According to Chromaway estimates, reduction of end-to-end property transaction time from weeks to hours will result in 100M EUR savings on insurance for safeguarding mortgage deed. The blockchain-based pension administration system in the Netherlands is expected to bring €500 million annually of savings on pension system administration. This corresponds to 50% decrease in costs from the actual level. These gains are attributable to all types of participating actors: public and private institutions and the citizens. In case of the Stadjerspas project, specific benefits such as improved redistribution and targeting of public funds are in fact attributable not only to the users but to the society as a whole.

Blockchain technology is expected to bring also a number of qualitative benefits. Storing transaction records in a shared ledger increases security and resistance to malicious behavior. The append-only way of updating blocks ensures irrevocability of records and increases integrity and auditability of data. All these benefits are provided directly by the technology itself, adding to the reliability and trustworthiness of governmental record keeping. Moreover, the analyzed services improve citizen experience from interacting with the public authorities. For example, Exonum system allows transferring a land title from home, without visits to the town hall or state registry. In the front end, the service has an attractive user interface, but in the back end, there is a private permissioned blockchain system operating. Users may not be aware about it, but it is a backbone of the entire service. Similarly, in the uPort project, users gain an ownership and control over their personal data. They may selectively disclose it to any third party via their mobile phone, without actually being aware that a distributed ledger ensures the reliability of exchanged data. These examples demonstrate the potential from integrating blockchain with other state-of-art technologies to provide new generation of highly reliable and trustworthy public services operated via personal devices.

4 Results and Discussion

In the current section, we elaborate on the two research questions posted in the introduction.

1. What patterns emerge from the current experimentation of governments with blockchain?

Pattern 1: Ongoing projects experiment with the full spectrum of blockchain functionalities.

Blockchain notarization enables verification of originality of a document and confirmation of the date of its creation and the owner. Decentralized notarization represents only incremental innovation and hence it brings only incremental value to centralized governmental services. The remaining two blockchain functionalities relay on programmable smart contracts. Smart contracts are implemented either as a shared database to facilitate exchange of information (in Pension Infrastructure or Stadjerspas) or as automated workflows to facilitate multiparty transactions (in Chromaway). Both functionalities offer higher stand-alone value and can facilitate or enhance wider range of governmental functions: internal data management, provision of information for ecosystem partners, redistribution of public funds or enforcement of regulations. Services leveraging smart contracts bring also concrete benefits to citizens such as reduced uncertainty and quicker settlement times.

Pattern 2: Type of implemented functionality affects the maturity of projects.

Services based mainly on plain blockchain notarization are relatively more mature, while services with the more advanced functionalities face challenges. Projects that rely solely on the proof of existence via verification of hash have quicker implementation times. They require less integration effort and may use existing software components. Projects which utilize smart contracts are less advanced in their lifecycle. This is expected, as these implementations have to reconcile possibly different needs in the ecosystem, integrate legacy systems of various actors through APIs and deliver mobile interfaces. In some cases, like in Chromaway project, blockchain functionalities already work well technically, but are not compliant with legal frameworks. The most common problem is legal non-equivalence of blockchain and traditional notarization as well as smart contracts and traditional contracts. Smart contracts do not have reconciliation and appeal mechanisms, which are required for legally binding contracts. These problems currently hinder the advancement of more advanced services beyond early pilot phase.

Pattern 3: Projects with a higher level of maturity tend to have less stakeholder complexity and more centralized governance.

The Pension Infrastructure project, which is in proof-of-concept stage, is the most complex in the sample. It has several types of stakeholders involved with varying business objectives and different legacy databases. On the other hand, Stadjerspas voucher system, Exonum land title registry or Blockcerts academic credentials have fewer stakeholder types. In addition, projects with more centralized governance structure are more advanced. More hierarchical decision-making processes in consortia that have a strong governmental leader is likely the cause.

Pattern 4: Services in production respond to clear business needs.

Two projects in our sample already deliver operational services. In both cases there is a strong technological partner, providing required integration with the legacy systems. Both projects also fit within the current technological limits. Exonum utilizes basic blockchain functionality, essentially time-stamped proof of existence. Stadjerspas utilizes an advanced programmable layer that allows for setting eligibility criteria and managing the use of subsidized services. Importantly, both projects have started from clearly defined ownership roles and business needs of the administration: registration and verification of land titles on a blockchain layer and more targeted allocation of vouchers according to specific criteria of beneficiaries.

Pattern 5. Blockchain is always just one layer of the developed service, dependent on non-DLT layers, which run legacy systems.

Blockchain is always one of several layers in the technical architecture. In all projects a centralized database is found that either stores user data or that feeds transaction data into the distributed system. In Exonum and Stadjerspas projects a centralized database is used to store transaction data. Blockchain protocol is used only to anchor hashes yet all the transaction details are stored in the databases of NAPR or DutchChain. The Uport project is an example of implementation where a centralized database is used to feed into the distributed system. Municipality checks the validity of the citizen's request and links own records with the Uport address, referred to as the blockchain identity.

Pattern 6. Blockchain technology does not pose a threat of disintermediation of existing public institutions.

In no case, blockchain substitutes any public institution. Chromaway is the only project that explicitly assumes disintermediation of traditional notary function. Blockerts project assumes elimination of one of the functions of national agency for academic credentials but this is unlikely to make the entire institution obsolete. The remaining blockchain-based solutions are either complementary to the existing administrative processes or partially substitutable. Complementary solutions build on top of existing processes, like in the Exonum project, which simply adds and independent content verification layer to centrally stored land titles. Partially substitute solutions propose new or changed way of providing an administrative function within institution. In the latter case, blockchain technology may take over some tasks, such as for example attestation of identity or eligibility check-up. These changes reduce paper work and generate time savings for administration, but does not threaten public institution's role as intermediary.

Pattern 7. Personal data is always stored off-chain.

The storage of personal data is carefully designed in all services. When permissionless or public blockchains are leveraged, user data is stored off-chain, either in centralized repositories, like in the Exonum project or locally by the users, like in the Blockcerts or uPort projects. When a private permissioned blockchain is used, private data in principle could be stored on-chain in an encrypted form. However sending large portions of data in the network is usually inefficient due to bandwidth restrictions. In the Chromaway project for example, a smart contract platform is used to connect centralized databases of participants and records statements about the new states in the workflow.

Pattern 8. Transaction throughput does not appear to be a major bottleneck.

A clear difference between permissioned and permissionless blockchains is observed with respect to the number of transactions that can be validated in a time interval. The throughput in permissionless blockchain protocols is significantly less than the permissioned blockchain protocols (up to 7 tps compared to 160–5000 tps). Projects that anchor transaction on public permissionless blockchains are in minority but they have designed ways to mitigate throughput constraints. For example, transactions are batched or the hash of total state of the system is recorded. Projects that use permissioned blockchains usually do not report any problems with a throughput however the most transaction-intensive projects, such as Pension Infrastructure, expect some scalability problems related to processing a large number of smart contracts.

2. What benefits blockchain may bring to the public sector?

Ongoing experimentation is still on a relatively early stage with only few operational implementations. The analyzed projects demonstrate however that blockchain technology offers potential benefits that may be allocated to administration, citizens and society as a whole. Services utilizing blockchain-based notarization increase the auditability of data and the transparency of administrative processes. Immutability of records on the ledger can possibly enlarge trust of citizens and companies in the governmental record-keeping. Blockchain can also increase reliability of markets on which governmental institutions participate as providers of information and facilitators of transactions. Besides trust and reliability, blockchain generates efficiency gains measurable in monetary terms. For example, streamlining mortgage handling and transfer of land titles in a smart contract workflow, shortens property transaction times from weeks to hours. Quicker settlement reduces property transaction costs and improves liquidity on the market, providing possibilities for more economic activity. Given the high value of traded properties, these savings may account for hundreds of millions of Euro annually. Blockchain based pension management system is another example of potentially high gains induced by smart contract workflow. Smart contracts allow for high level of process automation, which translates to lower administration costs, elimination of paper work and storage costs.

Shared ledger offers also new opportunities for governmental institutions in policy design and funding management. For example, an immediate access to information on the state of the pension transfers or taxed transactions among businesses will enhance ways, in which governments can counteract fraud and evasion from public liabilities. The smart voucher program for promoting social inclusion is another example of how management of transactions via smart contracts enhances effectiveness of administration. Besides elimination of human errors and cost savings on personnel due to automation of management process, smart contracts improve the allocative efficiency of public funds and their targeting to beneficiaries. From the citizen's perspective blockchain in combination with other digital decentralized technologies can eliminate excessive bureaucracy, hard copies or visits in the town hall. Most of the projects develop mobile app to serve as remote interfaces to interact with public administration. An important part of this new user experience links to citizen self-sovereignty. Thanks to blockchain-attested identity and local storage of personal records, citizens will become largely independent from central repositories.

Public permissionless blockchains seems to have a limited use for governments for their numerous economic and technical limitations, such as the use of built-in cryptocurrencies, network latency and possibility of untrusted writers. Nevertheless ongoing experimentation uses this design to some extent mainly to build an additional layer of trust on top of existing central registries. By recording extracts of documents on a public distributed ledger, which is opened to everyone, governments can increase reliability of the record keeping of their own centralized registries. Independently run and publicly accessible ledger is useful for verification of originality and integrity of the kept by citizens or governmental agencies. However even this rudimentary functionality requires additional non-DLT systems that actually store the records and authenticate users with government-attested identity.

Going beyond notarization via distributed consensus, the majority of analyzed services utilize blockchain to establish a shared database technology. This is a domain of private permissioned blockchains. Such database is a single source of truth that enables new service delivery and interactions within an ecosystem of organizations and actors. Sharing a ledger among certified and known nodes enables provision of new types of 'smart' services that are located outside traditional organizational boundaries. In some cases, the role of governments may be quite limited although critical for the whole value chain, like for example in property transactions where public institution simply submits a land title. In other cases, the role of governmental institutions is more profound, like for example in pension system where public institutions obtain powerful tools for regulatory oversight.

Our analysis confirms that important part of efficiency gains is attributable to smart contracts. There is however a second side of the coin. Smart contracts have to be carefully designed and properly coded to evoke an exact behavior at exact conditions. In real life implementations reconciliation mechanisms must be in place to correct for instances of improper outcomes or simply errors in code. Some applications, which use smart contracts for a simple task, such as eligibility check or store of personal identifiers, are already operable. Complex workflow-based applications have a longer way to the market. They require severe integration effort with different legacy systems and encounter non-compliance issues.

5 Summary and Conclusions

In this paper, we investigated a number of ongoing blockchain developments in the public sector in Europe in order to assess how blockchain technology could in practical terms change the operation of governments and what potential benefits it may bring. Analyzed projects experiment with three main groups of services: (1) social transfers and pensions, (2) citizen's records and public registries and (3) foundational components related to user identity and regulatory compliance. The data for the study was collected between February and April 2018 via structured interviews with the representatives of each project. Horizontal analysis of projects across different institutional, functional, technical and economic aspects was carried out in order to reveal current patterns of adoption of blockchain technology in the public sector.

We have found that all governments experiment with the three main blockchain functionalities: notarization, shared database and workflow automation. There are however some notable differences. Services leveraging blockchain notarization are relatively more mature, while more disruptive solutions face challenges in implementation, mainly related to incompatibility with the current administrative processes and regulatory noncompliance. Blockchain-based services that are already in operation respond to clear business needs. They also have an active public sector actor and a strong technological partner. Besides, projects with a higher level of maturity tend to have less stakeholder complexity and more centralized governance.

Blockchain implementations are predominantly based on open source software at the protocol level, but not necessarily at the application level. Some governments are pushing towards the publication of platform-agnostic open standards to minimize the risk of lock-in and to incentivize the adoption of the service by third parties. The majority of implementations use, at least partially, private permissioned blockchain. This design is best tailored to handle voluminous transactions between known nodes owned by government institutions and ecosystem partners. The distributed ledger is however always just one layer in the architecture and interconnects with non-DLT layers. Blockchain is dependent on inputs from centralized governmental databases or user wallets that provide storage of private data. Distributed ledger allow overcoming critical bottlenecks in the administrative process where attestation and verification of data is traditionally done by human work. Blockchain-based solutions do not threaten public institutions role as intermediaries. They are either complementary or partially substitutable for existing public services. Transaction throughput does not appear to be a major bottleneck for any of the analyzed projects. Those projects that anchor transactions on public permissionless blockchains have designed ways to mitigate throughput constraints.

Literature on new technology implementation within the public sector argues that institutional changes will follow with the introduction of new technologies. In our empirical research, we have yet to see these institutional changes proliferate with the implementation of blockchain. So far, blockchain implementations in the public sector seek mainly for efficiency enhancements in record-keeping and financial management. Existing projects experiment with automated enforcement of transactions and new service delivery models, which utilize mobile interfaces and shared databases. The outcomes are promising and demonstrate capability of blockchains to reduce bureaucracy and costs of administrative processes and break silos between governmental agencies. These efficiency enablers are available mainly in permissioned environments. These systems do not need to reproduce trust, but rather automate exchange of information between known nodes belonging to different ecosystem partners.

Some implementations demonstrate a capability to enhance experience from interactions with public authorities. For example, personal certificates and land titles issuance can be provided to the citizen automatically via mobile app, without a need to visit a town hall. Self-sovereign identity can also represent a real value for citizens, if it will serve as authentication gateway to large pool of digital services. These benefits for citizens or businesses would not be possible without other innovative digital technologies, pointing to the role of technological convergence as a general paradigm for citizen-focused services.

These potential impacts of blockchain technology look quite promising. Whether blockchain will disrupt the status quo with inefficient governmental processes is however uncertain at this point. The set of production implementations is very limited, which is an indication that technology has yet to mature. The technological landscape suffers from lack of standards and trusted hosting infrastructure as well as gaps in essential functionality (e.g., smart contracts). Challenges recognized by the project teams are scalability, governance, flexibility and interoperability. Without addressing these issues, blockchain will not become a transformative technology for governments.

6 Future Research

This research shows that current blockchain-driven innovation in the public sector mainly consists of automating the enforcement of transactions and that main benefit drivers are reducing bureaucracy and costs of administrative processes, like record-keeping or financial management. Some projects, such as identity management or academic credentials, highlight also a path for digital transformation of public services through self-management by citizens. However, a lack of standards and trusted hosting infrastructure as well as gaps in essential functionality are currently key inhibitors for blockchain to become a transformative technology for governments. We therefore suggest practical research into a trusted hosting infrastructure for public services using blockchain. In addition, we suggest research in technical standards and interoperability structures enhance the effectivity of this technology in the public domain.

Moreover, we acknowledge the fast-moving pace of this technology. The cases were analyzed mid-2018 and we suggest continued empirical research in this domain to revisit the current benefits and inhibitors of blockchain within the public sector.[2]

Acknowledgements This research was originally founded by the European Commission from the "European Location Interoperability Solutions for e-Government" (ELISE) Action of the ISA[2] Programme.

Annex: Characteristics of Individual Projects

Exonum Land Title Registry: Georgia

The National Agency of Public Registry (NAPR) of the Republic of Georgia partnered-up with Bitfuri Group in April 2016 to build a blockchain-based service for issuing digital certificates of land titles. The rationale for using blockchain was to increase public confidence in the property-related record-keeping, fight corruption and resolve disputes over contested property deeds. Solution based on Bitcoin protocol allows citizens and notaries to validate property-related certificates and make new registrations. The service allows for the registration of purchases and sales of existing land titles and a registration of new land titles. In the future, the system will

[2] For example, in 2019 the European Blockchain Partnership involving all EU Member States MS plus Norway and Liechtenstein started to build European Blockchain Services Infrastructure. EBSI will deliver EU-wide cross-border public services using blockchain technology. Three out of the four initial EBSI deployments that are underway: notarisation, diplomas and European self-sovereign identity represent clear scale-up attempts of the concepts analysed in this study. Deployment of these cross-border services will offer a unique opportunity to revisit some of the case studies presented here.

be extended to a registration of property demolitions, mortgages and rentals. The actual transaction validation occurs by a group of known servers or nodes. The transaction data is then hashed and recorded on the public Bitcoin blockchain. The hash is a cryptographic proof that transaction details match with the data recorded in the NAPR registry, without actually seeing it.

Blockcerts Academic Credentials: Malta

The Maltese government has launched a project that develops academic credentials verification using blockchain technology in October 2017. The Ministry for Education and Employment (MEDE) of Malta decided to use the Blockcerts open standard, developed in 2015 by Massachusetts Institute of Technology (MIT), for management of academic records. Blockcerts provides all aspects of the value chain: creation, issuing, viewing, and verification of the certificates, and uses blockchain technology as the infrastructure. The functionalities provided in the project include the issuance of academic credentials, the verification of certificates, and the storage of personal credentials in the user app. The Blockcerts app provides a wallet where the citizen has a full ownership of his records. System allows a citizen to control which third parties can see his academic records and verify their originality. By providing the URL of the certificate, one can verify the validity of the certificate, the owner of credentials, the issuing date, the issuing institution and the transaction ID. The system uses private permissionless design. The private blockchain network is composed solely of the certified institutions that participate in registering academic certificates using Blockcerts solution. The verification of the certificates is done on the Bitcoin network via the Blockcerts universal verifier. Anyone that has credentials of one of the consortia partners can apply for certificate and share it with any third party.

Chromaway Property Transactions: Sweden

The project was initiated in September 2016 by the Swedish Mapping, Cadaster and Land Registration Authority, Landshypotek Bank, SBAB, Telia, Chromaway and Kairos Future. The project was set-up to redefine real estate transactions and mortgage deeds. It aimed to address the main weaknesses of the current transacting system: lack of transparency, slow registration and transfer of land title and resulting high transaction costs. The underlying technology in this project consists of two main components: the blockchain platform (Postchain) and the smart contract workflow (Esplix). The smart contract workflow enables an automatic processing of transaction by the participants. The blockchain system uses private permissioned design. It combines the capabilities of centralized, relational databases with private blockchains. The shared database has capacity to store all transaction data, however in order to meet laws and regulations, the identifying (personal) data is stored off-chain and is represented on the blockchain by a hash. The solution introduces a completely new blockchain-based workflow that streamlines and secures the process of transferring a property title. Five types of actors are involved in the workflow: the buyer, the seller, the real estate agent, the banks and the land registry. The system interfaces to the Swedish Land Registry that is responsible for storing land titles. The blockchain updates state of the system after execution of each step in the workflow. In this way, synchronization among participants involved in the transaction is ensured.

uPort Decentralized Identity: Zug, Switzerland

In November 2017, City of Zug has launched a government-issued identity on the Ethereum blockchain, called uPort. The aim of the project is to provide a trusted and self-reliant blockchain-based identity to authenticate for e-government services and share personal data with third parties. uPort introduces a decentralized model of ownership, management and attestation of the identity of a person. It allows for a selective disclosure of specific information to particular companies or governmental institutions, giving citizens a full control over their personal data. Personal data is stored locally on the user's device in uPort application and anonymized before sending via network. Upon installation, the uPort application creates a unique private key, stored on a mobile device and two smart contracts running on Ethereum. The self-sovereignty property means that only the identity smart contract can make statements about a person's identity when interacting with other smart contracts or uPort users. These statements do not require confirmation from centralized certification providers. The identity contract is monitored by a controller contract. The controller contract grants or withdraws an authorization to sign statements. It also allows a citizen to recover identity access if a phone with the private key is lost. The city registration office has admin rights in the uPort application. After the verification, which has to be done in person in the town hall, the municipality issues an attestation signed with its private key. This implies that uPort is recognized as government-issued identity.

Infrachain Governance Framework: Luxemburg

The project started in November 2016 in Luxembourg. It aims to create pan-European host operator of blockchain network with certified nodes that comply with SLA-enforced governance. The certification will be based on the ISO27001 standard on the information security. Infrachain supports the creation of independent and incorruptible nodes involved in the operation of blockchain instances.

Infrachain develops a governance layer placed 'on top' of existing and future permissioned blockchains. The governance framework gives attention to privacy protection, cyber-security, law enforcement and business continuity to the same degree as centralized systems. The framework postulates a separation of service and network layers and the establishment of a reference blockchain infrastructure, composed of independent nodes, hosting different public and private services. Currently, individual private blockchain infrastructures comply with some security and confidentiality requirements, but there is no comprehensive set of shared rules followed by different implementations. This could be achieved via a virtual layer that serves as a host network operator with participating nodes operating under common service-level agreement (SLA). Because physical nodes are owned by different organizations, the host network would have a federated structure with a common governance framework. The host operator will offer high network stability and security, typical for public blockchains, and high performance required to host numerous private blockchain instances.

Pension Infrastructure: The Netherlands

The Pension Infrastructure project started in 2017 in collaboration with the two largest pension providers in the Netherlands. The Dutch National Government is involved in the project through the Dutch Authority for the Financial Markets (AFM) and the Dutch National Tax Office. The aim of the project is to build blockchain back-office for community-based pension administration. The system will allow for flexible and transparent pension administration for citizens, while reducing significantly pension management costs. The project has a variety of stakeholders, including employers, the national identity service, the tax authority, payroll providers, pension funds, technology providers and citizens. The system provides different functionalities based on the role of the actor. For the tax authority, for example, it provides an integral image of the contributions collected by a specific individual across many pension funds. For a citizen, it provides real-time insights into the evolution of their pension scheme and pension balance. Employers can directly introduce a salary change. Regulators do not have an active role, yet they can see part of the data. The project will create private blockchain architecture with a permissioned instance of the Ethereum protocol. The nodes in the network will have known identity and represent the stakeholders involved in the development of the infrastructure. Smart contracts are used to determine the rules for building up a pension balance for a citizen. They will also prescribe rules of who can view, change, and use the data. The project requires a combination of several blockchain functionalities: distributed registration, membership management, information exchange, automatic execution and digital fingerprints (hashing). The system is developed by setting up connections between the back-end systems of all the involved parties.

Stadjerspas Smart Vouchers: Groningen, The Netherlands

Stadjerspas is a fully operable service, developed by DutchChain. It uses blockchain infrastructure to distribute discounted services to low-income citizens of the Municipality of Groningen. The voucher system in Groningen was moved to a blockchain in 2016. The benefit of the blockchain-based system is the enhanced targeting of public money thanks to programmable money flows. Detailed spending conditions and eligibility criteria are set in the smart contract. Smart vouchers can be used, for example, in sport clubs, cinemas or for allocating subsidies to solar panels for homeowners. Stadjerspas ensures that public money reserved for a specified purpose is spent exclusively on that purpose and targeted at a desired group of beneficiaries. The municipality can provide eligibility criteria for users of smart vouchers, for example based on their residence, income, and number of children or any data linked to the resident number. Users of the system can see the vouchers they are eligible for in the mobile app or in the web portal, upon providing a QR code. The provider of the discounted service records each instance of a voucher use in the system. This blockchain implementation uses smart contract functionality and automatic payments. The blockchain system allows for transparency and programmability of public funding, specifically by adding functionalities of distributed registration, membership management, information exchange and automatic execution. The system uses public permissioned blockchain type. Initially the Bitcoin protocol was used, but the system has transferred to Zcash, which has significantly lower transaction costs. Every transaction is recorded in form of a hash, but the details of the transaction are not stored on blockchain.

References

Alammary, A., Alhazmi, S., Almasri, M., & Gillani, S. (2019). Blockchain-based applications in education: A systematic review. *Applied Sciences, 9*, 2400. https://doi.org/10.3390/app9122400

Allessie, D., Sobolewski, M., Vaccari, L., & Pignatelli, F. (2019). *Blockchain for digital government: An assessment of pioneering implementations in public services*. Brussels: Publications Office of the European Union. https://doi.org/10.2760/942739

Atzori, M. (2017). Blockchain technology and decentralized governance: Is the state still necessary? *Journal of Governance and Regulation, 6*(1), 45–52.

Batubara, F. R., Ubacht, J., & Janssen, M. (2018). Challenges of blockchain technology adoption for e-government: a systematic literature review, in *Proceedings of the 19th Annual International Conference on Digital Government Research: Governance in the Data Age* (p. 76).

Berryhill, J., Bourgery, T., & Hanson, A. (2018). Blockchains unchained blockchain technology and its use in the public sector. *OECD Working Papers on Public Governance, 28*, 53. https://doi.org/10.1787/3c32c429-en

Boucher, P. (2017). *How blockchain technology could change our lives*. European Parliamentary Research Service, Scientific Foresight Unit.

Casino, F., Dasaklis, T. K., & Patsakis, C. (2019). A systematic literature review of blockchain-based applications: Current status, classification and open issues. *Telematics and Informatics, 36*, 55–81. https://doi.org/10.1016/j.tele.2018.11.006

Davidson, S., De Filippi, P., & Potts, J. (2016). Disrupting governance: The new institutional economics of distributed ledger technology. *SSRN Electronic Journal*. https://doi.org/10.2139/ssrn.2811995

Davis, F. D. (1989). Perceived usefulness, perceived ease of use, and user acceptance of information technology. *MIS Quarterly, 1989*, 319–340.

Eisenhardt, K. M. (1989). Building theories from case study research. *Academy of Management Review, 14*(4), 532–550.

Gascó, M. (2003). New technologies and institutional change in public administration. *Social Science Computer Review, 21*(1), 6–14.

Grech, A., & Camilleri, A. F. (2017). *Blockchain in {Education} (Issue EUR 28778 EN)*. Inamorato dos Santos. Retrieved from http://nbn-resolving.de/urn:nbn:de:0111-pedocs-150132

Hughes, L., Dwivedi, Y. K., Misra, S. K., Rana, N. P., Raghavan, V., & Akella, V. (2019). Blockchain research, practice and policy: Applications, benefits, limitations, emerging research themes and research agenda. *International Journal of Information Management*. https://doi.org/10.1016/j.ijinfomgt.2019.02.005

Janowski, T. (2015). Digital government evolution: From transformation to contextualization. *Government Information Quarterly, 32*(3), 221–236. https://doi.org/10.1016/j.giq.2015.07.001

Janssen, M., & Van Veenstra, A.-F. (2005). Stages of growth in e-government: An architectural approach. *The Electronic Journal of E-Government, 3*(4), 193–200.

Konstantinidis, I., Siaminos, G., Timplalexis, C., Zervas, P., Peristeras, V., & Decker, S. (2018). Blockchain for business applications: A systematic literature review. In W. Abramowicz & A. Paschke (Eds.), *Business information systems* (pp. 384–399). Cham: Springer.

Lehdonvirta, V., & Robleh, A. (2016). Governance and regulation. In M. Walport (Ed.), *Distributed ledger technology: Beyond blockchain* (pp. 40–45). London: UK Government Office for Science.

Leitner, C., & Stiefmueller, C. M. (2019). Disruptive technologies and the public sector: The changing dynamics of governance. In *Public service excellence in the 21st century* (pp. 237–274). Cham: Springer.

McGhin, T., Choo, K.-K. R., Liu, C. Z., & He, D. (2019). Blockchain in healthcare applications: Research challenges and opportunities. *Journal of Network and Computer Applications., 135*, 62–75.

Meijer, D., & Ubacht, J. (2018). The governance of blockchain systems from an institutional perspective, a matter of trust or control? in *Proceedings of the 19th Annual International Conference on Digital Government Research: Governance in the Data Age* (p. 90).

Mik, E. (2018). Blockchains: A technology for decentralized marketplaces? *Impact of Technology on International Contract Law: Smart Contracts and Blockchain Technologies, 17*, 7.

Nakamoto, S. (2008). *Bitcoin: A peer-to-peer electronic cash system*. Retrieved from www.bitcoin.org

OECD. (2016). *Digital government strategies for transforming public services in the welfar areas*. Retrieved from http://www.oecd.org/gov/digital-government/Digital-Government-Strategies-Welfare-Service.pdf

Ølnes, S. (2016). Beyond bitcoin enabling smart government using blockchain technology, in *International conference on electronic government* (pp. 253–264).

Ølnes, S., & Jansen, A. (2017). Blockchain technology as support infrastructure in e-government, in *International conference on electronic government* (pp. 215–227).

Ølnes, S., Ubacht, J., & Janssen, M. (2017). Blockchain in government: Benefits and implications of distributed ledger technology for information sharing. *Government Information Quarterly, 34*(3), 355–364. https://doi.org/10.1016/j.giq.2017.09.007

Reijers, W., O'Brolcháin, F., & Haynes, P. (2016). Governance in blockchain technologies & social contract theories. *Ledger, 1*, 134–151.

Sandoval-Almazán, R., Luna-Reyes, L., Dolores, E., Luna-Reyes, D., Gil-Garcia, J., & Puron-Cid, G. (2017). Building digital government strategies. In *Public administration and information technology* (Vol. 16). Cham: Springer.

Swan, M. (2017). Anticipating the economic benefits of blockchain. *Technology Innovation Management Review, 7*(10), 6–13.
Szabo, N. (1997). The idea of smart contracts. *Nick Szabo's Papers and Concise Tutorials, 1997*, 6.
Tasca, P., & Tessone, C. J. (2019). A taxonomy of blockchain technologies: Principles of identification and classification. *Ledger, 4*, 1–39.

Maciej Sobolewski is a senior economist at the JRC, holding PhD in economics. Maciej specializes in economics of ICT and has scientific publication track record in online platforms and telecoms.His research interests include regulatory and competition policy for multi-sided markets, welfare impacts of zero-price digital services, online privacy, network effects and switching costs. Before joining the Joint Research Centre of the European Commission, he was assistant professor of microeconomics at the University of Warsaw and a research fellow at Digital Economy Lab established there. He also worked as a senior economist at Orange Labs R&D Centre. At the JRC he is involved in projects related to the economic impacts of emerging digital technologies, as well as competition and data issues in digital platforms.

David Allessie is a Senior Consultant at Gartner within the Digital Strategy practice. David is specialized in emerging technologies including Blockchain and other peer-to-peer technologies. David has experience in the field of digital strategy for clients in different industries, including the Public Sector, Financial Services, Oil & Gas and the Automotive industry. He holds a Masters in Systems Engineering from Delft University of Technology and has been a visiting researcher at the COSS lab at ETH Zurich.

Chapter 6
Who Supports Using Cryptocurrencies and Why Public Education About Blockchain Technology Matters?

Kristin Johnson and Brian S. Krueger

1 Introduction

Blockchain technologies offer the promise of transforming commercial, governmental, and individual interactions by offering secure transactions while circumventing the delay and cost of intermediary institutions or organizations. The most widely recognized use of this technology lies with cryptocurrencies. These currencies offer the potential for the development of parallel monetary systems replacing government issued legal tender. Another possibility for cryptocurrency is that it may assume the form of digital government backed alternatives to a largely dollar denominated international financial system. China, for example, is anticipated to launch a digital currency using blockchain technology in the near term (Elegant, 2019). The global proliferation of cryptocurrencies and startups using blockchain technology over the last decade is astounding: a brief survey of existing cryptocurrency exchanges at the time of the writing of this chapter identifies nearly 5000 available for purchase and exchange on the website coinmarketap.com. As recently as 2013, only 15 cryptocurrencies were listed for exchange and sale on the same site. Despite the substantial increase in cryptocurrency and blockchain startups, rapid adoption and use of cryptocurrencies has not occurred. Instead, the largest use of cryptocurrency resides with investors and speculators, with incipient expansion to financially excluded populations in the global south.

K. Johnson · B. S. Krueger (✉)
Department of Political Science, University of Rhode Island, Kingston, RI, USA
e-mail: Kristin_johnson@uri.edu; bkrueger@uri.edu

C. G. Reddick et al. (eds.), *Blockchain and the Public Sector*, Public Administration and Information Technology 36,
https://doi.org/10.1007/978-3-030-55746-1_6

Bitcoin offered the initial application of blockchain technology with the release of its open source code in 2008 (Nakamoto, 2008; Narayanan, Bonneau, Felten, Miller, & Goldfefer, 2016). While the initial hype and expectation of blockchain's potential for supplanting the role of financial intermediaries and the expansion of peer to peer financial interactions has yet to be realized, renewed attention to Bitcoin has been associated with significant variation in its trading value, particularly after its peak 2017 value of $19,783 per coin, despite significant subsequent volatility in value (Salzman, 2019). With the sharing economy estimated to expand to $335 billion dollars by 2025, blockchain is anticipated to revolutionize and expand peer to peer interactions (Lundy, 2016), particularly as consumers become more comfortable and reliant on the internet for consumer activity (Glaser, 2017).

However, most assessments of the scope of cryptocurrency indicate significant limits in its global use: a 2019 estimate suggests adoption is limited to 3% of the global population (CMS Law, 2019). Users of cryptocurrency remain comprised of unique population subsets, ranging from those lacking access to financial institutions in the case of Stellar's Lumens (XLM) to the more frequently identified investors and speculators in specialized currency and financial markets. Obstacles to the broader adoption of cryptocurrencies include a failure to understand and trust the underlying blockchain technology integral to its function. In the decade following the introduction of blockchain as a concept, its seemingly limitless potential applications are increasingly eclipsed by discussions of a failure to realize adoption on a broad scale (Treibelmaier, 2019). Systematic reviews of blockchain research identify concentrated discussion on (1) the technological challenges and opportunities of blockchain technology and (2) the transformative potential in applications ranging from tourism to voting and supply chain management (e.g., see Hughes et al., 2019).

Why is blockchain technology, particularly in the use of cryptocurrencies, experiencing adoption that significantly lags behind its technological potential? Large scale adoption of blockchain is often thought to be limited by negative public perceptions (Hawlitschek, Notheisen, & Tuebner, 2018; Hillman & Rauchs, 2017), largely conditioned on a lack of trust. Precedents to this study identify knowledge-based trust (understanding of technology) as a key determinant of use of new technologies (e.g. Lin, 2011). Though attitudes are identified as key to adoption decisions (Kietzmann & Archer-Brown, 2019), few, if any, empirical evaluations consider the specific information environment that effectively promotes or reduces the willingness to use blockchain. Our study remedies the gap in research by conducting a survey experiment focused on understanding how different, commonly encountered messages influence the openness to replacing the US dollar with a cryptocurrency. Among other findings, a key result suggests that messages including details about the security framework of blockchain technology increases openness to the use cryptocurrencies: explaining blockchain to a general audience using short messages is possible and it is persuasive. Further, we evaluate the social groups most likely to be open to cryptocurrencies. We find that social groups closer to the margins of the dominant economic, social and political institutions are most open to cryptocurrency adoption.

2 'All Money Is Made of Trust'—Yuval Harari, 2015[1]

Symbolic systems of exchange or value, such as currency, are predicated on trust.[2] The challenge experienced by cryptocurrencies in contrast to physical currencies, is that this trust relies on an understanding of blockchain technology and the ability of cryptocurrency to "compete" with other value based systems of exchange. Despite complex and transparent verification systems, including the ability to view any and all recorded transactions, individuals may lack familiarity with how blockchain's distributed ledgers work. The existing large literature on trust and blockchain primarily focuses on the technical vulnerability and design of the technology—information salient to experts, but not to the average potential adopter (e.g. see Angelis & da Silvia, 2019; Hughes et al., 2019). Very limited examinations of changing norms or attitudes necessary for the adoption of cryptocurrencies in social, legal, economic or other contexts exist (Hawlitschek et al., 2018). Expanding cryptocurrency will require two key facets of individual trust: first, individuals must trust the technology cryptocurrencies utilize, in addition, individuals must trust the monetary unit and system of exchange in order to commit their individual resources and utilize the currency.

In strong financial systems, individuals expect that currency will retain value within a set range of variation, allowing for economic transactions ranging from purchases, to wages, to investment, and savings.[3] The modern monetary economy relies on the strength of government regulation and institutions, and ultimately, individual confidence or trust, in their function (Alesina & La Ferra, 2002; Arrow, 1972). Numerous institutional remedies to support confidence in a currency exist, ranging from currency boards to exchange rate regimes: today these are nearly all built on a scaffolded structure of trust in foreign currencies or a selection of financial instruments rather than a prescribed connection to hard assets such as gold. Trust, in this case, is understood as both confidence in a political system for the regulation of the economy and perceptions of continued performance of financial institutions (Hetherington, 2005; Newton, 2007). Financial crises have profound impacts on trust in central banks: the 2008 economic downturn resulted in a report of only 27% of individuals polled in the US trusting the financial system, falling significantly below a previously reported cross national median of 55% reported by Gallup (Jacobe, 2002; Sapienza & Zingales, 2015). Established stable currencies

[1] Notable quote from a December 30, 2015 interview with Economist Yuval Harari on the ECON TALK Podcast December 30, 2015 on a return to the gold standard.

[2] Even asset backed currencies, for example adherence to a gold or other standard, require confidence in institutional transparence and enforcement of and maintenance of the codified standard. Recent currency crises, for example the 1997 Asian financial crisis, occurred in large part due to regulatory failures coupled with inadequate foreign reserve holdings. The crisis emerged as a lack of trust became widespread rather than as a function of fundamental adjustments in macro-economic structures.

[3] Future work examining predispositions to risk may also inform attitude formation surrounding blockchain and cryptocurrencies.

like the Euro or the US dollar demonstrate variance in public trust across countries over time—suggesting that an individual's overall evaluation of government and institutional performance fundamentally impact perceptions of monetary stability and support of a country's financial institutions (Eurobarometer, 2019; Kaelberer, 2007). This is particularly salient for currencies like the Euro, where member states lack overarching political control over financial instruments. Currency unions often reflect changing preferences among members: for example, a renegotiated agreement between former French colonies in African and France last year resulted in the CFA Franc, a French backed currency used by eight West African and six Central African countries, restructuring currency governance, renaming the unit and removing reserves and minimizing the role of France in maintaining value (Hoije, 2019).

This logic of trust is consistent across transactional contexts outside national monetary structures. For example, community currency programs, where local (municipal) currency rewards civic engagement and volunteering and accepted at town facilities or participating vendors, can facilitate relationships and strengthen networks (Richey, 2007; Seyfang, 2004; Izumi, 2002). With over 400 community currencies utilized throughout Japan, the inability to convert or use currency outside of municipal boundaries has not limited the trust associated with localized adoption in successful cases (Richey, 2007). In its continued use and reinforcement, community currencies both build generalized trust and reflect existing trust in local institutions (Richey, 2007).[4] In sum, trust in financial practice appears to be a consequence of repeated interactions and observation over time (Abramson, 1983; Newton, 2001, 2007; Newton & Norris, 2000; Hetherington, 2005). Similar patterns of trust are demonstrated consistently cross nationally, with trust identified as both consequence of and precursor to economic stability (Citrin & Green, 1986; van der Meer, 2017).

The uneven extension of access to banking and financial services and instruments across a population results in limitations for financially excluded populations to realize gains and access government services and economic opportunity; expanded financialization is a key way in which governments facilitate engagement and become relevant to their populations (for an extensive discussion see Herbst, 2000). Limited financialization can result in the reliance on alternative financial instruments, as financially excluded populations fail to benefit from institutions, regulation, and decreased transaction costs associated with government issued currency and regulated banking systems (Levi, 1998). Alternatives, existing in parallel with a formal monetary system, can emerge as substitutes for government issued currency. Empirically, this is observed in the use of mobile phone credits issued by Vodaphone's platform M-PESA, which functions as a parallel system of value-based exchange and savings in a number of East African countries. M-PESA's mobile phone credits comprise a substitute value-based systems of exchange, where

[4] Indeed, Japan's community currency programs were initiated in an effort to stimulate expanded social capital and civic engagement. While similar efforts have occurred in the UK and United States, the expansive nature and investment in community currencies is substantially more established in Japan (Izumi, 2002).

M-PESA users load credits (minutes of mobile phone time) purchased from a vendor onto their mobile phone account and can store or transfer credits for purchase or payment via text message—the platform requires a Vodaphone SIM card with users paying a fee per transaction (Hughes & Lonie, 2007). This use emerged as adaptation rather than by design; willingness to use M-PESA credits as a substitute for currency is based on both understanding of the use of mobile phone technology and incentives for efficiency encompassed by mobile phone transfers. M-PESA expands "banking" access to large populations lacking access to other secure banking or credit services.

Newton (2001) notes that trust is more likely to reflect an individual's access to benefits and services than be determined by individual characteristics such as political orientation, income, education, age, or race, observing that most societies have "winners" who are more likely to benefit from institutions and systems and are consequently more likely to trust them (such as currency and banking systems) and "losers" who do not. It is probable that those who lack access to or benefits from existing employment and financial systems are more open to alternative options such as the use and exchange of mobile phone credits as in the case of the widespread adoption of M-PESA in East Africa, or other forms of economic exchange including, possibly, cryptocurrency. Even in large economies where banking access is substantially supported, such as the United States, the Federal Reserve (2019) estimates in 2017 that over one-fifth of residents lacked full access to banking services. For those lacking bank accounts or credit cards, typical activities such as cashing a check, obtaining a pre-paid debit card, transferring money, or paying bills is costly and associated with a range of accompanying fees and requires additional time (Congressional Research Service, 2019). Barriers to obtaining fee-free bank accounts include a lack of credit history (more common among those with less education, immigrants, and those lacking co-signors), lacking a minimum daily balance, and reliance on sporadic and contract-based income, where regular deposits from an employer may be sporadic (Ibid). Financial exclusion, then, is likely to be characterized by lower levels of trust in monetary institutions and higher levels of openness to alternatives such as cryptocurrencies.

3 The Importance of Trust and Knowledge in Technological Adoption

A structural disadvantage in existing financial marketplaces alone is insufficient to prompt the adoption of a new system of value-based exchange and/or technological process. Why individuals choose to utilize a new platform or technology is a subject of substantial scholarship (e.g. see Venkatesh, Morris, Davis, & David, 2003). Most studies, however, review technological adoption as an extension of an existing service, for example the choice to use mobile banking compared to traditional banking services (e.g. Xiong, 2013). However, even studies examining this transition identify both perceived value and trust as significant factors motivating adoption (Ibid).

In most instances, individuals are choosing a service from an already known provider, in contrast to existing cryptocurrencies utilizing blockchain technology. A perhaps more appropriate parallel to understanding trust through networks and reputation is found in peer-to-peer based platforms that characterize the sharing economy.

Iterated trust is integral in the logic and design of peer-to-peer based platforms, where reputation and networks are critical to exchange and function. Services such as Air BnB, the use of rideshare services such as Lyft or Uber, or even Ebay or Etsy for the purchase and sale of goods rely on trust and reputation. These horizontal platforms facilitate the exchange of goods and services and may also encourage meaningful social connections through the reputation building and information sharing facets they require (ter Humme, Ronteltap, Guo, Corten, & Buskens, 2018). Requiring trust between both peers and interfaces, online engagement in the procurement of these services is conditioned by knowledge of transactional processes and trust in the interface (Gefen, 2002).

Hawlitschek et al. (2018) argue that while blockchain offers the potential to supplant shared economy platforms, "*it may require trust in an interface or technology and understanding to enjoy widespread adoption*" (pg. 60). A common and consistent theme in discussions surrounding the widespread adoption of blockchain technology is the assertion that increased knowledge and understanding of the technology is a critical element in facilitating expanded use (e.g. Hawlitschek et al., 2018; Kietzmann & Archer-Brown, 2019; Klarin, 2020). Unfortunately, available existing research on attitudes toward cryptocurrency adoption are largely inferred through limited yet thoughtful inferences from studies of share economies (Hawlitschek, 2018), based on substantial evaluation of existing literature on blockchain (Hawlitschek et al., 2018), or based on game theoretic applications (Roppelt, 2019).

An understanding of the attributes that characterize technological adoption, particularly for substantially new technologies, has significant implications for the adoption of cryptocurrency and acceptance of blockchain. Understanding how technology works is often a requirement for individuals in choosing online compared to face to face transactions (Gefen, 2002; Lin, 2011) and in transactions relying on automated or technological functions (Muir & Moray, 1996). Studies of ecommerce identify a positive relationship between knowledge surrounding online purchasing and trust in making online purchases (Wang, Chen, & Jiang, 2009). Online purchasing, particularly within peer to peer platforms carries higher uncertainty than conventional retail purchases (Li, Dong, & Chen, 2012). In studies examining why individuals eschew online financial platforms such as mobile banking systems, a lack of security, privacy, and confidence in systems are typically reasons associated with "opting out" (Lee & Chung, 2009; Lin, 2011). Trust in online environments is required in terms of both the transaction and in terms of the technology (Bart et al., 2005). In the following section, we detail existing work on the relationship between trust and technological adoption.

Innovation diffusion theory lends insight into challenges associated with the widespread adoption of blockchain technology and individual attitudes toward cryptocurrencies (Rogers, 1995), identifying two key conditions for individual willingness to adopt new technology: (1) knowledge based trust in the technology (Agarwal & Prasad, 1997; Lin, 2011; Moore & Benbasat, 1991; Papies & Clement, 2008; Tan, Thoen, & Ramanathan, 2001; Teo & Pok, 2003), and (2) the ease and advantage of using the new technology. Research on the adoption of mobile banking platforms informs probable determinants of cryptocurrency adoption across each of these dimensions (Venkatesh, Thong, & Xu, 2012).

Mayer, Davis, and Schoorman (1995) define knowledge based trust as a composite of three attributes: competence (the ability of the product to fulfill its anticipated function), benevolence (identification of the provider of the service as having good intentions), and integrity (that the provider of financial services is making agreements in good faith). Studies of mobile banking platforms suggest that a primary driver of non-adoption includes concerns surrounding security in transactions (Luarn & Lin, 2005). Prior work also indicates that trust and understanding decrease perceptions of risk in business transactions when uncertainty is present (Corriatore, Kracher, & Wiedenceck, 2003). Additional work suggests that the trust relationship between peer to peer or business to business transactions functions the same way, and does not require distinction (Li et al., 2012). Extensions of theories of technological adoption, for example the significant scholarship on the Universal Theory of the Acceptance and Use of Technology specifies that individually specific attributes (age, gender, education) moderate the effect of relative ease and benefit (along with a series of other characteristics) in technological adoption (Venkatesh et al., 2003). Our integration of individual trust attitudes from the public opinion literature provide more granular evaluations on why these individual attributes may result in differential openness to the adoption of cryptocurrencies, both as financial instruments and why the knowledge environment matters.

The spread of technological innovations occurs when technological innovation increases efficiency, quality, or offers expanded access to a service (Baptista, 1999; Stoneman, 1985; Stoneman & Battisi, 2010). Industries transfer technology as improved efficiencies derived from technological innovation increase competitive advantages (Stoneman, 1985). Consequently, the diffusion or distribution of technology can take the form of technology transfer across industries or individual adoption and use of the technology (Baptista, 1999). In the case of cryptocurrencies, technology has made small inroads within the fiscal and financial services industry with some limited extension to supply chain management (e.g. Ripple's XRP). This limited adoption has occurred despite clear efficiencies accompanying cryptocurrency use, realized in the form of eliminating currency exchange fees and transaction costs incurred in the use of monetary asset transfers.

Rapid adoption of new technology occurs the most readily when the technology offers access to a previously inaccessible service (Kietzmann & Archer-Brown, 2019). The only salient example we are aware of in the adoption of cryptocurrency lies with Stellar, a non-profit organization focused on increasing financial inclusion and providing banking to individuals lacking access. Stellar has partnered with the software company Oradian to support rural microfinance in Nigeria to those lacking access to alternate financial service provision (Ianskti & Lakhani, 2017). Stellar's platform uses an open source payment protocol that allows instantaneous transfers across currencies and across borders through its established cryptocurrency, Lumens. This has reshaped access to cash transfers and remittances in rural Nigeria, where previously remittances or cash payments had to be made in person (Shapshak, 2016). Adoption of this technology within the target population has been widely successful, reducing transaction costs and using a convertible cryptocurrency unit.

The utilization of private cryptocurrency (Lumens) or proxy system of exchange (M-PESA) are broadly facilitated by a lack of access to viable alternatives in existing financial service provision. While the lack of access facilitated widespread adoption, decreasing knowledge barriers and/or the utilization of familiar interfaces such as local microfinance institutions may also be critical factors in adoption (Nambisan & Wang, 2009). Adoption of alternative systems of economic exchange where access and alternatives exist is significantly more complex. Even when technologies offer advantages, in the presence of alternatives, knowledge-based trust in the technology or platform can be key to its adoption (Gefen, 2002; Hawlitschek et al., 2018; Laforet & Li, 2005; Lee & Chung, 2009; Lin, 2011).

These two salient case studies, M-PESA and Stellar are predicated by a gap in access to alternate services. While these perspectives are useful, they imperfectly inform determinants of openness to the adoption of cryptocurrencies and blockchain technology in locations like Europe or the United States. While studies of mobile banking inform our analysis, the public conversations surrounding the use of cryptocurrency and blockchain technology engage both a new technology for verification (blockchain's distributed ledger technology) and application (the substitution of a banking platform with peer to peer exchange in economic transactions). In contrast to mobile banking, where the majority of adopters are familiar with the institution providing the service or the technology, knowledge-based trust may be difficult to formulate.

4 Trust, Communication Environments and Individual Attitudes

The communication environment and nature of discussion surrounding complex technological issues is critical in individuals formulating responses to technology—ranging from adoption choices to risk perception (e.g. see Lin, 2011 in the regarding mobile banking; de Bruijin & Janssen, 2017 conveying cybersecurity threats, among others). When complex or unfamiliar technology or processes are involved in discussions of technology, describing the process of how the technology works can be important (Dolnicar, Hurlimann, & Nghiem, 2010). In the case of technological adoption such as mobile banking, both trialability through the demonstrated adoption by peers and demonstrated use facilitate widespread understanding and adoption of the technology. Because blockchain technology is foundational, resulting in the substitution of an entire system rather than a single product or application, the socio-technological element of adoption is also complex. Finally, the range of issues associated with the adoption of blockchain technology featured in the popular press and business news is largely unexamined (Shilkov, 2018).

Common concerns highlighted in discussions of cryptocurrency adoption and blockchain technology include a range of identified challenges ranging from concerns associated with movement away from government regulation to the support of illicit activity. The following section briefly outlines each concern and the potentially relevant trust environment associated with its implementation.

One frequent concern, or advantage, associated with current cryptocurrency is the reality that it is not controlled by a central government authority. We consider (in treatment 2) whether discussing the ability of governments to influence value, typically through inflationary monetary policy, may influence openness to substitution of government issued currency with cryptocurrencies (e.g. Elwell, 2013; Shilkov, 2018). Based on significant evidence noted earlier, we expect substantial variance in trust in central banks (Jacobe, 2002; Sapienza & Zingales, 2015).

A second concern associated with cryptocurrency use includes the security of blockchain technology. The United States and many countries offer deposit insurance for registered and certified banks through institutions like the Federal Deposit Insurance Corporation and National Credit Union Administration. Critiques of blockchain security are focused on a lack of understanding of the distributive ledger technology and the reality that at least for current cryptocurrencies, individuals act as their own banks outside the existing financial system. We consider the substantial literature on knowledge-based trust to identify if providing brief information about blockchain technology influences openness to its adoption in treatment 3 (Lin, 2011).

A practical consideration is the limited ability to currently use cryptocurrencies outside of coin exchanges. While several companies do accept Bitcoin, there are limited applications where individuals can utilize cryptocurrency in regular exchange. With noted exceptions such as the industrial adoption of Ripple's XLM in supply chain management (allowing the avoidance of exchange rates) and Stellar's Lumens for financial inclusions, use remains limited. This is addressed as a concern for adoption in treatment 4.

An additional issue associated with any currency adoption outside of legal tender is the potential for its use in illicit activity. While this has largely been confined in practice to alternative financial instruments such as prepaid visa cards in drug trafficking, large discussions focus on the legal risks to cryptocurrency users inviting additional scrutiny for its potential to support crime (Reiff, 2019; FBI, 2012; FinCen, 2013). This potential apprehension is addressed in treatment 5.

Finally, we consider the volatility in cryptocurrency value. One characteristic of the media coverage of Bitcoin features its dramatic rise and fall in value since its introduction in 2008. This newsworthy volatility does not conform to a core condition for a viable currency, a stable store of value. Several economists warn of asset bubbles associated with Bitcoin specifically (Joshi, 2020), which may hurt pro-adoption attitudes. We consider volatility in treatment 6.

In the subsequent sections, we evaluate how messages surrounding common concerns of cryptocurrency in comparison to the US dollar influence support for cryptocurrency adoption (Joshi, 2020; Shilkov, 2018). To our knowledge, our survey experiment offers the first investigation into attitudes toward the replacement of a national fiat currency with cryptocurrency within the US.

5 Methods and Data

To understand better the nature of public support for adopting cryptocurrencies, our research design is structured around two key objectives. Our first research objective is to assess how common contexts in which cryptocurrencies are publicly debated influence individuals' support for the replacement of the U.S. dollar with cryptocurrencies. To accomplish this goal we consider five distinct contexts that frequently compare cryptocurrencies to the U.S. dollar (e.g., see Shilkov, 2018): the centralization and control of the money supply; the safety of deposits; the degree of acceptance as a medium of exchange; the potential for use in illicit activity; and the stability of value. We attempted to reproduce the common discussion points in each of the above contexts. Because our goal was to assess how common discussion contexts influence cryptocurrency adoption attitudes, we prioritized trying to succinctly replicate the various common debates rather than describe in detail the technical characteristics of blockchain or central banking tools such as nuances related to open market operations. This also explains why we chose to use Bitcoin as an example of 'cryptocurrency' in our experimental design. Multiple reviews of the literature on blockchain demonstrate that nearly 1/3 of publications relate to Bitcoin and cryptocurrencies (Hughes et al., 2019). Bitcoin is indisputably the most widely featured cryptocurrency and has received exhaustive international media coverage.

Consequently, the use of Bitcoin as an example makes sense in framing questions surrounding cryptocurrency for a wide audience that may not recognize any other cryptocurrency or be familiar with the term cryptocurrency. Our second key research objective is to assess the types of people (social and demographic groups) that are most and least supportive of the transition from the U.S. dollar to a cryptocurrency. In summary, our research is designed to 1) assess how different messaging contexts influence support for cryptocurrencies, and 2) evaluate the association between societal groups and support for widespread cryptocurrency adoption.

To accomplish the two research objectives, an experiment was embedded into a 2018 U.S. national survey, with respondents randomly assigned to a control group or one of five treatment conditions that exposed the respondents to messages designed to capture the common debates contrasting the U.S. dollar and cryptocurrencies. YouGov, a leading online polling firm, conducted the nationally representative, matched, online survey. YouGov maintains an online panel of over one million individuals in the USA and uses their matching methodology to create nationally representative surveys. The 3000 respondents were matched to an appropriate sampling frame on gender, age, race, education, and political predispositions. The frame primarily was constructed using the 2010 American Community Survey. Data on political characteristics were matched to this frame using the November 2010 Current Population Survey and the 2007 Pew Religious Life Survey. Individuals take YouGov surveys online and are paid for participation. YouGov's survey methodology has been shown to be as or more accurate than traditional survey research firms (Rivers, 2016).

All randomly assigned treatments begin with the prefix below as well as *one* of the different context messages or the control group as seen in T1–T6. Note that T1 refers to the control group that does not include any context message for the respondent to read before answering a question about cryptocurrency.[5] For clarity, only the bolded text below was included in the survey.

We now have some questions about internet based cryptocurrencies like Bitcoin. Please carefully consider the following information.

T1: 'No message' control group

T2: The centralization and control of the money supply

The US dollar went off the gold standard decades ago, which means that the US dollar is not backed by gold. Today the dollar's value comes from people's faith in the dollar. The Federal Reserve, the central bank of the United States, has various tools for changing the money supply. The US dollar tends to lose buying power through inflation because the Federal Reserve has increased the supply of US dollars over the decades.

Bitcoin is not regulated by a central bank or other central authority. Cryptocurrencies like Bitcoin have a limited supply; for example, no more than 21 million Bitcoins will ever exist. Like the US dollar, Bitcoin's value is determined by the marketplace. Unlike the US dollar, no central authority will ever increase the supply of Bitcoins.

T3: The safety of transactions and deposits

Deposits of US dollars in US banks are insured by the FDIC, which was established during the Great Depression by the federal government to restore confidence in US banks. If a US bank fails, people with deposits in that bank don't lose their money.

Cryptocurrencies like Bitcoin are not insured by the FDIC nor held in banks. Instead Bitcoin uses ground-breaking blockchain technology that is considered extremely safe. Bitcoin transactions not only use cryptography but also are transparently stored across many computers making manipulation impossible.

[5] While a null (no message) treatment group is commonly employed as a baseline control group in experimental designs, different and relevant information could be gleaned by using a different control category. For example, a full message, using all of the information could be used as the control category. This could help understand how a fully engaged message would compare to some of the more narrowly targeted arguments. One limitation of using text in a survey as the treatments, as we do, is that messages should be short in length to avoid discontinuation of participation in the survey instrument. This could be an area for future research

T4: The degree of acceptance as a medium of exchange

The US dollar is the most widely used currency throughout the world. Cryptocurrencies, like Bitcoin are not accepted in nearly as many places as the US dollar. But cryptocurrencies are increasingly accepted for payment. Many mainstream businesses like Microsoft, Expedia and Subway now accept Bitcoin as payment.

T5: Potential for use in illicit activity

Cash transactions using the US dollar have long been used to avoid paying taxes to the US federal government. Cryptocurrencies, like Bitcoin may make it easier for these activities to occur because Bitcoin's decentralized blockchain technology places Bitcoin transactions beyond the reach of government-run financial systems.

T6: The stability of value

Although the US dollar has declined in purchasing power when viewed over many decades, dramatic swings in the value of the US dollar are extremely rare. Cryptocurrencies, like Bitcoin, have had enormous changes in value over a short period of time. This makes it hard to know how much a Bitcoin is worth from day to day and makes the trading of cryptocurrencies attractive to speculators. Proponents of cryptocurrencies like Bitcoin suggest that as the currency matures, the value will become much more stable.

After receiving one of the above randomly assigned treatments, respondents then were asked the following, which represents the dependent variable (percent of the sample in each category in parentheses):

We would be better off if a cryptocurrency like Bitcoin replaced the US dollar as the most widely used currency in the world.

Strongly agree (4.0%)
Agree (6.2%)
Neither Agree nor disagree (25.8%)
Disagree (20.7%)
Strongly disagree (43.3%)

Embedding randomized experiments in a nationally representative survey has distinct advantages. Because the experiments use a nationally representative sample for the subject pool, rather than a narrower pool of subjects (e.g., college students), the results of the analysis display a high degree of external validity. Moreover, because exposure to the stimulus is randomly assigned, rather than self-reported by the individual, and because the control results from randomized assignment to experimental groups, rather than solely from a list of control variables, the results should display a high degree of internal validity. However, revealed attitudes have limitations when what we probably most care about is behavior. Future studies should consider field experiments and other methodologies that capture how different messages and framing influence actual behavioral propensities.

A danger of all randomized experiments is that they may draw spurious conclusions about the relationships between variables if by chance the treatment groups over-represent individuals with certain characteristics that relate to the dependent variable. To protect against this possibility, we used a regression-based approach to interpreting the experiment. We modeled the dependent variable (degree of support for cryptocurrency to replace the US dollar) with dummy variables for each of the treatment groups as well as various variables for demographic and political characteristics. Statistically significant dummy variables representing the treatment groups imply that relative to the control group, exposure to the different messages influence individuals' perceptions about whether cryptocurrencies should replace the U.S. dollar. Ordered logistic regression is the appropriate methodological choice for our models since the five response categories range from strongly agree to strongly disagree. This methodological approach, which includes independent variables representing the treatments as well as controls for demographics, has another key advantage. Because the treatment conditions are included in the model, the demographic variable coefficients will represent the overall independent association between the control variable and support for cryptocurrencies replacing the U.S. dollar. This allows for estimating the independent association between social groups and support for cryptocurrency adoption. As is common in public opinion research, these demographic and predispositional variables include age, employment status, education, gender, racial or ethnic categories, voter/nonvoter, political ideology and presidential approval (i.e. Bafumi & Shapiro, 2009).

6 Results

We begin with the principal experimental results, which randomly assign respondents to different treatments. The treatments include messages that capture one dimension of the popular debate between cryptocurrencies and the US dollar; this primes the respondent to think about cryptocurrencies in the context of the specific debate and allows us to identify the arguments that most encourage support for cryptocurrency adoption. In other words, using this technique we can identify the arguments that most influence support or opposition to replacing the U.S. dollar with cryptocurrency. Table 6.1 displays the results from the ordered logistic regression analysis. The treatment coefficients are relative to the control group that received no priming message. The dependent variable response categories are ordered in a meaningful sequence, with higher scores representing greater opposition to replacing the U.S. dollar with a cryptocurrency.

T2 has a negative, statistically significant coefficient. Exposure to this treatment, relative to the control, associates with greater support for cryptocurrencies relative to the U.S. dollar. This suggests that support for cryptocurrencies increases when respondents are exposed to a message describing how the Federal Reserve has control over the supply of the U.S. dollar and that no central authority or other mechanism will change the supply of cryptocurrencies like Bitcoin. For most economists,

Table 6.1 Ordered logit models of opposition to cryptocurrencies replacing U.S. dollar

Variable	Coefficient (standard error)	First difference
Randomized groups		
T1: Control group		
T2: Money supply	**−0.476 (0.163)**	**−10.1**
T3: Safety of transactions	**−0.367 (0.161)**	**−7.8**
T4: Medium of exchange	−0.069 (0.164)	
T5: Illicit activity	−0.117 (0.167)	
T6: Stability of value	−0.015 (0.159)	
Age groups		
18–34		
35–45	0.128 (0.147)	
45–54	**0.440 (0.149)**	**9.7**
55–64	**0.600 (0.139)**	**13.4**
65+	**1.042 (0.152)**	**23.5**
Women	**−0.211 (0.096)**	**−4.6**
Education level		
No high school		
High school	0.176 (0.206)	
Some college	0.294 (0.206)	
College	**0.563 (0.223)**	**12.2**
Post-grad	**0.563 (0.246)**	**12.2**
Employed	0.037 (0.019)	
Racial/ethnic group		
White		
African American	**−0.960 (0.119)**	**−20.6**
Latino	**−0.697 (0.129)**	**−15.4**
Other	−0.163 (0.184)	
Political ideology		
Liberal		
Moderate	−0.197 (0.152)	
Conservative	0.353 (0.251)	
Pres. Trump approval	−0.089 (0.056)	
Non-voter	**−0.461 (0.121)**	**−10.1**
N	2300	
Prob of chi-square	0.000	

Bold indicates statistical significance. $P < 0.05$ (two tailed test)
First difference = percentage point change in 'strongly disagree' that cryptocurrency should replace U.S. dollar

though certainly not all, the ability of central banks to inflate or deflate the money supply is seen as a critical tool in regulating economies (e.g. Arrow, 1972) but for individuals, the supply stability of the described cryptocurrency may be an attractive feature. This conforms to the classic "public goods problem;" although countries and the overall economy may benefit from central banks controlling the money supply, typically through inflationary policies that make it easier for governments to pay their debts or stimulate the economy, individuals have an incentive to hold currencies that retain their value. This result suggests that Bitcoin's reputation as 'digital-gold' increases its appeal. Evaluating the first difference's column shows that the impact of exposure to a message describing control over the money supply has a substantial influence on attitudes; relative to the control group, exposure to the money supply treatment decreases strong opposition to replacing the U.S. dollar with a cryptocurrency by 10.1% points. This finding is wholly consistent with prior public opinion research surrounding approval of Central Banks and the Federal Reserve; these institutions experience variable trust based on perceived economic performance and regulatory efficacy (Jacobe, 2002; Sapienza & Zingales, 2015).

The coefficient for T3 is negative and statistically significant. Exposure to this treatment, relative to the control, associates with greater willingness to adopt cryptocurrencies. Support for cryptocurrencies is higher when respondents are exposed to descriptions of how FDIC insurance protects U.S. dollar bank deposits and how blockchain technology protects the security of transactions and deposits for cryptocurrencies. This result is important because it shows that simple and brief explanations of the key technology facilitating transactions and recordkeeping for cryptocurrencies can influence attitudes towards widespread adoption. The attitudinal impact of exposure to a message describing the safety features of blockchain is substantial; relative to the control group, exposure to the blockchain treatment decreases strong opposition to replacing the US dollar with a cryptocurrency by 7.8% points. This finding is consistent with the substantial body of literature focused on both knowledge-based trust demonstrated across models of technological adoption (Davis, 1985; Venkatesh et al., 2003), and Innovation Diffusion Theory (Rogers, 1995).

The final three treatments address common potential downsides to adoption of cryptocurrencies, seeming to favor the US dollar; the dollar is much more widely accepted and is a comparatively more stable store of value over the short term. We expected these conditions to push attitudes towards keeping the U.S. dollar dominance but these contexts were not efficacious in influencing attitudes. This result suggests that cryptocurrencies may be resilient to some of the criticisms commonly leveled against them.

Exposure to T4, the relative degree of acceptance of the US dollar and cryptocurrencies as a medium of exchange, had no significant effect on openness to cryptocurrency adoption. In models of individual willingness to adopt technology (highlighted in the previously discussed treatment), relative ease of use and comparative advantage of adoption are highly motivating factors in determining individual use (Lin, 2011; Laforet & Li, 2005; Lee & Chung, 2009). In offering Bitcoin as an alternative to the dollar, albeit with more limited potential in terms of ease of use, conditions of relative ease and comparative advantage identified as critical to motivate individual behavioral change were not satisfied; this explains why exposure to this treatment did not increase support for cryptocurrencies. But why would exposure to this message not decrease support for cryptocurrency? Perhaps some of the disadvantage may be attenuated by individuals thinking that wider cryptocurrency adoption could quickly snowball the number of outlets using it as a medium of exchange, making this just a short-term concern.

T5 focused on the potential for using the US dollar and cryptocurrencies in illicit activity; it had no statistically significant effect on attitudes. Substantial media attention focuses on the potential for Bitcoin to be used by criminal enterprises—for example—a January 2020 New York Times article discusses the attractiveness of Bitcoin to criminal enterprises with the alarmist headline "Bitcoin has lost steam. But Criminals Still Love it" generating an overall alarmist response. Cross national research on attitudes toward informal economic activity suggests that public opinion surrounding informal market activity is mixed (e.g. Berens & Kemmerling, 2019). With a "shadow economy" in the United States significantly larger than $1 trillion dollars, it is possible that this type of system of financial exchange is equated with largely victimless crimes; when the economy contracts informal work and off the books labor increases for individuals to retain their livelihoods while avoiding taxes. Certainly, attitudes toward the enforcement of labor protections and employment regulation varies across populations, however often it is the poor who benefit most from expanding informal economic activity (Berens & Kemmerling, 2019). While public opinion research suggests that the majority of Americans view tax evasion as morally wrong (71% in one Pew Study), less than half had a favorable view of the IRS (48%), the perceived beneficiaries of tax evasion varies along partisan lines resulting in a conflicting view of "winners and losers" associated with the informal or shadow economy (Motel, 2015).

Finally, Treatment 6 examines the historical degree of short-term stability in the value of the US dollar and cryptocurrencies. Despite highlighting the volatility of Bitcoin value, this treatment also did not have a significant effect. It is possible that acceptance of individual risk associated with the purchase of Bitcoin influenced this result. As with Treatment 4, we can similarly speculate that this volatility is discounted by individuals, who may perceive that the volatility would decrease dramatically upon widespread acceptance of a cryptocurrency as the new dominant medium of exchange.

Next, we turn to the analysis of the demographic and pre-dispositional variables. These results help us understand what demographic, social and political groups are most likely to support replacing the U.S. dollar with a cryptocurrency—particularly those most likely to experience financial exclusion. Each of the demographic variables are entered as a dichotomous variable and are interpreted either relative to the excluded reference category (i.e. the youngest age cohort) or as a stand-alone dummy variable (i.e. nonvoter). The pattern of the age group results is not surprising, relative to the youngest age cohort (18–34), those 65 and older, those 55–64 years and those 45–54 years of age are more likely to oppose replacing the US dollar with a cryptocurrency. However, those 35–45 years old did not have statistically significant differences in opinion compared to the youngest age group. What is perhaps remarkable is the magnitude of the generational effect. The older cohort (65+ years) was almost 25% points more likely to be strongly opposed to replacing the US dollar with a cryptocurrency compared to the youngest age group. The same effect is only about 10% points for those between the ages of 45–54. This result suggests that the strongest resistance to cryptocurrency adoption soon may fade as the oldest cohort shrinks due to generational replacement.

Critics of cryptocurrency conferences or new cryptocurrency leadership teams often point to gender imbalances, with men vastly outnumbering women even relative to other technology sectors (Hao, 2018). Because of this, we expected men to support replacing the US dollar with a cryptocurrency at higher rates than women. What we found was that women, relative to men, were more open to replacing the US dollar with a cryptocurrency. Although the effect size is not particularly large (4.6% point difference), the result suggests that women should not be underestimated as a driver of cryptocurrency adoption in the United States.

The education categories were compared to those without a high school education. What we found was that only those educational groups with a college degree, whether a bachelors or a graduate degree, held different opinions about cryptocurrencies relative to those without a high school education. Both of these college-educated groups opposed replacing the US dollar with a cryptocurrency relative to the no high school group. In addition, the effect of a college degree on this attitude was substantial, with college-educated groups being about 12% points more opposed to replacing the US dollar with a cryptocurrency.

With regards to racial and ethnic groups we had mixed expectations about the relative patterns of support. On the one hand, the overwhelming majority of the most prominent figures in the cryptocurrency field are white men. However, people of color are disproportionately represented in the unbanked population and the banking system has long history of redlining practices that target disadvantaged racial and ethnic groups; for this reason, blockchain technology may be particularly appealing to non-white groups because it offers the ability to impartially transact. What we found was that relative to whites, African Americans and Latinos were significantly more supportive of replacing the US dollar with a cryptocurrency. In addition, the magnitude of the effect was very large, with African Americans and Latinos 20.6 and 15.4% points respectively less likely to oppose cryptocurrencies replacing the US dollar relative to whites.

Voters and nonvoters are distinct across a wide range of characteristics; relative to voters, nonvoters are less likely to follow political news, more likely to feel disempowered, are much more disconnected from community life and are more likely to struggle to meet basic needs (Pew Research Center, 2017). In sort, nonvoters tend to be disconnected and marginalized. Everything else equal, we expected that nonvoters would be more open to the replacement of the US dollar with a cryptocurrency, as nonvoters tend to have weaker connections to major societal institutions. The significant coefficient for nonvoter conforms to this expectation. Nonvoters are about 10% points less opposed to replacing the US dollar with a cryptocurrency. Finally, several variables are not statistically significant, including employment status, political ideology and presidential approval. These findings suggest that, everything else equal, support for the widespread adoption of cryptocurrencies does not align with the standard political characteristics and may not result merely from a lack of economic prospects.

Overall, these patterns are similar to historical technological diffusions and are consistent with innovation diffusion theory. Often, those most advantaged within an existing system have little incentive to adopt new technologies outside of existing structures. Diffusion occurs when adaptation of those technologies is used to transform access (e.g. M-PESA, Lumens). Blockchain technologies are suggested to offer the potential for undermining the existing financial system that has recognized prejudices, one that often impose disproportionate costs on those from traditionally disadvantaged backgrounds.

7 Conclusion

Our study suggests that advocates for the use of blockchain technologies would be well served to consider the inclusion of educational information in efforts to enhance public acceptance of cryptocurrency. Our results are compatible with existing research on overall understandings of trust associated with value-based transactions in formal currency systems and within peer to peer platforms. Comparisons to the existing financial system, including reminders of the fiat nature of the dollar coupled with comparison of cryptocurrency to the existing financial system may be critical in framing messaging. As much of the literature indicates, understanding and knowledge associated with how distributed ledger technology works comprises one of the most important aspects of messaging. However, even though openness increases with knowledge, those benefiting from the existing financial system may be particularly resistant to accepting the shift or substituting government backed currency with an independent cryptocurrency like Bitcoin.

An emerging alternative for the use of blockchain technology for currency includes the development of an asset backed and/or government issued currency. Canada revealed in the fall of 2019 that it is considering adoption a digital currency using blockchain technology to use in conjunction with and ultimately as a substitute for its physical currency (Schwartz, 2019). Advantages to adoption include improved tracking on consumer activities, lack of forgery coupled with stronger verification systems for settlement, and efficiency in tax effort (Ibid), although the proposed digital currency would retain its fiat-based structure and the supply would be subject to government interventions. In contrast, China's cryptocurrency plans are at least rumored to include hard asset backing—either with gold or in combination with other commodities (Elegant, 2019). Whatever the veracity of the Chinese case, this type of virtual currency has the potential to rival the US dollar in the international economy, due to minimized volatility and valuation surety associated with asset backing, decreased transaction costs associated with existing exchange regimes, and protection from the US using these settlement regimes to wield political power. The consequences of this type of shift are evident for a range of commodities and international structures. For example, the valuation of the dollar is supported by both the exchange of dollar denominated commodities trade and in the reserve banking system. Elimination of one or both of these components requires institutional streamlining, likely escalates the cost of US debt, and also forces domestic scrutiny of monetary policy and regulation of the money supply. Either option would displace the dollar from its current dominance in international financial exchange, with subsequent consequences for the US economy, geopolitical influence and standards of living.

At the individual level, our results suggest that those most likely to be open to cryptocurrency adoption are the least advantaged by the existing financial system. Outside of speculative markets or supply chain applications, the only current societally widespread utilization of blockchain technology in cryptocurrency is financial inclusion for the unbanked in Nigeria. While it may appear that this is predominantly a concern of the global south, a recent study places at least 6% of the US population as unbanked with an additional 16% as underbanked (Federal Reserve, 2019). Nearly two fifths of the unbanked population use costly alternative financial instruments, including non-bank provided money orders, wire transfer services, or check cashing services and payday lenders and lack a bank account (Ibid). Those categorized as "underbanked" in the United States also utilize at least one of these services in addition to possessing a high fee checking account. In 2017, the FDIC found that the unbanked comprise 8.4 million households in the United States: major reasons cited for avoiding the banking system included a lack of trust in banks (a little over 30%) and complaints surrounding fees and unpredictable charges (between 20–25% respectively) (Apamm et al., 2018). The majority of unbanked households are characterized as low income and low education, with Latinos and African Americans comprising a larger section of the unbanked than their national population proportions (Federal Reserve, 2019). These are populations most likely to benefit from a reduction in use of a financial structure that is costly in terms of services (e.g. wire transfer services), and are most open to the adoption of cryptocurrencies in our analysis.

As with most technological innovations, first movers in adoption of blockchain distributed ledger technology are likely to be those most obviously benefitting from disruption of the status quo. The possibility of competitors utilizing this technology to challenge a dollar dominant international system (e.g. China) is consistent with the deployment of a foundational technology change. Similarly, those most likely to benefit from alternate financial instruments with reduced fees and transaction costs demonstrate the most openness to cryptocurrency replacement of the US dollar. Because of the established relationship between institutional performance, particularly financial performance, and trust in a system of exchange, these findings are not surprising. As evident in the proliferation and use of peer to peer transactions in the share economy, individual understanding of the nature of technology and systems of exchange are key to adoption; as the technology becomes increasingly familiar and better understood, the likelihood of adoption substantially increases.

This chapter addresses an understudied but important area: what influences attitudes towards the adoption of cryptocurrencies. As with all studies, it has limitations and room for future methodologies and approaches. Technological adoption can move slowly and then quickly and continued and updated assessments would be prudent. This study is a snapshot in time, about a decade after the financial crisis but undertaken prior to the COVID economic shock, with its associated unprecedented central banking operations. This new context may matter, as our work points to the importance of money supply concerns as a driver for positive adoption attitudes. Future work should build upon the attitudinal approach taken here and consider the factors that influence actual behavioral adoption. This could take the form of field experiments or lab-based experiments such as those used in behavioral economics. Ultimately, attitudinal openness is just a precursor to adoption. More than anything else, our study should demonstrate the relevance and insights that can be drawn from using interdisciplinary considerations of blockchain and cryptocurrency adoption.

References

Abramson, P. R. (1983). *Political attitudes in America: Formation and change*. San Francisco, CA: W.H. Freeman.

Agarwal, R., & Prasad, J. (1997). The role of innovation characteristics and perceived voluntariness in the acceptance of information technologies. *Decision Sciences, 28*(2), 557–582.

Alesina, A., & La Ferra, E. (2002). Who trusts others? *Journal of Public Economics, 85*(2), 207–234.

Angelis, J., & da Silvia, E. R. (2019). Blockchain adoption: A value driver. *Business Horizons, 62*, 307–314.

Apamm, G., Burhouse, S., Chu, K., Ernst, K., Fritzdixon, K., Goodstein, R., et al. (2018). *FDIC National Survey of unbanked and Underbanked households*. Washington DC: Federal Deposit Insurance Corporation.

Arrow, K. (1972). Economic welfare and the allocation of resources for invention. In *The rate and direction of inventive activity: Economic and social factors* (National Bureau Committee for Economic Research) (pp. 609–626). Princeton: Princeton University Press.

Bafumi, J., & Shapiro, R. Y. (2009). A new partisan voter. *The Journal of Politics, 71*(1), 1–24.

Baptista, R. (1999). The diffusion of process innovations: A selective review. *International Journal of Business Economics, 6*(1), 107–129.

Bart, Y., Shankar, V., Sultan, F., & Urban, G. L. (2005). Are the drivers and role of online trust the same for all wesbites and consumers? A large scale empirical study. *Journal of Marketing, 69*, 133–152.

Berens, S. Kemmerling, A. (2019). Labor divides, informality and regulation: The public Opinion on labor law in Latin America. *Journal of Politics in Latin America*. Online first.

Citrin, J., & Green, D. P. (1986). Presidential leadership and the resurgence of trust in government. *British Journal of Political Science, 16*(4), 431–453.

CMS Law. (2019). Cryptocurrency as a means of payment. https://cms.law/en/deu/publication/cryptocurrency-as-a-means-of-payment

Congressional Research Service. (2019). *Financial inclusion and credit access policy issues*. Washington, DC. https://fas.org/sgp/crs/misc/R45979.pdf

Corriatore, C. L., Kracher, B., & Wiedenceck, S. (2003). On-line trust: Concepts, evolving themes, a model. *International Journal of Human-Computer Studies, 58*, 737–758.

Davis, F.D. (1985, December 20). A technology acceptance model for empirically testing new end-used information systems: Theory and results. MIT Doctoral Dissertation.

de Bruijin, H., & Janssen, M. (2017). Building cybersecurity awareness: The need for evidence based framing stratgies. *Government Information Quarterly, 34*(1), 1–7.

Dolnicar, S., Hurlimann, A., & Nghiem, L. D. (2010). The effect of information on public acceptance – The case of water from alternative sources. *The Journal of Environmental Management, 91*(6), 1288–1293.

Econ Talk, (2015, October 15). Yuval Harari on Sapiens. Available at: https://www.econtalk.org/yuval-harari-on-sapiens/
Elegant, N.M. (2019, November 1). Why China's digital currency is a 'wake-up call' for the U.S. *Fortune*.
Elwell, C. K. (2013). *Economic recovery: Sustaining U.S. economic growth in a post crisis economy*. Washington, DC: Congressional Research Service.
Eurobarometer. (2019, June 7). Eurobarometer 479 in all the EU member states that have yet to adopt the Euro. European Commission Report.
Federal Bureau of Investigation. (2012, April 24) Bitcoin virtual currency: Unique features present distinct challenges for deterring illicit activity. http://www.wired.com/images_blogs/threatlevel/2012/05/Bitcoin-FBI.pdf
Federal Reserve. (2019, May). Report on the economic well-being of U.S. households in 2018. https://www.federalreserve.gov/publications/report-economic-well-being-us-households.htm
FinCen (Financial Crimes Enforcement Network) (2013). FinCen issues guidelines on virtual currencies and regulatory responsibilities. https://www.fincen.gov/sites/default/files/news_release/20130318.pdf
Gefen, D. (2002). Reflections on the dimensions of trust and trustworthiness among online consumers. *ACM SIGMIS Database, 33*(30), 38–53.
Glaser, F. (2017). Pervasive decentralization of digital infrastructure: A framework for blockchain enabled system use and case analysis. In *Proceedings of the 50th Hawaii International Conference on System Sciences*.
Hao, K. (2018). The first rule of being a woman in crypto is you do not talk about being a woman in crypto. *Quartz*.
Hawlitschek, F. (2018). Trust in the sharing economy: A behavioral perspective on peer to peer markets. Doctoral Dissertation, des Karlsruber Institut fur Technologie Wirtschaftswissschaften.
Hawlitschek, F., Notheisen, B., & Tuebner, T. (2018, May–June). The limits of a trust-free system: A literature review on blockchain technology and trust in the sharing economy. *Electronic Commerce Research & Applications, 29*, 50–63.
Herbst, J. (2000). *States & power Africa: Comparative lessons in authority and control*. Princeton, NJ: Princeton University Press.
Hetherington, M. J. (2005). *Why trust matters: Declining political trust and the demise of American liberalism*. Princeton, NJ: Princeton University Press.
Hillman, G., Rauchs, M. (2017). Cryptocurrency benchmarking study. University of Cambridge Center for Alternative Finance. Available at: https://www.jbs.cam.ac.uk/fileadmin/user_upload/research/centres/alternative-finance/downloads/2017-global-cryptocurrency-benchmarking-study.pdf
Hoije, K. (2019, December 28). Equatorial Guinea leader says French-backed currency is outdated. *Bloomberg*.
Hughes, L., Dwicedi, Y. K., Misra, S. K., Rana, N. P., Raghavan, V., & Akella, V. (2019). Blockchain research, practice and policy: Applications, benefits, limitations, emerging research themes and research agenda. *International Journal of Information Management, 49*, 114–129.
Hughes, N., & Lonie, S. (2007). M-PESA: Mobile money for the "unbanked". *Innovations, Winter & Spring*, 63–81.
Ianskti, M., & Lakhani, K. R. (2017, January–February). The truth about blockchain. Technology. *Harvard Business Review, 95*, 118–127.
Izumi, R. (2002). Trends in community currencies in Japan. *Self Government Research Monthly, 44*(511), 47–58.
Jacobe, D. (2002). EU 5 investors optimistic about U.S. markets. *Gallup*.
Joshi, D. (2020). How secure is cryptocurrency and blockchain technology? Security benefits and issues of DLT. *Business Insider.*
Kaelberer, M. (2007). Trust in the Euro: Exploring the governance of a supra-national currency. *European Societies, 9*(4), 623–642.
Kietzmann, J., & Archer-Brown, C. (2019). From hype to reality: Blockchain grows up. *Business Horizons, 62*, 269–271.

Klarin, A. (2020, July 20). The decade-long cryptocurrencies and the blockchain rollercoaster: Mapping the intellectual structure and charting future directions. *Research in International Business and Finance, 51*.
Laforet, S., & Li, X. (2005). Consumers' attitudes towards online and mobile banking in chain. *International Journal of Bank Marketing, 23*(5), 362–380.
Lee, K. C., & Chung, N. (2009). Understanding factors affecting trust in and satisfaction with mobile banking in Korea: A modified DeLone and McLean's model perspective. *Interacting with Computers, 21*(5), 85–392.
Levi, M. (1998). A state of trust. In V. Braithwaite & M. Levi (Eds.), *Trust & Governance*. New York: Sage.
Li, M., Dong, Z. Y., & Chen, X. (2012). Factors influencing consumption experience of mobile commerce: A study from experiential view. *Internet Research, 22*(2), 120–141.
Lin, H. F. (2011). An empirical investigation of mobile banking adoption: The effect of innovation attributes and knowledge-based trust. *International Journal of Information Management, 31*, 252–260.
Luarn, P., & Lin, H. H. (2005). Toward an understanding of the behavioral intention to use Mobile banking. *Computers in Human Behavior, 21*(6), 340–348.
Lundy, L. (2016). Blockchain and the Sharing Economy 2.0. IBM Developer Works. https://www.ibm.com/developerworks/library/iot-blockchain-sharing-economy/iot-blockchain-sharingeconomy-pdf.pdf.
Mayer, R. C., Davis, J. H., & Schoorman, F. D. (1995). An integrative model of organizational trust. *Academy of Management Review, 20*(3), 709–734.
Moore, G. C., & Benbasat, I. (1991). Development of an instrument to measure the perceptions of adopting an information technology innovation. *Information System Research, 3*(2), 192–222.
Motel, S. (2015, April 10). 5 facts on how Americans view taxes. *Pew Research Center.* https://www.pewresearch.org/fact-tank/2015/04/10/5-facts-on-how-americans-view-taxes/
Muir, B. M., & Moray, N. (1996). Trust in automation: Part II – Experimental studies of trust and human intervention in a process control simulation. *Ergonomics, 39*(3), 429–460.
Nakamoto, S. (2008). Bitcoin: A peer to peer electronic cash system. *Bitcoin.org*.
Nambisan, S., & Wang, Y.-M. (2009). Web technology adoption and knowledge barriers. *Journal of Organizational Computing and Electronic Commerce, 10*(2), 129–147.
Narayanan, A., Bonneau, J., Felten, E., Miller, A., & Goldfefer, S. (2016). *Bitcoin and cryptocurrency technologies: A comprehensive review*. Princeton/Oxford: Princeton University Press.
Newton, K. (2001). Trust, social capital, civil society, and democracy. *International Political Science Review, 22*(2), 201–214.
Newton, K. (2007). Social and political trust. In R. J. Dalton & H. D. Klingemann (Eds.), *Oxford handbook of political behavior*. New York: Oxford University Press.
Newton, K., & Norris, P. (2000). Confidence in public institutions: Faith, culture, or performance? In S. P. Pharr & R. (Eds.), *Disaffected democracies*. Princeton, NJ: Princeton University Press.
Papies, D., & Clement, M. (2008). Adoption of new movie distribution services on the internet. *Journal of Media Economics, 21*(3), 131–157.
Pew Research Center. (2017, September 14). *How 'drop-off' voters differ from consistent voters and nonvoters*. Washington, DC: Pew Research Center.
Reiff, N. (2019). Where is the cryptocurrency industry headed in 2019? *Investopedia.* Updated 24 Jan 2020.
Richey, S. (2007). Manufacturing trust: Community currencies and the creation of social capital. *Political Behavior, 29*, 69–88.
Rivers, D. (2016). Pew research: YouGov consistently outperforms competitors on accuracy. *YouGov.* https://today.yougov.com/topics/finance/articles-reports/2016/05/13/pew-research-yougov
Rogers, E. M. (1995). Diffusion of innovations: Modifications of a model for telecommunications. *Schriftenreihe des Wissenschaftlichen Instituts fur Kommunikationdieste, 17*, 25–38.
Roppelt, J. (2019). Security risks surrounding cryptocurrency usage: A study on the security risks of cryptocurrencies and how security perception affects usage. MA Thesis, University of Twente

Salzman, A. (2019, December 17). Bitcoin peaked 2 years ago. New competition is on the way. *Barron's*.

Sapienza, P., & Zingales, L. (2015). Economic experts versus average Americans. *American Economic Review, 103*(3), 636–642.

Schwartz, Z. (2019, October 15). Bank of Canada exploring digital currency that would replace cash, track how people spend money. *Financial Post*.

Seyfang, G. (2004). Working outside the box: Community currencies, time banks, and social inclusion. *Journal of Social Policy, 33*(1), 49–71.

Shapshak, T. (2016, February 2). Instant money transfer service Stellar launches for Nigeria's Rural Women. Forbes.

Shilkov, A. (2018). Governments and blockchain: The future is now. *Coinpress, 5*(12). https://coinpress.io/future/

Stoneman, P. (1985). Technological diffusion: The viewpoint of economic theory. In *Warwick Economic Research Paper Series* (Vol. 270).

Stoneman, P., & Battisi, G. (2010). The diffusion of new technology. *Handbook of Economics & Innovation, 2*(17), 733–760.

Tan, Y.H., Thoen, W., Ramanathan, S. (2001, June 25–26). E-everything: E-commerce, e-government, e-household, e-democracy. In *14th Bled Electronic Commerce Conference, Conference Proceedings*, Bled.

Teo, T. H., & Pok, S. H. (2003). Adoption of WAP-enabled mobile phones among internet users. *Omega, 31*(6), 483–498.

ter Humme, M., Ronteltap, A., Guo, C., Corten, R., & Buskens, V. (2018). Reputation effects in socially driven sharing economy transactions. *Sustainability, 10*, 1–19.

Treibelmaier, H. (2019). Toward more rigorous blockchain research: Recommendations for writing blockchain case studies. *Frontiers in Blockchain, 2*(3). https://doi.org/10.3389/fbloc.2019.00003

van der Meer, T. (2017). Democratic input, macroeconomic output and political trust. In S. Zmerli & T. van der Meer (Eds.), *Handbook on political trust* (pp. 270–284). Cheltenham/ Northampton, MA.: Edward Elgar Publishing.

Venkatesh, V., Morris, M. G., Davis, G. B., & David, F. D. (2003). User acceptance of information technology: Toward a unified view. *MIS Quarterly, 27*(3), 425–278.

Venkatesh, V., Thong, J. Y. L., Xu, & X. (2012). Consumer acceptance and use of information technolofy: extending the unified theory of acceptance and use of technology. *MIS Quarterly, 36*(1), 157–178.

Wang, C., Chen, C., & Jiang, J. (2009). The impact of knowledge and trust on e-consumers' online shopping activities: An empirical study. *Journal of Computers, 4*(1), 11–18.

Xiong, S. (2013, November 23–24). Adoption of mobile banking model based on perceived value and trust. International Conference on Information Management, Innovation Management and Industrial Engineering.

Kristin Johnson is Associate Professor of Political Science at the University of Rhode Island. There she directs the undergraduate program in International Studies and Diplomacy and the graduate program in International Relations. She is a political economy specialist and has an interest in developing economies, political and economic transitions, civil conflict and resource distribution.

Brian S. Krueger is Professor of Political Science and Associate Dean in the College of Arts and Science at the University of Rhode Island. He has an interest in political participation, public opinion, the impact of new technologies on political behavior and politics, survey research and government domestic monitoring.

Chapter 7
A Framework of Blockchain Technology for Public Management in Brazil

Benedito Cristiano Aparecido Petroni and Mariana Savedra Pfitzner

1 Introduction

Many breakthrough technologies and tools are responsible for data democratization and information widespread between the world population. These have been reducing the importance of national states to rule domestic economies. Some of the technologies are GPS, Artificial Intelligence, 5G, Blockchain and the tools embrace social networks and Internet broadcasters like Youtube and Netflix. When these technologies and tools operate together there is neither distance nor time lag for information sharing. In addition to that, Blockchain enables secure data and information dissemination, making whole production supply chain transactions trustable as well as increasing financial markets opportunities. Gatteschi, Lamberti, Demartini, Pranteda, and Santamaría (2018) suggest in greater details the general uses of Blockchain in the economy:

- **Government**: register citizens' votes, validate public policy or allow autonomous governance systems;
- **Intellectual Property**: ensure the authorship of a document;
- **Internet**: track the registered data in Blockchain;
- **Financial market**: transfer money among parties without depending on banks;
- **Commerce**: register the characteristics of different goods as well as their property, especially luxury goods, reducing fraud, robbery and product piracy;

B. C. A. Petroni
FATEC Jundiaí, São Paulo, Brazil

Universidade Paulista, Jundiaí, São Paulo, Brazil
e-mail: benedito.petroni@fatec.sp.gov.br

M. S. Pfitzner (✉)
Centro Universitário Adventista de São Paulo, São Paulo, Brazil

C. G. Reddick et al. (eds.), *Blockchain and the Public Sector*, Public Administration and Information Technology 36,
https://doi.org/10.1007/978-3-030-55746-1_7

- **Internet of Things (IoT)**: explore intelligent contracts to process automatically data from sensors;
- **Education:** store qualification background and ensure that people do not lie about their professional pathway. Human Resource Managers may use such data stored in the Blockchain to obtain information about candidate's real qualification and competencies.

Blockchain is a form of data existence (Pan et al., 2019) that doesn't require a centralized authority to guarantee transactions credibility. The technology stores information from different computers in the network and this only can be done if there is a consensus in such network (Ølnes, Ubacht, & Janssen, 2017). Blockchain offers non-repudiation of organized events embracing multiple servers under the control of many people in different places. Each of the participants in the network owns a "public account book" containing the registered information of all transactions in the Blockchain (Sullivan & Burger, 2017).

Hence Blockchain is more than a platform for cryptocurrencies. It is a safe way to exchange any type of goods, services and operations (Ahram, Sargolzaei, Sargolzaei, Daniels, & Amaba, 2017). The data traffic is assured by the so-called Smart Contracts, which are a kind of **appendix** of Blockchain technology.

On the one hand, Blockchain applications may validate economic transactions and reduce fraud in public services, production chains and information sharing. On the other hand, it may drastically change the processes and routines in Public Management bringing more transparency and operational efficiency.

This book chapter aims at discussing a potential implementation of Blockchain technology in Public Management, especially in public services provision, considering the Brazilian cases for healthcare and tax refund. These services have been chosen for two main reasons: (1) Availability of primary information, in other words, public servants in charge of these routines were opened to let the authors understand their routines through ethnography; (2) Existence of evidences, coming from secondary information sources, about problems of information asymmetries in healthcare services. The theory of information asymmetries was first developed by George Akerlof in 1970 with the so called "lemons market". It states that an imbalance in information between the parties (buyers and sellers) causes inefficient outcomes in several markets. This theory is also applied in public services reality, where the government owns more and better information than the citizens, leading the latter to make bad choices because of the lack of transparency and citizens' bounded rationality.

Therefore, this book chapter evaluates the major problems of Public Management in Brazil and proposes a technological framework for the usage of Blockchain in order to improve the quality of public services, independently from "subjective" decisions coming from political systems. This framework is based on Business Process Management (BPM) as an analytical tool to depict processes as they are ("as is") and as they will be ("to be"), after the implementation of Blockchain and Smart Contracts.

The Theory of Public Choice (TPC) states that politicians and public servants decide based on self-interest as well as the increase of personal power and department's budget (Mashaw, 2009; Oliveira & Filho, 2017). TPC comes from Economics and, among other themes, it expresses the Agent-Principal problem developed by Jensen and Meckling (1976), which means, the Agent (public servant) will not act in favour of the Principal (citizen) unless the action benefits him/her. The decision-making process in Public Management can also be justified by "Behaviour Economics", that describes individual behaviours as mirrors of cultural backgrounds (Mann & Wüstemann, 2010). As a matter of fact, cultural backgrounds can be well understood through a deep dive into public servant's routines through ethnographic research, supporting TPC's arguments.

The authors of this chapter use a bibliographic research focused on the state of art of Blockchain applications as well as a survey with public agents from local governments, entrepreneurs, students and scientists in Brazil. Ethnographic research was conducted in 02 (two) City Halls in Sao Paulo Province between 2016 and 2019, so that the authors could identify the way a political system operate, the key issues of Public Management and the routines of public servants to deliver public services.

Public Management comprises mandatory routines and procedures to provide public policies and services for the population related to health, education, social security, safety, housing, infrastructure services (garbage, water and sewage management/treatment), mobility and transportation. Some examples of Public Management routines are:

- Document validation (Sullivan & Burger, 2017);
- Development of more robust regulatory compliance frameworks (De Filippi & Hassan, 2016; Engelenburg, Janssen, & Klievink, 2017; Gerstl, 2016);
- Land and property management (Pichel, 2016).

Also, public services' procedures are supposed to regulate the expansion of economic and social activities regarding companies and people. In Brazil, IT systems and data are not integrated, leading to potential errors and fraud during information registration and sharing among public institutions. The widespread of Blockchain will assure correct information sharing between public institutions and requesting companies and persons. With respect to fraud in public administration, Smart Contracts technology can be applied to create secure public records. The use of Smart Contracts applied in specific Blockchain networks in some areas has been presented as a secure solution for recording network transactions, since everything is stored in a digital ledger.

A Smart Contract may have an arbitrary amount of operating conditions or may require no conditions other than its own initialization (Gilcrest & Carvalho, 2018), thereby representing its diversity, different possible means and application modes. Applications using Smart Contracts and Blockchain technologies, if properly configured and legalized, can help public managers mediate and reconcile administrative demands, thus ensuring less bureaucracy in public services as well as more security, integrity, transparency and availability of information.

Recent studies point that by 2025 Blockchain applications will account for 10% of world GDP. The online survey led by the authors suggest that Artificial Intelligence and Blockchain will be the most important technologies in public and private organizations within the next 10 years in Brazil.

Blockchain technology is the new value layer of the Internet, adding the so-called Ts2 trinity - trust, transparency and traceability - to any asset class (information, data and physical goods). Therefore, web transactions can be authenticated, validated, tracked and recorded in a distributed point-to-point digital accounting system (Lima, 2018).

The public sector is acting a little late in building competencies, including legal ones, and just looking at the opportunities to improve operational procedures (Rajamäki & Knuuttila, 2013), rather than paying attention to disruptive technologies such as Blockchain. For such reason, this book chapter analyses some issues on Public Management that can be solved by Blockchain, the state of art of Blockchain, the awareness of Blockchain and a technological framework for Blockchain in Public Management, based on Business Process Management.

After this Introduction, the authors explain the employed method (Methodology) to understand and explore problems of Public Management in Brazil and to build up a scalable technology framework for Blockchain. Thus, we discuss about Blockchain state of art through a deep literature review, the outcomes from the online survey and issues addressed by the ethnographic research (Discussion):

1. Public services in Brazil cannot be totally delivered to the population, which means they are not universal;
2. The lack of integration among public institutions and "subjective" decisions make the provision of public services uncertain.

Finally, the authors propose a Blockchain technology framework to mitigate the malfunctioning of Public Management in Brazil based on Ts2 trinity in healthcare and tax refunding routines (Results). For further research, the authors suggest a comprehensive application, validation and development of this Blockchain technology framework in many processes of Public Management as possible.

2 Methodology

The authors of this chapter have used different materials and methods to propose a technology framework for Blockchain in Public Mmanagement in Brazil. The research method can be summarized in three pillars, namely bibliographic research, ethnography and an online survey. These research methods are normally applied in qualitative research to explore and describe a social phenomenon (Cropley, 2019; Sellitz, Cook, & Wrightsman, 1975).

Moreover, this work was built up by five steps based on the following research question: "What are the main issues and challenges addressed in Public Management that can be solved by Blockchain technology in Brazil?"

In the **discussion session (Steps 1–4)**, we designed the problem and executed the research in three different forms (ethnography, literature review and survey). The ethnographic research, performed in the corridors and meeting rooms of two City Halls in Sao Paulo Province from 2016 to 2019, enabled the authors to understand the dynamics of Public Management, the influence of politics and bureaucracy on servant's routines.

According to Dalmolin, Lopes, and Vasconcellos (2002), ethnography helps researchers discover cultural patterns and social relations in a predetermined environment. Ethnography supposes also that the researchers are participants and co-creators of knowledge. This research method details uncertainty and complexity of micro-level processes like procedures and routines in Public Management. It also reveals hidden issues and people's perspectives beyond rationalization (Murto, Hyysalo, Juntunen, & Jalas, 2020).

In ethnography, the challenge is what to capture and how to capture for latter analysis, however the authors of this chapter have the appropriate knowledge background in economics, Public Management and engineering to observe, catch and ask for the right information.

Authors' prerequisites for such a sophisticated looking in ethnographic research were not only the knowledge background, but also: (a) previous review of all areas of Brazilian law and their Codes (Do all law areas have a Code/Manual? How about Public Management procedures?); (b) understanding of the main public services involved in Public Management routines (What do public servants do? How do they do? Why do they do so?); (c) literature review about the quality of public services in Brazil (How do other researchers evaluate the quality of public services in Brazil?) (*Step 1—Preparation*).

The ethnography consisted of observing behaviors attentively, discovering social relations by asking servants about routines and procedures of Public Management in 03 (three) years, taking notes on logbooks (*Step 2—Problem design*). The authors drove more attention to healthcare services and tax collection/refunding, asking and observing how public servants deliver such services to citizens.

These 02 (two) public services were selected for investigation because of servants' openness to let us research these specific processes as well as the existing evidences of information asymmetries in healthcare services in Brazil.

In addition to ethnography, the authors released an online survey with 30 respondents about breakthrough technologies that could help Brazil relieve its social problems (*Step 3—Survey*). This research raised awareness for the importance of Blockchain in the present decade.

The online survey comprised 05 (five) questions:

1. Type of institution of respondents;
2. Identify the most important technology with more diffusion in Brazil for the next 10 years (2020–2030), regarding its socioeconomic impacts in public and private environments;
3. Point the most required occupation for the next 10 years (2020–2030) in Brazil;
4. Point the most relevant application of Blockchain technology in Brazil considering the next 10 years (2020–2030);
5. Address the most important social challenge in Brazil for the next 10 years (2020–2030) as well as the technology to solve it.

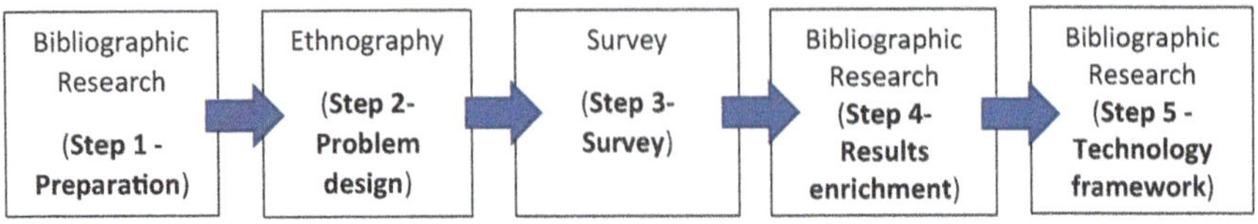

Fig. 7.1 Research method step by step

Through the combination of ethnography and online survey, the main issues and challenges of public administration could be mapped in a comprehensive way in addition to the technologies to cope with them.

The survey has helped authors to understand the most important technologies for the near future in Brazil (2020–2030), the role of Blockchain in Public Management and private organizations as well as the challenges of Brazilian's public services that can be solved *via* breakthrough technologies. These results were enhanced by a bibliographic research about Blockchain usages (*Step 4—Results enrichment*).

Thus, the authors combined the outcomes of the ethnographic research with a bibliographical research about Blockchain technology, its benefits and applications. In the **results session (Step 5)**, this chapter brings a **scalable technology framework** about the appliance of Blockchain technology in Public Management in Brazil, using healthcare services and tax refund as examples (*Step 5—Technology framework*). That means, this scalable framework will either be used in any public services in Brazil or even in external governments (Fig. 7.1).

The Blockchain framework built here is based on BPM, which focus on process description and analysis, comparing the present situation ("as is") with the desired one ("to be").

Herein the authors emphasize issues and problems raised from the survey, ethnographic and bibliographic researches that can be partially overcome through the implementation of Blockchain and Smart Contracts, however the success of the whole solution depends on people's willingness to improve their competencies and deliver better services for the citizens.

3 Discussion

3.1 Steps 1 (Preparation) and 2 (Problem Design): Issues and Challenges of Public Management in Brazil and Ethnographic Outcomes

In Brazil, almost every knowledge field of Law owns its Code with rules and principles just like the Civil Code, Criminal Code, Tax Code, Consumer Defense Code and so on. These Codes entail all norms and principles that strictly follow the Brazilian Constitution and frame human relations in the country. Then, the Union, its member provinces and municipalities establish their local laws derived from such Codes.

They work as practical "all in one" Law Manuals, because their content encompasses everything citizens need to know about "dues" and "rights" for a specific area of human relations. However, Public Management processes are principally based on the Brazilian Tender Law (Law Number 8.666, 1993) (Brazil, 1993) and the Rights of Public Servants (Law Number 8.112, 1990) (Brasil, 1990), which come from the Brazilian Constitution. These two laws concern to public procurement, contracts and human resources management within the public administration. Jurisprudence, doctrines and habits (behaviors) also shape the Brazilian Public Management.

Public Management processes consist of all types of procedures and routines of public servants to: (a) create public policies; (b) deliver public services properly for the population; (c) regulate relations among citizens, organizations and the State.

On the one hand, public policies and services refer to procedures of providing education, social security, public safety, health, infrastructure services (garbage, water and sewage management/treatment), mobility and transportation (a, b). On the other hand, public services' procedures are supposed to inspect and license economic organizations to ensure their local operation and foster economic growth, set/collect/refund taxes and protect the environment (c).

As mentioned above, behaviors, "local traditions" and "subjective decisions" also form procedures and routines of public servants in Union's member provinces as well as their municipalities. This behavior in Public Management fits to TPC, which states that public servants and politicians act based on self-interest aiming at the maximization of power, wealth and status (Mashaw, 2009).

The Theory of Public Choice represents the Agent-Principal problem (Jensen & Meckling, 1976), which comes from the separation of "control" and "management". In democratic regimes, the "control" of a nation belongs to its population, however, it delegates the "power" to managers (politicians and public servants). These act according to their own interest because they want to maximize their utility function represented by power, wealth and status. It is noteworthy that the decision-making process (economic choices) in Public Management is also founded in cultural behaviors. These are the missing link between the Theory of Public Choice and the reality in governmental institutions (Mann & Wüstemann, 2010).

In Public Management, there are two types of public servants, the career ones and servants in the so-called "positions of trust". Carneiro and Menicucci (2013) point that career public servants build their "own agenda", because of their job stability, which makes them think they have total control over public resources, budget and decisions. This leads them to act with operational inefficiency and disconnected from people's needs.

Servants in positions of trust are assigned to work for a limited period, which depends on political decisions of the "men in charge". During the ethnographic research, the authors found out that many people in positions of trust "erase" computer files and registers when they leave these positions, causing interruptions in many processes of Public Management and information asymmetries among public servants. There couldn't be identified a structured data policy to protect information integrity other than "antivirus" and "firewalls".

"Traditions", "subjective decisions", "self-interest", "musical chairs" of public servants from positions of trust and "operational inefficiency" of career servants are evidences for a gap of communication and integration amidst the multiple public institutions in different levels of the Federative Brazilian Republic. In addition to that, the decision-making process from public managers tend to be disconnected from societal demands. These gaps provoke information asymmetries and transaction costs for Brazilians. Transaction costs entail expenses generated by public services malfunctioning and opportunistic behavior of servants and politicians (Peres, 2007).

The authors of this book chapter have summarized the key problems of public services provision in two *corollaries,* using literature review to support the findings.

Corollary 1 *Public services in Brazil cannot be fully delivered to the population, which means they are not universal.*

TPC argues that public servants, politicians and voters, who belong to a political system, are moved by self-interest, which is materialized into an "objective function" of power, wealth and status (Mashaw, 2009; Oliveira & Filho, 2017). Then, the outcomes of national or local political systems just benefit individuals or selected groups, hindering laws and public services comprehensive dissemination to all citizens. Mann and Wüstemann (2010) state that information asymmetries between governments and citizens, which means, the fact that governments pursue more and better information than citizens, lead to the offer of poor services for the population.

In practical ways, this can be noticed in many areas of public services provision. For instance, the academic research of Leal, Esteves-Pereira, Viellas, Domingues, and Gama (2020) addresses that the lack of prenatal and birth care among users of public services in Brazil contributes for spontaneous preterm birth, infant morbidity and mortality. With respect to public education, there is also a shortage of kindergarden for toddlers: in 2018, only 34% of all Brazilian children from 0 (zero) to 03 (three) years go to kindergarden, according to the Brazilian Institute of Geography and Statistics. Even though it is a constitutional obligation of municipalities to provide daycare and kindergarden, more than the half of Brazilian children do not get access to such services.

These two examples show that social inequality begins at birth when public institutions fail to assure basic rights. As a matter of fact, the efficient allocation of proper public services for the population would mitigate poverty, regional and social inequalities.

Corollary 2 *Lack of integration among public institutions and "subjective" decisions make the provision of public services uncertain.*

The lack of integration among public institutions is led by the maximization of personal power and budget improvement of governmental bureaucracy. Mann and Wüstemann (2010) state that information asymmetry not only happen between government and citizens but it also takes place among governmental institutions as well.

The above-mentioned misbehavior and information asymmetries have impacts in government's operational efficiency for there is little interest in improving processes and reducing individual authority of making discretionary decisions. Every public institution has its own "practices" and "legacy systems" which do not (want to) communicate to others and, as a result, causes a lack of transparency to citizens and improves asymmetrical information between public servants and citizens.

The authors of this book chapter have noticed that the fast access to public services often come from "knowing someone" that may help the citizen. This problem is summarized as the Principal-Agent conflict, which indicates the Agent (public servant) will not act in the interest of his/her Principal (citizen) unless it fits to his/her own interest. It happens because everyone seeks to maximize its' own "utility function".

Requests for public services provision are presented as official petitions and forms by citizens. They come to the public institution, instead of using Internet applications to transfer documents, that it to say, citizens must come many times to different public departments, bringing signed documents and petitions, until he/she can get what he/she needs. A public servant can request many documents as he/she wants in order to examine a petition, under the argument of "legally asking" for "accessory obligations".

Frequently, citizens and private companies must ask for help to get access to public services because of the high complexity of bureaucratic demands and the lack of integration among public institutions. Such "subjectivity" in public-private relations can trigger corruption through bribes, that means, the Agent (servant) would be able to help the Principal (citizen) if he/she receives a "monetary incentive" in addition to his/her official loan (Oliveira & Filho, 2017). For instance, Sarmento Jr., Krishnamurti, Tomita, and Kos (2005) discuss that a patient of Brazilian's Public Health System has better chances to get hospital or clinical care if he/she knows a doctor that works in the medical institution. To avoid "subjective" relations in such cases, there is a Senate's law project which forces all local municipalities to publish queues for surgeries, containing patient's identity number, his/her queue position and a scheduled date for the surgery (Law Project 393, 2015).

3.2 Step 3 (Survey): Online Survey, Its Relevance and Outcomes

The authors of this chapter have sent an online questionnaire to researchers, students, public managers, teachers and entrepreneurs from Rio de Janeiro and Sao Paulo provinces to answer about breakthrough technologies and their applications, occupations of the future, social problems and possible technological solutions. Although these group of people is not statistically significant (N = 30), it is composed by well selected respondents who understand about the usage and development of new technologies, as a result, their answers represent a look into the future of Brazilian's technology evolution and social challenges.

1. ***Type of institution of respondents:***
   34.5% are service providers or handlers; 27.6% come from universities, 17.2% are public managers; 6.9% come from the industry and 13.8% belong to other institutions/sectors.
2. **Identify the most important technology with more diffusion in Brazil for the next 10 years (2020–2030), regarding its socioeconomic impacts in public and private environments**:
   This question indicates the awareness of Blockchain technology. Artificial Intelligence appears as the most relevant technology within the next 10 years indicated by 55.2% of the respondents, followed by Blockchain (27.6%), Machine Learning and Compliance for Data Security (10.3%) and Remote Sensing (6.9%).
3. **Point the most required occupation for the next 10 years (2020–2030) in Brazil:**
   The most cited occupation by 34.6% of the respondents is Data Scientist. They also expressed other professions that are tightly related to each other like Programmers (15.4%), IT professionals in general (11.5%), Traders (7.7%), DevOps Analysts (3.8%), Data and Security Information Analysts (3.8%), Developer of Autonomous and Semiautonomous Systems (3.8%), Chief Technology and Human Resources Manager (3.8%), Blockchain Developers (3.8%), Production Engineering (3.8%) and Psychologists (3.8%). Dealing with data (development, operation and security), multiple processes and people are the needed core competencies from the professions of the future.
4. **Point the most relevant application of Blockchain technology in Brazil considering the next 10 years (2020–2030):**
   "Security in digital file transfer" was cited by 38.7% of the respondents, followed by "Emission of electronical documents, notary office termination" (29.0%), "Tracking of trustable information about people, products and institutions" (29.9%) and "Business platform" (3.2%).
5. **Address the most important social challenge in Brazil for the next 10 years (2020–2030) as well as the technology to solve it.**

Table 7.1 indicates the key social challenges that Brazil will face within the next 10 years and potential solutions resting on technology. Some of the solutions mentioned are not correlated to a specific technology, they rather focus on economical and managerial practices like microcredit, transparency (reduce of information asymmetry), investment allocation, home-office and education widespread.

Cryptocurrencies were mentioned as a problem from one of the respondents. They lessen central authority, foster informal markets and tend to reduce tax payments. Blockchain may reinforce currency transaction in informal markets, that means, local communities may be able to create their virtual currencies, organize

Table 7.1 Social challenges and technology solutions

Social challenge	Technology solution
Potable water; food shortage	Better water management aiming at loss reductions; artificial food with nutritional value coming from laboratories
Diffusion of cryptocurrencies	(No solution cited)
Increase of productivity in agribusiness may lead to plague dissemination in crops	Artificial intelligence to eliminate plagues
Energy conservation	Consume behavior analysis and energy management
Administrative reform in public sector	Increase transparency in public accounts
Education (machine operation and programming; lack of skilled workers, low quality of education; technology management)	Home factory; artificial intelligence to improve knowledge diffusion; tools for education management and quality improvement of primary education
Corruption and frauds in production chains and elections	Blockchain for data tracking and security
Income inequality	Microcredit; tools to increase financial education to all citizens
Security in file transfer	Blockchain
Infrastructure	Widespread of communication networks; increase of people education to improve infrastructure conditions
Traffic/mobility	Blockchain for traffic control; home office
Too much bureaucracy	Efficient management; compliance of data security; data transparency
Crime	Artificial intelligence and machine learning
Universal access to sanitation	Decision tools to help allocate financial resources for public investment

Source: authors

their Initial Coin Offerings (ICOs)[1] and trade services on their own. Consequently, municipal governments—that run tax collection—may drastically lose revenues. The so-called "cripto-anarchist" vision behind the Blockchain technology supports the theory that Blockchain networks are powerful tools to decentralize political, economic and social infrastructure. Its "chains of blocks" are distributed transaction ledgers for a general purpose and may be used to represent any type of asset (Sclavounis, 2017).

In Brazil, cryptocurrencies appear as profitable investments, but these financial transactions are not regulated by the Brazilian Securities Commission, causing larceny and fraud from "cryptocurrencies' traders".

The respondents emphasize the role of Artificial Intelligence to control plagues in crops, prevent and mitigate crimes. Also, Blockchain will reduce fraud,

[1]The ICOs (Initial Coin Offerings) – which are similar to the famous company's IPOs (Initial Public Offerings) – refer to public offerings of new coins on virtual markets to raise funds, using Blockchain technologies, without the surveillance of a financial authority.

corruption and will enable "smart traffic". Moreover, the respondents pointed the synthetic biology to mitigate food shortage through "artificial food".

3.3 Step 4 (Results Enrichment): Literature Review on Blockchain, Smart Contracts and Business Process Management (BPM)

Routines and procedures to handle currencies, bonds, taxes and physical assets were configured by organizations, governments and people by technological developments over time. Institutions and people have always sought control and security in their transactions, even though they are carried out as a physical document indicating property registration.

Currently, driven by computer networks and the Internet, some technologies allow the replacement of the real world by the digital world through secure authentications, just exchanging information, such as the effective use Blockchain and Smart Contracts.

Blockchain technology fits into a new research area regarding forms and possibilities for applications in transactional systems. The rapid evolution of Blockchain, distributed ledger technology and its applications will require changes in business transactions and data recording (Hamilton, 2019).

Franciscon et al. (2019) report the existence of three different types of Blockchain structure: (1) centralized, when the block chain is stored in private mode; (2) distributed, when the block chain is stored in private or public mode on several servers and; (3) decentralized, when the block chain is public, all network nodes are interconnected and the consensus is based on visible nodes that are involved in each other. Table 7.2 depicts various definitions of Blockchain technology.

In its genesis, Blockchain technology was used only for financial and commercial transactions, but several studies have pointed that it can be applied to develop systems outside financial and commercial transactions (Andrian, Kurniawan, & Suhardi, 2018). According to Catalini and Gans (2019), when a distributed ledger is combined with a native cryptographic token (as in the case of Bitcoin), markets can be launched without the need of intermediaries, reducing network costs. This challenges some existing revenue models and the market power of incumbents, opening opportunities for new approaches of regulation, auctions and the provision of utilities, software, identity and reputation systems.

Blockchains allow us to have a distributed peer-to-peer network where non-trusting members can verifiably interact with each without the need for a trusted authority (Christidis & Devetsikiotis, 2016).

Taking into account actual heterogeneity of Blockchain solutions, application cases of Blockchain in Brazil are still modest (Rocha, 2019):

- **Transport industry**: realizes the Blockchain strategy with a great value to offer transparency regarding freight;

Table 7.2 Various definitions of Blockchain

Definition	Author (Year)
Blockchain is a public network. Anyone can view it at any time, as it resides on the network and not within a single institution in charge of audit	Tapscott (2016)
Blockchain can be defined as a continuously growing transaction ledger, distributed and maintained on a peer-to-peer network	Zheng, Xie, Dai, Chen, and Wang (2018)
Blockchain has restored the definition of trust through the encryption mechanism and embedded consensus, providing security, anonymity and data integrity without the need of third parties	Dai, Shi, Meng, Wei, and Ye (2017)
Blockchain is a technology that records transactions permanently, without being deleted, they can be only updated sequentially, maintaining an endless history track	Mougayar (2017)
As a resource, Blockchain has a consensus algorithm, applied to build blocks; entities involved (typically those involved in mining) check the consistency of transactions and their authenticity	Urien (2018)
Blockchain technology is fundamental for a trust model delivery provided by smart contracts	Destefanis et al. (2018)
Blockchain is the new wave of disruption that has already begun to redesign business, social and political interactions and any other form of value exchange	Singhal, Dhameja, and Panda (2018)
Blockchain is a growing list of records, called blocks, linked and protected using encryption and adopts the P2P protocol that can tolerate a single point of failure	Wang et al. (2019)
Blockchain has auditing as one of its main characteristics. After each transaction is validated, it registers in the current block with a timestamp and its users can track previous transactions and access the history of all transactions	Rouhani, Pourheidari, and Deters (2018)
Blockchain technology is a model of data persistence and software architecture designed to be essentially decentralized	Franciscon et al. (2019)
Blockchain is a technology containing ledgers distributed point to point that records transactions, agreements, contracts and sales	Leka, Selimi, and Lamani (2019)
Blockchain has shown its great potentials to meet the conflicting requirements of security, openness, scalability, and adaptability of BPM systems in a dynamic as well as a turbulent environment	Viriyasitavat, Xu, Zhuming, and Pungpapong (2019)
Blockchain introduces serious disruptions to the traditional business processes since the applications and transactions, which needed centralized architectures or trusted third parties to verify them, can now operate in a decentralized way with the same level of certainty	Casino, Daskalis, and Patsakis (2019)

Source: authors

- **Supply Chain**: Blockchain brings several benefits in terms of asset traceability and auditability;
- **Digital Records**: the technology registers works (such as books, brands and photos), signs documents, performs notary authentication and various other services, in addition to providing proof of authenticity;

- **Academy**: focus on education, with courses on various topics related to crypto, new business models and distributed accounting technologies;
- **Fund raising**: ICOs connect entrepreneurs and investors to social impact projects with difficult access to the traditional financial system.

The operation of a Blockchain network requires several computers (points or nodes in the network), considered as the backbone. Thus, it can be categorized in 03 (three) parts (Andrian et al., 2018):

- Smart Contracts;
- Blockchain as a peer to peer network - P2P and distributed system;
- Blockchain authentication or Blockchain encryption.

The technological scenario landscape is rapidly evolving as blockchain is being used in some fields other than cryptocurrencies, with Smart Contracts playing a central role. Smart Contracts were already defined in 1994 by Szabo, as cited in Casino et al. (2019): "a computerized transaction protocol that executes the terms of a contract."

Smart Contracts can store and change a given state of the Blockchain network with the execution of pre-configured transactions, according to predefined business rules. Programs containing Smart Contracts are executed in the Blockchain protocol and have their correct execution in a consensus-oriented network, as proposed by Szabo (1996), regardless of whether it is a permissioned network or not, where the consensus must come from the majority of connected nodes. Technically, the execution of Smart Contracts comprises pieces of code executed in a decentralized virtual machine that can be adapted to needs, according to operational models. Multiple definitions of Smart Contracts are in Table 7.3.

The use of Smart Contracts combines protocols with user interfaces to formalize and protect relationships through computer networks, and the objectives, business rules and principles for the design of these systems are derived from legal principles, economic theory and theories of reliable protocols and insurance (Szabo, 1996).

The entire sequence of actions performed in a Smart Contract is widespread by the network and/or registered in the Blockchain network, then they are publicly visible (Kosba, Miller, Shi, Wen, & Papamanthou, 2016).

Currently, Business Process Management as a managerial approach is based on the explicit definition of related roles and responsibilities, mainly focused on the internal operations of a company. Blockchain Technology can lead governments and companies to a more externally oriented self-governance model by means of smart contracts (Mendling et al., 2018). BPM governance refers to an appropriate and transparent accountability in terms of roles, responsibilities and decision-making processes for different programs, projects and operations (Rosemann & Brocke, 2015). Therefore, in a technical way, Business Process Management has several definitions and application contexts, as in Table 7.4.

Table 7.3 Various definitions of Smart Contracts

Definitions	Author (Year)
Smart Contracts are user-defined programs that specify rules and manage transactions, performed by a peer network	Bhargavan et al. (2016)
Users invoke Smart Contracts as in cryptocurrencies, sending transactions to the contract address, if, specifically, a new transaction is accepted by Blockchain and has a contract address as the recipient. All participants in the mining network will execute the contract code with the current state of the Blockchain and transaction payloads as inputs	Luu, Duc-Hiep, Olickel, Saxena, and Hobor (2016)
The advent of Smart Contracts can give governments and regulatory agencies the opportunity to reduce overall system costs and ensure competitiveness	Lee, Long, Burnap, Wu, and Jenkins (2017)
Smart Contracts can be encoded in blocks on the Blockchain to provide instructions for insurance, emergency contacts, wills and more. These Smart Contracts will be triggered by events that Blockchain can read from another web service	Karafiloski and Mishev (2017)
A Smart Contract is a self-executing computer program, capable of fulfilling the terms of a contract or a commercial agreement between two or more parties, having automated algorithms. Smart Contracts are executed when certain conditions are met	Gilcrest and Carvalho (2018)
A Smart Contract cannot be changed after the code is defined, and the code (source program) works as an agreement, available for anyone to use, therefore, its use is possible thanks to complete programming languages	Beck (2018)
A Smart Contract is automatically executed to transfer "assets", which is its essence	Liu and Liu (2019)
Smart Contracts contain modifiers that restrict access to methods based on the functions or status of your contracts, in addition, events are used to create notifications and keep records of important results and requests	Hasan and Salah (2019)
A Smart Contract is the key component of Blockchain, making it a technology beyond the scope of cryptocurrencies and with various applications, such as healthcare, IoT, supply chain, digital identity, business process management and more	Rouhani et al. (2018)

Source: authors

4 Results

4.1 Step 5 (Technology Framework): Blockchain Applied in Public Management

The current proposal from the authors aims to provide a framework based on Blockchain and Smart Contracts to improve public services provision, which is "uncertain" and "limited" (not universal).

In order to structure the framework, the authors applied the concept of Business Process Management and considered the routines of healthcare and tax refunding in Public Management. The adoption of BPM seeks to enhance productivity by increasing the operational efficiency through the combination of procedures, routines, governance and clearly defined process responsibilities (Gabryelczvk, 2018).

Table 7.4 Various definitions of Business Process Management

Definitions	Authors (year)
Business Process Management is closely related to disciplines from another areas, helping companies in their attempts to achieve customer satisfaction, loyalty, engagement and more sales	Prodanova and Van Looy (2019)
It involves the discovery, design and delivery of business processes. In addition, BPM includes excessive, administrative and supervisory control of processes	Business Process Modeling Notation Specification (2008)
Business Process Management is an approach to identify, design, execute, document, measure, monitor and control both automated and nonautomated business processes to achieve consistent, targeted results aligned with an organization's strategic goals	Viriyasitavat et al. (2019)
In the context of business process management, a "business process" is defined as end-to-end work which delivers value to customers	Bek (2014)

Source: authors

Process documentation provides a formal reference for everyone involved in BPM in Public Management and thus, managers can monitor entire processes, procedures, performances and their results. BPM is being adopted by an increasing number of institutions to achieve performance improvement and process (Malinova and Mendling, 2012), which meet the needs of the current research.

The modeling and optimization of operational processes comprises two major activities (Baldam, Valle, & Rozenfeld, 2009):

1. Describing the current process (as is);
2. Optimizing and modeling the desired process (to be).

The two activities will be described to propose a framework for a healthcare procedure (scheduling a surgery in Public Health System) and tax refund routines, using Blockchain and Smart Contracts.

4.1.1 Healthcare

Current Process (As Is)

According to the outcomes of ethnography and literature review, the "as is" processes (as they are currently) for "**surgery scheduling in Public Health System**" embrace the following actions:

1. Patient has an appointment with a physician from the Public Health System;
2. Physician recommends a surgery, but he/she doesn't schedule a date;
3. Patient must wait in a virtual "surgery queue", however he/she neither knows surgery's date, nor his/her queue position.

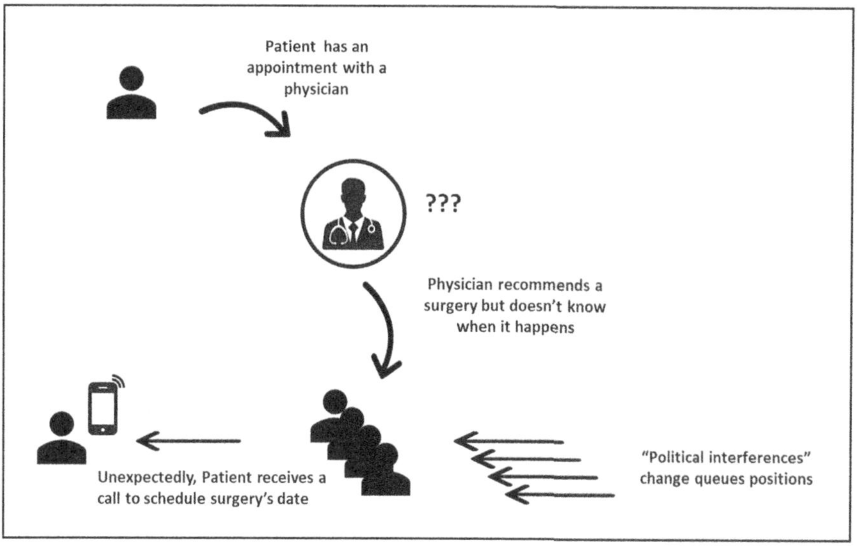

Fig. 7.2 "As is" for surgery scheduling in Brazilian's Public Health System

4. Patient waits, but "political interferences" changes queue positions to favor other patients;
5. Unexpectedly, Patient is called for the surgery.

Figure 7.2 represents the current procedures (as is).

Desired Process State (To Be)

The desired situation will occur if the Law Project PLS 393/2015 is approved and a Blockchain network starts to operate in the Public Health System. Therefore, everyone may see its positions in the virtual "surgery queue" and, through the generation of Smart Contracts no "political interference" can change the queue, otherwise everyone can see who has "interfered" and when:

1. Patient has an appointment with a physician from the Public Health System;
2. Physician recommends a surgery and he/she can schedule a specific date for the patient in a Platform of the Public Health System;
3. When the physician schedules the date in the Platform, a Smart Contract is generated and no one can change it;
4. Patient still has to wait, but he/she knows the date and his/her queue position;
5. Patient is operated.

Figure 7.3 shows an integrated Platform that works as a calendar to every physician who wants to schedule a surgery in Public Health System. The scheduled date turns into a Smart Contract that cannot be modified.

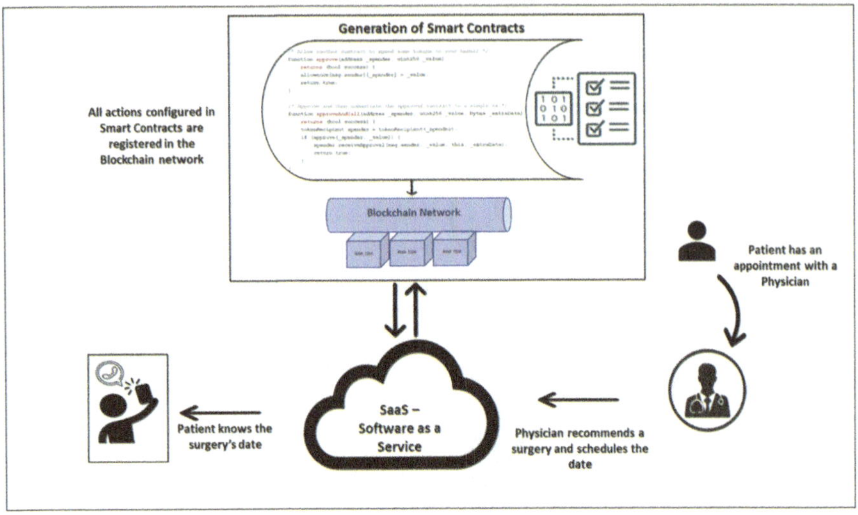

Fig. 7.3 To be for surgery scheduling in Brazilian's Public Health System

4.1.2 Tax Refunding

Current Process (As Is)

The current "**tax refunding**" process can be described as follows:

1. After receiving a charge for a particular tax, the taxpayer may request its review;
2. The taxpayer goes to the City Hall and brings a formal request addressed to the financial secretary, asking for a tax review;
3. The tax payer receives an identification protocol number;
4. The administrative secretariat, which received the request, forwards it for the analysis of the financial secretariat;
5. The request's merit is analyzed by the financial secretariat and forwarded to mediation;
6. There, attorneys analyze the request, accepting it or not;
7. The response is forwarded to the taxpayer by Press.

Figure 7.4 sums up the "as is" processes for tax refunding in a City Hall.

Desired Process State (To Be)

Here the authors present process improvements as a technology framework for tax refund:

1. After receiving a charge for a particular tax, the taxpayer can send a photo of the charge through a communication application;

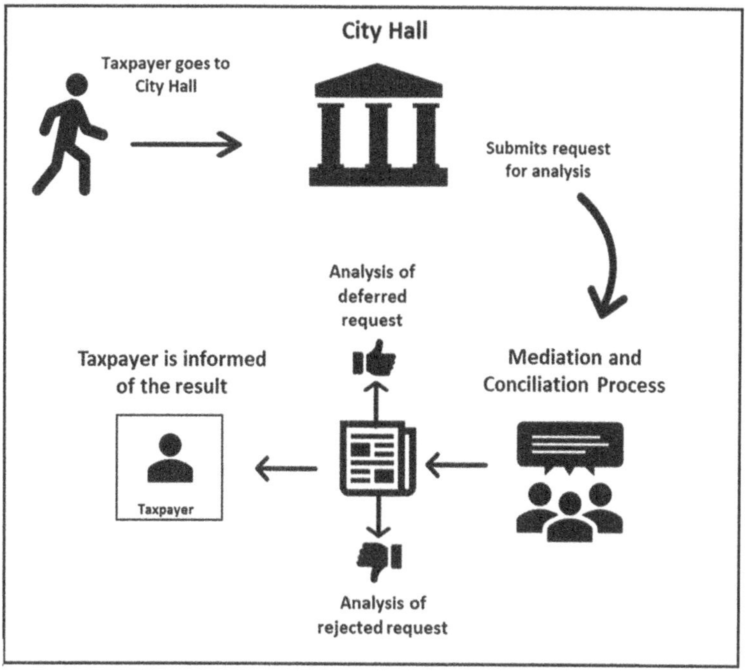

Fig. 7.4 As is for tax refunding in a City Hall

2. The software will receive it automatically, register a Smart Contract for the specific tax and make it available in the Blockchain network;
3. Analysts in the City Hall verify the request by examining its pertinence;
4. Analyst's evaluations are registered in Smart Contracts and made available in the Blockchain network;
5. The taxpayer receives through the application all information regarding the registration of his/her request.

If the citizen does not agree with the results, he/she can appeal, thus restarting the entire process before it comes to court. Figure 7.5 illustrates technology framework by using Smart Contracts and Blockchain technology with the expected improvements:

5 Final Considerations

Artificial Intelligence and Blockchain will the most important breakthrough technologies in Brazil within the next 10 years. They will help solve social problems and critical issues on public and private sectors, like frauds, corruption, crimes and the excess of bureaucracy. Blockchain is a technology or a "model of trust" composed

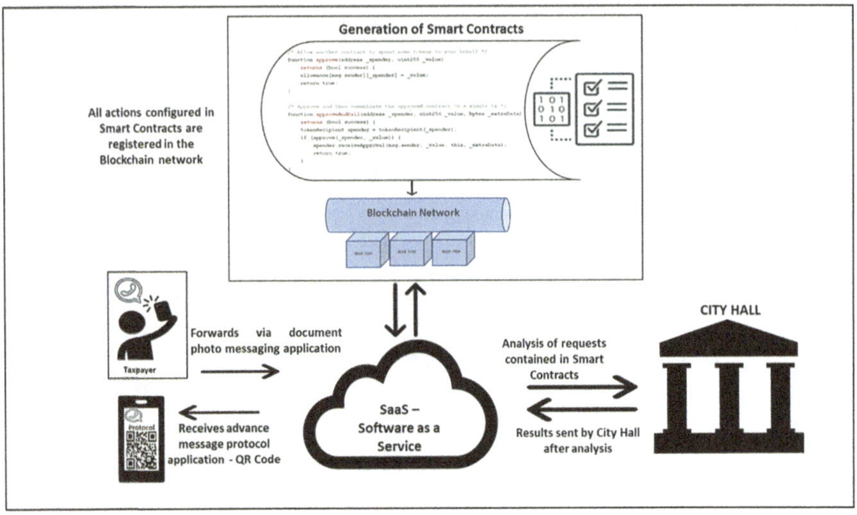

Fig. 7.5 To be for tax refunding in a City Hall

by ledgers that assure secure data transfer through Smart Contracts in a P2P network. Frauds and errors may not happen in a Blockchain network for all information is registered and can be tracked by everyone connected to such network. It tends to reduce information asymmetries within the government, leading to more operational efficiency in Public Management processes. Governments are supposed to help their citizens by means of public services. Blockchain is a way for Governments help themselves.

A Blockchain structure with the existing BPM routines will allow new constructions and extend the BPM as such because of Blockchain properties.

The research methodology, based on ethnography, survey and literature review, has allowed the authors to understand relevant challenges in Public Management, mostly associated with "uncertainty" and "lack of universality" of public services.

According to TPC, public servants and politicians are driven by self-interest, leading to the Principal-Agent conflict: the Agent (servant) does not handle in the interest of the Principal (citizen), unless it corresponds to his/her own interest. Therefore, the provision of public services could be more efficient and trustable with the employment of a Blockchain/Smart Contract framework in servants' processes and routines.

This chapter presented two possibilities of Blockchain applications, namely in healthcare and tax refunding using the BPM approach, which compares "as is situation" with "to be situation". These 02 (two) frameworks can be scalable and repeatable, which means then they can be employed in other routines/processes of Public Management to: (a) reduce the "Principal-Agent" conflict; (b) enforce data integrity and information transparency and; (c) foster a culture of fairness in public services provision.

References

Ahram, T., Sargolzaei, A., Sargolzaei, S., Daniels, J., & Amaba, B. (2017). Blockchain technology innovations. In *IEEE Technology & Engineering Management Conference (TEMSCON)*, Santa Clara, CA (137–141).

Andrian, H.R., Kurniawan, & Suhardi, N.B. (2018). Blockchain technology and implementation: A systematic literature review. In *International Conference on Information Technology Systems and Innovation (ICITSI)*, Bandung - Padang (370–374).

Baldam, R. L., Valle, R., & Rozenfeld, H. (2009). *Gerenciamento de processos de negócios BPM: Business Process Management*. São Paulo: Érica.

Beck, R. (2018). Beyond Bitcoin: The rise of Blockchain world. *Computer, 51*(2), 54–58.

Bek, I. (2014). *Business process management taxonomy in practice*. M.S. thesis, Masaryk Univ., Brno, Czechia, 2014. Retrieved from: https://is.muni.cz/th/420068/fi_m/thesis.pdf

Bhargavan, K., Delignat-Lavaud, A., Fournet C., Gollamudi, A, Gonthier, G., Kobeissi, N., et al. (2016, October). Formal verification of smart contracts: Short paper. In *Proceedings of the 2016 ACM Workshop on Programming Languages and Analysis for Security*, Vienna.

Business Process Modeling Notation Specification. (2008). *Business process model and notation, V1.1*. Needram: Object Management Group. Retrieved from: https://www.omg.org/spec/BPMN/1.1/PDF

Carneiro, R., & Menicucci, T. M. G. (2013). Gestão pública no século XXI: As reformas pendentes. In F. O. Cruz (Ed.), *A saúde no Brasil em 2030 - prospecção estratégica do sistema de saúde brasileiro: desenvolvimento, Estado e políticas de saúde [online]* (Vol. 1, pp. 135–194). Rio de Janeiro: Fiocruz/Ipea/Ministério da Saúde/Secretaria de Assuntos Estratégicos da Presidência da República.

Casino, F., Daskalis, T. K., & Patsakis, C. (2019). A systematic literature review of blockchain-based applications: Current status, classification and open issues. *Telematics and Informatics, 36*, 55–81. https://doi.org/10.1016/j.tele.2018.11.006

Catalini, C., & Gans, J. S. (2019). Some simple economics of the Blockchain. *NBER Working Paper Series*. Working Paper N. 22952. Retrieved from: https://www.nber.org/papers/w22952.pdf

Christidis, K., & Devetsikiotis, M. (2016). Blockchains and smart contracts for the internet of things. *IEEE Access, 4*, 2.292–2.303. Retrieved from: https://ieeexplore.ieee.org/document/7467408

Cropley, A. J. (2019). *Introduction to qualitative research methods*. Riga: Zinātne.

Dai, F., Shi, Y., Meng, N., Wei, L., & Ye, Z. (2017). From Bitcoin to cybersecurity: A comparative study of blockchain application and security issues. In *4th International Conference on Systems and Informatics (ICSAI)*, Hangzhou (pp. 975–979).

Dalmolin, B. M., Lopes, S. M. B., & Vasconcellos, M. P. C. (2002). A construção metodológica do campo: etnografia, criatividade e sensibilidade na investigação. *Saúde e Sociedade, 11*(2), 19–34. https://doi.org/10.1590/S0104-12902002000200003

De Filippi, P., & Hassan, S. (2016). Blockchain technology as a regulatory technology: From code is law to law is code. *First Monday, 21*. https://doi.org/10.5210/fm.v21i12.7113

Destefanis, G., Marchesi, M., Ortu, M., Tonelli, R., Bracciali, A., & Hierons, R. (2018). Smart contracts vulnerabilities: A call for blockchain software engineering? In *International Workshop on Blockchain Oriented Software Engineering (IWBOSE)*, Campobasso (pp. 19–25).

Engelenburg, S., Janssen, M., & Klievink, B. (2017, July). Design of a software architecture supporting business-to-government information sharing to improve public safety and security: Combining business rules. *Journal of Information Intelligent Systems., 52*, 595–618. https://doi.org/10.1007/s10844-017-0478-z

Franciscon, E. A., Nascimento, M. P., Granatyr, J., Weffort, M.R., Lessing, O.R., & Scalabrin, E.E. (2019). A systematic literature review of Blockchain architectures applied to public services. In *IEEE 23rd International Conference on Computer Supported Cooperative Work in Design (CSCWD)*, Porto (pp. 33–38).

Gabryelczvk, R. (2018). An exploration of BPM adoption factors: Initial steps for model development. In *Federated Conference on Computer Science and Information Systems (FedCSIS)*, Poznan (pp. 761–768).

Gatteschi, V., Lamberti, F., Demartini, C., Pranteda, C., & Santamaría, V. (2018, February). Blockchain and smart contracts for insurance: Is the technology mature enough? *Future Internet, 10*(2), 20. https://doi.org/10.3390/fi10020020

Gerstl, D. S. (2016). Leveraging Bitcoin Blockchain technology to modernize security perfection under the uniform commercial code. In A. Maglyas & A. L. Lamprecht (Eds.), *Software business. ICSOB 2016* (Lecture notes in business information processing) (Vol. 240). Cham: Springer.

Gilcrest, J., & Carvalho, A. (2018). Smart contracts: Legal considerations. In *IEEE International Conference on Big Data (Big Data)*, Seattle, WA (pp. 3.277–3.281).

Hamilton, M. (2019, November). Blockchain distributed ledger technology: An introduction and focus on smart contracts. *Journal of Corporate Accounting & Finance, 31*(2), 7–12. https://doi.org/10.1002/jcaf.22421

Hasan, H. R., & Salah, K. (2019). Combating Deepfake videos using Blockchain and smart contracts. *IEEE Access, 7*, 41.596–41.606.

Jensen, M., & Meckling, W. (1976). Theory of the firm: Managerial behavior, agency costs, and ownership structure. *Journal of Financial Economics, 3*(4), 305–360.

Karafiloski, E., & Mishev, A. (2017). Blockchain solutions for big data challenges: A literature review. In 17th IEEE International Conference on Smart Technologies, EUROCON 2017 – Conference Proceedings (pp. 763–768). https://doi.org/10.1109/EUROCON.2017.8011213

Kosba, A., Miller, A., Shi, E., Wen, Z., & Papamanthou, C. (2016). Hawk: The Blockchain model of cryptography and privacy-preserving smart contracts. In *IEEE Symposium on Security and Privacy (SP)*, San Jose, CA (pp. 839–858).

Law Number 8.112 (1990, December 11). Retrieved from: http://www.planalto.gov.br/ccivil_03/leis/l8112compilado.htm

Law Number 8.666 (1993, June 21). Retrieved from: http://www.planalto.gov.br/ccivil_03/leis/l8666cons.htm

Law Project Number 393, 2015. Retrieved from: https://www25.senado.leg.br/web/atividade/materias/-/materia/121974

Leal, M. C., Esteves-Pereira, A. P., Viellas, E. F., Domingues, R. M. S., & Gama, S. G. N. (2020). Prenatal care in the Brazilian public sector. *Revista de Saúde Pública., 54*(8). https://doi.org/10.11606/s1518-8787.2020054001458

Lee, T., Long, C., Burnap, P., Wu, J., & Jenkins, N. (2017). Automation of the supplier role in the GB power system using blockchain-based smart contracts. *CIRED - Open Access Proceedings Journal, 1*(10), 2.619–2.623.

Leka, E, Selimi, B., & Lamani, L. (2019). Systematic literature review of Blockchain applications: Smart contracts. In *International Conference on Information Technologies (InfoTech)*, St. Constantine and Elena Resort, Varna (pp. 1–3).

Lima, C. (2018, November). Developing open and interoperable DLT. *Blockchain Standards in Computer, 51*(11), 106–111. https://doi.org/10.1109/MC.2018.2876184

Liu, J., & Liu, Z. (2019). A survey on security verification of Blockchain smart contracts. *IEEE Access, 7*, 77.894–77.904. https://doi.org/10.1109/ACCESS.2019.2921624

Luu, L., Duc-Hiep, C., Olickel, H., Saxena, P., & Hobor, A. (2016). Making smart contracts smarter. *IACR Cryptology ePrint Archive*.https://doi.org/10.1145/2976749.2978309

Malinova, M., & Mendling, J. (2012). A qualitative research perspective on BPM adoption and the pitfalls of business process modeling. In M. La Rosa & P. Soffer (Eds.), *International Conference on Business Process Management* (Vol. 132, pp. 77–88). Springer, Berlin, Heidelberg.

Mann, S., & Wüstemann, H. (2010). Public governance of information asymmetries: The gap between reality and economic theory. *The Journal of Socio-Economics, 39*, 278–285. https://doi.org/10.1016/j.socec.2009.10.009

Mashaw, J. L. (2009). Public law and public choice: A critique and rapprochment, Chap. 1. In D. A. Farber & A. J. O'Connell (Eds.), *Research book on public choice and publix law*. Cheltenham: Edward Elgar.

Mendling, J., Weber, I., Aalst, W., Brocke, J., Cabanillas, C., Daniel, F., et al. (2018). Blockchains for business process management - Challenges and opportunities. In *ACM Transactions on Management Information Systems*. In press, accepted. https://doi.org/10.1145/3183367

Mougayar, W. (2017). *Blockchain para negócios: promessa, prática e aplicação da nova tecnologia da internet*. Rio de Janeiro: Alta Books.

Murto, P., Hyysalo, S., Juntunen, J.K., & Jalas, M. (2020). Capturing the micro-level of intermediation in transitions: Comparing ethnographic and interview methods. In *Environmental Innovation and Societal Transitions*. In press, accepted. https://doi.org/10.1016/j.eist.2020.01.004

Oliveira, C.B., & Filho, J.R.F. (2017), July/August. Agency problems in the public sector: The role of mediators between central administration of city hall and executive bodies. *Brazilian Journal of Public Administration*. Rio de Janeiro, 51(4), 596–615.

Ølnes, S., Ubacht, J., & Janssen, M. (2017). Blockchain in government: Benefits and implications of distributed ledger technology for information sharing. *Government Information Quarterly, 34*(3), 355–364. https://doi.org/10.1016/j.giq.2017.09.007

Pan, Y., Xiaosong, Z., Wang, Y., Zhou, S., Guanghua, L., & Bao, J. (2019). Application of Blockchain in carbon trading. *Energy Procedia, 158*, 4.286–4.291. https://doi.org/10.1016/j.egypro.2019.01.509

Peres, U. D. (2007). Custos de Transação e Estrutura de Governança no Setor Público. *RBGN, São Paulo, 9*(24), 15–30.

Pichel, F. (2016). Blockchain for land administration. *GIM International, 30*(9), 38–39.

Prodanova, J., & Van Looy, A. (2019). How beneficial is social Media for Business Process Management? A systematic literature review. *IEEE Access, 7*, 39.583–39.599. https://doi.org/10.1109/ACCESS.2019.2903983

Rajamäki, J, & Knuuttila, J. (2013). Law enforcement Authorities' legal digital evidence gathering: Legal, integrity and chain-of-custody requirement. In *European Intelligence and Security Informatics Conference*, Sweden (pp. 198–203).

Rocha, L. (2019). *7 blockchain businesses in Brazil run by women*. Retrieved from: https://www.criptofacil.com/confira-7-negocios-de-blockchain-no-brasil-comandados-por-mulheres/

Rosemann, M., & Brocke, J. (2015). The six core elements of business process management. In M. Rosemann & J. Brocke (Eds.), *Handbook on business process management 1: Introduction, methods and information systems* (pp. 105–122). New York: Springer.

Rouhani, S., Pourheidari, V., & Deters, R. (2018, August), A case study of execution of untrusted business process on permissioned blockchain. In 2018 IEEE International Conference on Internet of Things (iThings) and IEEE Green Computing and Communications (GreenCom) and IEEE Cyber, Physical and Social Computing (CPSCom) and IEEE Smart Data (SmartData), (pp. 1588–1594).

Sarmento Jr., K. M., Krishnamurti, M. A., Tomita, S., & Kos, A. O. A. (2005). O problema da fila de espera para cirurgias otorrinolaringológicas em serviços públicos. *Revista Brasileira de Otorrinolaringologia, 71*(3), 256–262. https://doi.org/10.1590/S0034-72992005000300001

Sclavounis, O. (2017, November). *Understanding public blockchain governance*. Oxford: Oxford Internet Institute. Retrieved from: https://www.oii.ox.ac.uk/blog/understanding-public-blockchain-governance/

Sellitz, C., Cook, S. W., & Wrightsman, L. S. (1975). *Métodos de pesquisa nas relações sociais*. São Paulo: EPU e EDUSP.

Singhal, B., Dhameja, G., & Panda, P. S. (2018). *Beginning Blockchain: A Beginner's guide to building Blockchain solutions*. Bangalore: Apress.

Sullivan, C., & Burger, E. (2017). E-residency and blockchain. *Computer Law & Security Review., 33*(4), 470–481. https://doi.org/10.1016/j.clsr.2017.03.016

Szabo, N. (1996). Smart contracts: Building blocks for digital markets. *EXTROPY: The Journal of Transhumanist Thought, 16*, 18.

Tapscott, D. (2016). *Blockchain: como a tecnologia por trás do Bitcoin está mudando o dinheiro, os negócios e o mundo*. São Paulo: SENAI-SP Editora.

Urien, P. (2018). Blockchain IoT (BIoT): A new direction for solving internet of things security and trust issues. In *3rd Cloudification of the Internet of Things (CIoT)*, Paris (pp. 1–4).

Viriyasitavat, W., Xu, L. D., Zhuming, B., & Pungpapong, V. (2019). Blockchain and internet of things for modern business process in digital economy—The state of the art. *IEEE Transactions on Computational Social Systems, 6*(6), 1.420–1.432. https://doi.org/10.1109/TCSS.2019.2919325

Wang, S., Ouyang, L., Yuan, Y., Ni, X., Hang, X., & Wang, F. Y. (2019). Blockchain-enabled smart contracts: Architecture, applications, and future trends. *IEEE Transactions on Systems, Man, and Cybernetics: Systems*.https://doi.org/10.1109/TSMC.2019.2895123

Zheng, Z., Xie, S., Dai, H., Chen, X., & Wang, H. (2018). Blockchain challenges and opportunities: A survey. *International Journal of Web and Grid Services, 14*, 352. https://doi.org/10.1504/IJWGS.2018.095647

Benedito Cristiano Aparecido Petroni PhD in Production Engineering (Software Management and Interactive Media), Master in Computer Systems—IA, Postgraduate in Internet Design and its Applications and Bachelor in Systems Analysis. Full Professor at Universidade Paulista, Professor at FATEC in Jundiai, Sao Paulo. HTCIA member: International High-tech Criminal Investigation Association. Member of the ABNT/CEE-307 Committee—Blockchain and Distributed Registration Technologies. Specialist at ASC Academy—Cisco Academy. He researches the areas of Information Security, IoT, Blockchain and Artificial Intelligence. Prof. Dr. Benedito Petroni develops activities as Judicial Expert for Federation Courts of Justice and Procedural Technical Assistance. He works with Computer Forensic Consultancy and Expert Reports against Technical Reports and Opinions.

Mariana Savedra Pfitzner PhD in Scientific and Technological Policy from Unicamp, Master in Professional Education and Human Resources Management—Otto von Guericke Universität—Magdeburg (Germany), Bachelor in Economics from the State University of Campinas. Prof. Dr. Mariana worked with market analysis, project management, intellectual property, spin-offs and technology transfer for companies in Brazil and Germany. She also worked as analyst and consultant in companies such as Vale, Thyssen Krupp, Bosch and Eletrobras with technological forecasting, corporate governance, technological planning, design thinking and innovation management. She taught Economics and Management in several private universities and was Director of Economic Development in the Municipality of Campinas, Sao Paulo. There, Mariana worked with the formulation and execution of Science, Technology and Innovation policies. Currently, she is Director of Science and Technology in Jundiai City Hall, gathering 20 years of experience in Public Management, policy design and development of R&D projects.

Chapter 8
Blockchain Enabled Digital Government and Public Sector Services: A Survey

Anwitaman Datta

1 Introduction

Over the last two decades, the proliferation of Internet has changed almost every aspect of how modern societies function. This includes how the government functions, interacts with the various stakeholders and delivers public services. It gained momentum (Heeks, 2001; OECD, 2014) with the creation of IT infrastructure to support the government's own internal processes (e-government) which the OECD defines as '*the use by the governments of information and communication technologies (ICTs), and particularly the Internet, as a tool to achieve better government*', and the delivery of government services (e-governance) (Field, Muller, & Lau, 2003). The scope has now expanded significantly, leading to the advent of what is often termed as 'digital governance', which the OECD defines (OECD, 2014) as "use of digital technologies, as an integrated part of governments' modernisation strategies, to create public value. It relies on a digital government ecosystem comprised of government actors, non-governmental organisations, businesses, citizens' associations and individuals which supports the production of and access to data, services and content through interactions with the government".

The terms e-government/governance[1] and digital government/governance are often used interchangeably, nevertheless, the distinct OECD definitions help capture subtle yet fundamental changes that have emerged over time. Prominently,

[1]The distinct terms e-government and e-governance are sometimes used to distinguish the use of technology for managing the government's internal activities versus service delivery to citizens. Nevertheless, for brevity, in this paper, we will use the term e-government, and likewise, digital government, to capture both meanings.

A. Datta (✉)
School of Computer Science and Engineering, NTU Singapore, Singapore, Singapore
e-mail: anwitaman@ntu.edu.sg

C. G. Reddick et al. (eds.), *Blockchain and the Public Sector*, Public Administration and Information Technology 36,
https://doi.org/10.1007/978-3-030-55746-1_8

while the core mission of catering to the public at large remains the same, the means has expanded in its scope, and the emphasis has shifted from the governments delivering it on their own to creating an environment, where it can be done using public-private partnerships, as well as by facilitating purely privately funded efforts to flourish. This is being achieved by creating an ecosystem comprising digital infrastructure and regulatory frameworks on which the diverse participants can build upon.

Smart city initiatives such as mobile app based urban transportation solutions and sharing economy in general (Heinrichs, 2013; Martin, 2016) exemplify such a model of moving up the data value chain. There are several intertwined and cascading factors at play in this evolution. What started as a move from paper-based workflows to digitization, led to creation of a huge volume of data that is readily available for automated processing. The infrastructure to store and process humongous volume of data started to mature, even as the volume of data being acquired also keeps rising by leaps and bounds. This data comes from a plethora of sources, and is very diverse in nature—social media, sensors deployed for monitoring the environment, cities, buildings, financial records, health records, to name just a few. Analysing this data yields intelligence, and creates opportunities, both for solving (and identifying) problems, as well as the positive societal and financial impact such solutions yield.

A common underlying theme in all this is the availability and sharing of (good quality of) data. However, there are several challenges that hamper this, to name a few prominent ones: data integration and portability (Doan, Halevy, & Ives, 2012), privacy, distributed control, provenance and data usage transparency.

There are numerous privacy issues, and not all the issues are even well understood. This includes questions of access control (who should get what data), information leak and side channels (even if a specific data in itself may not prima facie reveal something, in conjunction with some other information, it may reveal something more than what each of the individual pieces of information disclosed). Even within different government agencies, sharing certain data may be violative of the rights of a citizen as per the laws of the country. Sharing it with non-government entities compound the concerns. Lack of (well thought of) regulations also lead to many grey areas. Furthermore, individual data aggregators need to satisfy the associated privacy and security requirements, and they may also want to control the data they own in a manner where they can account for its usage.

For whichever reasons, the data in the system may be of poor quality, or outright wrong. Even otherwise, it would be reasonable to expect certain accountability on the source of the information. Thus, data provenance and lineage, along with ability to trace who all have accessed said data, and for which purposes, are also essential.

Technological solutions are thus needed to store, process, and share data in a secure manner, balancing the needs (aspirational, as well as, often, regulatory) of utility and privacy in a highly distributed environment, involving many autonomous entities, which may not (fully) trust each other. Blockchain technologies have emerged as a potential candidate providing a framework to address several of these concerns. At this juncture, it is worth emphasizing that, blockchains (1) may not be the only way, or the best way, to solve the mentioned problems, (2) may not even be solving all the problems enumerated here (let alone other issues not mentioned).

Nevertheless, it is a candidate solution that can naturally address issues such as distributed control among untrusted entities, and provides certain extent of flexibilities, which is why they are being tried out in a plethora of application domains.

It is in this background, prompted both by need and potential but also hype, that several governments and public service providers have started pilot projects of using blockchains (Hileman & Rauchs, 2017). National Institute of Standards and Technology (NIST, U.S. Department of Commerce) defines blockchains as "tamper evident and tamper resistant digital ledgers implemented in a distributed fashion (i.e., without a central repository) and usually without a central authority (i.e., a bank, company, or government)" (Yaga, Mall, Roby, & Scarfone, 2018). Blockchains may be viewed as one specific mechanism (using an append-only model) to realize what are more generally known as distributed ledgers, which realize a trustable distributed database even in an environment where individual nodes storing the data cannot be trusted, and may operate under different administrative control (Hileman & Rauchs, 2017).

Broadly, as shown in Fig. 8.1, blockchains can be categorized (Daniels, 2018) based on the nature of entities that are storing and validating the information (validators) to be added to the blockchain, and by who can access the data stored in there. The governance model of the blockchain depends on the trust on the validators, and whether any arbitrary entity can participate or not, leading to the dichotomy between permissioned and permissionless blockchains. Who can view (read) the data being stored on the blockchain, and whether the access is restricted, for example using smart contracts, determine a further dimension to differentiate blockchains into being public or private.

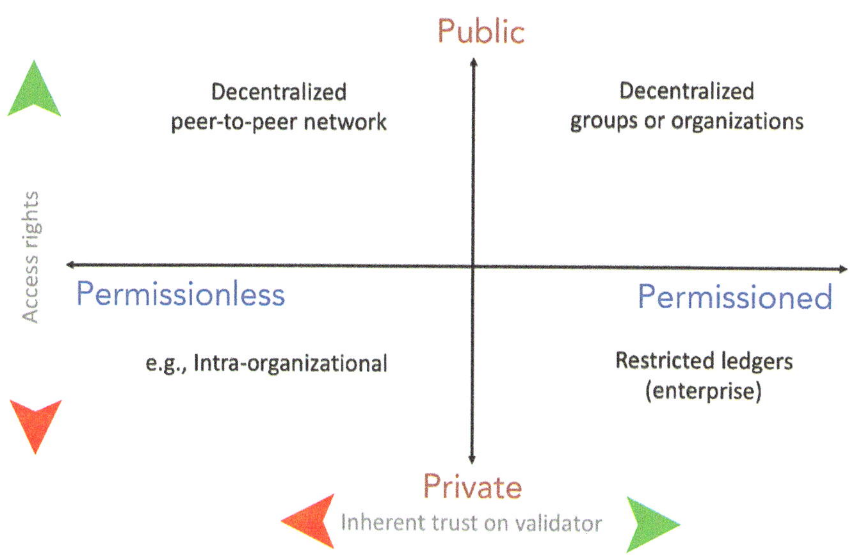

Fig. 8.1 A dichotomy of blockchains

Next, in Sect. 2 we categorize the primitive functionalities that blockchain provide, and how these are leveraged to create further building blocks and overlying applications; discussing then particularly in the context of government use cases and public services. In discussing those examples, our treatment is non-exhaustive, but we have tried to keep the case studies representative. Subsequently, in Sect. 3 we critique the existing initiatives and draw our conclusions.

Note:

- Despite the subtle distinction between distributed ledgers (DLT) and blockchains, for the rest of this paper, we use the terms interchangeably.
- All web resources cited in this paper were last accessed on 20th February 2020.

2 Use Cases

In Warren et al. (2019a), the perceived values of using blockchain from across a spectrum of industries have been identified by conducting a survey of industry representatives. The prominent identified benefits and drivers included (1) full traceability of any information on the blockchain, (2) ability to ensure data has not been tampered with, (3) smart contracts and automation, (4) increased speed and efficiency, (5) increased security and (6) a holistic view with transparency for all appropriate parties.

Traceability and tamper resistance (evident) were among top three drivers in most industries, including in public services as per (Warren et al., 2019a). These provide means to bring transparency and address trust deficit that government bodies may otherwise suffer from. In the context of public services, increased speed and efficiency was additionally identified among the top three drivers in Warren et al. (2019a). Separately, in Scholl and Bolívar (2019) a meta-level study of topics in academic literature associated with both blockchains and public sector/digital government was studied, and cost reduction, innovation, regulation, taxation, security, privacy, transparency were determined to be some of the most prominent topics of interest. Another study explored potential factors that may drive the adoption of blockchains in public sector (Reddick, Cid, & Ganapati, 2019)—and cybersecurity, government effectiveness, and political stability were found to be potential predictors from among six original factors investigated which also included control of corruption, e-government development and democratic participation. This provides an interesting insight of contrasts, namely, while transparency and addressing trust deficit may be perceived immediate benefits of using blockchains, based on the results from (Reddick et al., 2019), control of corruption is apparently not an explicit driver for governments to adopt it.

Several of these desirable properties such as traceability and tamper resistance are key inherent features of blockchain and distributed ledger technologies, while others such as increased speed and efficiency, information reconciliation and a culture of information sharing are by-products that result from multiple data driven services, and multiple stake-holders participating through a single blockchain infrastructure, and the associated transparency and accountability. For example, such benefits of blockchains to manage intragovernmental transfers in the US have been explored in Booz Allen Hamilton (2019a), and it has been argued that because of the guarantees of data traceability, and automation achieved using smart contracts, audit and reconciliations can be carried out more efficiently and in (almost) real time, eliminating intermediaries and third parties, all leading to a boost in speed and efficiency. Likewise, Booz Allen Hamilton (2019b) notes that traditionally, organizations trying to collaborate among each other face several challenges, including reconciliation of information, identifying a single source of truth and facilitating accountability, which can be done more readily and efficiently by leveraging blockchains.

One way to look at the blockchain based government and public service applications is to consider that the inherent characteristics of a blockchain can be harnessed to achieve two primitive services—a notary service for time-stamping, and a (multiparty) data management platform with a single source of truth facilitated by traceability. On top of this, certain basic building blocks such as digital identity, digital registry, digital certificates, ledger service to store interactions or transactions are realized. These are applications on their own right, but they furthermore support each other, leading to a degree of entanglement among the modules, e.g., digital ID and registry services are interdependent; furthermore, enable other overlying applications that leverage on these underlying primitives and building blocks. This (conceptual) layered view is depicted in Fig. 8.2.

2.1 *Notary (Time-Stamping) and Registry Services*

A natural digital government service of blockchain is a time-stamping notary service. Any information or digital document can be time-stamped.

Drawing on this, registry for any real-world assets can also be built using a blockchain. This is indeed one of the canonical use cases of blockchain being piloted in many places. Land and real-estate property registries have emerged as one of the most explored genres of use-case. Potential benefits include efficiency and transparency in determining ownership and carrying out property transfer and reducing the chances of fraud and human errors. Secondary benefits include ease in accessing credit (Kriticos, 2019). Different variations exist, some are government led or backed initiatives, while there are also efforts where private entities mirror the government's land registry record on a blockchain. Partial lists of projects that have implemented blockchain based land registries can be found at (Eder, 2019; Müller & Seifert, 2019; Perez, 2019).

However, it needs to be emphasized that a blockchain is only a part of the solution for land or real-estate assets management, which needs to be complemented by other technological, legal and institutional mechanisms. For instance, from a technological perspective, proper digitalized cartography is essential. Some of the legal

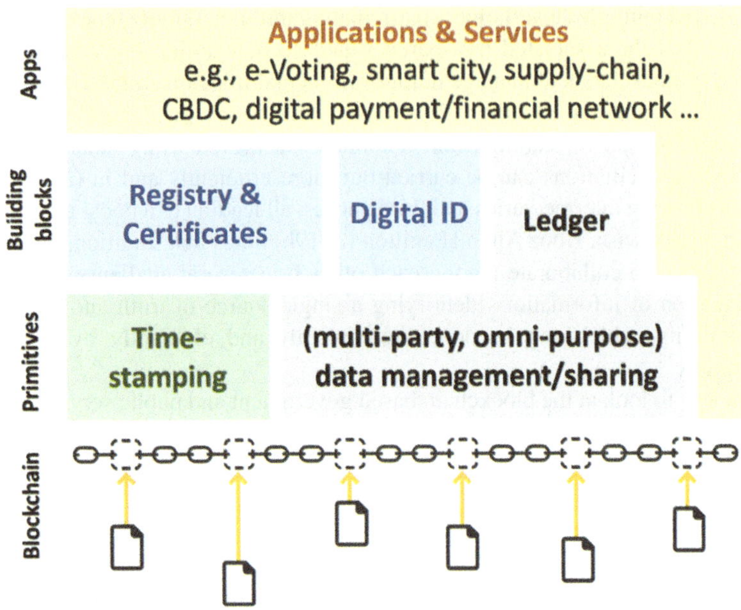

Fig. 8.2 A layered view of blockchain enabled government and public sector services

and institutional issues include the legal validity of 'smart contracts' manipulating the digital records, governance of the blockchain infrastructure to manage the registry and enforcement on the ground. Mendez (2018) makes this case that though sometimes the 'code is the law' view of blockchain is purported but it is in fact not aligned with the role that land registries play in a state, and argues that while blockchain can help automate some of the processes, the guarantees are not automatic, and accordingly the author identifies some of the other legal and institutional gaps that need to be addressed for blockchains to be successfully deployed to realize a land registry service.

Naturally, registry services of all sorts can be realized using blockchain. For example, Dubai and Malta have implemented registry of companies based on blockchain (SmartDubai.ae, 2016; The Malta Independent, 2019). The Singapore Shipping Association (SSA) is developing a blockchain based registry for ships, called International E-Registry of Ships (IERS), to "streamline, standardize and drastically improve the currently laborious ship registration and renewal process" (Singapore Shipping Association, 2019).

Such registry services rely on some form of identity or other. Likewise, facets of a digital identity themselves might be established with the use of time stamping and registry services. We next discuss this intertwined building block of digital identity.

2.2 Digital Identity

Identity is an essential enabler for many services (including registry services discussed above), and as such, the application of digital identity management has been identified severally (Lyons, Courcelas, & Timsit, 2018a; Mark et al., 2018; Morris, Mirkovic, O'Rourke, & Cayholl, 2018; Warren et al., 2019b) as a key application of blockchain in government. An individual's identity can be characterized in many manners. In Morris et al. (2018) identity has been characterized in terms of the nature of origin of identity and the dynamicity with which said information changes. These two dimensions are shown in the horizontal plain in Fig. 8.3. For instance, the date of birth of a person is something inherent, while the educational qualification,

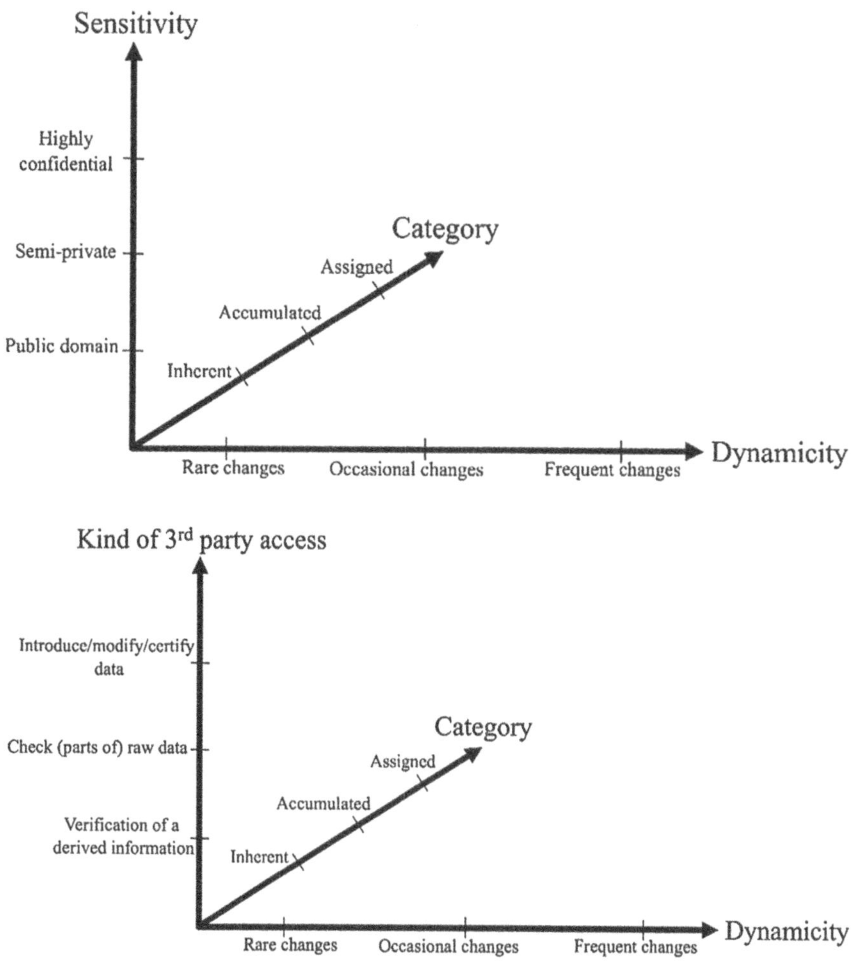

Fig. 8.3 A dissection of identity information

ownership of assets, health history are acquired, while a social security number or a licence number are assigned. Likewise, some information such as one's name or educational qualification may change rarely, while one's address or employer information may change occasionally, while one's credit record or health record might change frequently.

We add to these further dimensions, in terms of the sensitivity of the information as well as in terms of the kind of restricted access to various third parties that ought to be considered. For instance, some information, such as a person's name, family members or employment may not be very sensitive and are of public knowledge, though some of these semi-private in nature, while other information such as health or financial records may be confidential. We note that this categorization is orthogonal to a further dimension (not shown in the figures), that relates to personally identifiable information (PII)—and in fact, how PII is handled in turn determines whether sensitive information is exposed. Who handles various information, and how, where handling includes various actions such as storage, transmission, processing, modification, etc. is another relevant dimension. In that context, Mark et al. (2018) notes that "If PII is managed by a blockchain then users of the chain can be assured that the managed PII are as originally recorded and that all recorded PII are present in the chain. While blockchain's organic integrity assurance is a natural draw for PII management, there is a consequence to the immutability of the managed PII". The consequences arise from legal requirements for correction of record, or even deletion of records (e.g., 'right of erasure' under the European Union enacted the General Data Privacy Protection Regulation (GDPR)), which are at a first glance at odds with the immutability property of blockchains. Examples demonstrating how even indirect referencing (also called, tokenization) mechanisms may not always be adequate from providing adequate defence against PII leakage are also discussed in Mark et al. (2018).

Notwithstanding some of the outstanding technical challenges, particularly pertaining to the privacy concerns and legal restrictions, numerous blockchain based solutions are being explored. See for example (Sabadello, 2020) for a large yet non-exhaustive list. Many projects are still work in progress, but many others have already been deployed. Some prominent pilot cases include e-voting[2] and bike rental[3] applications tried in Zug, Switzerland; worker training certification and check-in/check-out at work sites carried out by Swiss railways,[4] debit cards for refugees without other documentations or bank account in Finland.[5] All the three use cases from Switzerland mentioned here used a public blockchain based decentralized identity service (https://www.uport.me), while the Finnish initiative was in

[2] https://medium.com/bitrates-news/swiss-city-of-zug-successfully-completes-blockchain-based-e-voting-trial-b7b312e5cdc0.

[3] https://medium.com/uport/zug-residents-can-now-ride-e-bikes-using-their-uport-powered-zug-digital-ids-7ed31ac9d621.

[4] https://medium.com/linum-labs/swiss-federal-railway-trials-first-digital-identity-pilot-on-ethereum-4a3cb3c6621.

[5] https://www.wired.com/story/refugees-but-on-the-blockchain/.

liaison with a private enterprise, Moni. Estonia, considered a pioneer in digital identity, uses a blockchain variant called KSI (Keyless Signature Infrastructure), created by Guardtime (e-estonia.com, 2008), and uses this digital identity for delivering a wide range of services including enabling electronic voting. The United Nations Joint Staff Pension Fund (UNJSPF) has in a board meeting in August 2019 (United Nations Joint Staff Pension Fund, 2019) informed about the use of biometrics such as facial recognition, geo-location and blockchain technologies in conjunction to administer their pension disbursal system.

The European Union regulation eIDAS (electronic IDentification, Authentication and trust Services) mandates a digital identity system that interoperates across EU, however it somewhat predates the recent hype around blockchain technologies, and it does not utilize blockchain as the core infrastructure to realize it, but use of and with blockchains is under deliberation (Servida & Munoz, 2018). The examples discussed so far realize digital identity using blockchains, some of which are permissionless, others permissioned. Irrespective of the governance model of the underlying blockchains, the identity layer in these cases are typically administered centrally. In the context of government and public services, a more federated mechanism would provide greater flexibility and allow diverse applications to leverage in a single identity service (Morris et al., 2018)—where, for example, various kinds of government IDs such as driving licence, passport, tax identifier, etcetera are managed by respective agencies.

Pushing this idea of decentralization further, the idea of 'sovereign identity' has been proposed (Allen, 2016), where the identity information is administered by the individual, in a manner unshackled from and administrative authority. For the purpose of government and public services, the intermediate level of distribution, with federated administration of identity information might suffice while keeping the system design and usage complexity reasonable. Indeed, Schwabe (2019) argues (in general, and not specifically for digital identity) that public agencies play an important role in blockchain consortia used for public services, including as a supplier of data and a source of trust guaranteeing the quality of information, and furthermore driving the use of said data. Thus, even as blockchain can be used as a tool for governance, public sector entities may in turn play the role of governing the blockchain. This duality has been remarked previously variously, e.g., in Ølnes, Ubacht, and Janssen (2017).

2.3 *Digital Certificates and Records*

The ideas of a registry service combined along with identity naturally extends to a repository of certificates and records. The suitability of storing the spectrum of such records over blockchain, considering the issues of sensitivity and personally identifiable information, and meeting access control, confidentiality, (system) access and change logging, and content update dynamics that achieve legal and ethical constraints require further exploration. In the meanwhile, blockchains are already in use for managing certificates and records for a wide range of applications. We provide a few illustrative examples to emphasize the diversity of possible use cases.

Use of blockchain to curb degree fraud has been proposed in countries as diverse as Malaysia[6] and Malta (Patel, 2018).

Hash based integrity check and logging is used for Estonia's electronic health records,[7] Synaptic Health Alliance is using a permissioned blockchain to create a platform for sharing reliable and accurate data across the healthcare ecosystem, The U.S. Food and Drug Administration's (FDA) Oncology Center of Excellence operates an information exchange platform based on blockchain (Booz Allen Hamilton, 2019b) and many healthcare industry use cases from drug traceability[8] to insurance (Deloitte, n.d.) are expected to improve the quality of data, service and cost to deliver the same.

The then Chief Information Officer of the Government of Canada announced in May 2019 (Benay, 2019) "Blockcerts, a permanent, self-owned and secure record of their skills and experiences" which would help professional in providing proof of their skills and experiences, which in turn is expected to facilitate better mobility.

2.4 (Multi-Party, Omni-Purpose) Data Management and Ledger

Despite the traditional view point that draws implicit equivalence between blockchains and distributed ledgers, in this work we use the term 'ledger' in a more restrictive sense. Specifically, we consider it to comprise a special class of data which is transactional (but need not be financial) in nature. As such, we consider it as a subset of a wider range of data that could be logged on a blockchain. For instance, in a smart grid system, a multitude of data from Internet of Things (IoT) devices operated by numerous autonomous entities may be logged into the blockchain, and various smart contract based actuations may be carried out; these would fit the more 'catch all' data management layer in our view of the architecture shown in Fig. 8.2. The ledger layer, in contrast, will capture the energy trading activity information. Given this nuanced view, where the ledger is subsumed by the (multiparty) data management layer, but it also captures a special subclass of dataset, we coalesce the two, even while depicting them across layers. We reiterate that the ledger could include financial transactional information too, but is not restricted to it.

A multi-stakeholder data sharing platform can act as a natural aggregator of data, and allow secure and transparent data management, for instance, facilitating data

[6] https://www.nst.com.my/news/nation/2018/11/429615/university-consortium-set-authenticate-degrees-using-blockchain.

[7] https://e-estonia.com/solutions/healthcare/e-health-record/.

[8] https://www.ibm.com/blogs/blockchain/2018/12/what-are-the-use-cases-for-blockchain-tech-in-healthcare/.

owners sovereignty over said data, with abilities for users to determine provenance of the data, have proof of use or access of data, etc. Such a platform can thus enable both digital government as well as non-governmental applications (this is termed as 'Blockchain platform as a service' in Lyons et al. (2018a). It can be viewed as the holy grail for a blockchain in the government technology stack. Several governments, at city, state, country as well as supra-national levels, have deployed, started developing or expressed interest in exploring the provisioning of such multi/omni-purpose blockchains. Examples of some early initiatives include Dubai (SmartDubai.ae, 2016), State of Illinois (Morris et al., 2018), Estonia (eestonia.com, 2008), Switzerland (Swisscom, 2018), Australia,[9] and EU through European Blockchain Partnership.[10]

A very wide range of applications are potentially feasible. We mention some applications that have been tried out but using dedicated blockchains (or piggybacking on an existing one) to give representative examples and emphasize the potential diversity of applications that can benefit from a 'blockchain as a (public) service' platform.

In the U.S. Department of Health and Human Services the grant administration run by the Administration for Children and Families is exploring the use of blockchain (Booz Allen Hamilton, 2019b), The Treasury Department, Bureau of the Fiscal Service is using blockchain for tracking mobile devices (Booz Allen Hamilton, 2019b).

Port of Valencia and Port of Genoa are using blockchains for managing parts of their supply chains and activities such as container management and inter-entity operations (Hewett et al., 2019).

In Alladi, Chamola, Rodrigues, and Kozlov (2019), different use cases of blockchain for smart grids are discussed—this includes smart meters and billing integrated with payment mechanisms (including with cryptocurrency) and energy exchange, spanning countries spread globally, such as the Netherlands, South Africa and Australia.

A multi/omni-purpose blockchain would support wide range of applications, and because of the logical (though not necessarily physical) co-location of data and services, it would provide a multiplier effect in terms of value. However, for certain sensitive applications, for example, catering to defense sector, where some existing use of blockchain includes data sharing, supply chain management for 3D printing aided additive manufacturing and secure communication to name some (3dprintingindustry.com, 2019; Mearian, 2020), private blockchains operated exclusively in isolation for specific purposes might also make sense. Similar to cloud computing, where public, private and hybrid cloud models all have their own pros and cons, and corresponding use cases; in the context of blockchains, a similar parallel can be drawn.

---

[9] https://www.minister.industry.gov.au/ministers/karenandrews/media-releases/advancing-australias-blockchain-industry.

[10] https://ec.europa.eu/digital-single-market/en/news/european-countries-join-blockchain-partnership.

2.5 *Digitizing Currency and Financial Transactions*

Given that blockchain's popularity in the past decade originates from the success of cryptocurrencies, use of blockchain to support digital sovereign fiat currencies (aside the many private sector financial technology innovation attempts) is natural. Banking and financial services are an important aspect of public services, and many central banks are involved in exploration of blockchain technologies in that context. Here, we highlight a very few distinct approaches that have been attempted. An in-depth review on central bank digital currency (CBDC) can be found at (Lannquist, 2019).

Sinagpore's project Ubin (The Monetary Authority of Singapore, 2017), under stewardship of the Monetary Authority of Singapore and in collaboration with major financial institutions (the Association of Banks in Singapore (ABS)) carried out pilot studies of inter-bank transactions using digital ledger technologies, and developed three models for decentralised inter-bank payment and settlements. While the Singapore project used the blockchain technology solely as a distributed ledger for recording the transactions using tokenized coins, "Crypto Franc" was proposed as a bond,[11] with its value pegged to the Swiss franc on a 1-to-1 basis (such a pegged model of cryptocurrency is sometimes termed as 'stable coin'), where permissioned nodes federating Swiss Cantons were proposed to enforce the adherence to regulatory requirements, and to maintain the ledger. The status of this proposal is ambiguous at the time point this article is being written, and in general, there seems no government level support or intent for a sovereign Swiss digital currency.[12]

A notable but dubious (because of the political background) and apparently defunct attempt was Venezuela's Oil and Mineral backed Petro currency. Marshall island, through Sovereign Currency Act of 2018 (Republic of the Marshall Islands, 2018), introduced a new blockchain based currency called the Sovereign ('SOV'), but ironically, with a plan to also issue physical notes for the digital currency.[13]

Bank of Canada, Bank of England and Monetary Authority of Singapore have carried out a collaborative project exploring international fund transfers (KPMG Services, 2018), and government agencies led (or backed) as well as private initiatives supporting international financial transactions is another key area where blockchains is useful in supporting crucial public services.

---

[11] https://www.swissinfo.ch/eng/stable-coin_crypto-bond-catapults-swiss-franc-onto-blockchain/44512880.

[12] https://cointelegraph.com/news/state-issued-digital-currencies-the-countries-which-adopted-rejected-or-researched-the-concept.

[13] https://www.prnewswire.com/news-releases/tangem-to-produce-physical-blockchain-banknotes-for-the-marshall-islands-digital-currency-legal-tender-300784876.html.

3 Critique: State and the Blockchain

The embrace of blockchains in the government technology stack is in its nascence.

Consequently, despite numerous news articles, press releases and white papers, actual technical details regarding most of the initiatives are often sparse, sometimes contradictory, or just absent from the public domain. Furthermore, since there are no well validated and established best practices, and almost every effort is exploratory in nature, design and decisions may just not yet be finalized, and so things naturally change. While we have tried our best to filter out the latest relevant and correct information, it is thus apt to note at this juncture that some of the points we make here may inadvertently be somewhat off the mark, or may become obsolete over time.

Just like we see diverse forms of economic systems in general, where core services for citizens (such as health care, transportation, financial services, utilities) are provided in some instances by solely government agencies, in others, by only private entities, in yet others, in private-public partnerships, and finally, also in forms where private and government run entities both operate and compete in the market; from the examples we have discussed above, we see an echo of similar different formats in the government technology (GovTech) space in general, and for blockchains for GovTech in particular.

For the rest of our discussions here, we focus on three aspects: (1) blockchain support for sovereign digital currency, (2) blockchain as a platform for digital identity, and (3) the nature of the underlying blockchain infrastructure used as an omnipurpose platform. The other specific use cases, such as registry services or repository for digital records, all in turn rely on the underlying infrastructure and the identity service and are thus not explicitly discussed. We conclude with a discussion on a few recognized as well as potential pitfalls that need to be considered when deploying a blockchain based solution.

3.1 Sovereign Digital Currency

In Lyons et al. (2018a), the following argument is forwarded "Another important building block, in our opinion, is having digital versions of national currencies on the blockchain, for example through blockchain-based central bank digital currencies (CBDCs). Making it possible for legal tender to become an integral part of blockchain transactions will make it easier to reap the benefits of new technologies like smart contracts. On a systemic level, CBDCs could bring the benefits of decentralisation to inter-bank payments and real-time gross settlement systems, among other things".

There are several cryptocurrency flavoured approaches to realize a digital sovereign currency, Venezuela's Petro (now apparently defunct) and Marshall Islands' 'the Sovereign' (which also is planned to come with physical 'banknotes') come to mind. While there is some level of enthusiasm about such digital sovereign currencies (to be distinguished with the non-state-backed cryptocurrencies), it is rather unnecessary and a tokenization-based approach showcased in project Ubin is a pragmatic solution to realize central bank digital currencies (CBDCs).

To quote (The Monetary Authority of Singapore, 2017): "the SGD-on-ledger is a specific use coupon that is issued on a one-to-one basis in exchange for money. The coupons have a specific usage domain - in our case for the settlement of interbank debts - but no value outside of this. One is able to cash out by exchanging the coupons back into money later... SGD-on-ledger has three useful properties that make it suited to our prototype. First, unlike money in bank accounts, we do not receive interest on the on ledger holdings. The absence of interest calculations reduces the complexity of managing the payment system. Second, to ensure full redeem-ability of the SGD on-ledger for money, each token is fully backed by an equivalent amount of SGD held in custody. This means that the overall money supply is unaffected by the issuance of the on ledger equivalents since there is no net increase in dollar claims on the central bank. Third, SGD-on-ledger are limited use instruments and can be designed with additional features to support the use case—such as security features against misuse."

The three highlighted properties from the project Ubin report emphasize the importance of responsibly using blockchain without creating instability while solving actual pain points of digital financial activities that exist with legacy infrastructure: particularly that the processes are unnecessarily complex with respect to the functionalities provided, making the solutions inefficient (slower and/or expensive). Such a tokenized approach also allows a natural integration of the currency with other workflows and functionalities that may be carried out over a multi/omni-purpose blockchain platform.

Overall, using a tokenized representation of real-world currency, where a distributed ledger (realized over a permissioned blockchain) is used for record keeping, automation and integration with other services looks like the most pragmatic approach forward, instead of creating new forms of currencies.

3.2 Digital ID in a Multi-Stakeholder Environment

Digital identity has been repeatedly emphasized as one of the 'killer apps' of government blockchains. For instance, to quote (Morris et al., 2018): "A citizen-centric digital identity model based on distributed ledger technologies could be used to consolidate disparate data that currently exists across multiple agencies and layers of government into a network cantered around a citizen's or business' credentials, licenses and identity attributes. It would enable citizens to view their public service identity via an identity app on their smartphone and share relevant data with government to access public services." A European Union Blockchain Observatory & Forum report (Lyons et al., 2018a) likewise states "One of the most important requirements in building a digital economy and society is viable digital identities for all participants, whether individuals, companies, public agencies or, increasingly, machines and other autonomous agents. The need to be able to identify ourselves and others is so important, in fact, that it is considered the essential prerequisite for most use cases." Many other whitepapers (Allen, 2016; Australia Post, 2016; The World Bank Group, 2018; Willars, 2019; World Economic Forum, 2016) have likewise elaborated the importance of digital identity in the recent years.

The Estonian blockchain at its core deals with digital identity (e-estonia.com, 2008), and several of the proposed government run blockchains aim to provide and utilize digital identity in some manner. Yet, some of the world's largest digitalized identity systems are in fact not blockchain based. This includes EU's electronic IDentification, Authentication and trust Services (eIDAS[14]), India's Aadhaar[15] which is the world's largest world's largest biometric ID system managed by Unique Identification Authority of India (UIDAI) and China's social credit system (The Economist, 2016). So, the performance at scale, or the multi-stakeholder usage scenarios in themselves do not necessitate the use of a blockchain. One argument for using blockchains is the notion of 'self-sovereign digital identity' (Allen, 2016; Willars, 2019). In this (as well as many other security benefits that are assumed and/or promised with blockchain, such as more generally data sovereignty, portability, privacy and security, integrity and audit trail), the nuances of how the underlying infrastructure is actually designed, deployed and used determines whether the security guarantees are actually realized. It is too early to comment on how (ID2020.org, 2014) or (DIF, 2017) technology stack evolves. Thus, while blockchain based distributed ledger technology can be used to support digital identity, it is not a singular option to do so, nor are all the assumed security guarantees inherent invariants. We will discuss more on the potential gaps and pitfalls that need careful navigation when deploying a blockchain based solution.

3.3 Blockchain as a Platform

In February 2019, the European Medicines Verification System (EMVS)[16] was launched.[17] Such an application perfectly fits a blockchain use case, given the scale and multi-stakeholder nature of the system. It (to the best of our understanding) however does not use blockchain technologies. Many large-scale multi-stakeholder systems in general exist. While technologically not singular, and many other alternative realizations are possible (as exemplified by deployed systems), one argument in favour of a blockchain is to expose it as a platform or service, where new applications can be modularly integrated, rather than having to design and deploy different

[14] https://ec.europa.eu/digital-single-market/en/trust-services-and-eid.

[15] https://uidai.gov.in/my-aadhaar/about-your-aadhaar.html.

[16] https://emvo-medicines.eu/mission/emvs/.

[17] https://emvo-medicines.eu/new/wp-content/uploads/EMVO-Press-Release-EMVS-Launch.pdf.

systems from scratch for individual applications. Incidentally, since such systems are being built ground up, they are in a position to avoid some of the problems faced by many legacy systems, such as poorly structured, non-standardized data, interoperability across systems (though blockchain interoperability is still an open research in itself (Buterin, 2016; Dinh, Datta, & Ooi, 2019; Lyons, Courcelas, & Timsit, 2018b; Rutter, 2017)) and the ability to migrate the data to/from another system. While these are not inherent properties of blockchain, the creation of a new digital infrastructure ground up provides a coincidental opportunity.

In Lyons et al. (2018a, 2018b), some design dilemmas are discussed at length. For instance, a top-down approach where the government deploys (and possibly enforces) the usage of a single blockchain for every government related purpose, will help with the aforementioned standardization by default, and yet, it may lead to a single vendor lock-in, while lacking the flexibility to accommodate all possible use cases. Many of the national blockchain initiatives (eestonia.com, 2008; SmartDubai.ae, 2016; Swisscom, 2018) appear to be following this approach of a single standardized blockchain. In contrast, uncoordinated experimentations of different technologies by different agencies may lead to duplication of effort, as well as fragmentation of platforms. In Lyons et al. (2018a) a middle ground is advocated: "flexible, cloud based shared infrastructure that hosts different protocols as well as developer tools, and an integrated development and operations environment". The authors further add "A shared "sandbox" approach, even one featuring multiple technologies, should also foster knowledge sharing and make it easier for agencies to work together to ensure interoperability". Particularly for a supra-national set-up such as the EU, this approach may be inevitable, since individual member states would likely embrace a spectrum of blockchain solutions.

To wrap up this discussion, we refer to (Fan et al., 2019) where a multi-stake holder blockchain based solution for data management approach is studied and contrasted with centralized approaches. It has been argued in Fan et al. (2019) that in a centralized solution where a single entity manages all the data, citizen's privacy may be at risk because of aggregation of all information and the system may also suffer from lack of transparency of usage of the data, issues which a blockchain deployed across multiple parties may mitigate. Use of blockchain is thus a promising alternate to traditional IT infrastructure deployment models and provides opportunity to mitigate trust deficit between governments and citizens to certain extent. From this point of view, blockchain may serve as a new tool for governance (Ølnes et al., 2017), provided it can overcome technical challenges, as well as organizational inertia in adopting new governance model (Batubara, Ubacht, & Janssen, 2018). In terms of technical challenges, there are scalability, performance and security issues, which amplify the issue of the challenges of governance (Rikken, Janssen, & Kwee, 2019) of the resulting blockchain based IT infrastructure (recall the governance duality noted between blockchains and public bodies in Ølnes et al. (2017), both because some of the technological challenges are not yet well understood and there might be organizational inertia in embracing new governance models; furthermore, it has been noted in Rikken et al. (2019) that unlike in non-blockchain applications, there is strong entanglement between the applications and infrastructure, complicating the governance of the resulting IT infrastructure. Whether this is an inherent behaviour of blockchain based systems, or an artefact of current deployments would need more research. We speculate that the modular layered model advanced in this article (see Fig. 8.2) will help reduce if not eliminate such entanglement, thus simplifying the IT infrastructure governance challenges.

3.4 *Mind the Gap*

While the above design dilemmas are relevant, in this paper, we want to highlight a few other, arguably more critical issues, that needs careful attention.

Consider the KSI blockchain used in e-estonia.com (2008), quoting (Guardtime, 2015) regarding data privacy guarantees: "KSI does not ingest any customer data; data never leaves the customer premises. Instead the system is based on one-way cryptographic hash functions that result in hash values uniquely representing the data but are irreversible such that one cannot start with the hash value and reconstruct the data—data privacy is guaranteed at all times." Since the blockchain does not store the actual data, prima facie data privacy is achieved using the blockchain, while also validating data integrity. However, depending on the nature of the data/application if it is something that resides on an off-chain storage repository and is corrupted, the blockchain would be able to detect such corruption upon usage of said off-chain data, but it does not support prevention or correction (for which, out of chain mechanisms would be required in a well-designed system). Likewise, the confidentiality of such data may still be violated if the off-chain repository is breached. Moreover, even the meta-information, depending on the nature of said meta-information, may lead to leakage of critical information, as has been emphasized with examples in Mark et al. (2018). For the electronic voting system i-Voting, (e-estonia.com, 2008) states: "the Estonian solution is simple, elegant and secure. During a designated pre-voting period, the voter logs onto the system using an ID-card or Mobile-ID, and casts a ballot. The voter's identity is removed from the ballot before it reaches the National Electoral Commission for counting, thereby ensuring anonymity. With any method of remote voting, including traditional postal ballots, the possibility of votes being forced or bought is a concern. Estonia's solution was to allow voters to log on and vote as many times as they want during the pre-voting period. Since each vote cancels the last, a voter always has the option of changing his or her vote later." However, such broad and strong claim of security calls for scepticism. For instance, side-information such as time of authentication/communication might reveal who a specific person voted for, even if that information is not explicitly stored. We are not asserting that the Estonian blockchain deployment in their e-Government technology stack necessarily suffers from all these vulnerabilities, and in fact, it is very likely that some of these concerns have been investigated and many further layers of protection have been deployed. The purpose of this discussion using hypotheticals is to emphasize that the blockchain does not and cannot provide a range of security guarantees in a stand-alone manner, yet we often see a marketing pitch in the lines of 'its secure because it is a blockchain', which has the risk of creating a false and misplaced sense of security.

In e-estonia.com (2008) it is further stated: "With KSI blockchain deployed in Estonian government networks, history cannot be rewritten by anybody and the authenticity of the electronic data can be mathematically proven. It means that no one—not hackers, not system administrators, and not even government itself—can manipulate the data and get away with that."

However, the claim that data is immutable because it is on a blockchain (which is the one fundamental functionality a blockchain is supposed to provide) may overlook some fundamental issues. In the specific case of (e-estonia.com, 2008), the blockchain is further published in the physical media (newspapers), which are subscribed by many libraries spread worldwide, creating a globally dispersed 'physical backup' which is nigh to impossible to tamper.

Public blockchains are hugely inefficient for the purposes of many e-Government use cases. From usability and cost perspectives, the sole rational choice in most if not all cases would be to use permissioned (and even private) blockchains. For instance, Swisscom (2018) states "Swiss Post and Swisscom are connecting their existing private infrastructures for blockchain applications. On the basis of distributed ledger technology, the two instances check each other and thus help to establish trust. In contrast to "public blockchains" (e.g. Bitcoin and Ethereum), this private blockchain infrastructure requires much less energy, since it can only be used by identified users who have a contractual relationship with the providers of an application. This enables more efficient agreement procedures as well as significantly higher security and performance. This is an important prerequisite for many companies to launch their own applications based on blockchain technology."

The participating entities in such permissioned or private blockchains can collude together, or may be forced by a (hypothetical, dystopian) government, to manipulate the data. Furthermore, in many such deployments, the software running at all sites are sourced from the same vendor. So, a software (update) run by all the sites from a malicious or compromised vendor would be sufficient to subvert the whole blockchain's integrity. These are some very critical issues that need more attention, particularly in the context of blockchain use in the government technology stack. An approach like (e-estonia.com, 2008) utilizing off-chain globally dispersed physical back-up is a nifty safeguard for this concern. Doing so individually for every private blockchain, while feasible, may still be cumbersome for respective stakeholders.

Smart contracts can be used over a 'Blockchain platform as a service' to automate many tasks, including, near real time monitoring and actuation of action plans, and in the longer term, to enhance workflows and decision processes further driven by analytics (artificial intelligence). Such automation can significantly improve the cost effectiveness and quality of service that can be delivered. However, the opportunities to leverage such data using the blockchain infrastructure directly may also be constrained, depending on the nature of the blockchain deployment. For example, if the actual data is stored off-chain, and tokenization is used, then the nature of tokenization would influence the versatility of applications that can be built on top of the blockchain. This is not necessarily a bad thing, nor does it add fundamental limitations in creating decentralized applications leveraging the troika of blockchains, smart contracts and artificial intelligence. In Lopez, Montresor, and Datta (2019), an argument for (a network of) blockchains being utilized as a glue to bind actual data and services that are off the chain (to realize better data sovereignty), and likewise keeping the logic also at the edge (which is where the data originates and/or is utilized) is forwarded.

To wrap-up, we reiterate the observation from Mendez (2018) regarding the need to complement the technological opportunities with institutional readjustments. This includes the legal frameworks. For instance, the use of blockchain based digital ID for the voting in Zug foremost required local legislative adjustment so that such a digital identity can be deemed legally valid. The state of Illinois enacted the Blockchain Technology Act which went into effect on 1st January 2020 (Illinois General Assembly, 2019). It is essential to address such legal gaps, in addition to the technological gaps, in order to properly harness the potential of blockchain technology in government and public services.

References

3dprintingindustry.com. (2019). *Blockchain secures distributed additive manufacturing in the U.S. air force*. Retrieved from https://3dprintingindustry.com/news/blockchain-secures-distributed-additive-manufacturing-in-the-u-s-air-force-160928/

Alladi, T., Chamola, V., Rodrigues, J. J., & Kozlov, S. A. (2019). Blockchain in smart grids: A review on different use cases. *Sensors, 19*(22), 4862.

Allen, C. (2016). *The path to self-sovereign identity*. Retrieved from http://www.lifewithalacrity.com/2016/04/the-path-to-self-soverereign-identity.html

Australia Post. (2016). *A frictionless future for identity management: A practical solution for Australia's digital identity challenge* (Tech. Rep.). Author.

Batubara, F. R., Ubacht, J., & Janssen, M. (2018). Challenges of blockchain technology adoption for e-government: A systematic literature review. In: *Proceedings of the 19th Annual International Conference on Digital Government Research: Governance in the Data Age* (pp. 1–9).

Benay, A. (2019). *Securing the future of talent mobility in the government of Canada*. Retrieved from https://tbs-blog.canada.ca/en/securing-future-talent-mobility-government-canada

Booz Allen Hamilton. (2019a). *Blockchain and intragovernmental transfers* (Tech. Rep.). Report for the Bureau of the Fiscal Service.

Booz Allen Hamilton. (2019b). *Bringing blockchain into government* (Tech. Rep.). Data Foundation.

Buterin, V. (2016). *Chain interoperability* (Tech. Rep.). R3 Reports.

Daniels, A. (2018). *The rise of private permissionless blockchains*. Retrieved from https://medium.com/ltonetwork/the-rise-of-private-permissionless-blockchains-part-1-4c39bea2e2be

Deloitte. (n.d.). *Blockchain in insurance*. Deloitte white paper.

DIF. (2017). *Decentralized Identity Foundation: DIF*. https://identity.foundation/

Dinh, T. T. A., Datta, A., & Ooi, B. C. (2019). *A blueprint for interoperable blockchains*. arXiv ePrint 1910.00985.

Doan, A., Halevy, A., & Ives, Z. (2012). *Principles of data integration*. Saint Louis: Elsevier.

Eder, G. (2019). Digital transformation: Blockchain and land titles. In: *OECD Global Anti-Corruption & Integrity Forum.*

e-estonia.com. (2008). *KSI blockchain.* Retrieved from https://e-estonia.com

Fan, L., Gil-Garcia, J. R., Song, Y., Cronemberger, F., Hua, G., Werthmuller, D., et al. (2019). Sharing big data using blockchain technologies in local governments: Some technical, organizational and policy considerations. *Information Polity, 24*, 419.

Field, T., Muller, E., & Lau, E. (2003). *The e-government imperative*. OECD Publishing.

Guardtime. (2015). *KSI data sheet: Keyless signature infrastructure*. Retrieved from https://m.guardtime.com/files/KSI_data_sheet_201509.pdf

Heeks, R. (2001). *Reinventing government in the information age: International practice in it-enabled public sector reform* (vol. 1). Psychology Press.

Heinrichs, H. (2013). Sharing economy: A potential new pathway to sustainability. *GAIA - Ecological Perspectives for Science and Society, 22*(4), 228–231.

Hewett, N., Wolfgang, L., Yingli, W., DiCaprio, A., Leong, A., Guinard, D., et al. (2019). *Inclusive deployment of blockchain for supply chains* (Tech. Rep.). World Economic Forum (White Paper).

Hileman, G., & Rauchs, M. (2017). *Global blockchain benchmarking study* (Tech. Rep.). Cambridge Centre for Alternative Finance.

ID2020.org. (2014). *ID2020.* Retrieved from https://id2020.org

Illinois General Assembly. (2019). *Blockchain technology act.*

KPMG Services. (2018). *Cross-border interbank payment and settlements* (Tech. Rep.). Monetary Authority of Singapore (project Ubin report).

Kriticos, S. (2019). *Keeping it clean: Can blockchain change the nature of land registry in developing countries?* Retrieved from https://blogs.worldbank.org/developmenttalk/keeping-it-clean-can-blockchain-change-nature-land-registry-developing-countries

Lannquist, A. (2019). *Central banks and distributed ledger technology*. World Economic Forum whitepaper.

Lopez, P., Montresor, A., & Datta, A. (2019). Please, do not decentralize the internet with (permissionless) blockchains! In: *IEEE International Conference on Distributed Computing Systems (ICDCS).*

Lyons, T., Courcelas, L., & Timsit, K. (2018a). *Blockchain for government and public services* (Tech. Rep.). The European Union Blockchain Observatory & Forum.

Lyons, T., Courcelas, L., & Timsit, K. (2018b). *Blockchain scalability thematic report scalability, interoperability and sustainability for interoperability government and public sustainability services blockchains* (Tech. Rep.). The European Union Blockchain Observatory & Forum.

Mark, G., Melinda, N., Lisa, P., George, B., Jonathan, D., Kaivan, R., et al. (2018). *Blockchain and suitability for government applications* (Tech. Rep.). United States Department of Homeland Security.

Martin, C. J. (2016). The sharing economy: A pathway to sustainability or a nightmarish form of neoliberal capitalism? *Ecological Economics, 121*, 149–159.

Mearian, L. (2020). *U.S. air force to pilot blockchain-based database for data sharing.* Retrieved from https://www.computerworld.com/article/3519917/us-air-force-to-pilot-blockchain-based-database-for-data-sharing.html

Mendez, F. P. (2018). Smart contracts, blockchain and land registry. In: *International Federation of Surveyors (FIG).*

Morris, C., Mirkovic, J., O'Rourke, J., & Cayholl, C. (2018). *Illinois blockchain and distributed ledger task force final report to the general assembly.* State of Illinois Government Report.

Müller, H., & Seifert, M. (2019). Blockchain, a feasible technology for land administration? In: *OECD Global Anti-corruption & Integrity Forum.*

OECD. (2014). Recommendation of the council on digital government strategies. *Public Governance and Territorial Development Directorate*.

Ølnes, S., Ubacht, J., & Janssen, M. (2017). Blockchain in government: Benefits and implications of distributed ledger technology for information sharing. *Government Information Quarterly, 34*, 355.

Patel, N. (2018). Malta pilots blockchain-based credentials program. In: *IEEE Spectrum.*

Perez, E. (2019). *Blockchain registers for recording ownership rights around the world.* Retrieved from https://cointelegraph.com/news/blockchain-registers-for-recording-ownership-rights-around-the-world

Reddick, C. G., Cid, G. P., & Ganapati, S. (2019). Determinants of blockchain adoption in the public sector: An empirical examination. *Information Polity, 24*, 379.

Republic of the Marshall Islands. (2018). *Declaration and issuance of the sovereign currency act 2018.* Retrieved from http://law.sov.global/law.pdf

Rikken, O., Janssen, M., & Kwee, Z. (2019). Governance challenges of blockchain and decentralized autonomous organizations. *Information Polity, 24*, 397.

Rutter, K. (2017). *The myth of easy interoperability* (Tech. Rep.). R3 Reports.

Sabadello, M. (2020). *Blockchain Identity project list.* Retrieved from https://github.com/peacekeeper/blockchain-identity

Scholl, H. J., & Bolívar, M. P. R. (2019). Mapping potential impact areas of blockchain use in the public sector. *Information Polity, 24*, 359.

Schwabe, G. (2019). The role of public agencies in blockchain consortia: Learning from the Cardossier. *Information Polity, 24*, 437–451.

Servida, A., & Munoz, C. (2018). The eIDAS regulation, and how it may be linked to blockchain. In: *EU Blockchain Forum Workshop 5 Report on e-Identity.*

Singapore Shipping Association. (2019). *International e-registry of ships (IERS). Press release, Singapore, 14 October 2019.*

SmartDubai.ae. (2016). *Dubai blockchain strategy.* Retrieved from https://www.smartdubai.ae/initiatives/blockchain

Swisscom. (2018). *Swiss Post and Swisscom launch a 100% Swiss infrastructure for blockchain applications.* Press release. Retrieved from https://www.swisscom.ch/en/about/news/2018/12/post-swisscom-blockchain-infrastruktur.html

The Economist. (2016). *Big data, meet big brother: China invents the digital totalitarian state.*

The Malta Independent. (2019). Retrieved from http://www.independent.com.mt/articles/2019-05-08/local-news/Registry-of-Companies-to-be-first-agency-in-the-world-run-by-a-Blockchain-based-system-6736207848

The Monetary Authority of Singapore. (2017). *Project Ubin: SGD on distributed ledger.* Monetary Authority of Singapore and Deloitte report.

The World Bank Group. (2018). *G20 digital identity onboarding.* World Bank Group Report.

United Nations Joint Staff Pension Fund. (2019). *Modernizing pension processes: UNJSPF and ICC launch pilot project for facial recognition.* Retrieved from https://www.unjspf.org/modernizing-pension-processes-unjspf-and-icc-launch-pilot-project-for-facial-recognition/

Warren, S., Deshmukh, S., Whitehouse, S., Treat, D., Worley, A., Herzig, J., & Nolting, G. (2019b). *Building value with blockchain technology* (Tech. Rep.). World Economic Forum (White Paper).

Warren, S., Deshmukh, S., Whitehouse, S., Treat, D., Worley, A., Herzig, J., et al. (2019a). *Building value with blockchain technology* (Tech. Rep.). World Economic Forum (White Paper).

Willars, E. (2019). *Self-sovereign and shared ledgers: A new dawn for digital identity? Innovate Identity* (http://www.innovateidentity.com) whitepaper.

World Economic Forum. (2016). *A blueprint for digital identity.* World Economic Forum Report.

Yaga, D., Mall, P., Roby, N., & Scarfone, K. (2018, October). *Blockchain technology overview* (Tech. Rep. No. NISTIR 8202). NIST. NISTIR 8202.

Anwitaman Datta is an associate professor in the School of Computer Science and Engineering at Nanyang Technological University, Singapore. Anwitaman's core research interests span the topics of large-scale resilient distributed systems, information security and applications of data analytics. Presently, Anwitaman is exploring topics at the intersection of computer science, public policies & regulations along with the wider societal and (cyber)security impact of technology. This includes the topics of social media and network analysis, cyber risk analysis and management, cryptocurrency forensics, the governance of disruptive technologies, as well as impact and use of disruptive technologies in digital societies and government.

Chapter 9
"Blockchain-Based Identity: The Advantages and Disadvantages"

Clare Sullivan

1 Introduction and Chapter Overview

This chapter examines blockchain-chain based identity and its specific advantages and challenges for identity management, from the perspectives of governments, businesses and individuals. This examination is then used as the basis for determining the policy and legislative reforms needed to underpin effective blockchain-based identity systems.

The chapter defines identity and digital identity for the purposes of the discussion because there is often lack of clarity, and hence confusion, about what constitutes identity and its legal standing and importance. The chapter then examines existing paper-based identity authentication and verification including the Know Your Customer (KYC) protocols that are in place in most jurisdictions around the world. The discussion contrasts identity authentication and verification under a paper-based system with a blockchain-based system, to identify the specific changes brought by blockchain. Using that discussion as a foundation, the advantages and disadvantages of existing paper-based identity management systems are compared with a public blockchain-based system which is considered more secure than a private blockchain. The interests and the legal duties and rights of these stakeholders, including developing rights and duties under international law, are considered, particularly the impact of blockchain on current data protection and privacy legislation in place in most jurisdictions. That legislation is predicated on an approach to data management and control, and the traditional roles of data controller and data processor, that are effectively up-ended by blockchain-based systems.

Having examined the overall changes brought by blockchain and the advantages compared to the disadvantages, the chapter examines the policy and legal changes

C. Sullivan (✉)
Law Center, Georgetown University, Washington, DC, USA
e-mail: Cls269@georgetown.edu

C. G. Reddick et al. (eds.), *Blockchain and the Public Sector*, Public Administration and Information Technology 36,
https://doi.org/10.1007/978-3-030-55746-1_9

needed to support blockchain-based identity. The chapter concludes with a call for action by policy and law makers to provide a sound legal foundation for these new systems including protections for government, businesses and individuals relying on blockchain-based systems.

2 Implications for Digital Identity

This section defines digital identity for the purposes of the discussion; and examines existing paper-based identity authentication and verification requirements and procedures. The discussion contrasts identity authentication and verification under a paper-based system with a blockchain-based system, to identify the specific changes brought by a blockchain-based system, particularly public blockchain for identity authentication.

2.1 Digital Identity in Context

Depending on context, the term digital identity can have different meanings for different people. A sociologist may use this term to refer to a person's online persona, for example. In this chapter, however, digital identity is used to describe the group of information that is required to establish one's identity for official business purposes. It is the group of identity information that is used to conduct a commercial transaction.

As I have explained in earlier scholarship, historically identity has not had an important role on commercial dealings. For much of legal history it has been amorphous and its legal standing and role have been very unclear. This is especially so in common law jurisdictions and those with a common law legacy. It is surprising to many that contract law in these jurisdictions is not usually concerned about the identity of the parties. Instead the law is concerned as to whether there is genuine agreement between the parties and usually presumes that in face-to-face dealings each party intends to deal with the person who is physically present, though this presumption can be rebutted by clear, admissible evidence to the contrary. Similar reasoning is also evident in other branches of the common law such as the law of agency in relation to the doctrine of undisclosed principal. In summary, a person's identity, its composition and legal role and standing has been largely unimportant and as a consequence, nebulous.

In the digital age, dealings conducted in person have been almost entirely replaced by dealings conducted without a history of personal acquaintance, or even any human to human interaction; and digital identity is routinely required for both private sector and government transactions. This has made digital identity both important and necessary if an individual is to be able to conveniently access most services and commodities. It also became imperative that an individual have one digital identity for transactional purposes, whereas traditionally at common law that was not a requirement.

While law is still developing, the importance of digital identity was formally recognized in 2017 by the United Nations in its sustainable development goal (SDG) 16.9. This goal is "By 2030, provide legal identity for all, including birth registration." Although "legal identity" is not defined in SDG16.9, this goal is, for all practical purposes, a digital identity for all, and significantly SGD 16.9 recognizes the information recorded at birth as critical. This is a major step along the road to formal legal recognition of the role, nature, and importance of digital identity.

2.2 Digital Identity Defined

The most significant set of information that is common to all digital identity schemes is 'transaction identity' because it is the information that a person must provide to transact. This set of information comprises full name, date of birth, usually gender and at least one piece of identifying information i.e. information that is regarded as unique to the individual such as a PIN, signature, identifying number or sometimes a biometric. The scheme and the value and type of transaction, dictate the identifying information required including whether more than one piece of identifying information is necessary.

The set of information that constitutes a person's digital identity for transactional purposes is therefore, a small, defined, set of identity information. This information is largely derived from a person's birth certificate. It is significant that in the digital age is still the seminal identity document in most jurisdictions including the U.S. Digital identity is also very different from traditional legal notions of identity because digital identity is comprised of information which does not just have meaning – it also has function. When the information is entered, it is used by the system to first to recognize the particular identity from the many registered digital identities on record, and then to enable the requested transaction.

The other information which makes up digital identity is more extensive and dynamic. It sits behind transaction identity and is essentially a person's transactional history and usually other associated information including administrative information. This information will vary depending on the type of scheme but it is personal information that is linked to an individual by, and through, his/her transaction identity.[1]

[1] For a more detailed discussion see, Sullivan C, Digital Identity: An Emergent Legal Concept, 2010: ISBN 978-0-9807230-0-0 (electronic), ISBN 978-0- 9807230-1-4 (paperback) (2010) and http://www.adelaide.edu.au/press/titles/digital-identity/.

2.3 Digital Identity Schemes and Identity Authentication and Verification

All digital identity schemes for transactions (as distinguished from social media, for example), depend on two processes. The first process which occurs at the time a person registers, is authentication of identity. The second is verification of identity which occurs once a person has registered and uses the registered digital identity for a transaction. Verification occurs each time the transaction identity information is used to transact.

At the time of registration, information is collected and checked to determine the authenticity of the person's identity.[2] This is done by the individual providing original documentation which typically begin with the birth certificate and include driver's and other licenses, marriage certificate if there has been a name change as a result of marriage, passport and other official documents such as those issued by government authorities, stating name and address. As mentioned, the birth certificate is the most important identity document from which most of the key information for other required identity documents such as licenses and a passport, are derived. This document checking generally follows the Know Your Customer (KYC) requirements for identity authentication that are required under Anti-Money Laundering/Counter Terrorism Financing (AML/CTF) legislation that was widely adopted in the U.S. and most nations to address money laundering. The KYC protocols, also commonly referred to as the 100-point identity check, typically include an in-person interview at which time the applicant provides a range of specified identity documents that are ranked in terms of their standing to establish his/her identity. Originals of the identity documents are presented in-person by the applicant and copies of those documents are made at that time by the authenticating agency for their record as required by the AML/CTF legislation and are cross checked against official and other records.

The thoroughness and integrity of identity authenticity checking on registration is crucial because the information registered establishes an individual's digital identity, and most importantly, his/her transactional identity. In addition to establishing and recording the person's full name, gender, and date of birth, the required identifying information i.e. signature, photograph, and biometrics such as a face scan, iris scans and fingerprints, are recorded as part of registration and other identifiers such as a number or PIN are also assigned at this time. The primary role of the identifying information is to the link to the individual who presented the information with the registered digital identity. At the time of registration, the digital identity comes into

[2] A familiar example in the U.S. is the identity verification process that is required to obtain a driver's license, open a bank account, obtain a credit card or apply for a passport. In some jurisdictions, like the U.S., registration must be done at different public and private sector organizations but many countries have, or are moving to, centralized national identity schemes where registration is done by one body, usually a government department, and the issued identity can be used for a full range of public and private sector transactions.

effect and the recorded identifying information is then inseparably associated with the individual. This is so even if there is error or fraud in the process.

Once registration is completed, transaction identity becomes the primary means by the individual transacts. Identity is verified for transactions when all the required transaction identity information as presented matches the information on record. Transaction identity operates much like a key opening a door to allow access to the system to enable transactions. First, a single digital identity is found amongst all the identities registered under the scheme, then that identity is verified to enable it to transact under the scheme. Identity is verified by matching the transaction identity information as presented at that time, with the information on record. If all that identity information matches the information on record, then the system automatically authorizes the transaction. Of course, the assumption is that the dealing is with the person who presents the transaction identity but the system actually deals only with the digital identity, in other words with information presented in digital form. The transaction is with the registered identity via transaction identity, not with the individual represented by that transaction identity. This is an important point because it lies at the heart of how identity theft and fraud and error, can occur. Transaction identity functions independently of a human being. The system presumes that the person who is registered to a particular digital identity is presenting the information, but that is not necessarily the case. [3]

The nature and functions of transaction identity, and its significance in the digital era means that the consequences of system error, or fraud are serious, especially for the individual who is associated with the identity used for a bogus transaction.

2.4 *Blockchain Technology Transforming Digital Identity Schemes and Identity Authentication and Verification*

Blockchain and other distributed ledger technology (collectively referred to as blockchain technology in this chapter) has much to offer in improving identity authentication and verification by fundamentally transforms the way identity information is controlled, authenticated, and verified. The way this can work is that an individual's identity attributes are distributed across the blockchain, and individual determines decides what identity attributes are shared, when, and with whom. This puts control in the hands of the individual and for this reason this approach is referred to as self-sovereign digital identity.

While the use of blockchain in this context has been presented as a way of creating alternative regimes that operate outside existing legal frameworks and beyond the reach of regulation, blockchain technology can be established within existing

[3] This discussion is an updated and summarized version of the more detailed conceptual analysis in Sullivan C, Digital Identity: An Emergent Legal Concept, 2010: ISBN 978-0-9807230-0-0 (electronic), ISBN 978-0-9807230-1-4 (paperback) (2010) and http://www.adelaide.edu.au/press/titles/digital-identity/. See also, Sullivan (2018), pp. 723–773.

legal frameworks to address the security vulnerabilities inherent in existing procedures for identity authentication and verification. This is especially needed because digital identity, particularly the information required to transact, is susceptible to fraud, misuse and mistake in the initial authentication process, and subsequently when digital identity is verified for transactions.

Blockchain technology can improve security and give individuals more control when and how their identity information is disclosed. For example, consider the registration process described above. Originals of the required identity documents including the most important birth certificate, are provided to authenticate identity. Copies of these documents are taken at that time and are scanned into the records that an authenticating entity must keep as part of the registration process including those prescribed by KYC requirements. This process is carried out when opening a bank account, applying for a loan, when buying and selling real estate and other prescribed property, and when applying for a driver license, to mention just some of the many occasions when identity must be verified. The result is that in the U.S. and most other countries, there are multiple records of these documents held by a wide range of public and private sector bodies that increases over time. While some of the required documents change over the years such as when a person obtains a new passport for example, the seminal identity document, the birth certificate, remains the same so over the course of a person's life time that document will be copied on multiple occasions and copied stored in literally hundreds of data bases. The security of those copies and the information they contain is largely dependent on the protocols used and enforced by each entity and even when those protocols are strong, they are never infallible. The more copies are held in multiple data bases, the greater the possibility of an important identity document like a birth certificate and the information it contains, being compromised, whether by hacking, fraud including employee fraud, system error or system failure.

Blockchain technology, while not perfect,[4] does offer a relatively more secure alternative to storing and accessing important identity documents such as those required for identity authentication including the KYC protocols, and offers greater protection for a person's birth certificate and other documents required to establish i.e. authenticate identity. A block chain is a public ledger distributed across many computers[5], using cryptography to provide confidentiality and security. It is touted as being essentially trust-based, the trust being in the network of servers and the software system, rather than a particular organization like a bank or government department, for example.

There are many approaches that have been suggested for the broader use of blockchain including to identity, but public blockchain is perhaps the most promising in terms of improved security for identity documents and because it enables an individual to control and monitor access.

[4] There are security risks even with private permissioned blockchain networks, particularly unauthorized access.

[5] The distributed nature of the ledger means that the network can still operate even if a node is unavailable.

3 Public Blockchain and Identity Authentication

This section examines the nature of public blockchain, and outlines in simple terms how it works and its application to digital identity, particularly for identity authentication i.e. the registration process described in the preceding section. The advantages of public blockchain are compared to the current paper-based identity authentication still required to in most jurisdictions. This discussion provides the basis for the following section which examines consequences.

3.1 Public Blockchain for Identity Authentication and Verification

Public blockchain is the technology that underpins Bitcoin which is most notable because it enables users to transact without using a traditional intermediary such as a bank or government body. A public blockchain does not have access restrictions whereas a private blockchain controls access. A private blockchain may be presumed to be more secure because of controlled access but the opposite is true. This is because of the nature of blockchain technology. A public blockchain is more secure because of it is decentralized, with information encrypted and stored on multiple devices.

The way this works is through a chain of linked records called blocks, hence the term blockchain. As data is added new blocks are added to the chain. Each block has a hashed[6] key that links it to the preceding block, a time stamp for when it was added or altered, and transaction data. With a blockchain-based system, the source documentation such as identity documents, can be stored off of the blockchain, the document hash can be compared to the hash on the blockchain, and the comparison can be stored on the blockchain. The benefits of this approach are that the authenticating organization can prove by a ledger entry on the blockchain, that the KYC checking has been done, without the need to handle paper documents or the scanning and storing of copies. This is a much more secure approach that also gives the individual much more control over crucial identity documents and the information they contain.

While there are still points of attack, blockchain is consensus-based and a majority of nodes comprising the blockchain would have to collude to remove or change data, so in theory fraud is relatively easier to detect. Moreover, access rights enable the individual to control access to the data via encryption, instead of identity provider-enforced policy. Most public blockchain systems use keys and signatures to control the shared ledger. Each blockchain node within the network has its own

[6] In simple terms, a hash is a value from a string of text that is generated using a mathematical function. The formula generates the hash, which helps to protect the security of the transmission against tampering

copy of the ledger, and data added to the ledger is sent to all participating nodes so the data appears in all copies of the blockchain. Any of the participants can add data to the blockchain, and algorithms aggregate data in 'blocks.' These blocks are added to the chain of existing blocks, using a cryptographic signature. For public blockchains, that signature includes a proof of work and that makes it cryptographically unlikely that anyone can alter the prior blocks. The overall result is that public and distributed nature of the blockchain makes it difficult to have a false block accepted by the network. This is the immutability feature of blockchain.

An individual can encrypt select data on the blockchain belonging to the subject and the subject can select who gets the key/s to decrypt the data. The way this works for identity authentication is that instead of a person taking his/her identity documents like a birth certificate, to the authenticating organization such as a bank, and having that organization take copies for its records, the individual could simply allow the bank to view his/her birth certificate through the public blockchain. The source document such as a birth certificate is stored off of the blockchain, but the document hash can be compared to the hash on the blockchain, and the comparison stored on the blockchain to show that the document has been checked and validated at part of the identity authentication such as is required for KYC, for example. Blockchain technology can also be used for identity verification i.e. use of an individual's transaction identity i.e. the specific set of identity information required for transactions, though the main advantage of the public blockchain is it's use for identity authentication, particularly in relation to important identity documents like the birth certificate.

However, while there is no doubt that blockchain provides more security, it is important to note that it is not infallible. Moreover, the immutability feature of blockchain can have a significant downside in that it makes errors and inaccuracies recorded on the blockchain difficult (though not necessarily impossible) to remove or otherwise correct. The most serious consequence is creation of a digital identity that is not accurate by enshrining those errors, or creating a false identity through the use of identity documents and information that are fabricated. Once that information is recorded on the blockchain, it is accorded a level of permanency and assumed authenticity, that can create a digital identity for many years if not for the person's lifetime.

In most developed nations and increasingly in many developing nations, digital identity is the primary means by which an individual is acknowledged to exist and to have standing to transact with a range of public and private sector organizations, so an inaccurate digital identity has serious consequences, especially for the individual concerned. The consequences are even more concerning if the error results in another person being able to use an otherwise valid digital identity as can happen if there has been identity theft, or if there has been system error where records have been incorrectly assigned to another person. The consequences are concerning and the situation is difficult to fix in any event, but when the information is on the blockchain it is more difficult to correct. The affects are broad. While there is clear impact on individuals, there are also the broader consequences of bogus transactions for businesses and other organizations including those in the public sector, and wider societal implications.

3.2 *Public Sector Use of Blockchain for Identity Authentication*

The emergence of digital identity and realization of its increasing significance has led to use of blockchain for identity authentication. Estonia is a leader in its use of blockchain, and is a pioneer in its early use for digital identity in relation to its national identity scheme for its citizens and permanent residents, and for the Estonian e-Residency program that extends to non-Estonian citizens located outside the country. In Estonia, a one-way hash[7] of the data it wants to protect is generated and combined with prior hashes, and then published on a blockchain-like chain of hashes.[8]

In the U.S., use of blockchain beyond Bitcoin has gained momentum. In April 2019, the Brookings Institute classified U.S. States in terms of the extent to which they have embraced and engaged blockchain technology for public sector activities and responsibilities. According to this study, the level of uptake is not especially strong. Only six States were considered to be actively engaged, in that they use blockchain for government functions; and only a few are considered to be recognizing innovation potential.[9] Most notable amongst the latter, is Illinois. The State established the Illinois Blockchain Initiative (IBI) consisting of members of the State's general assembly, as well as representatives from public entities, in 2016 to conduct a number of use-case pilot programs.[10] One of these use cases is a pilot with the Department of Health, to examine the use of blockchain in relation to digital identity. This pilot examines a blockchain-based birth registry/ID system to provide

[7]A one-way hash is a mathematical function that converts a variable-length input string into a fixed-length binary sequence. Since it is one way, it is virtually impossible to derive the original text from the string and therefore is more data protective and secure.

[8]E-Estonia, "Estonian Blockchain Technology" https://e-estonia.com/wp-content/uploads/2019 sept-nochanges-faq-a4-v03-blockchain-1-1.pdf.

[9]Desouza, K C. Chen Y, and Somvanshi KK, "Blockchain and U.S. state governments: An initial assessment", April 17, 2018 at https://www.brookings.edu/blog/techtank/2018/04/17/blockchain-and-u-s-state-governments-an-initial-assessment/.

[10]Although there were initially six cases covering a wide range of uses as part of the pilot, it is significant that according to Jennifer O'Rourke, business liaison for IBI, that "[o]ver the course of the past six months, we found all of these use cases - despite being broad and diverse - could be distilled into one singular use case, which is digital identity. As broad as they are, they essentially come down to saying, 'I am who I am, and I need to prove that using identity in certain ways as I interact with very different parts of government through different phases of my life." See, Friedman S, "Illinois builds momentum for blockchain", February 5, 2018 at https://gcn.com/Articles/2018/02/05/Illinois-blockchain.aspx.

a secure 'self-sovereign' identity for Illinois citizens during birth registration.[11] Government agencies can authenticate and subsequently verify birth registration information cryptographically, including digital identity attributes such as full name, date of birth, gender and even biometrics.

This use case is significant in that it specifically addresses birth registration as the time a person's digital identity is established. The motivation is to structurally address the issues relating to digital identity, by developing a framework that examines identity from its inception at birth, because identity is the basis of access to most government and private sector services.[12] The IBI site explains that in the proposed framework, "government agencies will verify birth registration information and then cryptographically sign identity attributes such as legal name, date of birth, sex or blood type, creating what are called "verifiable claims" or attributes. Permission to view or share each of these government-verified claims is stored on the tamper-proof distributed ledger protocol in the form of a decentralized identifier... This minimizes the need for entities to establish, maintain and rely upon their own proprietary databases of identity information."[13] The approach is to "take the source data from the passport office, from the DMV, from the post office, from the utility companies, and using that to prove granular things about a person's identity."[14] The overall objective is to place control in the hands of the individual. "Self-sovereign identity refers to a digital identity that remains entirely under the individual's control. A self-sovereign identity can be efficiently and securely validated by entities who require it, free from reliance on a centralized repository."[15]

A report on the pilot study was presented by the IBI in 2018, with one of the proposals being creation of a secure platform to enable irrevocable digital identities.[16] The IBI summarizes its findings: "[T[his Task Force believes that blockchain technology and its built-in encryption can facilitate highly-secure methods for interacting with government and keeping paperless records, increasing data accuracy

---

[11] As reported, Douglas T, Illinois Announces Key Partnership in Birth Registry Blockchain Pilot, September 8, 2017 https://www.govtech.com/data/Illinois-Announces-Key-Partnership-in-Birth-Registry-Blockchain-Pilot.html.

[12] According to Jennifer O'Rourke, Blockchain Business Liaison for IBI. See the Illinois Blockchain Initiative https://illinoisblockchain.tech/illinois-partners-with-evernym-to-launch-birth-registration-pilot-f2668664f67c.

[13] The Illinois Blockchain Initiative https://illinoisblockchain.tech/illinois-partners-with-evernym-to-launch-birth-registration-pilot-f2668664f67c.

[14] The Illinois Blockchain Initiative https://illinoisblockchain.tech/illinois-partners-with-evernym-to-launch-birth-registration-pilot-f2668664f67c.

[15] The Illinois Blockchain Initiative https://illinoisblockchain.tech/illinois-partners-with-evernym-to-launch-birth-registration-pilot-f2668664f67c.

[16] See, House Joint Resolution 25, "Illinois Blockchain And Distributed Ledger Task Force Final Report to the General Assembly", January 31, 2018 https://www2.illinois.gov/sites/doit/Strategy/Documents/BlockchainTaskForceFinalReport020518.pdf. See also, Department of Innovation and Technology, "State of Illinois Releases Blockchain Task Force Report-*Distributed Ledger Technology Poised to Strengthen Security and Bring Economic Opportunity,*" January 31, 2018 https://www2.illinois.gov/Pages/news-tem.aspx?ReleaseID=15316.

and providing better cybersecurity protections for Illinois residents. Though the technology still needs refinement, government has an opportunity to help shape and adopt innovative solutions." The report does not set out a plan for how this will be achieved but there is clear interest in exploring the potential to harness the benefits of blockchain, and the IBI states that "continued development of blockchain pilot projects is expected to further the exploration of distributed ledger technology in Illinois."[17] It is acknowledged, however, that while the technology is exciting in its possibilities, it is important to be thoughtful in its application."[18]

Caution is needed because use of blockchain, especially for identity documentation and information, profoundly changes the status quo, especially in terms of control by individuals, their rights; and the duties of public and private sector organizations in relation to digital identity.

4 The Impact of Blockchain on Rights and Duties

This section builds on the preceding discussion, to examine the consequences of the use of public blockchain for identity from the perspectives of government, business, and the individual. Blockchain was originally designed to remove the need for a traditional intermediary. It is designed to put control back into the hands of individuals. This approach fits well with identity and similar notions of control that are grounded in autonomy, and with data protection and privacy. Control by the individual is important on many levels, including who accesses an individual's identity documents and identity information and when that access is permitted. The blockchain also provides the individual with timely information about access.

This section examines the impact of blockchain on current data[19] protection and privacy legislation in place in most jurisdictions around the world; and then developing rights and duties under international law, particularly the emerging right to digital identity. This discussion of the rights around digital identity is based on international rights because as discussed in the next section, that is the foundation of most privacy and data protection regulation around the world; and because this law upholds basic rights for all people as international standards.[20]

[17] House Joint Resolution 25, "Illinois Blockchain And Distributed Ledger Task Force Final Report to the General Assembly", January 31, 2018 https://www2.illinois.gov/sites/doit/Strategy/Documents/BlockchainTaskForceFinalReport020518.pdf.

[18] Friedman S, "Illinois builds momentum for blockchain", February 5, 2018 https://gcn.com/Articles/2018/02/05/Illinois-blockchain.aspx.

[19] Data and information are usually used interchangeably in data protection legislation and are similarly used interchangeably in this chapter.

[20] This is in contrast to tortious claims for example, which although seemingly close in nature, have a fundamentally different basis and different objectives, Tortious claims are usually under domestic law and usually require some notion of harm, whereas an infringement of a human right, of itself, is all that is needed.

4.1 Data Protection and Privacy Implications

Most countries have data protection and privacy legislation based on the European Union (E.U.) model,[21] the most notable exception being the U.S. that does not have a national equivalent. However, the recent enactment of the new Californian Consumer Privacy Act of 2018 has narrowed the gap, not just because of its requirements[22] but because other U.S. States are already following California's lead. Even more significantly, this development of similar but different State laws is leading to renewed calls for a Federal statute, to provide uniformity. If that occurs it is likely to also follow the E.U. model, particularly the General Data Protection Regulation (GDPR), if only broadly.

Most nations have data protection laws based on the E.U. 1995 Data Protection Directive, and are now updating their domestic legislation to more closely follow its successor, the GDPR which came into effect in the E.U. in 2018.[23] It can be expected that the E.U. will continue to set the standard for data protection, and that the changes in the GDPR will continue to inform law reform outside Europe.

This section examines the impact of the GDPR that like its predecessor, the 1995 Directive, gives effect to the European Convention for the Protection of Human Rights and Fundamental Freedoms (ECHR) particularly Article 8. This Article sets

---

[21] The reasons are pragmatic. The E.U. has required that countries wishing to do business with the E.U. have similar data protection standards and the E.U. data protection requirements provided a comparatively early model. Australia for example, was one of the first nations outside Europe implement data protection legislation based on the E.U. model and over time Australia has updated its Privacy Act 1988 (Cth) to align with E.U. requirements in order to facilitate business with the E.U.

[22] The CCPA creates new consumer rights for Californian residents relating to the access to, deletion of, and sharing of personal information that is collected by businesses i.e. for-profit entities. The CCPA is more basic and limited than the GDPR. The definitions of "personal information", data "processing" and data "collecting" are broadly similar. The CCPA sets out some of the basic rights provided to data subjects but they are much more rudimentary than those in the GDPR. For example, the CCPA requires a business to:

- Inform the data subject it collects personal information either before or as that information is collected.
- Inform the data subject of the types (though not the names) of third parties with whom it shares your personal information but only when asked by the data subject.
- Provide a data subject with ways to opt out of having his/her personal information sold to, or shared with, third parties and must honor a request to opt-out. Businesses must put a link to their opt-out page on their homepage informing individuals of this right.

The CCPA also gives data subjects the right to tell the business to delete their personal information. The relevant point for this discussion if that these rights and requirements do not present any conceptual issues for blockchain especially as it applies to digital identity.

[23] The Directive established a data protection standard to be incorporated into domestic law but gave discretion to member nations as to how that was done, but the GDPR as a Regulation, now applies directly as law in the E.U.

out the right to respect for private and family life[24] and has been interpreted as providing individual privacy and data protection rights. Recital 1 of the GDPR specifically provides that "[t]he protection of natural persons in relation to the processing of personal data is a fundamental right. [2]Article 8(1) of the Charter of Fundamental Rights of the European Union (the 'Charter') and Article 16(1) of the Treaty on the Functioning of the European Union (TFEU) provide that everyone has the right to the protection of personal data concerning him or her."

This human rights basis and focus, influences the law in adopting nations including those that do not have a human rights heritage. Australia for example, does not have this legal tradition, nor a formal national human rights regime established under its Constitution or through regional treaty, but as a consequence of following the E.U. model for its national law, Australia has effectively imported the applicable human rights, and human rights concepts such as balancing the privacy and data rights of a data subject with the public interest.

This raises the question as to how blockchain and identity integrates with data protection law, especially law based on the E.U. model that is followed by most jurisdictions. In determining the applicable law, the type of identity scheme is major factor, particularly whether the blockchain is owned and operated by government or is outsourced to the private sector, and the location and control of the blockchain ledgers. The GDPR, and similar domestic legislation that regulates data processing in most jurisdictions, apply when the personal data of an individual is processed.[25] The E.U. model is based on three key players – the individual who is referred to as the "data subject" [26], the data "controller" [27], and the data "processor". The model is predicated on the assumption that the controller and processor are dealing with the personal data of the data subject and requires that they do so in accordance with specified data protection principles. Control is presumed to be in the hands of controllers and processors that are typically organizations, not the individuals who are the data subjects. The legislation therefore seeks to redress the power imbalance by giving individuals basic rights in respect of the processing of their personal data."[28] Blockchain changes this premise and the balance of power so that in effect the individual becomes the data controller. Nevertheless, for the most part, regulations like the GDPR apply and can do so without major issues.

---

[24] Formally, the Convention for the Protection of Human Rights and Fundamental Freedoms, which was signed by all Council of Europe member States in 1950, became effective in 1953 (at http://www.echr.coe.int/Documents/Convention_ENG.pdf).

[25] Under the GDPR, an E.U. data subject is a data subject in the E.U.

[26] A data subject is defined as a natural person who is identified or identifiable by the data. See Article 4 (1) of the GDPR.

[27] A controller is typically defined as "the natural or legal person, public authority, agency or other body which, alone or jointly with others, determines the purposes and means of the processing of personal data." See Article 4 (7) of the GDPR.

[28] A processor is defined as "a natural or legal person, public authority, agency or other body which processes personal data on behalf of the controller." See, Article 4 (8) of the GDPR. Typically, the data controller is primarily responsible for compliance, though the GDPR extended accountability to include processors.

Data "processing" is typically defined broadly [29], as is "personal data". "Personal data" is defined in Article 6 of the GDPR for example, as "any information relating to a data subject"[30] while Article 6 of the GDPR defines "data subject" as "an identified natural person or a natural person who can be identified, directly or indirectly, by means reasonably likely to be used by the controller or by any other natural or legal person, in particular by reference to an identification number, location data, online identifier or to one or more factors specific to the physical, physiological, genetic, mental, economic, cultural or social identity of that person."

Although current data protection and privacy regulations around the world have not been designed with blockchain in mind, in many ways blockchain furthers the primary objectives of the law which is to give individuals more control in relation to the processing of their personal information. The E.U. data protection model for example, is predicated on the basic principles set out in Article 5 which are lawfulness, fairness and transparency, purpose limitation, data minimization, accuracy, storage limitation, integrity and confidentiality, and accountability. The GDPR gives effect to these principles by setting conditions for lawful processing, requirements for individual consent, specific rights of data subjects in respect of their personal data, required data security and protection including privacy by design and default, and compliance requirements.

Although the traditional roles of data controller and data processor are fundamentally changed by blockchain-based systems, which are designed to remove intermediaries, the data protection principles remain relevant and for the most part can still be applied effectively. Indeed, blockchain can assist in providing the required data protection which is important for all personal data but is crucial for digital identity information.

There are many examples of how blockchain can assist in achieving the established data protection objectives but the most important is data subject consent. A general principle of all data protection regulations is that processing an individual's person information should be with consent of the data subject or otherwise only done when necessary for legitimate interests or in the public interest.

---

[29] Data "processing" is defined in Article 6 as "any operation or set of operations which is performed upon personal data, *whether or not by automatic means*, such as collection, recording, organization, storage, adaptation or alteration, retrieval, consultation, use, disclosure by transmission, dissemination or otherwise making available, alignment or combination, blocking, erasure or destruction." (emphasis added).

[30] If the personal information is categorized as sensitive, then processing is only permitted in limited circumstances set out in Article 9 (2) and its equivalents. Under the Article 9 (1) of the GDPR, sensitive data is data consisting of "racial or ethnic origin, political opinions, religious or philosophical beliefs, or trade union membership, genetic data, biometric data, data concerning health or data concerning a natural person's sex life or sexual orientation." One of the specified grounds is explicit consent of the data subject that typically requires that the data subject consents by taking affirmative action after being clearly informed of the use of the data. Most of this sensitive information is not part of transaction identity, the major exception being biometrics which are used in some digital identity schemes.

When blockchain is used, data subject consent is easier to verify because its audit trail and immutability enables transparent tracking, and it is easier to demonstrate regulatory compliance. Article 6 of the GDPR for example, allows processing of personal data when "the data subject has given consent to the processing of his or her personal data for one or more specific purposes."[31] Under Article 4 (11) the GDPR, "consent" of the data subject means any freely given, specific, informed and unambiguous indication of the data subject's wishes by which he or she, by statement or by a clear affirmative action, signifies agreement to the processing of personal data relating to him or her.[32]

Processing is permitted in the absence of the explicit consent of the data subject in limited circumstances which are typically where the processing is necessary for the purposes of the legitimate interests pursued by the controller or by a third party; or when the processing is necessary for the performance of a task carried out in the public interest.[33] Blockchain also assists in meeting the requirements for this data processing including data subject notification and associated rights of the data subject to rectify errors and inaccuracies and to request data removal, often referred to as the right to be forgotten.[34] Even though the immutable nature of blockchain may seem to present a challenge for these latter rights, data correction and removal can be done if the personal information is stored off chain and only the cryptographic hash exposed to the chain is used for authentication.

As to the legitimate interests ground, Article 6(1)(f) of the GDPR which is replicated in most similar legislation around the world, specifically allows processing that is "necessary for the purposes of the legitimate interests pursued by the control-

[31] Article 7 requires that "2. If the data subject's consent is given in the context of a written declaration which also concerns other matters, the request for consent shall be presented in a manner which is clearly distinguishable from the other matters, in an intelligible and easily accessible form, using clear and plain language. Any part of such a declaration which constitutes an infringement of this Regulation shall not be binding. 3. The data subject shall have the right to withdraw his or her consent at any time. The withdrawal of consent shall not affect the lawfulness of processing based on consent before its withdrawal. Prior to giving consent, the data subject shall be informed thereof. It shall be as easy to withdraw consent as to give it. 4. When assessing whether consent is freely given, utmost account shall be taken of whether, inter alia, the performance of a contract, including the provision of a service, is conditional on consent to the processing of personal data that is not necessary for the performance of that contract."

[32] The GDPR places the onus on the data controller to demonstrate the data subject's consent is informed and not coerced. The GDPR now clarifies that consent will not considered to be freely given if the data subject has no genuine and free choice; or is unable to refuse or withdraw consent without detriment; and where there is a clear imbalance between the data subject and the controller, though this is particularly stated in relation to a public authority. See Recitals 42 and 43 of the GDPR.

[33] Article 6 (1) of the GDPR.

[34] These rights have limited application to identity information especially that which is derived from birth registration, but recording mistakes can occur at the time of birth that need to be rectified.

ler or by a third party,[35] *except where such interests are overridden by the interests or fundamental rights and freedoms of the data subject which require protection of personal data, in particular where the data subject is a child*." (my emphasis) This ground can be invoked to process identity information so the exceptional reference to the fundamental rights of individuals, especially children is significant. This provision also links to the human right to identity, including digital identity, that is explored later in this chapter. Similarly, processing "necessary for the performance of a *task carried out in the public interest* or in the exercise of official authority vested in the controller..." [36] (my emphasis), can apply to the processing of digital identity information. This ground also reflects the basic tenant of private international law that the public interest can override individual human rights. It is highly relevant to all the human rights that form the basis of the GDPR and to the specific data subject rights set out in the Regulation and its international equivalents, including the rights to be informed of data processing, the rights to access and correct personal data, right to data portability, and the right to be informed of a data breach.

For the present discussion, the important point is that blockchain assists in achieving the requirements of data protection legislation like the GDPR including data subject rights and in monitoring regulatory compliance. By contrast, as discussed, the nature of current paper-based system, especially for KYC, makes it difficult for the data subject to know exactly what data is being processed, how and when and where[37] it is processed, and if the required data protections are in place and are effective. All these factors impact data subject rights and make it more difficult for an individual to know if there is non-compliance and if steps need to be taken to enforce his/her rights in respect of identity information and other personal data. The use of blockchain for identity information and other personal data also

[35] The GDPR requires notification of a data subject when personal data is obtained without data subject consent. Article 13 covers the information to be provided where the personal data are collected from the data subject whereas Article 14 covers personal data not obtained from the data subject. These Articles require that the data controller notify the data subject of the purpose of the processing, the recipients of the data; and in the case of Article 14 the period of data storage; and the "legitimate" interests of the controller or third party that provide the legal basis for the data processing. Article 14 (3) requires that the controller provide the information to the data subject "(a) within a reasonable period after obtaining the personal data, but at the latest within one month, having regard to the specific circumstances in which the personal data are processed." Article 14 (5) sets out the circumstances in which the notification is not required, i.e. where the data subject already has the information; or provision of such information proves impossible or would involve a disproportionate effort. In such cases the controller is required to take appropriate measures to protect the data subject's rights and freedoms and legitimate interests.

[36] See for example, Article 6(1)(e) of the GDPR. Notification of the data subject is not usually required.

[37] The location of processing is important especially considering the increased extra territorial operation of many data protection regulations, including the GDPR. Whereas the predecessor to the GDPR applied to organizations based outside the E.U. when they did business in the E.U., the GDPR applies to organizations processing personal data of an E.U. data subject wherever that occurs, regardless of the organization's geographical base and area of operation. See Article 3 of the GDPR.

accords with another important requirement of the GDPR which is being replicated in data protection regulation in other jurisdictions, i.e. data protection and privacy by design; and the new emphasis in the GDPR[38] on data pseudonymisation,[39] anonymisation,[40] and encryption.

However, the rights to privacy and data protection, by their nature, as recognized by laws like the GDPR, can be readily overridden by rights of others including the public. It is not difficult to think of instances where the greater public good can, and should, outweigh an individual's right to data protection and privacy; and as a consequence, these rights are not very robust. In comparison to data protection and privacy rights, the right to identity is much less likely to be overridden by public interest, making it an especially robust human right and a better means of protecting identity.

4.2 An Emerging Right to Digital Identity and Why it Is Needed

An international human right to digital identity is now emerging and this section discusses its legal basis and nature. The development of this right is important because it is an acknowledgement of the importance of digital identity particularly to an individual. Although the authenticity and functionality of an individual's digital identity is important for both public and private sector organizations, it is crucial for the individual. Moreover, the human right to identity fits well with the use of blockchain for identity authentication in that it reinforces individual autonomy and control.

The human right to identity is much more robust than an individual's rights to data protection and privacy. While it is easy to envisage circumstances where other interests override the individual rights to data protection and privacy, it is extremely challenging to imagine a situation when removing or interfering with a person's identity can be legitimately justified. Loss of privacy can be legitimately be total as in the case of a person incarcerated for example it is difficult to imagine a situation

[38] And other regulations in other jurisdictions that follow this model.

[39] Under the GDPR, pseudonymized data is data where identifying information has been replaced with alternative identifiers that do not identity the person i.e. data subject. Pursuant to Article 4 of the GDPR pseudonymization is "...the processing of personal data in such a manner that the personal data can no longer be attributed to a specific data subject without the use of additional information, provided that such additional information is kept separately and is subject to technical and organisational measures to ensure that the personal data are not attributed to an identified or identifiable natural person." Recital 26 of the GDPR makes it clear that pseudonymised personal data remains personal data within the scope of the GDPR.

[40] Under the GDPR, anonymisation is the process of removing all identifying information. Anonymised information is not considered to be personal information that attracts the protections of the GDPR but data is only considered anonymised if it is impossible to re-identify, even when cross referenced with other data. See also Recital 26 of the GDPR.

in a democratic society when it is, or should be, lawful to interfere with, or remove, a person's identity. This is even more so now considering that digital identity effectively gives a person legal standing in the digital era. Digital identity is now the primary means by which a person is recognized as exiting and having the ability to transact.

As to the basis of the right, an individual right to identity clearly exists under international law in the Convention on the Rights of the Child [41](CRC) and arises at birth under Article 8.[42] The Convention also clearly distinguishes the right to identity from the right to privacy which is set out in Article 16. It should be noted that the CRC sets out rights of minors, though of course a right to identity established in childhood continues into adulthood and this is especially so for digital identity which has its basis in birth registration information. This view is by the strengthened European Court of Human Rights recognizing the right of identity for minors and adults under Article 8 of the European Convention Protection of Human Rights and Fundamental Freedoms which is similarly worded. The expanding importance of digital identity, and SGD 16.9 i.e. a "legal identity for all, including birth registration" by 2030, provide additional impetus.

The CRC is also the most widely ratified convention with every country except the U.S., ratifying it. This is a notable exception however, and it means that the U.S. is not bound by the CRC. The importance of identity, especially digital identity and its seminal roots in birth registration, may provide new impetus for the U.S to ratify the CRC.

In any event, arguably the individual right to identity that includes digital identity can also be recognized under another international convention, the International Covenant on Civil and Political Rights (ICCPR). The ICCPR has been ratified by the U.S., although the ICCPR is not as widely accepted by other nations as the CRC. While the right to identity under ICCPR is less clear and is not as developed as the right under the CRC, the ICCPR is capable of development that acknowledges the new significance of digital identity.

The most relevant provision is Article 1(1) which states that "[A]ll peoples have the right of self-determination. By virtue of that right they freely determine their political status and freely pursue their economic, social and cultural development." The basis of the argument is individual autonomy. The right to self-determination as set out in Article 1 of the ICCPR, is generally regarded as encompassing self-determination.[43] It is postulated that in an era where digital identity is the primary

[41] Adopted by United Nations General Assembly resolution 44/25 of 20 November 1989, entered into force 2 September 1990.

[42] Article 8 was included in the CRC as the result of a campaign by the grandmothers of 'The Disappeared' in Argentina for the right to identity. They argued that the country's adoption laws enabled concealment of children's true identities and the creation of false identities Their campaign led to Argentina recognising a constitutional right to identity.

[43] It has to be said, however, that the exact nature and extent of the rights under ICCPR Article 1 are unclear. The Committee on the Elimination of Racial Discrimination (CERD) has postulated that the Article has both internal and external aspects.

means by which an individual is recognized, and by which he/she has transactional standing, autonomy must now necessarily include the right to an accurate, functional digital identity. This ties in with notions of individual autonomy that lie at the heart of democracy where "[T]he individual sector" that is, according to legal theorists like Charles Reich, the "zone of individual power" that is "absolutely essential to the health and survival of democratic society." [44] Reich maintains that this autonomy is necessary for the healthy development and functioning of the individual and that aspect is directly relevant to identity, especially digital identity. The argument that can be advanced is that identity is now clearly the most important part of individual power because identity and specifically digital identity. must be provided for virtually every significant function including voting, travelling, and most transactions with both public and private sector organizations. The right to identity, especially the right to digital identity, is clearly now an essential part of individual autonomy – perhaps more so than in any other time in history, although the recognition of this under ICCPR will need to evolve over time.

The development of the right to identity is important because it can provide a legal basis for recognition of the rights of individuals in relation to his/her digital identity and the duties of public and private sector organizations in relation to that identity and the information it comprises. This is important no matter what technology is used to store and transmit the information but it is especially important when blockchain is used. This is because the human right to identity provides an obligation to protect identity and to address issues that impact its authenticity and functionality. In some cases, the convention enables legal action under the convention itself by the individual or a representative body; or as a result of the convention being incorporated into the law of the nation. It should be noted however, that although infringement of some human rights involve damages awards as well as penalties,[45] the primary theoretical objective of international human rights is to set standards and regulate State conduct.[46] The ICCPR, for example, impacts State conduct mainly through the United Nations Human Rights Committee (UNHRC) monitoring and reporting on its national implementation.[47]

[44] Reich (1991), pp. 1409–1448.

[45] This is often set out in derivative law. An example is the GDPR which gives effect to the protection of natural persons in relation to the processing of personal data, as a fundamental human right. Article 8(1) of the Charter of Fundamental Rights of the European Union and Article 16(1) of the Treaty on the Functioning of the European Union provide that everyone has the right to the protection of personal data concerning him or her. See Recital 1 of the GDPR.

[46] This can include the content, enactment, and application of relevant national law.

[47] Nations bound by the ICCPR must report on their implementation of ICCPR Article 1 to the United Nations Human Rights Council (UNHRC). This reporting is required every four years and the UNHRC publishes its findings and any concerns about compliance. It is important to note that although there is an individual complaint procedure established by the Optional Protocol to the ICCPR, at present the UNHRC will not consider complaints from individuals for infringement of ICCPR Article 1. The UNHRC will only consider individual complaints based on ICCPR Articles 6 -27. However, this may change as the importance of an accurate and functional digital identity is fully realized.

5 Framework for a New Approach

Having examined the overall changes brought by blockchain and the advantages compared to the disadvantages, this section examines the policy and legal changes needed to support blockchain-based identity. Overall, existing data protection and privacy legislation which mostly follows the E.U. model, can accommodate the use of blockchain for identity; and blockchain can assist in achieving data protection principles such as those in the GDPR and other requirements.

The main area in need of review is the KYC requirements. The present KYC requirements for identity authentication under (AML/CTF) legislation were put in place in over 190[48] countries following the 9/11 attacks in the U.S., to address the laundering of money to finance terrorism. Although there is a high degree of international commonality in the requirements, they are enacted and enforced locally so there are national, and even organizational, differences in the way the law is interpreted and applied. For example, in the U.S. four data points are usually the minimum requirement while in the Peoples Republic of China which has a national identity scheme, only requires name and ID number.

A recent report highlights some key implementation issues and concerns that are relevant to this discussion of blockchain and identity.[49] A major concern is the time and resources consumed by KYC and the impact on costs and efficiency. Current KYC processes tend to be manually intensive and time consuming and the absence of a single client view for all data and documentation makes the process more challenging. Identity authentication is also generally taking longer. A concerning perception is that the procedures have become check-box exercises, rather than a thorough process to authenticate identity and mitigate risk. There is a further concern about the quality of data and documentation used to authenticate identity, particularly that they are not of high quality. There are also issues with legacy systems such as limitations on the ability to a full-field scan and store restrictions, for example. In summary, an overhaul of how KYC can, and should be done, is needed. Central to this review is how technology especially new technological developments, can be used to improve the effectiveness and efficiency of KYC requirements.[50]

As is the case with privacy and data protection, blockchain generally complies with the objectives and concepts that underpin current KYC checking requirements; and improves compliance. Blockchain can address many of the issues that affect current KYC and can improve its effectiveness and efficiency. As discussed, blockchain can also provide a comparatively high degree of privacy and data protection

[48] In the U.S., the Patriot Act includes the Customer Identification Program which sets out the KYC requirements.

[49] See International Regtech Association and Protiviti, "An Urgent Call for KYC Optimization- A global study calling for KYC innovation and collaboration", 2019: https://www.protiviti.com/US-en/insights/urgent-call-kyc-optimization-protiviti-study.

[50] See International Regtech Association and Protiviti, "An Urgent Call for KYC Optimization—A global study calling for KYC innovation and collaboration", 2019: https://www.protiviti.com/US-en/insights/urgent-call-kyc-optimization-protiviti-study, particularly pages 5, 8, 18 and 25–26.

and security as well as an in-built audit trail, However, international standards are needed for operational integrity and to engender confidence in this approach. There are international organizations that can spearhead this initiative including the Financial Action Task Force (FATF), the International Organization of Securities Commissions (OSCO), the Financial Stability Board (FSB), the Bank for International Settlements (BIS), the Wolfsberg Group, and the International Institute of Finance.

To be most effective, development of the standards should involve national governments, national and international regulators, financial institutions, consumers and other stakeholders such as platform providers, to capture best practices as well as regulator expectations. While a detailed discussion of the content of the standards is beyond the scope of this chapter, they should cover technical specifications, not permit storage of identity information and documentation on the chain, clarify system ownership and the responsibilities of all stakeholders including for public/private sector collaborations, for maintenance and system failure. It is also crucial to include a liability model that satisfies all stakeholders and includes the human right to identity as well as rights to privacy and personal data protection.

6 Conclusion

This chapter has examined the nature and functions of digital identity, particularly transaction identity and its increasing importance to individuals and public and private sector organizations; and how blockchain can be used to support identity authentication especially the KYC procedures. Blockchain can address many of the factors that reduce the efficiency of the current paper-based approach and make the process more effective.

Blockchain is comparatively more secure and is more protective of personal data and individual privacy than the current approach. This use of blockchain is in-line with established and developing data protection and privacy legislation around the world. Although regulations like the GDPR and similar legislation around the world is predicated on a different conceptual basis than exists for blockchain, the data protection principles and regulatory requirements can generally be applied. In fact, the use of blockchain can assist in achieving the objectives of the regulations. It is clear, however, that the protection provided by the individual rights to data protection and privacy that are the foundation of regulations based on the E.U. model, are not robust. The right to identity that currently exists under international law is far more resilient. Considering the importance of digital identity in determining whether an individual has standing to transact in this era, there is a strong argument that this right now includes the right to digital identity. It is crucial however that all stakeholders recognize the right to identity and its nature and that it differs significantly from the rights to privacy and data protection which have limitations. The acknowledgement of the importance of identity in SGD 16.9 is a major step in this regard, but it is just first step.

Blockchain for identity authentication has many advantages over the present paper-based systems but a sound legal foundation is needed, particularly an international standard that as discussed above, includes technical and procedural specifications, responsibilities, and a liability model. Achieving this may seem daunting but international cooperation established KYC procedures around the world. Now the next step is to use technology like blockchain to improve the efficiency and effectiveness of those procedures.

References

Reich, C. (1991). The individual sector. *Yale Law Journal, 100*(5), 1409–1448.
Sullivan, C. (2018). Digital identity—From emergent legal concept to new reality. *Computer Law and Security Review, 34*, 723–773.

Clare Sullivan is a cyber-lawyer specializing in digital identity, international privacy and data protection, blockchain and cyber security. She is a Visiting Professor at the Law Center, a Fellow at the Center on National Security, and Managing Director of Cyber SMART Research Center, all at Georgetown University. At Cyber SMART she also leads the cyber law and digital identity research teams. An attorney with many years in international legal practise, Professor Sullivan has advanced degrees in law including a PhD in cyber law, and has been awarded both a Fulbright Scholarship and an Endeavor Fellowship. Professor Sullivan is the author of "Digital Identity" the first text to define and examine digital identity from a legal perspective and its implications for government, business and individuals. She has authored internationally published articles and book chapters on digital identity, blockchain, privacy, and cyber security; and reports covering those areas for the U.S., U.K. and Australian governments, for the Commonwealth Secretariat, and for the World Bank.

Chapter 10
Analyzing the Case for Adopting Distributed Ledger Technology in the Bank of Canada

Christopher G. Reddick

1 Introduction

Distributed ledger technology (DLT), a type of blockchain technology, is a peer-to-peer computing technology platform and was first introduced to the world by Bitcoin in 2009. This system was a breakthrough because it demonstrated a way to maintain a ledger of information between parties in such a way that no one oversees the system. The ledger can be credibly updated and agreed upon by members of the Bitcoin system even though no one trusts any other member to act honestly (Chapman, Garratt, Hendry, McCormack, & McMahon, 2017).

DLT is heralded to revolutionize industry and business and to drive economic change on a global scale (Lucas, 2017). DLT is "immutable, transparent, and redefines trust, enabling secure, fast, trustworthy, and transparent solutions that can be public or private" (Underwood, 2015, p. 15). DLT involves a distributed database maintained over a peer-to-peer network of computers to record and transfer *digital assets* through blockchain (GAO, 2014). Through a computer algorithm-based consensus mechanism, the network nodes validate financial transactions. Hence, DLT enables the network to share and retain identical, cryptographically secured records, so-called distributed ledgers, in a decentralized manner.

This emerging disruptive digital technology is said to be poised to transform service operations of the banking industry and financial markets (Christensen, 1997). The disruptive technology facilitates the transfer of *digital assets*, including cryptocurrencies, in near real-time, to support payments, clearing, and settlement which do not require a central coordinating governance structure (GAO, 2017a, 2017b). Hence, the potential impact of disruptive DLT technologies on central coor-

C. G. Reddick (✉)
Department of Public Administration, The University of Texas at San Antonio, San Antonio, TX, USA
e-mail: chris.reddick@utsa.edu

C. G. Reddick et al. (eds.), *Blockchain and the Public Sector*, Public Administration and Information Technology 36,
https://doi.org/10.1007/978-3-030-55746-1_10

dinating governance organizations such as central banks worldwide is unimaginably large and would have significant implications for national and international financial and monetary transactions and economic stability.

Disruptive innovations through DLT either create growth in the industries they penetrate or introduce entirely new industries through new digital business models for products and services which are significantly less costly, better, and offer greater customer value (Kostoff, Boylan, & Simons, 2004). In addition, to potentially creating business value, DLT's potential transformational power in creating public value such as trust, transparency, and accountability was underscored in a 2016 UK government report entitled, *Distributed Ledger Technology: Beyond Block Chain* (UK Government Chief Scientific Advisor, 2016).

Not surprisingly, fintech firms in the financial industry have begun to invest in this new technology for radical and architectural innovations in faster payments and other services (Gomber, Kauffman, Parker, & Weber, 2018). Major stock exchanges have announced the use of blockchains in trading corporate equities and tracking their ownership (Yermack, 2017). However, disruptive technologies need "to move from the conceptual phase into actual use" (Zamani & Giaglis, 2018, p. 645). Moreover, the DLT use by financial regulators such as central banks worldwide would have significant strategic implications for governance, regulations, and public policies as well as practical managerial implications for information systems, accountants, and finance professionals (Dai & Vasarhelyi, 2017; GAO, 2018; Pachamanova, Mancha, & Kokina, 2017).

Leadership in central banking has an enormous impact on stability in financial markets and financial institutions. Central banks differ from commercial banks. A central bank is responsible for regulating the banking and monetary system for the national government. The most difficult challenge facing a central bank under uncertain impacts of disruptive peer-to-peer DLT platform technologies is maintaining its leading market regulatory position. Particularly, when rapid technological evolution continually tests the ability of the central bank to rapidly adapt and stay ahead in exploring and understanding the opportunities and challenges of disruptive technologies and exploiting their potential benefits to the nation.

Despite the potentially impacts of the blockchain/DLT on central banking performance, the literature is relatively scarce on DLT use cases in central banking. To fill the research/practice gap we raise the following research question (RQs):

RQ1: *What impact can DLT have on improving the Bank of Canada's performance?*

In this paper, we answer these RQ in the context of the Bank of Canada's so-called "Project Jasper" which consists of four phases of proof-of-concept projects from March 2016 to 2018. Theoretically, we apply the disruptive innovations theory to our case study. Methodologically, we adopt qualitative case study research to investigate the Bank of Canada's exploration of the disruptive blockchain/DLT. Then, we perform an analysis of case interview data, secondary source data including the Project Jasper documents, media debriefings, and industry analyst reports for our case study.

The rest of this paper is organized as follows. The second section reviews the existing literature on blockchain/DLT and disruptive innovations. The third section describes the use of a qualitative case study research methodology. The fourth section presents the background of the Project Jasper and the important timelines. The fifth presents the answer to our research question. The sixth section concludes the paper, including the contribution to the literature, our research limitations, and future research directions are discussed.

2 Literature Review

2.1 Blockchain and Distributed Ledger Technologies

Blockchain is a form of Distributed Ledger Technology (DLT) that has introduced different payment characteristics compared to existing payments systems. Central banks have experimented with DLT to try to capture the benefits that the Blockchain introduces to payments while avoiding the costs (Wadsworth, 2018). Although blockchain is still an emerging technology, strong public interest in cryptocurrencies, such as *bitcoin* powered by blockchain, has popularized the term blockchain. Despite the growing interest in the trendy term, however, *ISO/TC 307 Blockchain and Distributed Ledger Technologies* standing committee identified the key challenge in defining and standardizing blockchain and distributed ledger technologies consistently across the countries (International Organization for Standardization, 2016). The National Institute of Standards and Technology (NIST) at the U.S. Department of Commerce considers blockchain as a type of DLT. NIST defines blockchain as "a distributed ledger which is decentralized, peer-to-peer, tamper-evident/resistant, and synchronized through consensus" to "facilitate transactions between mutually-distrusting entities without the need for a trusted arbiter" (Regenscheid, 2017).

The DLT system is distributed, which means records are not held centrally and communicated to nodes by a central authority. A key feature of the technology is that it removes the need for users to trust a centralized payment authority to conduct a transaction and replaces that with an architecture that creates trust through consensus (Wadsworth, 2018). DLT consists of (1) an electronically distributed ledger to store a verified set of transaction records, (2) a network of participants or nodes which are connected to the network to share the replicated distributed ledger, (3) a consensus mechanism, a set of algorithms, for achieving consensus among nodes on the validity of records to be stored in the ledger, and (4) cryptography applied to the records to ensure secure storage and privacy (Australian Securities & Investments Commission, 2018). As for a network of participants, the network can consist of individuals, businesses, or financial entities (GAO, 2017a, 2017b) which underscores a consensus mechanism as the important process of DLT in affecting the potential value of DLT application systems.

To further understand different types of Distributed Ledger Technology, four design choices are particularly important in how some forms of DLT are similar to existing payment systems, while other differ considerably (see Table 10.1). To understand how these key elements matters, consider the example of Blockchain, which is a permissionless, public, non-hierarchical, and open-source DLT while other DLTs that have permissioned, private, hierarchical elements create secure transaction. The combination of elements is particularly important in determining how the validation process occurs. Permissioned, private and hierarchical DLT is used in environments where a trusted third party already exists and validation can be faster and cheaper, which can occur in financial transactions of banks (Wadsworth, 2018).

Since 2009, in a relatively short period, more businesses are accepting cryptocurrency payments, including Bitcoin and Ethereum. It has been predicted that industrial applications and use cases will likely increase because DLT can record not only cryptocurrencies but also other digital assets, such as securities and supply chain transactions. Hence, DLT can redefine near-real-time digital transactions by removing the costly and time-consuming back-office processes and can affect structural change by removing the need for third-party 'middlemen' in many transactions (Anjum, Sporny, & Sill, 2017). Similarly, the disruptive potential of DLT exists to shape the future of the financial services in securities post-trading (Pinna & Ruttenberg, 2016) and faster payments and inter-bank transfers and settlement (Brühl, 2017). DLT embedding trust in decentralized networks has the potential to radically change markets and businesses, although many governance and regulatory issues remain unresolved (Zamani & Giaglis, 2018). While blockchain is widely viewed as potentially disruptive Risius and Spohrer (2017) conclude that there is a lack of understanding of where and how blockchain is most effectively applied with potential business effects. They show that while prior research has predominantly focused on technological questions of design and features, it has neglected application and governance questions as we explore in this chapter.

2.2 Disruptive Innovations

Disruptive innovation is defined as "an innovation that changes the performance metrics, or consumer expectations, of a market by providing radically new functionality, discontinuous technical standards, or new forms of ownership" (Nagy, Schuessler, & Dubinsky, 2016, p. 122). The theory of disruptive innovation (Christensen, 1997) is a highly cited theory not only by researchers but also by business leaders. By reviewing a sample of disruptive technologies from the 1980s to the mid-1990s, the theory of disruptive innovation aims to explain why even great incumbent firms fail to harness disruptive technologies in dynamic environments.

The theory consists of four underlying assumptions: (1) incumbents' sustaining innovation, (2) sustaining innovation's overshooting customer needs, (3) the emergence of a disruptive innovation to which incumbent firms have the capability to respond, and (4) incumbent firms' "floundering" by the disruptive innovation (King

Table 10.1 Distributed ledger technology key elements

Permissionless	Any node (computer) can download the ledger and validate transactions
Permissioned	Permission is required to download the ledger and validate transactions
Public	Any node can read and initiate transactions on the ledger
Private	Only a selected group of nodes can read and initiate transactions
Non-hierarchical	Each node has a full copy of the ledger
Hierarchical	Only designated nodes have a full copy of the ledger
Open source	Anyone can suggest improvements to the code underpinning the ledger platform
Closed source	Only trusted entities can see and add improvements to the code underpinning the ledger platform

Source: Wadsworth (2018)

& Baatartogtokh, 2015, p. 80). Despite the popularity of this theory, its validity and generalizability have not been rigorously tested in the academic literature (King & Baatartogtokh, 2015). Importantly, it is doubtful that all the firms have the necessary capabilities to respond to a disruptive technology in the same way.

Similarly, the diffusion of innovation (DOI) theory Rogers and Shoemaker (1971) posits that innovation adoption and diffusion does not occur simultaneously in a social system. DOI theory explains how, over time, an innovation such as a new idea, behavior, or product gains traction, spreads, and diffuses through a specific population or social system. The key to the adoption decision-making process is the individual's perception that the idea, behavior, or product is new or innovative. DOI theory postulates that individuals vary in innovation adoption speed; some are faster than others (Chatfield & Reddick, 2018).

DOI theory further postulates that the characteristics of adopters, the rate of adoption, and the adoption decision-making process tend to vary across these adopter categories. Finally, the DOI theory identifies five innovation-specific factors that influence innovation adoption and diffusion: relative advantage, compatibility, complexity, trialability, and observability. The last factor measures the extent to which innovation generates tangible benefits to the adopter. While the theory is one of the most widely applied theories in social sciences, it takes into account neither the effect of an individual adopter's resources nor institutional resources as a determinant of innovation diffusion. Moreover, the DOI theory does not take into account external factors such as industry competitive pressures or societal pressures for change (Chatfield & Reddick, 2018).

Rasool, Koomsap, Afsar, and Panezai (2018) propose a five-step framework of Market observation, latent needs, customer value, idea generation, and disruptive potential scale to help firms develop disruptive innovations and to offer a scale for evaluating their disruptive potential. In other words, it proposes a practical framework to assist in developing disruptive innovations or waiting to face the dilemma of whether to act against innovations or ignore them (Table 10.2).

Finally, the innovation landscape map model also proposes four different types of innovations: (1) *routine innovations* which leverage existing technical capabili-

Table 10.2 Five steps framework of disruptive innovations

Step1: Market observation	The author state that by dividing customers into four categories according to their demand for product features (low, medium, high and very high demand customers) and then focus on serving low and medium demand customers. The low and medium demand customers are generally the first to adopt disruptive products, as such tend to be simpler, cheaper and sufficient to satisfy their needs
Step 2: Latent needs	Acquiring customer needs start by gathering data and as a result of this activity, firms can adopt available tools deem appropriate for their project. Otherwise, a large number of innovation projects fail to succeed in the market due to the inability to understand customer needs
Step 3: Customer value	Customer value in disruptive innovations do not focus on any existing product or competitor; instead, these focus on customers' (existing and future) and their needs. Then, the customer expectation canvas is drawn. This canvas will assist firms to understand the level of each feature that customers expect from a future offering. In other words, customers require this level of service from each attribute or feature. This canvas will also highlight the most important features of the offering for each customer segment
Step 4: Idea generation	Idea generation is the most important activity during the innovation process and many of the new offerings introduced to a market fail due to wrong or immature ideas. Therefore, it is argued that the difference between a successful and a failed product is the idea generation stage, whereas the other stages of innovation development are the same. Once introduced in the market, disruptive innovations follow a different diffusion pattern than sustaining innovations
Step 5: Disruptive potential scale	Once an idea has been developed for a new disruptive product, it needs to be verified; in other words, ideas need to be assessed for disruptive potential. After passing the disruptive potential scale, firms are ready to shift gears from the planning phase of disruptive innovation to the development and market launch phases

Source: Rasool et al. (2018)

ties and an existing business model, (2) *disruptive innovations* which leverage existing technical capabilities but at the same time shift towards a new business model, (3) *radical innovations* which leverage an existing business model and create new technical capabilities, and (4) *architectural innovations* which create new technical capabilities and create a new business model (Pisano, 2015). The author argues that these four distinct types of innovations indicate the imperative for an innovation strategy in close alignment with the type of technological innovations to make sound benefits-risks trade-off decisions. This author also identifies *the* leadership challenge in governing a complex innovation project which cuts across many functions.

In terms of disruptive technology use cases on blockchain or DLT, there is a very limited number of empirical studies on the inhibitors in the academic literature. However, one recent research found four inhibitors. The inherent risk of the technology, infrastructure requirements, skepticism of decision-makers, and the lack of required new skills and competencies deterred organizations from further developing decentralized trusted peer-to-peer transaction ledger systems that could lead to sustainable business models (Zamani & Giaglis, 2018). Moreover, the study found that many regulatory issues remain unresolved. Similarly, another study on the non-fiat, decentralized digital payment systems found that Canada's challenge was to find the right balance between disruptive innovation and oversight. Specifically, the government's role was complex; on the one hand, it fosters innovation and on the other hand, it concurrently strengthens governance and regulations for public safety (Ducas & Wilner, 2017). The need for regulation of fintech payment innovations was also examined (Chiu, 2017). As for the potential impact of blockchain and DLT on disintermediation, the study concludes that there is a lack of evidence for complete disintermediation, suggesting the possibility of new types of intermediaries in mediating blockchain-based economic transactions (Zamani & Giaglis, 2018).

3 Methodology

While research interests on blockchain have surged since 2015, research on DLT is very new and still very limited in the number of journal articles published. We selected Canada, out of 35 countries which is a participating member of the International Organization for Standardization (ISO) Standing Committee on *ISO/TC 307 Blockchain and Distributed Ledger* Technologies (International Organization for Standardization, 2016).

Our sampling rationale is that Canada is more advanced in research, exploration, and exploitation of DLT than non-participating countries of ISO/TC 307 Standing Committee. Moreover, Canada is a member of the Group of Seven (G7) nations, representing the seven largest advanced economies in the world. Table 10.3 shows the sample characteristics of the Bank of Canada in total assets (Bank for International Settlements, 2016; United Nations, 2016) E-Government Development Index (EGDI) Global Ranking (United Nations, 2016), and its URL. EGDI provides a comprehensive measure of IT use in public service delivery and citizen e-participation at the national government level with Canada ranked in the top tier.

Our data collection focused on secondary data which could be collected from the website above, including technical reports on blockchain and DLT, corporate documents on strategic planning, ICT, and innovation, annual reports, and public speeches delivered by central bank governors and other senior executives. We also collected news releases and media reports of the central bank DLT use cases. We then developed a curated list of text data to conduct a thematic analysis (Eisenhardt, 1989). Thematic analysis plays an integral role in qualitative text data analysis to identify, examine, and record patterns (or "themes") within text data that are relevant to describe a phenomenon of interest and are related to a specific research question. We conducted these thematic analyses for the Bank of Canada each on

Table 10.3 Sample characteristics

Country	Central Bank (official acronym)	Assets 2016 (billions of U.S. dollars)	2016 global ranking of e-government	Central Bank URL
Canada	Bank of Canada (BOC)	4179.5	14	https://www.bankofCanada.ca/

their DLT use cases to answer our research question. Finally, interviewed with the Director of Project Jasper to learn more about the development of this project.

4 Bank of Canada Case Analysis Results

4.1 *Charter and Governance*

The Bank of Canada (BOC) is the central bank of Canada and was chartered in 1934 under the *Bank of Canada Act*. BOC's four main areas of responsibility are monetary policy, financial system regulation, currency, and funds management. The BOC is led by the Governing Council, the policy-making arm of the Bank. It is made up of the Governor, Senior Deputy Governor, and four Deputy Governors. The BOC is a special type of Crown corporation (semiprivate entity) established by an act of parliament owned by the federal government and reports to the minister of finance but has considerable independence to carry out monetary policy.

As the central bank, The BOC's core functions and main responsibilities include monetary policy, the financial system, the distributions of currency, and funds-management services for the Government of Canada as well as other clients. The objective of monetary policy is to preserve the value of money by keeping inflation low by enacting policy reforms to hit the 2% inflation-control target. The BOC promotes the economic and financial welfare of Canada by conducting research analysis as well as overseeing the stability and efficiency of the financial system which includes financial markets, credit unions, as well as clearing and settlement systems. The BOC also acts as a regulatory agent and conducts oversight of the financial market infrastructures and payment systems (this includes the Large Value Transfer System and the Automated Clearing Settlement System which is owned and operated by Payments Canada). The bank does this by providing liquid funds to the financial system and acting as a lender-of-last-resort to prevent instability. The BOC is the sole authority for issuing banknotes as well as responsible for the distribution of the Canadian dollar. The BOC supplies banks notes and ensures confidence in the currency by developing banknotes that are difficult to counterfeit, and by conducting verification of banknotes by retailers and the public. The last core function of the BOC is funds-management services for the Government of Canada, which mostly include treasury management and reducing risk in the financial system.

4.2 *DLT Exploration and Exploitation: Project Jasper*

The BOC's Project Jasper aims to explore the technological feasibility, financial performance, and market opportunities and capability challenges associated with introducing DLT in the central bank's high-volume transaction environments and hierarchical regulatory environments. The Project Jasper consists of four phases.

Based on the case interview analysis and project document analysis, Project Jasper's timeline has been captured and summarized in Fig. 10.1.

Figure 10.1 shows that Bitcoin introduces Distributed Ledger Technology (DLT) to the world which is a blockchain technology that saves identical copies of a ledger which updates independently and is managed and distributed by many peer-to-peer networks. In March 2016 (Phase 1) Payments Canada in conjunction with the Bank of Canada and R3 labs launch Project Jasper which attempted to further research DLT in hopes to find what benefits blockchain technology offers for the future of payments between large banks and possibly commercial use for consumers. In September 2016 Phase 2 of Jasper was launched and transitioned from Ethereum platform to R3's Corda platform embedded with liquidity-savings mechanism (LSM) which settles payments between 2 or more parties when certain conditions have been met. In May 2017, the Bank of England published a blueprint for Real-Time Gross Settlement Service (RTGS) which can be used to transfer funds of high value. In October 2018 Phase 3 is launched Payments Canada, the Bank of Canada, and TMX Group announced an integrated securities platform for Jasper and in Phase 4 a Cross-Border Interbank Payments report which discusses the future of using blockchain technology for payments between banks across borders.

4.3 *Project Jasper Phases*

4.3.1 Phase 1: DLT-Based National Inter-Bank Wholesale Payments Using the Ethereum Platform

In 2016, Payments Canada, the BOC, and Canadian commercial banks that are members of the R3 global consortium, and a group of academics initiated an experi-

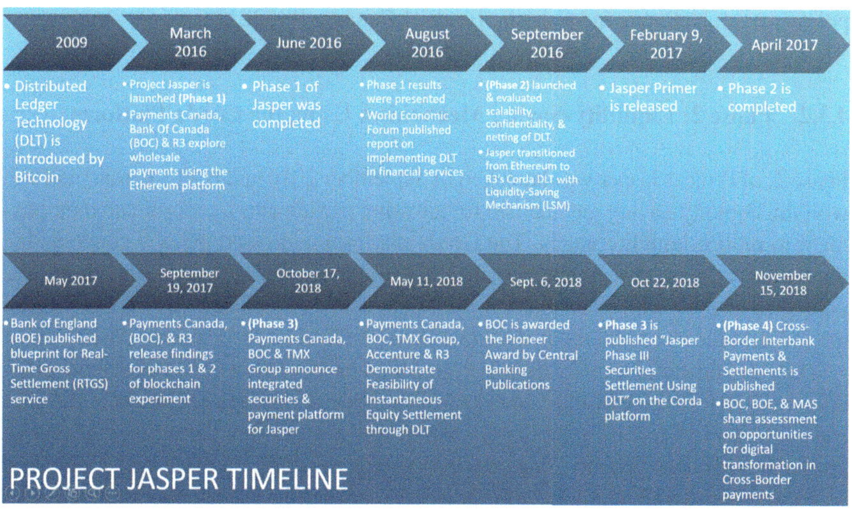

Fig. 10.1 Project Jasper timeline

mental proof-of-concept (POC) project Jasper to explore the feasibility of a DLT-based wholesale payment (Chapman et al., 2017). Payments Canada runs the national interbank payment system that clears more than 175 billion Canadian dollars a day (Ho, 2017). Payments Canada is accountable to the Minister of Finance and its core payment system is overseen by the BOC.

Initially, they were looking for an interbank payment system related to the Payments Canada modernization project in Phase 1, March 2016 to June 2016, Project Jasper built a proof-of-concept system for payment settlement controlled by the Bank of Canada. An Ethereum platform was built, the Ethereum solution provided full visibility into the central ledger for all participants in the system. Although this transparency helped to monitor the status of all participants in the system, the platform did not support participant requirements for data privacy (Canada & R3, 2017). The Ethereum platform made the system more resilient, but would be costly and raised key issues of privacy.

The four-main area of focus for guiding hypotheses in phase I is cost; the overall cost of the system per participant will be less with DLT solution than with a centralized system, Resilience; A DLT system will be more resilient than a centralized system due to the distribution of technology across participants, Accessibility; barriers to entry will be reduced in a DLT system relative to a centralized system, allowing for an increased number of direct participants, and Control; Information will be protected/released in a more granular and policy-determined manner (Canada et al., 2017).

Phase 1 efforts include building a framework to evaluate the suitability of a central bank-issued asset transferred between participants on a distributed ledger network for Canadian domestic large-value wholesale payments. Project Jasper's efforts have focused on evaluating the suitability of DLT for the issuance, transfer, and settlement of Canadian payments from a business, technical, operational, monetary policy and regulatory perspectives. Results and insights will provide valuable input on domestic payments regulation, financial system stability and monetary policy research (Payments Canada, Bank of Canada, R3, 2017).

4.3.2 Phase 2: Liquidity-Saving Mechanism Using the Corda Platform

Phase 2, of Project Jasper was launched in September 2016 and built a Corda platform with the liquidity-saving mechanism for allowing participants to coordinate their payment to reduce liquidity needs. The Corda platform addressed privacy concerns but made the system less resilient (Ho, 2017). From Phase 2, a longer white paper was published in 2017 which outlined Project Jasper's first two phases and implications of the project outcomes (Payments Canada, Bank of Canada, TMX Group, 2017).

Data-driven simulation exercises were completed in Phase 2 to evaluate the operation and performance of the Jasper platform. Specifically, the operation of the central queue and payment-matching algorithm was evaluated under a range of unique circumstances. As well, the payment-processing capacity of the broader platform was evaluated using simulation by drawing on much larger data sets reflective of daily transaction volumes observed in the Large Value Transfer System (LVTS) today (Canada et al., 2017).

In 2016, the LVTS processed the value of a total payment of $175.245 billion each day, on average, representing more than 34,000 transactions. The maximum daily value cleared by the LVTS in 2016 was $271.797 billion and more than 53,000 transactions. At some points in 2016, the LVTS was processing up to 14 transactions per second, in addition to addressing other queries that may have been run at the time. Payments Canada maintains a firm commitment to business continuity and disaster recovery planning for the system, given the importance of the LVTS to the Canadian economy and its role as a centralized infrastructure (Canada et al., 2017).

In the Corda platform used in Phase 2 of Project Jasper, this is done via a notary node that is trusted by everyone. Finally, these systems dispense with the concept of a blockchain and replace it with a ledger that is still distributed among the nodes, but where each node has access only to necessary data. This affords less transparency across the system and allows more privacy for participants (Chapman et al., 2017).

In contrast, notary based DLT systems, such as Corda, permit increased privacy because a trusted third party (e.g., the Bank of Canada) helps validate all transactions. In other words, these new distributed ledger systems allow access only to a restricted set of trusted counterparties. However, the lack of transparency in the Corda system implies that no node in the system, with the possible exception of the notary, has all the information. Therefore, if the information at one or more nodes is corrupted, it may not be possible to reconstruct the entire network since even the notary does not have a full copy of the ledger. This creates the need for backups of individual nodes and a loss of the economies of scale associated with centralized systems (Chapman et al., 2017).

In phase 2, a key conclusion of Jasper Phase II was that the material benefits of a DLT-based financial system might be realizable if the scope of the DLT system included the settlement of multiple assets. Phase II also showed that it was possible to have a liquidity savings mechanism for netting transactions. The conclusion was that significant efficiency gains were likely to be realized only if multiple assets were settled on the same distributed ledger system (Bank of Canada, TMX Group, Payments Canada, Accenture, R3, 2018).

The overall conclusion from the first two phases was that the Corda and Ethereum platforms for DLT would not provide overall strategic benefits substantially over the existing centralized interbank systems (Ho, 2017). The perceived strategic risk involved switching to a DLT system which is highly decentralized, from extant payment system which is very centralized through the use of traditional accounting-based ledger systems, while the BOC needs to retain some of the centralized core functions of the extant system (Chapman et al., 2017). In an interview with an official at the Bank of Canada, he believes that the BOC was not convinced at this time that a distributed ledger system or a blockchain system will be much better than a centralized system that we now operate (S. Hendry, personal communication, October 10, 2018).

4.3.3 Phase 3: Securities Clearance and Settlement Using the Corda Platform

Phase 3 is to determine if the new business value in terms of greater speed and efficiency can be achieved through the DLT-based automation of the securities settlement process. On the one hand, phases 1 and 2 of Project Jasper had the participants exchanging Canadian dollars for digital tokens, which could then be transferred across the distributed ledgers within the computer networks. On the other hand, Phase 3 tests a hypothesis on whether DLT can provide improvements of the settlement process for the financial system in times of financial stress with faster settlement times, reduced settlement risk, and ultimately lower transaction costs for securities transactions (Christopher Jeffery et al., 2018). It was hypothesized that this implementation would enable the following benefits as outlined in Table 10.4 (T. G. Bank of Canada, Payments Canada, Accenture, R3, 2018).

The BOC launched Phase 3 of Project Jasper in 2017. The purpose is to learn more about DLT application to a wider set of functions within the Canadian financial system (Payments Canada, Bank of Canada, TMX Group, 2017). DLT is used to create a proof-of-concept (POC) for the clearing and settlement of securities using a central bank cash-on-ledger model, in collaboration with the TMX group which operates the Toronto Stock Exchange (Christopher Jeffery et al., 2018).

The use of DLT was important for creating a loose integration of the Large Value Transfer System (LVTS) and Canadian Depository for Securities (CDS) that achieved delivery versus payments (DVP1) settlement with only DVP2 input of liquidity. This loose integration framework left the two authorities involved—the Bank of Canada for cash and CDS for equities—in full control of their respective instruments or tokens. The platform was also capable of handling the different participant sets between the LVTS and CDS such that each participant was only capable of performing those functions for which they were authorized. Finally, the

Table 10.4 Benefits of DLT for securities clearance and settlements

Technical efficiencies	• An integrated financial market infrastructure (FMI) solution may reduce technical frictions that exist in the current market infrastructure, resulting in better and more efficient securities and cash interactions among participants • The Corda DLT platform enables loose coupling of the components controlling cash, equities, and positions in the ecosystem. This simplifies integration with the different participants' existing systems and is expected to ease extension to additional asset and transaction types
Operational efficiencies	• Common processing conditions, executed over a common computer network, may reduce participant costs to validate and reconcile delivery vs. payment transactions • One of the project's hypotheses stipulated the potential for reconciliation benefits for settlement participants, which was deduced from the inherent characteristic of a shared ledger in providing transactional transparency and trusted records to participating entities
Cash and collateral efficiencies	• FMI integration may also bring opportunities to consolidate and optimize collateral requirements between large-value interbank payments and securities settlement systems

project scope was not sufficiently broad to determine whether DLT would yield significant cost savings or efficiency gains (Bank of Canada, TMX Group, Payments Canada, Accenture, R3, 2018). The BOC has seen many pluses and minuses still probably looking at having to expand the scope of these projects to really realize significant value (S. Hendry, personal communication, October 10, 2018). The conclusion was that significant efficiency gains were likely to be realized only if multiple assets were settled on the same distributed ledger system (Bank of Canada, TMX Group, Payments Canada, Accenture, R3, 2018).

4.3.4 Phase 4: Cross-Border Interbank Payments and Settlement

Cross-border payments and settlements have not kept pace with advances in domestic payments and continue to be based on the correspondent banking model, which has not changed materially over the decades. Managing issues in the cross-border payment and settlement space is a more challenging proposition than domestic payments and settlements because of the lack of standardization between jurisdictions in terms of regulatory requirements, data standards and operating hours. In particular, a collective action problem exists in the cross-border payment and settlement space that does not occur on the same scale in the domestic payment and settlement landscape (Bank of Canada, Bank of England, Monetary Authority of Singapore, 2018).

Based on current cross-border payment and settlement flows, this report identified some key challenges affecting end-users, commercial banks and central banks: End-users of cross-border payments do not have clarity on the time required for payments to complete or on the fees that will be imposed. Commercial banks are unable to provide this visibility and require manual operational efforts to process such transactions. Central banks provide the domestic real-time gross settlement (RTGS) systems that are essential for the processing of cross-border payments (Bank of Canada, Bank of England, Monetary Authority of Singapore, 2018).

This report identifies the future-state capabilities expected of a cross-border payment system model to address these challenges and resolve underlying root causes which include extended availability of domestic and international payment capabilities, visibility of payment statuses, and certainty of outcome; consistency of payment standards and greater transparency of regulatory differences and regulatory requirements across jurisdictions, as well as direct, peer-to-peer payment and settlement; and lastly an enhanced technical infrastructure of payments systems RTGS increase stability and resilience, widen access and foster innovation (Bank of Canada, Bank of England, Monetary Authority of Singapore, 2018).

The Project Jasper noted several strategic benefits for Canada through the DLT system (Payments Canada, Bank of Canada, R3, 2017). There are (1) improved back-office payment processing and reconciliation performance, (2) reduced likelihood of costly errors and disputes in the settlement process, (3) providing clear and consistent audit trails for financial transactions, (4) greater transparency in monitoring of the BOC and its regulators, (5) information privacy, and (6) increased efficiency through improved automation (Payments Canada, Bank of Canada, R3, 2017). The strategic risks as previously noted are (1) privacy issues, (2) performance, and (3) moving from a highly centralized interbank system to a decentralized DLT system. While these strategic benefits are noted there is still much focus centered around the improvement of all phases especially in phase 4 (S. Hendry, personal communication, October 10, 2018).

When it comes to Cross-border payments and settlements have not kept pace with advances in domestic payments and continue to be based on the correspondent banking model, which has not evolved materially over the decades. Managing issues in the cross-border payment and settlement space is a more challenging proposition than domestic payments and settlements because of the lack of standardization between jurisdictions in terms of regulatory requirements, data standards and operating hours. In particular, a collective action problem exists in the cross-border payment and settlement space that does not occur on the same scale in the domestic payment and settlement landscape (Bank of Canada, Bank of England, Monetary Authority of Singapore, 2018).

5 Discussion

Project Jasper represents an opportunity for Canadian industry members to work together to investigate opportunities that will benefit all players in the payments settlement space (Bank of Canda, R3, 2017). In addition to industry-level recognition of the potential value of DLT to drive efficiencies and support innovation, many Canadian financial institutions are members of the R3 consortium and have benefited from R3's global perspective and focus on DLT initiatives.

Project Jasper maintains a keen interest in understanding how emerging technologies such as DLT could transform the future of payment (Bank of Canda, R3, 2017) that allows data and assets to be transferred online without the need for intermediaries. The first two phases of the project focused on the clearing and settlement of high-value interbank payments using distributed ledger, or blockchain, technology. However, Phase 2 was launched in September 2016 to build on the learnings from Phase 1. A major goal of Phase 2 was to evaluate the scalability and flexibility of DLT by moving to an alternative technology platform and by continuing to build in more of the functionality observed in today's interbank settlement solutions.

Table 10.5 provides DLT-based BOC central banking innovations using the cycle time for four innovation adoption/diffusion phases. Canada took a broad approach involving various stakeholders; central banks, payments systems, retail banks, and other important interest groups. Canada initiated these projects with pressures to innovate and disrupt the existing process, with the idea of DLT being an important driver of improving the payments process and bringing it into the twenty-first century from a centralized payments system to decentralized faster payments platforms.

In Phase 2, Canada's central bank announced the development of a DLT-based project. Project Jasper completed 2 phases of POC in 2017 to build Ethereum and Corda platforms for payments. BOC launched its phase 3 POC DLT for securities settlement in collaboration with the TMP Group which operates the Toronto Stock Exchange in 2017. Canada and these platforms had similar issues in that it was not robust enough to replace the existing payments system with DLT technology. It called for a collaborative action from the payments industry ecosystem including consumer groups, federal and state government agencies, regulators, standards bodies, industry trade organizations, consultants, and academics.

In Phase 4, we examined a shift from the POC DLT project to production. As of April 2018, we could not find evidence for Canada's central bank in replacing their existing payment systems or platforms with a full-fledged DLT system. Despite some of the setbacks with the earlier phases of Project Jasper, however, BOC is trying a different approach to a DLT-based securities settlement, which is an important part of innovation. Finally, while DLT-based solutions can meet the current performance needs of the existing RTGS systems using liquidity saving mechanisms and DLT-based solutions were resilient to the failure of the individual network nodes.

The first two phases of the project have been completed and have delivered substantial understanding and accomplishments regarding this emerging technology. Specifically, the project team had the opportunity to explore and compare the capabilities of two distinct DLT platforms, the Ethereum and Corda platforms to build out this settlement functionality (Bank of Canda, R3, 2017). In addition, Phase two of the project took on the learnings from phase 1 specifically. It sought to mitigate the problems of high liquidity requirements and transparency of sensitive information. To do this, Project Jasper used closed-source DLT platforms and designed them to be private, permissioned, and hierarchical (Wadsworth, 2018).

The third phase involved creating a proof of concept for the automation of the securities settlement process. It builds on the work of the first two phases, as well as experiments being performed by other central banks, such as the Monetary Authority of Singapore, the European Central Bank and the Bank of Japan, and the South African Reserve Bank (T. G. Bank of Canada, Payments Canada, Accenture, R3, 2018).

In accessing cross-border payments, the collaboration between Bank of Canada and Monetary Authority of Singapore has successfully proven the ability for settlement of tokenized digital currencies across different blockchain platforms. The Jasper-Ubin project is experimental, and whether we will eventually use blockchain technology for high- value cross-border payments remain to be seen. However, technology exploration and experimentation will continue because of the potential

Table 10.5 DLT-based central banking service innovations

Phases of development	Timeline
Phase 1: First public innovation announcement	Yes, BOC and Payments Canada take lead in 2016
Phase 2: Publicly pronounced DLT project to start	Yes, Project "Jasper" announced in 2017
Phase 3: Proof-of-concept DLT project completed	Yes, completed 2 phases (Ethereum and Corda) in 2017 and currently working on phase 3 in 2018
Phase 4: From proof-of-concept to production	Not yet, but anticipated with the TMX in securities settlement starting in 2018

in this technology (Bank of Canada, Monetary Authority of Singapore, 2019). Both projects unilaterally aimed to develop more resilient, efficient and lower-cost alternatives to today's financial systems based on central bank-issued digital currencies. According to Bank of Canada, Monetary Authority of Singapore (2019) and Singapore (2019) further questions to pursue are the complication that will arise with a large number of jurisdictions, legal aspect to be considered, and research in DLT interconnectivity mechanisms and alternative network models which represents opportunities for further collaboration among central banks, financial institutions, and FinTech firms should be considered.

Overall, Project Jasper and Project Ubin achieved some of the benefits of Blockchain, including faster settlement, fewer reconciliation requirements and high visibility of the payment status. However, it also resulted in greater visibility of sensitive information between participants and greater liquidity requirements compared to existing payments infrastructure (Wadsworth, 2018).

Our cross-case analysis findings on the DLT use cases by Canada's central bank and found similar challenges related to the uncertainty of the relatively new DLT and its perceived risks on process disruptions. Our findings are consistent with the DOI theory, given the speed of innovation adoption of Canada's central bank. In addition, our findings suggest the relative importance of the governance structure in steering POC DLT projects successfully. On the one hand, Canada has a single board that is proactive towards exploring DLT innovations despite its known technological immaturity.

Next, we applied the innovation landscape map (Pisano, 2015) to an emerging DLT landscape to Canada's central bank (Table 10.6). This map shows *Routine Innovation* that leverages existing technical capabilities and existing business models. We also found evidence of *Radical Innovation*, which not only leverages existing business models but also creates new technological capabilities, in BOC with project Jasper. Canada's central bank created new technical capabilities through the exploration and exploitation of DLT. We did not find any evidence of *Architectural Innovation* from our case studies. Overall, Table 10.6 indicates that Canada's central bank did not adopt DLT for bank settlements, but the potential exists for other areas such as cross border settlements.

As shown in this paper, the central bank's role in DLT innovation is complex. On the one hand, as Ducas and Wilner (2017) note the government fosters innovation. On the other hand, it concurrently needs to strengthen governance and regulations for public safety. This balancing act makes it difficult for these central banks to embrace DLT-based innovations.

In consequence, the BOC has taken a more incremental approach to innovation.

Table 10.6 DLT-based disruptive innovation for Bank of Canada

	Creating new technical capabilities through DLT
Leveraging existing business model	*Routine and radical innovation* Jasper Phases I & II (BOC)
Shifting to new business model	*Architectural innovation* No evidence found

Pisano (2015) argues the leadership challenge in governing technological innovations. We also observed in the formation of different forms of collaborative network governance within the nation of Canada, these collaborative network governance structures may be required to move forward to the next level and co-create value—both business values and public values—for example, Canada's central bank real-time gross settlement platform and faster payments platform participants.

As Pisano (2015) expressed, it is important to understand how innovation will create value for potential customers. For example, Bank of Canada case study focuses on transforming the future of payments (Bank of Canda, R3, 2017), One of the main lessons from this experiment is that the versions of distributed ledger currently available may not provide an overall net benefit when compared with existing centralized systems for interbank payments. However, there may be benefits for the broader group of payment system participants and the entire financial system from a DLT-based wholesale payment system in terms of savings from reduced back-office reconciliation and improved interaction with a larger DLT ecosystem of financial market infrastructures (Chapman et al., 2017). Just like Pisano (2015) expressed is it important in choosing what kind of value your innovation will create and sticking to it is critical.

6 Conclusion

This paper analyzed the Bank of Canada innovations into DLT. Overall, our analysis shows that there is no imminent future full deployment of DLT-based platforms for the central banking core functions in high-volume and high-value payments, clearing, and settlement, despite the successful proof-of-concept DLT projects. However, against the disruptive innovation theory, Jasper Phase 3 successfully demonstrated that a DLT platform can be used for a payment and securities settlement system. The POC platform processed key functions, such as pledging and redeeming cash and equities and performing settlement transactions, in a manner aimed at respecting the privacy and scalability requirements of the Canadian system (Bank of Canada, TMX Group, Payments Canada, Accenture, R3, 2018). While the smallest country such as Canada is currently integrating DLT in the securities settlement platform.

While the challenges for Canada's central bank are noted; the key strategic risk challenge in moving from highly complex centralized payments systems to new near-real-time payments platforms, and to DLT-based highly decentralized autonomous networks without a central control mechanism. The role of the board leadership in steering DLT innovations in uncharted waters would be also the complex challenge for the central bank. The technological uncertainty, issues of security and privacy, and the leadership challenge characterized by the board's technical competencies may explain the slower speed with which Canada's central bank is adopting DLT innovations in comparison to the agility and flexibility of fintech firms that embraced blockchain and DLT more fully (Gomber et al., 2018). In this regard, our cross-case analysis results on the value network governance challenges facing central banks are consistent with prior research on DLT-based innovation challenges in the different research contexts (Brühl, 2017; Chiu, 2017; Ducas & Wilner, 2017).

Banking systems are highly regulated which may further stifle DLT-based radical and disruptive innovations unless the board with technical competences leads the development of an effective form of collaborative network governance (Chatfield & Reddick, 2018; Ojo & Mellouli, 2016) in the balancing act of leveraging the new DLT for disruptive innovations or radical innovations and performing the central banking roles in services and regulations. In this complex and challenging DLT innovation landscape, what is interesting is that the board of the Bank of Canada has reached out to the private sector partner, TMX Group that operates the Toronto Stock Exchange to leverage DLT for its radical innovations as a way to minimize the technological and business risks.

Disruptive technologies such as blockchain and DLT provide both fintech firms and incumbent firms with strategic options to pursue different types of innovations (Pisano, 2015). How DLT is used in value networks in the financial and banking sectors have significant strategic and economic implications and practical managerial implications (Dai & Vasarhelyi, 2017; GAO, 2018; Pachamanova et al., 2017). Despite the growing interest in DLT-based service innovations among fintech firms, incumbent firms, and academics over the recent years, prior research has identified the need to better understand DLT benefits and challenges through actual use cases (Zamani & Giaglis, 2018). By focusing on the DLT use cases in central banking service innovations and by comparing Bank of Canada's response to DLT-based innovation opportunities, this research has contributed to the literature on disruptive innovation and disruptive technology governance in the central banking context.

There are some limitations to this study. First, we only focused on Canada's central bank, and many other countries that are currently experimenting with DLT and payment systems. Second, we relied on secondary data without conducting field case study interviews with those involved with these projects, especially in Canada with their proof-of-concept projects completed. From these limitations, future research could provide a comparative case study analysis of innovations in DLT in other central banks.

Acknowledgements I appreciate the insight from Mr. Scott Hendry, Senior Director Financial Technology for the Bank of Canada. The views expressed in this chapter are those of the author and do not reflect the views of the Bank of Canada or its staff.

References

Anjum, A., Sporny, M., & Sill, A. (2017). Blockchain standards for compliance and trust. *IEEE Cloud Computing, 4*(4), 84–90.

Australian Securities & Investments Commission. (2018). *Evaluating distributed ledger technology* (p. 219). Retrieved from https://asic.gov.au/regulatoryresources/digital-transformation/evaluating-distributed-ledger-technology/

Bank for International Settlements. (2016). *Fast payments: Enhancing the speed and availability of retail payments*. Basel: Committee on Payments and Market Infrastructures.

Bank of Canada, Bank of England, & Monetary Authority of Singapore (2018), https://www.bankofengland.co.uk/news/2018/november/boe-boc-mas-joint-reportdigital-transformation-in-cross-border-payments

Bank of Canada, & Monetary Authority of Singapore. (2019). Jasper—Ubin design paper: Enabling cross-border high value transfer using distributed ledger technologies. Retrieved from https://www.mas.gov.sg/-/media/Jasper-Ubin-Design-Paper.pdf

Bank of Canada, TMX Group, Payments Canada, Accenture, & R3. (2018). Jasper phase III securities settlement using distributed ledger technology. Retrieved from https://www.payments.ca/sites/default/files/jasper_phase_iii_whitepaper_final_0.pdf

Bank of Canada, & R3. (2017). Project Jasper: A Canadian experiment with distributed ledger technology for domestic interbank payments settlement. Retrieved from https://www.payments.ca/industry-info/our-research/project-jasper

Brühl, V. (2017). Virtual currencies, distributed ledgers and the future of financial services. *Intereconomics, 52*(6), 370–378. https://doi.org/10.1007/s10272-017-0706-3

Chapman, J., Garratt, R., Hendry, S., McCormack, A., & McMahon, W. (2017). Project Jasper: Are distributed wholesale payment systems feasible yet? *Financial System Review*, 59–69.

Chatfield, A. T., & Reddick, C. G. (2018). All hands on deck to tweet #sandy: Networked governance of citizen coproduction in turbulent times. *Government Information Quarterly, 35*(2), 259–272. https://doi.org/10.1016/j.giq.2017.09.004

Chiu, I. H. Y. (2017). A new era in fintech payment innovations? A perspective from the institutions and regulation of payment systems. *Law, Innovation and Technology, 9*(2), 190–234. https://doi.org/10.1080/17579961.2017.1377912

Christensen, C. (1997). *The innovator's dilemma: When new technologies cause great firms to fail.* Boston: Harvard Business Review Press.

Christopher Jeffery, D. H., Hardie, D., King, R., Mendez-Barreira, V., Yeung, I., Clark, J. & Carlyle, T. (2018). Central Bank of the Year: Bank of Canada. Retrieved from https://www.centralbanking.com/awards/3348626/central-bank-of-the-year-bank-of-canada

Dai, J., & Vasarhelyi, M. (2017). Toward blockchain-based accounting and assurance. *Journal of Information Systems, 31*(3), 5–21. https://doi.org/10.2308/isys-51804

Ducas, E., & Wilner, A. (2017). The security and financial implications of blockchain Technologies: Regulating merging technologies in Canada. *International Journal, 72*(4), 538–562. https://doi.org/10.1177/0020702017741909

Eisenhardt, K. M. (1989). Building theories from case study research. *The Academy of Management Review, 14*(4), 532–550. https://doi.org/10.5465/AMR.1989.4308385

GAO. (2014). *Virtual currencies emerging regulatory, law enforcement, and consumer protection challenges* (p. 496). Washington, DC: United States Government Accountability Office.

GAO. (2017a). *Financial technology: Information on subsectors and regulatory oversight* (p. 361). Washington, DC: United States Government Accountability Office.

GAO. (2017b). *Financial technology. information on subsectors and regulatory oversight. Statement of Lawrance L. Evans, Director, Financial Markets and Community Investment.* In: Testimony, H. Before the Committee on Banking, and Urban Affairs, Senate (Eds.), Washington, DC: United States Government Accountability Office.

GAO. (2018). *Financial technology: Additional steps by regulators could better protect consumers and aid regulatory oversight* (p. 254). Washington, DC: United States Government Accountability Office.

Gomber, P., Kauffman, R. J., Parker, C., & Weber, B. W. (2018). On the fintech revolution: Interpreting the forces of innovation, disruption, and transformation in financial services. *Journal of Management Information Systems, 35*(1), 220–265. https://doi.org/10.1080/07421222.2018.1440766

Ho, S. (2017). *Canadian trial finds blockchain not ready for bank settlements.* Toronto: Reuters.

International Organization for Standardization. (2016). *Blockchain and distributed ledger technologies.* Geneva: ISO.

King, A. A., & Baatartogtokh, B. (2015). How useful is the theory of disruptive innovation? *MIT Sloan Management Review, 57*(1), 77–90.

Kostoff, R. N., Boylan, R., & Simons, G. R. (2004). Disruptive technology roadmaps. *Technological Forecasting and Social Change, 71*(1), 141–159. https://doi.org/10.1016/S0040-1625(03)00048-9

Lucas, M. (2017). *Blockchain: The most disruptive tech in decades*. Hong Kong: Computerworld.

Nagy, D., Schuessler, J., & Dubinsky, A. (2016). Defining and identifying disruptive innovations. *Industrial Marketing Management, 57*(C), 119–126. https://doi.org/10.1016/j.indmarman.2015.11.017

Ojo, A., & Mellouli, S. (2016). Deploying governance networks for societal challenges. *Government Information Quarterly, 15*(4), 681–697. https://doi.org/10.1016/j.giq.2016.04.001

Pachamanova, D., Mancha, R., & Kokina, J. (2017). Blockchain: Emergent industry adoption and implications for accounting. *Journal of Emerging Technologies in Accounting, 14*(2), 91–100. https://doi.org/10.2308/jeta-51911

Payments Canada, Bank of Canada, & TMX Group. (2017). Payments Canada, Bank of Canada and TMX Group announce integrated securities and payment platform as next phase of Project Jasper. Retrieved from https://www.payments.ca/about-us/news/payments-canada-bank-canada-and-tmx-group-announceintegrated-securities-and-payment

Payments Canada, Bank of Canada, & R3. (2017). Project Jasper: A Canadian experiment with distributed ledger technology for domestic interbank payments settlement. Retrieved from https://www.payments.ca/industry-info/our-research/project-jasper

Pinna, A., & Ruttenberg, W. (2016). Distributed ledger technologies in securities post-trading—Revolution or evolution? *IDEAS Working Paper Series from RePEc*.

Pisano, G. (2015). You need an innovation strategy. *Harvard Business Review, 93*(6), 44–54.

Rasool, F., Koomsap, P., Afsar, B., & Panezai, B. A. (2018). A framework for disruptive innovation. *Foresight, 20*(3), 252–270. https://doi.org/10.1108/FS-10-2017-0057

Regenscheid, A. (2017). *Blockchain and distributed ledger technologies: Opportunities, challenges and future work*. Cryptographic Technology Group, National Institute of Standards and Technology, Technology Administration, U.S. Department of Commerce.

Risius, M., & Spohrer, K. (2017). A blockchain research framework. *Business & Information Systems Engineering, 59*(6), 385–409. https://doi.org/10.1007/s12599-017-0506-0

Rogers, E. M., & Shoemaker, F. F. (1971). *Communication of innovations; a cross-cultural approach*. London: Collier Macmillan.

Singapore, M. A. O. (2019). Central Banks of Canada and Singapore conduct successful experiment for cross-border payments using distributed ledger technology. Retrieved from https://www.mas.gov.sg/news/media-releases/2019/central-banks-of-canada-and-singapore-conduct-successful-experiment-for-cross-borderpayments

UK Government Chief Scientific Advisor. (2016). Distributed ledger technology: Beyond block chain. Retrieved from https://www.gov.uk/government/news/distributed-ledger-technology-beyond-block-chain

Underwood, S. (2015). Blockchain beyond bitcoin. *Communications of the ACM, 59*(11), 15–17. https://doi.org/10.1145/2994581

United Nations. (2016). UN e-government survey 2016: E-government in support of sustainable development. Retrieved from https://ictlogy.net/bibliography/reports/projects.php?idp=3082

Wadsworth, A. (2018). Decrypting the role of distributed ledger technology in payments processes. *Reserve Bank of New Zealand Bulletin, 81*(5), 3–20.

Yermack, D. (2017). Corporate governance and blockchains. *Review of Finance, 21*(1), 7–31.

Zamani, E. D., & Giaglis, G. M. (2018). With a little help from the miners: Distributed ledger technology and market disintermediation. *Industrial Management & Data Systems, 118*(3), 637–652.

Christopher G. Reddick Ph.D., is a Professor in the Department of Public Administration at the University of Texas at San Antonio, USA. Dr. Reddick's research interests are in information technology and public sector organizations.

The manufacturer's authorised representative in the EU is Springer Nature Customer Service Centre GmbH, Europaplatz 3, 69115 Heidelberg, Germany. If you have any concerns regarding our products, please contact ProductSafety@springernature.com

Printed and bound by CPI Group (UK) Ltd, Croydon, CR0 4YY
28/09/2026
02224090-0008